# Grey Aliens and the Harvesting of Souls

"Nigel Kerner's shocking new book totally redefines the nature of the alien presence on our planet. In a detailed study that is certain to send shockwaves throughout the world of UFO research, Kerner offers a terrifying theory to explain the presence of the so-called extraterrestrial Greys on our world. Far from being the benevolent visitors that many abductees believe them to be, in reality aliens are cold and clinical creatures whose stark and terrible task is to reap and manipulate our very life force—the human soul—for purposes both nefarious and ominous. A book that should, and must, be read."

NICK REDFERN, AUTHOR OF *FINAL EVENTS: ALIEN ABDUCTIONS, THE GOVERNMENT, AND THE AFTERLIFE*

# Grey Aliens and the Harvesting of Souls

## THE CONSPIRACY TO GENETICALLY TAMPER WITH HUMANITY

## Nigel Kerner

Bear & Company
Rochester, Vermont • Toronto, Canada

Bear & Company
One Park Street
Rochester, Vermont 05767
www.BearandCompanyBooks.com

Bear & Company is a division of Inner Traditions International

**Library of Congress Cataloging-in-Publication Data**

Kerner, Nigel.
  Grey aliens and the harvesting of souls : the conspiracy to genetically tamper
with humanity / Nigel Kerner.
      p. cm.
  Includes bibliographical references and index.
  Summary: "Exposes the agenda behind the bio-robotic grey aliens' genetic
manipulation of certain human races"—Provided by publisher.
  ISBN 978-1-59143-103-9 (pbk.)
  1. Alien abduction.  I. Title.
  BF2050.K47 2010
  001.942—dc22

                                                            2009045520

Printed and bound in the United States by Lake Book Manufacturing

10  9  8  7  6  5  4  3  2  1

Text design by Jon Desautels and layout by Priscilla Baker
This book was typeset in Garamond Premier Pro with Agenda and Avenir used as
display typefaces

To send correspondence to the author of this book, mail a first-class letter to the
author c/o Inner Traditions • Bear & Company, One Park Street, Rochester, VT
05767, and we will forward the communication.

*Is God willing to prevent evil, but not able?*

*Then he is not omnipotent.*

*Is he able, but not willing?*

*Then he is malevolent.*

*Is he both able and willing?*

*Then whence cometh evil?*

*Is he neither able nor willing?*

*Then why call him God?*

EPICURUS, GREEK PHILOSOPHER,

341–270 BCE

## NOTE TO THE READER
### Author-Coined Terms

In this work, the author has coined or provided specialized defi-nitions of certain words that are unique to this discussion, such as *Brind* (brain mind) and *Godverse* (a universe that is eternal and thus timeless, where all the extremes of values that are per-fect are inherent and free). A complete list of these terms and their meanings has been provided in the Glossary at the back of the book for your ready reference.

# Contents

# Introduction

I was passing through the East End of London with my fellow school-mates, on our way to see the famous Tower of London. The year was 1960. I was fourteen years old, and we were all, my mates and I, full of the exuberances of youth that were natural at that age. There was excitement, even joy, in the form of a zest running like soft brush strokes of stinging nettles around the extremities of my body, joy in anticipation of what was waiting for us all just a few meters ahead on one thousand square meters of pure history—history wrapped up in ghosts and human ghouls that marked the jagged desultory corridors of a British past.

Prior to that day, I had never taken ghosts as a phenomenon seriously enough to give even a lingering thought to them. I had always been a dreadful cynic. My mind has naturally never had a penchant for the belief in anything that I could not see, feel, or touch. Ghosts were definitely out. But something really strange happened on that first trip to the Tower. I suddenly felt real fear at one point on the tour. I remember feeling annoyed at myself at not being able to explain why. The fear arose just there, at a particular location, and nowhere else. There was nothing forbidding about the place, it was a kind of lobby from which a staircase descended. The fear was completely irrational, and this irritated me more.

Reason had been my lifelong agent of assurance, but reason deserted me at that point. It was inexplicable. There was of course the underlying

1

prompt suggesting that I was subconsciously tapping into all I had heard about ghosts and the Tower. This was possible, but it was intriguing that I felt no fear whatsoever in any other part of the Tower. I have since been back to the ancient edifice several times and on every single occasion felt the same gut-wrenching fear at that particular spot.

This curious phenomenon was the only strange inexplicable experience in my life, till much later. The lack of resolution of this mystery annoyed me for a long time, but it did trigger a sort of perverse fascination with things inexplicable, setting a route forward for me to a much more open mind about such things, particularly the nature of our reality. Despite my experience in the Tower, as I continued with my education, science was my root and branch, and the simple questions of everyday physical reality were settled with the equations that balanced this reality on either side of an equal sign.

Then, when my son was about the same age, he posed a question to me that led me to a discovery that blew my mind and called into question all that I had previously believed to be real. My son's mind had my respect. He was not a frivolous boy by nature. A studious and highly intelligent young man, he would always pose questions that required some pretty nifty thinking to find an answer. The answer to this particular question took twenty-two years, and when it finally arrived, it was most certainly not the answer I expected. The question was: "Dad, are UFOs real?"

I first set out to investigate the UFO phenomenon to prove to my son that it was all nonsense and that the world was full of timid, gullible, paranoid sorts who would believe anything that would cause raised eyebrows in the interest of conversational anecdotes, party pieces, and downright attention seeking. I thought that all it would take was some clear coherent study and painstaking research and I would soon see off these prophets of doom, despondency, and distortion. I saw it as a lesson for my boy, which as a father I would be proud to offer. I set a strict scale of objectivity, and with a super ferret for a senior researcher, I set out to blow the lid off the canard I thought it all to be.

Within one year of seriously looking at it all, I was folded up like a dead spider in ignominious retreat from this point of view. My research revealed that not only was the UFO phenomenon true—beyond a shadow of a doubt—but also that the whole thing pointed to the most deadly secret in the world. It was a secret that turned known human history on its head and revealed a conspiracy so terrifying that it struck at the very root of the value of our existence as a species. It cut through the bases of all religions, science, and social semantics. The range of concatenate associations and knowledge fields I had to look at turned out to be so vast that it took me nearly two decades to do the subject justice.

I came to the inescapable conclusion that not only were UFOs real, but that *Homo sapiens sapiens*—which we call the primary controlling living species on this planet—is a genetically farmed species, farmed for the utilitarian purposes of the occupants of the UFOs: alien extraterrestrials. Our awesome vanity as a species, it seems, has prevented us from seeing what has been in front of our very noses for millennia. We have known nothing about it, just as a laboratory rat knows nothing about the fact that it is in an artificial environment. The rat has not decided to be in the laboratory; it knows nothing about its genetically determined body with red eyes and white fur. It goes about its business in its cage thinking that this is all there is to its world. It has no clue that a strange species alien to its own is giving it and its companions time to be themselves, providing food, and then making them pay the price. The price is capture and, if they are unlucky, pain. Their bodies are used as measuring devices for someone else's end.

Yes, folks! It is my contention that we were farmed into existence in our present form as the species *Homo sapiens sapiens* by a superior alien intelligence just as we, in turn, farm other animal intelligences less than ours, in farms and laboratories all over the world.

This book is my insight into the frightening phenomenon of alien abduction and interception in the affairs of the human race. Abductees report the removal of sperm and ova and the making of hybrid babies.

The abduction phenomenon cannot, it seems, be explained away as the aberration of an unbalanced mind or the result of a state of "sleep paralysis." Over a million people in the United States alone report the same experiences with the same key factors present. The book takes a serious look at the situation in terms of the sociological consequences of this profound threat to our humanity, with strict recourse to purely scientific rather than mystical paradigms.

The position is taken that this is a purely physical phenomenon. The grey aliens are similar to the probes we send to planets like Mars. In the course of the book, I will explain what I have discovered about how and why they were sent out to explore a hostile universe and the wide-ranging nature of their interceptions in human affairs. For example, the book proposes that racism and other forms of discrimination might well have their origins in the programming of humanity by this alien species, which has tried to prevent interbreeding in order to protect the experimental integrity of specific isolated groups of humanity. Hitler reportedly saw these beings, who then showed him their ideal future man—blonde and blue-eyed, the Aryan ideal. The properties of the skin pigment melanin, which surrounds a cell nucleus and thus protects the DNA of those who have darker skins against alien interference, is discussed as a plausible reason for the fact that alien abduction is far more prevalent in the northern hemisphere than anywhere else on the planet.

I am only too aware that I am treading an unfamiliar path and in many cases laying down new paths in previously uncharted territory. For this reason, I have been careful to base my conclusions about grey alien interceptions on actual reports from reliable witnesses, among them doctors, teachers, policemen, pilots, and high-ranking military officials. These reports describe encounters with alien craft and alien abduction. Additionally, I present accounts of a certain category of near-death experience that strangely seems to mirror the abduction experience.

Many years before *The Da Vinci Code* and the issues surrounding it became a hot controversial topic, I suggested—citing evidence from the Gospel of John and the Book of Revelation—that Jesus Christ may well have left a biological line into the future. In this book, I will present this evidence in the context of my thesis that the *immaculate* biological line of Jesus Christ was a line free of alien genetic manipulation. Citing the fact that the human body is 65 to 75 percent water, I suggest that the *living water* of which Jesus spoke expressed the potential of this biological line to clean up the alien-intercepted lines of humanity.

My previous book, *The Song of the Greys,* was a serious look at the UFO phenomenon as a signal that extraterrestrial intercession in the affairs of humankind by alien beings had really happened and is, in verifiable truth, happening on this planet. It drew so much controversy and raised so many questions—both for myself in the writing and through intelligent public comment—that I was compelled to take on certain derived implications with this book.

I have been stunned by what I have discovered regarding the likely consequences for all of us in the family of humanity of the greatest secret kept from us by our governments. The earth *was* our home. It is now theirs. I do not wish to be chilling in this scenario, but it does prompt conclusions that force us to take a long hard look at the entire existential vista that we have taken for granted over the millennia. If I am right, history as we know it is bunk. As a father, I sincerely hope that I am wrong and that in future moments, when we look at our children and grandchildren in pride, admiration, and love, we will still be able to smile.

Through most of my life I have been allergic to organized religion. It has been this way since my childhood. Nothing and no one was able to make me see past the rational and look at the behests of religious polemics that demanded faith, belief, and unconditional trust in what I saw as mostly needs-based social drivel steeped in unreason. But when I started to look deeply into the UFO phenomenon, I found I was being inexorably drawn into taking a look at religious premises I would never have dreamed were relevant. In time, it forced me to look carefully at the record of the great religious teachers and their sayings and their works. It required a detailed examination of their plausibility and veracity.

To my astonishment, the UFO phenomenon became more and more the first cousin of religion, particularly in relation to the great prophets and teachers of the great religions, a cast of main players in the drama of discovery. I looked at all the personal information about them that I, myself, and my researchers could lay eyes on over the fifteen years it took to research the subject. I looked at both the conventional party line of the various organized religions and the noncanonical texts, which I found in many cases to provide more accurate descriptions of the great teachers and their works. And the world of religious knowledge exploded in my face. It did so particularly in the name of Jeshua Ben Joseph and Siddhartha Gautama, commonly known as the Buddha. The process of re-reading what the great teachers meant in the light of modern scientific discoveries has taught me that knowledge is the key to it all: there is nothing more worthwhile than the search for and discovery of the truths of our existence.

Yet it seems that only the scientific outlook drives most of the minds leading the edges of discovery on our planet and that curious principle we call truth. Every newborn baby now faces its first breath at the behest of this axiom. All power to achieve is slowly being siphoned and bottlenecked in a resolution that points to no meaning and purpose beyond the day's own troubles. The highs and lows of mental resolve are tacitly assumed to be no more than the result of purely chemical functions that drive a carcass that begins rotting the moment it is conceived. From this perspective, our ultimate legacy is a dead, go-nowhere, existential paradigm that questions no more why poets hide in the places where a lark sings or a rainbow sleeps. Nothing could be further from the truth. To truly see reality, we need to look at our existential situation from all points of view at once, combining the views of the physicist, biologist, sociologist, philosopher, poet, and priest.

If you are a brave soul, let me take you into a sensational story. Let me put before you something that took me over a decade to believe and come to terms with, even after I had all the evidence to suggest that I should have believed it in the first place. It might change the very base of your thinking, as it did mine. I cannot promise you the last word in truth. I can promise you an interesting quest, at least. I can also promise you a glimpse at the glory of your own mind, as you unravel with me answers that I might not have seen and you might have spotted, perhaps for the very first time in the history of our precious humanity—at least this time around!

# 1

# A Beginning of Sorts

Of all unexplained phenomena, UFOs and alien abduction seem to arouse the greatest popular intrigue, when judged from the number of hits on the subject collated from the Internet.

The sighting of mysterious craft in the sky and encounters with strange, nonhuman, extraterrestrial entities have been described for millennia. Cave paintings and petroglyphs dated from 40,000 years ago show nonhuman beings that are often depicted with strange craft that are quite clearly not planetary bodies. A large number of ancient historical and theosophical texts describe beings from the sky coming to this Earth and investing their ways within indigenous primal societies on this planet.

It is clearly an enigma that humankind, now seen to be of a lineage of some five million years, could not, until relatively recent times, develop such a simple artifact as the wheel. This gives rise to questions such as: What prompted the sudden and totally unprecedented surge in technological development that was the signature tune of Cro-Magnon man's appearance in the fossil record thirty to forty thousand years ago? Why, even after this, did it take tens of thousands of years of plodding technological progress before the genus *Homo sapiens sapiens* suddenly progressed from throwing stones and flying kites made from stretched bat wings to launching rockets into space? What produced the remarkable surge of development in the last two hundred years or so that now allows us to explore the outer planets in our solar system, when we achieved, in terms of technological progress, virtually nothing before that? We have gone from the cotton jenny to a Cray computer in just three human lifetimes, from the merest sense of the rudiments of life to the threading of polypeptide chains of amino acids for the creation of life, from the primitive understanding of a cell to the cloning of an entire animal through DNA transfer from the cell nucleus.

Is our accession through time, as a species of sentient, intelligent, living beings, an independent development isolated to natural processes and procedures on this planet, or has something out of this world inter-cepted us and provided aids and prompts to our development? Are we now a sponsored species, lab rats used and secured for the purposes of entities of extraterrestrial origin? Could they be far more intelligent and have their own agenda that might have involved genetically engineering a monkey to produce our genus?

The thesis of evolution put forward by Charles Darwin is commonly used to explain concatenate development to betterment. Development comes with the passage of time through the natural survival of the *fit-test* and therefore the *best*. This is regarded as an incidental and fortu-itous process that depends on mere chance to genetically bring about the development of the larger brain capacity that makes us capable of better and better things. As an aside, it might be worth asking why Neanderthals did not go to the moon before we did, since their brains were larger than ours!

In my last published book, *The Song of the Greys,* I put forward my own reasons for believing the explosive notion that evolution as it is commonly interpreted (and not in the original way in which Darwin actually described its philosophical treatise) is bunkum. I hasten to add that I also see great logical inconsistencies in the theories of creationism and intelligent design—the time-honored rivals to evolutionary theory. I will elaborate on all this later, but for now I would like to introduce my suggestion that no such thing as evolvement to betterment is pos-sible in light of the universal law underlying it all, the second law of thermodynamics (SLOT). The SLOT breaks down all physical things in the universe into greater situations of randomness and chaos with time, decaying all things into smaller and smaller parts till no*thing* exists anymore.

We all rot the moment we are conceived. When left on their own, without any tending or replenishment, all things go one way: from a better arrangement of constituent parts to a worse one. The clash of opposites is always finally settled on the side of the SLOT, when the entire span of creation is said to devolve into a dark cold nothingness: a purposeless universe of purposeless things, defining a purposeless end. This indeed is the latest assessment of the guardians of sense themselves, the scientists. The meaning of all physical verifiable existence all comes to *non-Sense*. To *no-thing*. They call it the *cold death* of the universe.

What then are *we,* that we progress to know so much when the end of it all, as science prescribes, is meaninglessness dressed up in nonsense? It's all quite mad put that way isn't it? Yet this is the final result based upon the very latest research in cosmology. Something is quite clearly wrong here. Something hidden. Something not open to the scientific process of discovery. Something strange and so massive in its implications that it might ironically be right before our eyes, to such an extent that we cannot see the forest for the trees.

Could there be something else other than that which is prescribed by the physical universe and its artifacts? Could the way we see it be upside down? Have the discoveries of science in our modern world led us to a point where we are going to have to radically rethink the entire existential base, as it has been revealed to us by science, religion, and philosophy in the past? Are UFOs real, and are they the hint that forces us to take a long, long look at all we have accepted and taken for granted through the millennia as the *Truth*?

Most of us have asked the questions: Who are we? Why are we here? Where are we going? These questions are set at the deepest root of our existential base as human beings.

To some of us, these questions have no pertinence or interest value at all. Events in our day-to-day lives progress inevitably and are enough, it seems, to occupy and fulfill our humanity. But to some, these questions provide an incessant prompt that continues within to tax our mind, our sense of ourselves, our sense of others, and the way we relate to our physical and emotional environment. With some of us it goes even deeper, reaching into the final definitions of our very being, in a quest that takes us out of physical sensory perspectives to a horizon that reaches beyond those limits. In my quest to discover the truth about UFOs, I found that I had to look at these questions and see if the grand visions of a world beyond sight, touch, taste, hearing, and smell are simply founded in the abstractions of faith, belief, and trust, or if they are more fundamentally verifiable through our capacity for reason and logic.

Why did we have a Jesus Christ, a Mohammed, a Buddha? Were these seemingly wondrous expressions of humanity a collection of dreamers, fools, and charlatans, mere respondents to the hard defines of a physical world that all too easily provided pain and emotional suffering for so many as the norm of daily living routine? Or, were they truly the most glorious pioneering revealers of a wonderful truth that most of us have not discovered? Were they indeed what they claimed to be in their own terms?

All through the centuries, human beings have sought truth. History, as we may know or reveal it within accepted human capability, is a chronology of effect, judged in event perspective. We have judged these events in terms of a reality based overwhelmingly on the physical, so the derivatives of tens of thousands of years of such observation are reflected now in the loss of what might be termed the more ephemeral, aesthetic, and spiritual value outlook and our settlement, instead, for the object-oriented materialistic outlook. This is not a question. It is a charge.

This result is an inevitable outcome of the ongoing dismantling of order into chaos throughout the physical universe, defined by science in the second law of thermodynamics with the concept of entropy. Entropy is the measure of disorder in any given situation and the consequent reduction in final value terms, judged against the only real ultimate value—existence itself. We have set our store in the narrower perspective of a unit of flesh, a perspective that describes the square meter of space that includes our physicality and is dominated by it.

I am writing this on a plane, high above the terrestrial space we call France. Her meaning is an effect of the eye, set in rigid geometric patterns of brown and green, anonymous arrangements that from the window of the aircraft seem little more than the markings on a giant counterpane. Yet, upon it rests the glory of a million you's and me's: tiny points so small that my vision, my hearing, my sense of smell, of touch, or taste, may never discern them. In my thoughts, the bland checkerboard lives—France lives in the smile of a child down there, in the weathered furrows of a farmer's face, the gay swirling skirt of a woman awash with her beauty, the downed head of a mother alone, abandoned with her starving infant in some tenement in Toulouse. When viewed as physical entities with the physical eyes that *see,* they are less than specks of dust on my French counterpane. But when viewed through the mind's abstract eye, these are human beings, each magnificent. Such is discernment without the physical senses.

In terms of atoms, we are all physical, insignificant, minute. If this is true in our local planetary perspective, how much smaller in meaning is physical sensibility when placed against the size of the stars, galaxies, and the expanse of the universe? But in *thought,* we are grander than the universe, because we can stretch our perspective to include every galaxy, every star, every planet. In the human mind's eye, the scope is grander than the universe. In the human physical eye, it is reduced to a speck we cannot even see.

Why do we let the minute dominate the vast? In the materialistic outlook so prevalent in what we call the developed societies, we confine our perspective to more and more limited horizons—horizons as confined as the property of an atom, the smallest signature of force that, in conspiracy with all of its own kind, provides the vast forces that now dominate the physical universe of matter and therefore us. In the tragedy of all trag-edies, the materialistic outlook increasingly limits even the perspectives of the mind's eye to the directives of the second law of thermodynamics.

At the same time, all things can be seen as immortal in apparent con-tradiction to the second law. A seed continues in subsequent generations of seeds. We may be said to continue in the seed of our sons and daugh-ters. Yet, the crucial question is: What about individuality and individ-ual knowing? Why do we dream unique dreams, plan unique schemes: dreams and schemes that are ours—yours and mine, in our personal terms—and no one else's? What of the glories of Mozart, Michelangelo, da Vinci, Shakespeare, Tagore? Are these unique geniuses all just inciden-tal means for the neutral expression of the universe to live and die, with no more permanent result than the physical products of their genius?

A tree flourishes and dies, leaving no more mark on the world than its few square meters of spread. It cannot reach out and touch and change a single value outside its canopy. It is endlessly static, restricted—going nowhere. And so it will remain, till a man cuts it down or a flood washes it away, with no hope of renewal out of its own aegis, and no hope of a change it can dictate. Its seed, dry and hard, takes its identity, a fitting eulogy to its restricted scope. How different is a man, a woman. We can see forever, if we choose. The living seed we carry within, warm, motile, resolute, and vital, flourishes with the zest of an ancient promise—that we can beat death itself and gain a view from beyond the body, limp and ended, and start again somewhere else, maybe.

It's this *maybe,* this *somewhere* of uncertainty, that points a finger of eternal or temporal result. Why the maybe? Where is the somewhere?

Some of the most respected intelligences on Earth hail Darwin's the-ory of evolution and accept the progressive making of better situations for living platforms within an overall situation of gathering chaotic ameliora-tion. This has been mistakenly taken to mean that the improvement is intrinsically, existentially, from zero to better. Nothing could be further from the truth. Scientists would have us believe that we evolved in a pro-cedure from less to more, into our present structures—species of living beings, be they amoeba, tree, dog, or human—in an ongoing sequence of improving movement that has in billions of years produced, through a lottery of chance, a human. But the universe hasn't existed long enough for chance to have produced even the most basic rudiment of life—a polypeptide chain of amino acids. Even Einstein confirmed the numbers just don't fit. But much beyond that, we are supposed to believe that the immense intricate complexity of a human came out of a system that exponentially promulgates more and more chaos the longer it exists.

Any serious investigator of such a claim using mathematical logic as a tool will soon throw out evolution as *we* generally understand it (not as Darwin wrote it), having discovered an endless series of maybes, some about as plausible as flying icebergs, involving fantastic juxtapositions of excruciatingly contrived situations. Many of these, if set to laws of probability, would require the universe to be $10^{1000000} + n$ years old.

This may be why we see so few mathematicians—who tend to test speculations with the cold dispassionate eye of the purity of reason—among these purveyors of nonsense. Why do the leaders of thought bend the straight lines of reason to a kind of safety pin of emotionally comfortable nonsense? And why do we believe them? Perhaps our sense of self-preservation cannot permit us to believe that we humans aren't anything but the best, any place, any time. In this most basic instinctive belief, we delude ourselves into the most ludicrous denial of reason and build theses galore to try to disprove what we have striven to prove beyond a shadow of a doubt, namely that the sole business of the universe is to provide a fabulous engine for the dismantling of order into and through the infinite states of suborder in the randomized chaotic momentum of subversion we call entropy.

"*Out of chaos comes order.*" This is an anthem of the mad. Anyone that would try to account for the order we see in the universe as a product of chaos must bear the medallion of a fool. The same property has systematically taken from our midst all the lovers of reason that simply claimed the order in the universe was, and is, generated from *outside* it and not from *within* it.

Scientists commonly believe that the universe was born from a point so unimaginably small as to be *nothing*. The primal identity thus emerged from what is described by science as the *cataclysm primus,* which provided an unimaginably hot sheet of plasma that differentiated in the first microseconds into the phenomenon of parts, creating space and time as measures and measurers of such a phenomenon. Like a tree bursting forth into branches and leaves from a tiny seed, so the universe was deployed into action in the inertia of something, or somewhere, to continue seemingly endless demarcations into fractions of a prior amalgam. But what was the amalgam prior to *nothingness*? What was the cause of this fantastic happening? It is logically undeniable that what was prior had the greater union of parts. In fact, parts happened as a phenomenon of the universe's emergence from this prior state, or effect, or whatever it might have been.

Any search that might lead to the truth has to be investigated with the two main existential dispositions of humanity: the physical and the psychological. But some of the regions of the whole existential outlay that must be investigated are inherently unsure, and they are referenced against the most unreliable investigative tools. On the one side, the tools that are materially derived—the physical senses—are notoriously misleading information-gatherers, as any lawyer or scientist will tell you. On the other side, mentally derived verifications provide equally nebulous effects: thought-propagated incidental feelings, inspirations, visions, and revelations.

So how and where can our species find reliable definitive answers to our existential predicament? Can these answers be objectively confirmed, or must they remain subjective envisioning that each of us must bear within, to be confirmed or denied without tests and verifications that provide results that are common to all?

There is really only one final yardstick against which final truth may be seen. It is the most simple and, therefore, the most profound yardstick against which all effect is to be judged. When you clear away all the humbug—the falsely contrived chaotic ameliorations provided by the entropic momentum—that yardstick, stated simply, is: If you are there—you can know!

What constitutes simply *being there*? This is the only important question open for answer: *What allows you to be there, for as long as possible, so that you can know as much as possible?* This defines the highest existential margin. I have sought all my answers in the spirit of this alma mater.

The current ascendance of science in defining and hallmarking quantitative and qualitative truths has generated a storm force of denial of the previous foundation of human thinking—religious beliefs and religious belief systems. People are thoroughly confused about what to believe. Such is the grand predicament we all share. As the spiritual, metaphysical perspectives lessen, the atomic and thus enforced perspectives are more firmly consolidated, driving away our ephemeral humanity and supplanting it with our physicality. This exchange has one end: the death of our humanness. It can be seen in the expression of systems that devalue our grander perspectives.

This is the exchange of *heart* mind for *machine* mind. Life and living are measured in value against a system set in machines, with the precision-ground exactness of straight-line geometrical certitudes. This is the ecology and economy of the slide rule and binomial theorem. Could it be that the strange, seemingly emotionless, robotic creatures that have been witnessed by so many abductees are to a great extent responsible for all of this? Could they, for some reason, be shaping us in their image and likeness, grooming us to become as close to their machine-like nature as possible?

The harrowing experience of abduction has been endured by millions of our human species all over the world now, many times over by some individuals. It points to the presence of something more advanced than humanity. It remains a mystery to this day, though dismissed by the scientific cartel that sees it as something manufactured by the human mind. I have to confess that this was my view for a long time. I lumped so called "abductees" among those ingenuous cranks and charlatans who claim all kinds of paranormal and supernatural experiences and, in so doing, give ammunition to the congenitally cynical and skeptical, who claim that all extraordinary paranormal experience is untenable and unreal.

Now, however, after many years of carefully looking at the evidence, I have to say unequivocally that there is no doubt whatsoever in my mind that this is a real physical experience and, further, that it is also the most profound and significant experience of our times. It does not surprise me in the least that the renowned and brave Harvard psychiatrist John Mack affirmed the abduction phenomenon to be a genuine one, not to be grouped with psychopathological or other aberrant psychological conditions.

Mack pointed out that any theory that would begin to explain the abduction phenomenon as anything but literally true would have to account for five basic dimensions:

1. The high degree of consistency of detailed abduction accounts, reported with emotion appropriate to actual experiences told by apparently reliable observers.
2. The absence of psychiatric illness or other apparent psychological or emotional factors that could account for what is being reported.
3. The physical changes and lesions affecting the bodies of the experiencers, which follow no evident psychodynamic pattern.
4. The association with UFOs witnessed independently by others while abductions are taking place (which the abductee may not see).
5. The reports of abductions by children as young as two or three years of age.[1]

David M. Jacobs, Ph.D., associate professor of history at Temple University in Philadelphia, is a leading academic authority on UFOs and alien abductions. Since 1986, he has been conducting hypnotic regressions with abductees. When he was asked in an interview whether he believes that it is possible that experiences with alien craft and alien beings could be psychologically contrived manifestations, his answer was the following:

> What you have to remember is the sheer enormousness of the abduc-
> tion phenomenon; millions of people are being abducted. Moreover,
> in abductions people are typically missing from their normal envi-
> ronment. Others notice that they are missing. There are multiple
> abductions. People may see other people being abducted, and may or
> may not be abducted themselves. There are situations where some-
> body sees somebody else being abducted, and is abducted him or
> herself. Years go by and person A has a hypnotic regression, remem-
> bers seeing the other person. Person B, 3,000 miles away in another
> city, and for another reason has a hypnotic regression, remembers
> the abduction and sees person A there as well. And neither of them
> know that they have been regressed remembering this same abduc-
> tion. To make that psychological, we have to live in a different infor-
> mational world of how the human brain operates.
>
> Furthermore, abductees come back from an abduction event
> with anomalous marks on their body, scars on their body, scar-tissue
> that was literally formed the night before. They came back wearing
> somebody else's clothes, they came back to somebody else's house by
> accident. People see UFO's in the air, hovering directly over the per-
> son's house when they're describing being abducted, neighbors who
> have nothing to do with it see this. There is a very, very, very strong
> physical aspect to this, that is completely non-existent in all of the
> other dissociative behavior that we see.
>
> The interesting thing about all these questions is, if this were psy-
> chological, if people were dreaming it up, we wouldn't be asking any
> of these questions, we'd know all the answers. We'd ask people, why
> do you think they're doing this? And they wouldn't tell you, because
> that's the way the brain works. In channeling for example, all ques-
> tions are answered, all ends are tied up, and it's all roses and light.
> With the abduction phenomenon we just don't know.[2]

In 2007, Professor Jacobs wrote a report called "A Picture We May Not Wish to Gaze Upon," outlining the changes in abduction accounts he has noticed over the past ten years. This is one of the most alarming reports I have read on the subject. I quote:

> All of these accounts, to put it bluntly, point to a future in which human-looking hybrids will be here amongst us. The evidence is now so strong I can no longer look at alternative motivations for them. Everything I have learned about this subject in the past 20 years inexorably points to this conclusion. I cannot escape it.
>
> I have heard everything about abductions many times over in the past 20 years. I have investigated over a thousand abduction accounts. In the standard abduction scenario, procedures continue according to a set, albeit flexible, plan. Therefore, the accounts in which I hear the same thing repeatedly help in building up verification and validation. After one researches abductions in a systematic way and learns what happens in them, one finds that the information flow to the researcher proceeds at glacier-like speed. Only about every seventh session would I hear something I have never heard before. It might be a procedure the aliens did a little differently, or a new way of doing something, or it might be something else that was related to the standard procedures that I had not heard before. That would keep my interest up and help to propel me forward intellectually. Now I am constantly hearing things I have never heard before. All sorts of people who for many years had been telling me primarily the standard abduction procedures now tell me new things. And new people with whom I have just begun to work tell them to me too. Furthermore, people with whom I have not had a hypnosis session for many years, come back and want to have a session so that they can fully remember the new and extraordinary events that have happened to them recently.
>
> Why is this happening? Is something changing? Are we in a new phase now? In my research in the mid-1990s, I had heard the aliens

talking about what they called "The Change" when they would be here with us. What this meant exactly I was not sure. I was even less sure when it would happen. They used the term "soon" which is somewhat meaningless. I thought that if this were to happen, perhaps it would take 30 years or so to begin. Now I am not sure. Now I think that the evidence indicates "The Change" might be happening a lot sooner than I had thought. It was not very long ago, when people would ask me if I thought hybrids were walking around in normal human settings, that I would answer, "Of course not!" To me, the evidence had never indicated that. And I knew that to answer affirmatively would label me even more fringy than I already sounded. Even then, however, I would think to myself, "Maybe I am wrong. Maybe they have learned how to do a job interview. Maybe they are walking around in human society." But I never voiced this publicly because the evidence was not strong enough for me. Now what I hear is much more about interfacing with hybrids, and teaching hybrids, and getting hybrids "ready," and making sure everything is all right.[3]

Jacobs goes on to say: "Budd Hopkins and I have been doing this work for a cumulative total of over forty-five years. We have interviewed, listened to, read letters from, and worked with thousands of abductees and we still do not know why the aliens have initiated this program." Both Hopkins and Jacobs have contributed hugely to our knowledge of the abduction phenomenon through their brave research. In this book, I hope to answer their questions about the whys and wherefores of what they have discovered.

The terrifying thing that is pointed to by the abduction phenomenon taken together with the UFO phenomenon is the most significant occurrence in the existential base and affairs of humankind, calling for a full exploration of truth on several levels: the physical, the nonphysical, the metaphysical, the abstract, and the spiritual.

# 2

# The Truth about UFOs

The evidence for the physically real existence of UFOs is now sufficiently overwhelming to suggest the presence of a huge and powerful
deliberate conspiracy to present the phenomenon as something that
is only believed by cranks. Why is this so? Any physical disease, for
instance, that can threaten the welfare of humanity is looked at very
closely by many people. It begs the question why the existence of a
super-intelligent extraterrestrial power among us doesn't come under
closer scrutiny. Could it be that these superintelligent aliens are making
sure that they are not discovered? How then would they do it?

I again quote Professor David Jacobs, from his 2000 treatise entitled
*Some Thoughts about the Twenty-First Century:*

> Most commentators have concentrated on the coming wonders
> that aliens and hybrids plan a possible integration or colonization
> of human society. I have come to agree with them. I have arrived
> at this extreme view cautiously after spending over thirty-five years
> studying the subject—the last eighteen of which I have spent con-
> centrating almost exclusively on abductions. It is not a view of which
> I am very fond. It makes me seem as if my quality of mind is lacking
> and my judgment is severely impaired. It destroys my credibility in
> virtually all areas of my intellectual life as a professor of history.
> Yet I must adhere to it because I have found the evidence for it

so compelling, even though I have struggled against the evidence of this train of thought.[1]

In fact, Professor Jacobs' quality of mind might be of a particularly perceptive genre, of the same quality as the greatest minds in history who at one time or another ran contrary to the accepted norms of their peers and were finally found to be right. This, by the way, includes practically every scientist who has ever made a significant breakthrough. Professor Jacobs joins a very illustrious crew of original thinkers because he dares to look at and see and believe what is dangerous and deadly to the welfare of us all. It is a brave and resourceful act of the greatest service to humanity. Most of those who seek to ring these alarm bells are crushed daily in all their efforts, and it is done so cleverly nobody notices.

All this might seem utterly bizarre—this is how I viewed it when I first started investigating the UFO phenomenon. I was an utter cynic about the whole phenomenon. It was only after many, many years of painstaking research into the available archives and access to information trawled from contacts, some in high and secret places of many countries, that I am unalterably convinced of the veracity of my claims. Extraterrestrial alien-sponsored UFOs on this planet are a real phenomenon. Real in our reality terms. They do not belong in some esoteric library of the mind that conjures them up in the imagination. Before I illustrate my point with reference to the evidence for UFOs, let me say that I really do not think that a single person will ever be allowed to provide tangible definitive proof of the existence of a single extraterrestrial alien in the affairs of our species. The scale of their interception of humankind is awesome because it is so fundamental and so cleverly covert.

Everyone I am sure has heard of the famous Roswell incident that happened in New Mexico in the United States in 1946, when the U.S. government covered up the alleged crash landing of a UFO. Hundreds of books have been written about the incident, and it is one of the most talked about events on the Internet to this day. I have written about it in my previous book, *The Song of the Greys,* so here I will simply say that it demonstrates the power governments have to lie, cheat, deny, and cover up things that have perhaps the most crucial bearing on the lives of their citizens, their children, and their future. The whole Roswell saga teaches us all a lesson about how futile it can be to try to expose what governments do to us.

However, I am by no means suggesting that all claimed encounters with alien phenomena are authentic. A truly neutral skepticism is utterly essential. Those who are sincere seekers are true guardians of the truth and contribute to the benefit of us all. Our physical senses are notoriously fallible. And the world is full of liars. Human vanity and a natural sense of physical vulnerability tend to make some people prone to hyperbole and careless recall. "Look at me, I have something special to say" is an axiom that seems to lead the personalities of many people. We need to ensure that information is accurately reported, especially information that is not tangible, that cannot be readily, repeatedly, and objectively demonstrated.

Many so-called skeptics tend to be deeply committed to hidden prejudices, or are manipulated in various ways to tow a party line that represents the interests of individuals and organizations for whom the revelations of certain truths might be inconvenient or downright disadvantageous. This disadvantage might be measured as fiscal in nature. More commonly, the truth would be detrimental to the assertion of power and control over others. The verity of the UFO phenomenon is steeped in consequences to both categories. So, too, is the verity of the existence of a world beyond the atom and a world beyond death.

For all these reasons I have looked for the testimony of those who have nothing to gain and everything to lose in reporting encounters with UFOs or alien beings: individuals such as pilots, air traffic controllers, or military personnel, highly trained eyes that are not given to frivolous observations. These men and women have to have the finest of tested characters, trustworthy enough to be given daily charge of missiles that travel at near bullet speeds with hundreds of lives on board.

They know what is truly unusual and can easily distinguish between a phenomenon that is controlled and one that is random and weather produced, such as ball lightning or earth-shift-engendered plasma balls. Many professionals have been warned not to report UFO confrontations, with the implied or explicit threat of negative impacts on their careers. The power of such threats is so great that most bow to the pressure, but some brave souls still speak up. Read on and see what you make of the evidence that I will now cite, both for the veracity of the phenomenon itself and the astonishing extent of the effort to cover up its exposure to the public.

An event that took place in the United Kingdom far more recently than Roswell is even more convincing, simply because those who verify it are among some of the most important people in the security "food chain" of the nation. The Rendlesham Forest incident (reported on at www .rendlesham-incident.co.uk/rendlesham.php) is considered the United Kingdom's Roswell. It also demonstrates vividly the power and scale of cover-up that takes place when an event purporting to be the landing of a UFO takes place in modern times.

Woodbridge and Bentwaters Air Force bases were a joint NATO-incorporated facility, in the English county of Sussex. Here U.S. personnel, numbering in the thousands, were stationed to supervise and guard the storage of nuclear weapons and their delivery systems. The bases were also a facility for operating A10 tank-buster jets capable of delivering battlefield nuclear weapons in the event of a war in Europe. Nuclear weapons with hundreds of thousands of kilotons of explosive power were stored in huge underground bunkers, fortified with layers of steel, concrete, and earth. The base was manned by highly skilled airmen with cool clear heads who were trained to deal with life-and-death situations. What happened there on Christmas night in 1980 was to make thick-skinned military men shudder.

It was a clear cold night, and Airman John Burroughs and Sergeant Bud Stevens were patrolling the perimeter areas of the base. Rendlesham Forest, a thick wooded area, surrounded the periphery. The men decided to drive into the forest part of the patrol area. They noticed strange lights in the woods, just off the road. It was an unusual sight, and the men decided to investigate it with a closer look. As they approached, they felt a real sense of danger. The lights were of different colors and blinking on and off. Alarmed, the men decided to speed back to the gate and get in touch with the base through a secure phone. They did not want to broadcast the information over the open radio line.

They spoke to the staff commander at Central Security Control (CSC), who dispatched Sergeant Jim Penniston to the site. Penniston and a driver arrived at the east gate, where they met the two airmen, Burroughs and Stevens. They directed his view to the lights in the trees. Penniston thought the red and yellow lights might be a downed aircraft, and he called CSC for clearance to investigate this possibility. Stevens told Penniston that it wasn't a crashed aircraft and that—whatever it was—it had landed. Penniston, Burroughs, and the driver decided to head toward the lights, and Stevens returned to his post.

The three airmen drove as far as the road would let them, and from there they continued on foot about fifty yards. As they walked, they noticed that their radios were encountering stronger and stronger interference. Penniston felt an electric charge in the air. It was far more than an adrenalin rush. It felt as though his clothes, his face, and his hair were electrically charged. The closer they got to the lights, the more apparent it became it was not a crash site. They finally emerged into a clearing. There was a sudden, bright, almost blinding light, which then dimmed; they could then make out an object about ten feet away. Sergeant Penniston took photographs with the military-issue camera he always carried on investigative trips.

He saw a triangular craft that measured, he estimated, nine feet on each side and about eight feet high. He could not identify a front or back. There were no protrusions that looked like engines or a cockpit. The whole craft was smooth on the outside. He circled the craft, writing notes on a pad. He noticed that his handwriting deteriorated as he got closer to it. He then reached out to touch it. He found it as smooth as glass and warm to the touch. What looked like lights on the craft were somehow part of its fabric. Penniston noticed symbols on the side of the object, which he copied down in his notebook. He described them as markings, not numbers or a language. There were six or seven symbols, each three feet wide.

The object suddenly emitted a blinding flash of light. The men dove for cover, and the craft lifted up above the trees. Penniston reported that he had never seen anything move so fast in all his life, and that in a blink of an eye it was gone. When the men got to their feet, they saw another light in the distance. They noted that this light was the Orford Ness Lighthouse, about five miles away.

Burroughs and Penniston checked out their radios. They were working again. It was 5 a.m. in the morning. Two hours had passed since they first noticed the strange lights. They reported to CSC, and their commander ordered them to rendezvous with the security team at the east gate.

Later, in their debriefing, they were unsure what to report. They realized it was not a good career move to say what they had actually seen. They gave a sanitized version. There was a veiled threat by their staff commander who said, and I quote: "Project Blue Book ended in 1969 and sometimes, gentlemen, things are better left alone."

The whole incident began to obsess Sergeant Penniston. He returned the next day to search for tangible evidence. He thought the craft he had seen must have left some indentations in the ground. He indeed found and made molds of three indentations, each about two to three inches deep, spaced evenly apart. Penniston now had photographs and three plaster molds to back his story up. At the time he didn't know that corroboration was going to come from someone in one of the highest posts at the base: the deputy commander himself, who became an eyewitness two nights later when the UFO made a return visit.

On the evening of December 27, 1980, Deputy Base Commander Lieutenant Colonel Charles Halt was at the officers' club when an excited airman interrupted a holiday party being held there. The man, in a state of shock and excitement, reported personally to Halt that the UFO had returned. Lieutenant Colonel Halt decided to investigate the matter himself.

He assembled a team of three security men and headed for the site. When they arrived there, a security cordon had already been set up. He was told that the UFO was no longer visible. Very high radiation readings were found on the trees surrounding the site. All kinds of animal sounds were coming from a nearby farm, as though the animals were in a very agitated state. The lights that the team was using were subject to inexplicable outages. They also were experiencing radio interference about 150 feet from the suspected impact point, the same place where Burroughs and Penniston had reported seeing the mysterious craft two days previously. There were deep gashes in the trees surrounding the site. Halt took pictures of the indentations in the trees.

One of Halt's men then pointed out a light in the distance. It was a bright red light, with a dark red center, about 150 yards ahead of them. It looked like an eye. The red light had a yellow tinge. As they watched, the light got bigger; they realized it was coming closer. It was moving through the trees toward them, in a dipping motion, zigzagging as it approached. The lighted object was dripping what appeared to them to be molten metal. Halt and his entourage chased the light, which moved away from them into a farmer's field and stayed there for about twenty to thirty seconds. Suddenly and silently the object exploded and broke into several white objects. They went into the field to search for any burnt areas and to see if they could find the dropped matter but found nothing. But one object was overhead. It made a sudden turn and approached them at very high speed. It then stopped overhead and sent out a beam, which Halt described as a sort of laser, a "steady, constant beam." The beam then swept over the base. It seemed to focus with special attention on the area where the nuclear weapons were housed. Halt and his crew were mesmerized. The object then sped away and continued beaming the light down as it went into the distance.

John Burroughs, one of the men who had seen the actual craft on the ground two nights earlier, then arrived at the site. He noticed that all the men in Colonel Halt's party were, as he put it, "weird." As he looked away he saw a blue light in the clearing that Colonel Halt had just examined. The Colonel authorized a Sergeant Adrian Bustinza to investigate the light. They went toward the strange glow in the field. As they got closer, the blue light disappeared and the whole area was in darkness again.

Debriefing followed. This was generally straightforward, but Sergeant Penniston, who had actually touched the craft, said that things "got heavy." Two weeks after the initial interview, people from the Officers' Special Investigation Unit came to interview them. The investigations took a sinister form, with the authorities using sodium pentathol to extract information. The whole questioning approach was shaped to leave the suggestion that there was no UFO and that the light that had been seen was nothing more unusual than the lighthouse at Orford Ness. What of the photographs taken by the cameras as the whole experience unfolded at Rendlesham? I'll give you three guesses. They all turned out blank. But who developed them? You guessed it! The authorities on the base.

For days afterward there was a lot of secret to-ing and fro-ing from the site of the occurrences, with squads of personnel and helicopters sweeping the area. Colonel Halt confirms this in a memo he wrote to the British Ministry of Defense (MOD), outlining the whole experience. Then the whole affair was closed.

None of this would have made it to the public eye if not for Larry Warren, an airman who worked in security at the base for years. Three years later he leaked the story of what had happened at the base. Using the Freedom of Information Act, Warren got a copy of Halt's memo to the MOD, which was published in 1983 by a British newspaper, the *News of the World*.

Warren had a story of his own to tell. He was one of the airmen at Bentwaters ordered from his post to help Colonel Halt's initiative in investigating the strange lights two days after the day Halt had gone out himself. Warren claimed that on reaching a clearing on December

29, he saw a group of military personnel surrounding a glowing object; as he drew nearer the object, he saw three small glowing entities with humanoid shapes standing in the light. He watched as an officer started communicating with the entities.

The whole Rendlesham event underwent a huge verification process, years afterward, when a concerted effort was made to debunk it. All kinds of bizarre suggestions to account for it have been made, some of them concocted years later. But they could not break the stories of the main individuals involved, including Colonel Halt, who all verified that the whole thing happened as they reported. The firsthand witnesses have all maintained their story to this day. I find them brave and noble individuals. The whole human race will one day see what they owe them for fighting against those who deliberately seek to obfuscate the real evidence, which shows that this world of ours is a stage for a deadly cohort, a stage set up and designed to make fools of all who seek to expose what they are up to.

Despite the government pronouncements about the Rendlesham forest incident, one man whose views cannot be ignored is the late Lord Peter Hill Norton, chief of staff of the British Armed Forces.

It seems to me that something physical took place, I have no doubt that something landed at this U.S. Air Force Base and I have no doubt that it got the people concerned, the Air Force people and the Commanding General at the base, into a very considerable state. My view is that the Ministry of Defense, who are repeatedly questioned about this, not only by me, but by the other people, have doggedly stuck to their normal line, which is that nothing which was of defense interest took place on that occasion. My position about this is quite clear and I have said this both in public and on the television and on the radio and I said it face to face to Lord Trethgowan when we met—either large numbers of people, including the Commanding General at Bentwaters, were hallucinating and for an American Air Force Base this is extremely dangerous, or what they say happened did happen and in either of those circumstances there can only be one answer and that is that it was of extreme defense interest to the U.K. and I have never had a satisfactory rebuttal of that view.[2]

Colonel Halt and Admiral Hill Norton—high-ranking military personnel—staked their reputations to declare out loud that a real and solid phenomenon unlike anything they had experienced in their careers as frontline defense personnel is taking place on this planet. I believe that the forces that know the phenomenon is real are centrally powerful in every major country. They are backed by an outlay of extraterrestrial intellect and power that can make it well nigh impossible to discover any smoking gun that will put the presence of this power beyond doubt.

Of course there are many who say: "No smoking gun means no alien presence on Earth." They use this pretext to counter every anecdote, every personal experience of extraterrestrial contact, no matter how compelling or how reputable the contactee might be. There is no way that any single mouse is going to bell this particular cat. What is needed is for the numbers of mice trying to do it to become so overwhelming that the sheer weight of number and the sheer zeal of the effort is so great and pervasive that the magnitude of the push to lay it all bare overcomes the awesome conspiracy to keep it all hidden.

Even so, there are now well over 7,500 pilot-reported confrontations with UFOs to date that catalogue in-air encounters all over the world since regular air flights began.

In January 2001, the leading international news service Agence France Presse reported that a Siberian airport was shut down for an hour and a half while a luminescent unidentified flying object hovered above its runway. A compelling October 2000 study by a retired aerospace scientist from NASA-Ames Research Center shows that similar incidents have occurred in American skies over the last fifty years. *Aviation Safety in America—A Previously Neglected Factor* presents over one hundred pilot and crew reports of encounters with unidentified aerial phenomena (UAP) that appear to have compromised aviation safety.[3]

Author Dr. Richard F. Haines, formerly NASA's Chief of the Space Human Factors Office, documents how, in stunning detail, pilots and crew describe a range of geometric forms and lights inconsistent with known aircraft or natural phenomena. All the reports quoted in the next few paragraphs are referenced in his report. They include bizarre objects pacing aircraft at relatively near distances, sometimes disabling cockpit instruments, interrupting ground communications, or distracting the crew. Fifty-six near misses are documented; in a few cases the pilot's reaction to approaching high-speed objects caused passengers to be thrown from their seats or crew to be injured. In 1997, a Swiss Air Boeing 747 over Long Island just missed a glowing white, cylindrical object speeding toward the plane. According to an FAA Civil Aviation Security Office memorandum, Pilot Philip Bobet said that "if the object had been any lower, it might have hit the right wing."

While flying over Lake Michigan in 1981, TWA Captain Phil Schultz saw a "large, round, silver metal object," with dark portholes equally spaced around the circumference, which "descended into the atmosphere from above," according to his handwritten report. Schultz and his first officer braced themselves for a midair collision; the object suddenly made a high speed turn and departed. Veteran Japan Airlines 747 Captain Kenju Terauchi reported a spectacular, prolonged encounter over Alaska in 1986. "Most unexpectedly two space ships stopped in front of our face, shooting off lights," he said. "The inside cockpit shined brightly and I felt warm in the face." Despite the FAA determination that he and his crew were stable, competent, and professional, he was grounded for speaking out.

Ground systems operators have also been affected by these craft. "The element of surprise means a decrease in safety because it diverts the attention of air traffic controllers that should be focused on landing planes. That is a danger," says Jim McClenahen, a recently retired FAA air traffic control specialist and NARCAP technical advisor. *Aviation Safety in America* does not attempt to explain the origin of these mysterious objects. But Haines writes that hundreds of reports, some dating back to the 1940s, "suggest that they are associated with a very high degree of intelligence, deliberate flight control, and advanced energy management."

In the 1950s, pilots and crew reported seeing flying discs, cigar-shaped craft with portholes, and gyrating lights, all with extraordinary technical capabilities. Documents show that the unexplained objects were considered a national security concern. By order of the Joint Chiefs of Staff, commercial pilots were required to report sightings. At the same time, the unauthorized release of a UFO report could cost them ten years in prison or a $10,000 fine. To keep this information from the public, officials ridiculed and debunked legitimate sightings, angering some pilots. According to the *Newark Star-Ledger* in 1958, over fifty commercial pilots who had reported sightings, each with at least fifteen years of major airline experience, blasted the policy of censorship and denial as "bordering on the absolutely ridiculous."[4]

These pilots said they were interrogated by the Air Force, sometimes all night long, and then "treated like incompetents and told to keep quiet," according to one pilot. "The Air Force tells you that the thing that paced your plane for 15 minutes was a mirage or a bolt of lightning," he told the *Star-Ledger*. "Nuts to that. Who needs it?" As a result, many pilots "forget" to report their sightings at all, one pilot said.

According to a 1952 Air Force Status Report on UFOs for the Air Technical Intelligence Center, pilots were so humiliated that one told investigators: "If a space ship flew wing-tip to wing-tip formation with me, I would not report it." The vast majority of sightings by American pilots are still not reported. The media perpetuates the censorship and ridicule, handicapping the collection of valuable data.[5]

A 1999 French study by retired generals from the French Institute of Higher Studies for National Defense and a government agency with the National Center for Space Studies examined hundreds of well-documented pilot reports from around the world. The study could not explain a 1994 Air France viewing of an object that instantaneously disappeared as confirmed by radar and a 1995 Aerolineas Argentinas

Boeing 727 encounter with a luminous object that extinguished airport lights as the plane attempted to land. "Aeronautic personnel . . . must be sensitised and prepared to deal with the situation," the report states. They must first "accept the possibility of the presence of extraterrestrial craft in our sky." Then, "it is necessary to overcome the fear of ridicule."

In 1997, the Chilean government formed the Committee for the Study of Anomalous Aerial Phenomena (CEFAA) following publicly acknowledged observations of unidentified flying objects at a remote Chilean airport.

Both the French group and General Ricardo Bermudez Sanhuesa, president of the CEFAA, have made overtures to the U.S. government for cooperation on this issue, with no response. General Bermudez Sanhuesa, and Air Force General Denis Letty, chairman of the French group, stated in recent interviews that the Haines study has international significance and should be taken seriously. Brian E. Smith, current head of the Aviation Safety Program at NASA-Ames, agrees. "There is objective evidence in pilot reports of unexplained events that may affect the safety of the aircraft," he says. "Yet getting people to take an objective look at this subject is sometimes like pulling teeth."[6]

To further illustrate the extent of the cover-up, let's have a look at a subject that has received a good deal less public attention than the UFO phenomenon. I refer to the phenomenon of Unidentified Submarine Objects (USOs). These are craft that seem to appear out of, or disappear into, bodies of water. Given the fact that about three-quarters of the Earth's surface is covered by water and that many areas of water are so deep that they have not yet been explored, a convincing case could be made to suggest that an underwater harbor for alien craft would be ideal for their purposes, if they wish to remain out of sight as much as possible.

The USS Franklin D. Roosevelt was an experimental floating laboratory for the U.S. Navy from the 1950s until it was decommissioned in 1977. It was the first U.S. carrier to carry nuclear weapons. For some reason—and many have speculated that this reason might center on the ship's advanced technology and the fact that it carried nuclear weapons—the USS FDR seems to have been a central focus point for UFO activity. Chet Grusinski was an engineer on the vessel between January 1958 and December 1960. In September 1958, Grusinski was on the vessel as it cruised Guantanamo Bay near Cuba. Notes Grusinski: "I was down below when I was told to go topside to see something strange. So I went up and couldn't believe my eyes."[7] The encounter lasted for forty-five seconds. Grusinski saw a cigar-shaped craft with no accompanying sound. He could see a row of windows on the craft through which he could see "silhouettes of figures looking at us. They had no features and you could tell they weren't human. I could feel the heat on my face and these figures looking at us. Then the bottom turned cherry red and it vanished in a flash." Grusinski says that at least twenty-five of his shipmates witnessed the event, but these crew members were quickly transferred off the FDR. Within hours the ship's log had been altered so that no mention was made of the incident.

Harry Jordan was a radar operator on the FDR between 1962 and 1965. From 1961 to December 1965, Jordan served aboard the destroyer escort USS Laffey, destroyer USS Loeser, and aircraft carrier USS Franklin D. Roosevelt. He served in the operation's intelligence division on all three ships, to display, analyze, report, and record radar, radio, and electronic emission data. For this he received extensive training at the Naval Station, Newport, Rhode Island. While on the FDR he served two cruises in the Mediterranean. After discharge from active duty he worked as an instructor at Jones Point Naval Reserve, Alexandria, Virginia, on the use of navigational equipment particular to radar intelligence, testimony to his expertise in his field, especially regarding the detection of surface or air objects as far away as 300 miles.

On October 2, 1963, Jordan detected a large UFO off the coast of Sardinia. Apparently fifteen other seamen witnessed the event with binoculars. He provided the Senate Intelligence Committee with an affidavit detailing his experience. According to his own account: "During this particular cruise there were several photographers on board to document the NATO fleet operations. They were present on board the night of my contact on radar. I was told in no uncertain terms to keep my mouth shut for 20 years." The following is Jordan's firsthand account of the UFO encounter, the text taken directly from his testimony before a U.S. Senate UFO hearing in the summer of 1998:

> Late one night while operating off the coast of Sardinia at approximately 02.00 hours Zulu time I was standing mid watch on an SPA-8 repeater and height finding equipment. My IFF box was enabled and in the process of challenging an aerial contact approaching the ship from a bearing of 012 degrees relative to our course. The aerial contact was detected at 600 miles according to the calibration rings on my scope. I made several adjustments to the calibration settings because I didn't believe I detected such a contact at that distance. The aerial contact was at a height of 80,000 then dropped to 65,000 feet in about 20 seconds where the contact then hovered for about ten minutes.[8]

The original height of eighty thousand feet was an impossible height for any conventional aircraft at the time. Jordan goes on to say:

> During this period the watch officer woke the Division Commander and informed him of our situation. U.S. Naval Task Forces operating in the Mediterranean in those days were being subjected to frequent flyovers by Russian Bear aircraft with electronic warfare capability. It was my job to stay alert for such a scenario. The Division Commander came into CIC, observed the radar returns, expedited his own ECM scan of the contact and then informed the orderly standing watch at the Captain's stateroom. The Captain was appraised of the situation, ordered a course change into the wind and increased ship's speed to launch aircraft. During this time I was continuing to observe the contact and watched the Phantom F4Bs

once they attained sufficient altitude. The Phantoms went to after burners vectoring to a course straight for the bogey on my scope. After a period of about 15 to 20 minutes the F4Bs were within 200 miles of the bogey due north of our course. They turned on their conical scan radar, the bogey disappeared from my scope. The pilots did not detect any contact on their scope, were turned by the Air Ops C.O. and headed back to the ship. The Captain had kept the ship on a heading into the wind during this entire operation so aircraft could be launched or recovered at will.

The Phantoms returned to the ship and were recovered. About five minutes after the recovery of the last aircraft and during the process of turning the ship back to our original course the contact winked back on again! This time it closed from a distance of 600 miles from the ship to right above us in about 1 minute. The bogey was traveling around 3,600 miles an hour at an altitude of 30,000 feet. I never saw any heat signature. Someone in CIC yelled out, "damn it what the hell is that!" I couldn't determine who made the comment. Lookouts on the port and starboard look out wings of the conning tower could not see anything above the ship with their binoculars. The situation was bizarre and watch personnel looked scared but calm.[9]

Jordan later mentioned in a television interview that the immense speed and right-angled turns made by the craft in a Z pattern would "have crushed any man-made aircraft." He also says that he has personally witnessed on radar all kinds of aircraft, Soviet and Chinese included, plus meteor phenomena, but this particular contact was "nothing like it." The commanding officer, a Commander Gibson, burst in after the incident was over and asked him what he had put in his log. When Jordan showed him his record of the incident he was told to take out all mention of it. Jordan queried this, saying that surely it was an unidentified craft that had been witnessed. The commander's reply was, "Yeah, that was what it was, but no, Jordan, nobody else is to know."

Jordan expressed his dismay at the situation in the TV interview in the following way: "This is a historical moment for the U.S. Navy and it is left out of the log."

Six similar events have been cited on the USS FDR. One of the most remarkable was the multiple sighting that occurred during the NATO Operation Main Brace in 1952.[10] Main Brace was the first multilateral maneuver after World War II. It was a NATO fleet exercise near the coast of Denmark involving two hundred ships, one thousand planes, and eighty thousand men from NATO member nations. The USS FDR led the way to seal off Russian submarine access through the North Sea into the Atlantic. On September 13, 1952 Lieutenant Colonel Schmidt Jensen and his crew members on a Danish destroyer saw a luminous triangular-shaped object moving above the water in close proximity to the main fleet. The object moved westward and then southeast toward the FDR. During the following week many more sightings were reported.

On September 20 at 7:30 p.m., several officers saw a small disc-shaped object rise out of the water and head for the FDR. The object went east and then disappeared into the cloud layer. The next day, September 21, 1952, British officers flying over the North Sea saw a shiny object come out of the water. They gave chase to it but it evaded their pursuit. According to a witness report, given to Harry Jordan, at one point an object a quarter of a mile wide actually dented one of the ships and the damage was later reported as the result of a collision between two destroyers. During Operation Main Brace there were multiple sightings by crew members on the FDR. A journalist on board, Wallace Litvin, managed to photograph the disc on September 20. The U.S. Navy was given the photo to study.

It seems that USOs change and displace the surface of the water. The Tully Nests off the Coast of North Queensland in Australia are a case in point. Cane farmer George Pedley was driving his tractor through a neighboring farm when he suddenly developed problems with the tractor and heard a high-pitched hissing noise in the distance. Twenty to thirty feet away from him, rising from the lagoon was a thirty or forty foot metallic disc. It took a shallow dive into the water and then took off at high speed. The disc left an imprint on the lagoon surface like a whirlpool, which lasted for days. Half a dozen other "water nests" were found in the area, and samples of the water were sent to Brisbane University for radiation testing. The tests proved positive for beta radiation, but the samples mysteriously disappeared.[11]

The numerous signs of extraterrestrial presence on our planet are summarily dismissed or suppressed by every governmental authority of any size and importance. It is apparent from my research that the intelligence of these visitors is so supreme they have control of all the governments of any significance on this planet, through cartels of their agents at the center of most administrations. These individuals have been placed there for just such a reason: to dismiss and obscure any revelations that might identify an alien extraterrestrial hand in the affairs of humanity. It is done with very few individuals. They only have to be placed at the articulation points of administration: the joints, not the long bones.

The dissemination of information around the world can be narrowed down to very few central portals of origin. All of the main publishing agencies of the world's media are finally owned by the security and intelligence services of the United States and a few others in the major countries such as the Soviet Union, Britain, Germany, France, and China, through myriad of doglegs of ownership. This is a startling revelation to the public at large and of course should be proved with evidence. But just suppose someone attempted to do this. If the all-powerful security services of the United States, with their power to control even sovereign governments, deem it a taboo subject, there would be no way any journalist would stand a bat's chance in hell of getting any of this evidence to public notice, never mind proved. There are too many points along the way at which the process could be stopped. Most media editors of any prominence value their status and livelihoods if not their lives too much. Part of the reason for the adoption of antiterrorist laws may well have been to stop such an eventuality.

Evidence is plentiful. Getting it to the public notice with any power to impress is plainly and simply getting more and more impossible each day. There are too many stooges in the information-dissemination pipeline, with their foreheads branded with CIA, KGB, MI6, Mossad, RAW, Surette, and all manner of other national covert spying organizations. They ensure that a headline such as "This World is Run by a Race of Super Roboids" will never appear in the places that count. Stooges act as front men, whose job it is to see to it that editorial control is maintained by more stooges who have one all-encompassing priority: make sure nothing ever definitively reveals the presence of an alien intelligence in the affairs of our species.

The fakers and the New Age proselytizers who weave endless lies and bizarre imaginary socio-religious tapestries only help with the cover-up. In fact, deliberate and carefully planned fake reports are a favorite ploy used by the powerful secret-keepers to disillusion the public at large. UFO sightings are manufactured, made to look convincing, and then debunked by the so-called experts called in. Millions of people are fooled into accepting the party line of huge power groups, and maximum coverage worldwide is given to the well-coached liars who represent them. If you think governments aren't capable of such subterfuge, think: "Iraq." A single word encapsulates all I mean.

Most of the infamous internationally significant incidents have their original authorships in the occidental or white-run governments and countries of the world, with the blame for the responsibility for these acts put on the shoulders of Third World countries as the culprits. Referring to the old Southern racist adage "nigger in the wood pile," which suggests that somehow, somewhere, there would always be a black person to blame for any trouble, the late James Cameron, the illustrious journalist and columnist, once told me years ago that, on the contrary, I should look for the "white man in the wood pile" where evil rules the day. He was convinced that I would never find any "niggers" there. The entire Iraq engagement is a vivid example of how powerful these groups are in getting their way. Exposed now the world over as a huge conspiracy, full of double-talk, misinformation, and downright lies, the United States, Britain, and a few of their more racially and tribally motivated allies carried out an attack on a sovereign country in opposition to the will of the vast majority of the people of the world.

This is a vivid example of the extent to which the Anglo-Saxon cartel of humanity, through the U.S. and British governments, will go to produce the result they intend to get. It forever indicts anything they claim in the future. You believe them at the risk of your children's welfare. The families of nearly five thousand soldiers of U.S. and British dominion are now living their lives in the tears of their loss, while the perpetrators plan the next hall of victimization—Iran. They have already begun the demonization of this nation as they did with Iraq before they went in. The lies and obfuscation of the truth are cleverly postured in the media. It happens every day all over the world. It is the daily business of national intelligence agencies to set things up for their own governments, so that individuals and enemy countries get the blame in the public mind for their own evil acts. Your news is managed in their interests.

How, then, can we hope to know the truth?

# 3

# **What Is Truth?**

You sit there reading this presumably with a mind that can make sense of what I am writing. You do this with a consciousness and an awareness that you take for granted and presume is part of the physical infrastructure of your being. You are what we commonly call human and live on a place in the universe we call a planet. You and the place you live are made of atoms, and these atoms give rise to and compose a substantiality that defines our reality as material and physical. It is touchable, tangible, and in this context, verifiable.

I ask you to pause a moment now and consider all this as deeply as you can. Consider first your reality. Consider how you know this reality and verify it. How do you define this reality? How do you measure it? How are you aware of it?

There you sit, implicitly and tacitly measuring how you know and judge your situation as a living being. You are in some sort of physical placement while you are doing all this. Perhaps you are sitting down, or lying down, maybe in a room somewhere, or in the open air. You are surrounded by the paraphernalia of life. You may be physically comfortable. You may be uncomfortable. You may be feeling a soft cushion against your back, possibly tasting a drink of coffee as you read. You are measuring it all, either consciously or subconsciously. In other words you *know* all this to be true in these moments.

Let's now consider the elements that allow you to do this, and how

41

each functions in itself, out of itself, and in interplay with the other, to make the whole you. We can start with the dictionary definitions:

Truth: *The state of being the case, the fact. The body of real things, events, and facts. Actuality. A transcendent fundamental or spiritual reality. The property of being in accord with fact or reality, in accord with reason or correct principles, or an accepted standard.*

The definitions are rather imprecise. They pass the buck. We now have to look up what *fact* is and what *reality* is. What constitutes *correct principles* and *accepted standards?* Truth will naturally vary according to what standards and principles are applied. Whatever definition we accept, it is likely to provide an existential compromise. In other words, what is true in one culture may not be in another; what is truth to a priest or an artist is likely to be fallacy to a scientist. To an artist, or to someone with an extended sense of meaning, a leaf might be the most beautiful representation of form, structure, and arrangement, while to a scientist it is more likely to be defined as something that cows eat!

On the face of it all we seem to live to die and not to exist. In this madness no more value is placed on our being than that of the day's own troubles. But it is only the madness of those who won't or can't see past the face value of anything, those not capable of perceiving and asking the simple questions that logically deny this premise, such as: Why do we dream? Why is there song, poetry, imagination, and the capacity to change the natural course of anything, if it is all as meaningless as we are told by scientists now? If, in other words, the inherent drive of the whole physical existential scale is finally to take out meaning itself? How true and reliable is this premise broached in madness? It is all we have if science is to be believed, if we all seek truth with the hard-wired resolutions of the physical senses. Yet these are the premises increasingly accepted these days. In fact it may be said that the power of scientific endorsement is now the most significant power ruling the lives of human beings on the planet. It used to be religious belief once upon a time. In contemporary times the parameters for believing in most things are getting more and more narrow, and the scientific ethic of empirical provability increasingly determines what we finally accept as truth.

The lords of science say that the whole of physical creation is defined by the laws of physics. These doyens of rationally expressed meaning claim that the truths that underpin our reality can only be affirmed by science. Actually, the business of science is only to affirm that which pertains to force, that which is physically real and substantial. In other words it is *objective* in its approach. There is no room for the *subjective* in science. The strongest implication of all that scientists say and do is that whatever is not physically verifiable with their tools is unreal and thus *untrue*.

This single-dimensional approach to truth, when used as a means of control, can be devastating to the aegis of living beings with rational choice-making capability. It tends to lump everything together in reductionist modes that fail to see the whole multidimensional nature of all things. Such an approach can only finally recognize humanity and never human beings. Even worse, science today is more likely to be in pursuit of funding than truth. This further sharpens the reductionism.

The universe can be viewed as a brick that broke up at its inception and has ever since then been broken up into smaller and smaller pieces, in greater and greater states of chaotic amelioration from each other. In some areas of this "Universe of Parts," the pieces are more stuck together than in others. Scientists are like more aggregated pieces riding on more broken-up pieces, using the broken pieces to try to figure out what "brickness" was in the first place. Mystics, philosophers, and seers know what brickness is all about. Scientists, and all who think like them, seem to have lost the ability to know; they look for the answers while sitting on the grains of sand that once made up the brick.

However, there are notable exceptions to this even within the scientific community. Among them stands distinguished physicist Professor Russell Stannard, who points out in his book *Doing Away With God:* "Science cannot say what anything is. At a fundamental level, it cannot say what anything actually is." He clearly illustrates this point in the following way:

(You can say) that matter is made of atoms; an atom is made of a nucleus and electrons; the nucleus is made of protons and neutrons; and protons and neutrons are made of quarks. So, everything is made of electrons and quarks. So, there we have it. What is matter? It's a pile of electrons and quarks. But does that really tell us what matter is? No, not at all. We haven't said what quarks and electrons are—other than that they are point-like somethings.

There are of course additional statements we can make about them. We can say for example, that each electron and quark spins about on its axis like a top. But that still does not throw light on the nature of the *stuff* out of which the tiny top is made.

Or we can say that the particles carry electric charge. But that only gets us into deeper water still. It raises the question: What is electric charge? Again, we can't actually say.

We introduce the notion of electric charge because it helps us to understand the movement of the particles better. For example, it is noticed that when two electrons are placed close to each other, they tend to try and move away from each other. Why do they do that? We say that they each carry an amount of negative electric charge and that like charges repel each other. Good. That explains the motion of the electrons. But it does not tell us anything about what electric charge is—any more than it helps us to understand what the matter is that carries the charge.

Talking about motion brings us up against yet more unknowns. The motions are in space and time. But what actually is space? What actually is time? We know how to measure them. We can assert that the distance here called a meter, is a 100 times that one called a centimeter; or that an hour is 60 times as long as a minute, but the actual nature of space and of time? They remain a mystery.

So, if science is fundamentally incapable of explaining what anything actually is, what does it explain?

It describes how things behave. That's all science ever does. It describes how point-like objects behave in space and time and it manages to do that without ever coming clean about the nature of the *stuff* that makes up either the objects, or the space, or the time. Put that way, it can sound like a pretty modest enterprise.[1]

A new edition of *The New Physics,* first published in 1989, was published in 2006 and is entitled *The New Physics for the Twenty-First Century* (Gordon Fraser, Cambridge University Press). According to Robert Matthews, science writer, reviewing the new edition in the *New Scientist*:

> It remains hard to escape the conclusion that there just hasn't been much progress toward answering the Big Questions since the publication of the first edition. That is not to deny that some very significant discoveries have been made. But all too often these discoveries have shown that physicists are far from reaching their summit, and in some cases may be on the wrong path altogether.[2]

Key cosmic parameters such as an accurate determination of the age of the universe have been determined since the book was first published, but Matthews is careful to point out that:

> The determination of these key parameters is undoubtedly a landmark in cosmology, but the implications, as Freedman and Kolb are quick to point out, are disquieting to say the least. Put simply, the measurements point to a universe filled with a kind of matter we have never seen and propelled by a force we do not understand. Such a revelation is progress of a sort, but it hardly suggests that the peak of Mount En-lightenment is just over the next hump. . . . The impression is one of physicists not so much approaching a beckoning peak as wandering about in a thick fog.[2]

Apparently, at a conference discussing superstring theory (December 2005) a pioneer of the theory admitted: "We don't know what we're talking about." Matthews concludes his review with the following sardonic remark: "Who knows, perhaps physicists are about to reach the broad sunlit uplands of cosmic insight." Don't hold your breath, though. The latest edition of *The New Physics* suggests too many of them are stumbling about with their eyes aimed straight at their boots.

We have to resist the explanation of truth in terms of the scientific way alone, or we will be looking at it in the most limited of ways. If a truth as an axiom is anything at all, it has to be the final arbitration of what a thing is in its completeness. That is, it has to be able to be expressed for all to know in all possible ways and not in any specific way. It has to reflect the whole story of any particular thing with all the connections of and to it, because nothing stands alone. Let's therefore try to be as simple as we can in explaining and defining these ways, so that as many of us as possible can get our minds around them and see them as completely and as holistically as possible.

This is something science can never do. Science is not very intelligent in believing that empirically verified truth is all that is true. By intelligence I mean the ability to assemble collected information so that the meaning of this information can be gleaned in its ultimate aspect and totality. To do this requires a systematic approach. That approach is provided for by what we commonly term logic. Logic may be seen as the connection of connectable facts so that they are in their ultimate value set in their most economic and ergonomic potential. Intelligence and logic go hand in glove (not hand in hand).

If intelligence is applied to the premise that truth is only what is discernable through our physical senses, it reveals that something essential has been left out. No physical sense can empirically detect the very thing that gives meaning to any truth—*thought*. Thought lies in the realm of the ephemeral and the implied. Yet, with the mightiest of ironies, thought is the foundation of all that is accepted by science. The famous French mathematician and philosopher Descartes retorted to a challenge to affirm his existence by saying: "I think therefore I am." In these words he defined his existence in the simplest possible way. He thus affirmed his existence as the product of an abstraction. The two clue words he used to do this were "think" and "am." Thus Descartes did not describe the physical material being that science defines us to be. Instead he defined the presence of his being as the verification of something that thinks.

Thought is the central aegis that we all use to apply the intelligence that makes reasoned sense of anything. The hand in the glove of all meaning is made known through thought. There you have it: thought and intelligence—through which all truth is perceived and discerned—are themselves never provable through the methods science uses to establish truth. How then can thought exist? How can it manifest and, how is it the basis that provides the means to give value to anything through intelligence?

Thought has been attributed to the mechanism we call "mind." But how do we define mind? Can we separate it from the body? The first place to look is of course the dictionary. This tells us that the mind is the seat of volition, thought, and feeling. But where precisely is this absolutely final seat, this power that arbitrates all knowing? Where do we find it or pinpoint it? No one knows precisely where the mind exists. We do know it is not physical or substantial, nor is it a single elemental entity that we can find through the mechanisms we use to define physical material things. We know that it is ephemeral, abstract, and insubstantial, yet it manifests to support all our capacities to know anything. It is the final paradox. We can use it to manifest and understand everything that defines our physical living being and its environment, but we may, it seems, never know it in terms of its own intrinsic reality as an entity in itself.

How then does the physically unreal exist and allow us to know about all that exists and existence itself? If the physically unreal, namely the mind, defines all our reality, surely that which is finally true ought to be of a metaphysical, ephemeral, abstract, nonphysical nature, rather than of a "hard," enforced, verifiable one. The logic of it all by implication makes this undeniably true. But the two states of reality, the physical and the "nonphysical," seem so wrapped in each other that we may not separate them.

The general consensus seems to be that the mind is likely to be located in the brain. We know that our thinking process is altered if we put a physical probe in the site of the brain and stimulate it electronically. This does not happen with any other organ of the body. We thus say the brain is the site of the mind. We sense with our brain. We think with our brain . . . or do we? I hope to show you in this book that we really think with *all* of our being.

The information on which we might decide any truth is seen or perceived against a background screen we call consciousness. This in itself can only be tacitly proven because we know it is going on subjectively and only subjectively. We can never know it is going on objectively. We can never know if anyone else's actions are conscious, or whether they are derivations of a program that makes them happen through the mere promulgation of nonbiological forces acting upon their bodies (like a robot for instance). Yet we believe with only subjective affirmations that while we are alive we are conscious.

There is argument and speculation in the world of science that a kind of consciousness might be created out of a "framed mathematical symposium, a state at some sort of quantum level of interaction where quarkiness deploys to mathematical statements and gives a field of coherence." This gobbledygook is a statement made by an eminent neuroscientist in a desperate effort to explain the manifestation of consciousness as a product of an atomic hive.

But other scientists have been proving this stance wrong. Mexican neurophysiologist Jacobo Grinberg-Zylberbaum conducted an experiment in which he demonstrated that consciousness can cross physical barriers of separation. In this experiment, two subjects meditated together with the intention of establishing direct communication. They were separated and put in electromagnetically insulated chambers and wired up to separate electroencephalogram (EEG) machines. When one of them saw a series of light flashes, it evoked a potential in his brain's EEG that was reflected, in a similar phase and strength, in the other subject's EEG. Control subjects did not show a transferred potential.

Thus the brains of the two experimental subjects were correlated via conscious intention.[3] If consciousness were purely a product of brain function, the results of this experiment would be impossible.

The great teachers of philosophical and religious truth all hailed a world beyond the physical as the final experience of all experiences. They affirmed this as a world with magnitudes that surpassed our physical, matter-based "real world." These sometimes fabulous, but mostly marvelous, teachers encouraged us to guide our behavior and our focus for future behavior, with resolute affirmation of the physically unreal. They insisted that the realms of the physical and nonphysical were so inextricably intertwined that behavior within the one decided existential status within the other. They spoke of a world that exists beyond atoms, and some of them manifested markers of that world with a physically real phenomenon known as transfiguration.

These teachers affirmed the existence of numerous rhetorically and metaphysically real processes and procedures such as soul transmigration and reincarnation. Some were so filled with the reality of the other, next, or final world that each step they took in this one was carefully and precisely designed to gain entry to, and ensure that they would never return from, the world that they described beyond this temporal Universe of Parts and diminishing returns.

The one phenomenon above all others that defines our existence in this universe is the phenomenon we call *force*. The universe is made of various aggregations of force set in an overall binding composed of gravity, the electromagnetic force, the atomic strong force, the atomic weak force, and the nuclear force. This universe of "en-forced" or enforced phenomena is made up of a number of basic entities called subatomic particles or waveforms. These are packages, or vibrating discrete locations of tension, or potential tension, that change—when forced, either from within themselves or by external contrivance—into the various physical manifestations we see and know as our solid material world. The basic building block of this materiality, the atom, has itself been found to be made out of subatomic minutia, entities called protons, neutrons, electrons, and, on an even smaller scale, quarks, bosons, leptons, gluons, and photons. These, when taken down even further, define the very space and time in which we exist.

Take an average glass of water and hold it before you. If you completely release the force bound up in the atoms of water in that glass you will destroy the city in which you live, no matter how big that city is. How therefore does water exist in a form that does not destroy? Indeed, how does anything physical or material exist? If the force that makes the water in the Caspian Sea, for instance, were not kept in a state of inertial balance, the release of all the force holding together and making up the atoms would make our planet vanish. It could be said, if the scientists are to be believed, that the entire universe is a package of force, inertially bound in and out of itself, that only exists in purely enforced physical terms for itself. But nothing can be further from the truth. The scientists' idea of the universe is only partially true.

Most of us believe utter illogical nonsense. Most of us cherish, fight for, and die for beliefs that—when looked at carefully and with meaning and pristine mathematical implicate logic—are seen to be postulations of utter drivel that are worthy of the repeat mechanistic reactive mentalities of baboons and apes. Why do we do this? Indeed, what makes so many of us do this, even if some of us have mentalities that are apparently capable of the highest values of logic and its manifestation in mathematics, art, music, engineering, and philosophy?

In travels around the world I have met many a clever mind steeped in the highest university degrees, alumni reflecting learning in the disciplines of the real physical world of medicine, physics, chemistry, and biology, men and women of great eminence in their fields. To my astonishment, many consult astrologers and holy men before they take any important steps in their personal lives. In other words, they consult subjective modalities of thought and opinion unverified through logic and in some instances plainly illogical. They will yet walk into their laboratories the next day and verify as truth things they can measure, see, taste, feel, and touch, and totally dismiss any claim, hunch, or feeling their colleagues might have unless it is verifiable and physically definite. Why is this contradiction so prevalent? What instinct leads us despite ourselves to see nature as more than just the physically verifiable? What leads us to such contrary stances in seeing, sorting out, and accepting what might be regarded as true?

If all things have meaning then there must be the means of divining it out of and from all things that exist. But what things exist truly in their own terms and are forever, and what things only exist as a reference against others? It all comes down to the nature of awareness, thought, knowing, and will, and how these capacities manifest in the first place. Do thought and knowing come from the context of atoms or are they a product of the interface of a paradigm of no force acting on paradigm of force?

We now tend to depend on modern science for all the answers that we once accepted on trust, faith, or forced belief in the past. The main expressers of these truths were the religious, who, under the authority of their gods or demons, promulgated their various party lines under the sanction of negative results to the offender or disbeliever, be these results hell fire and damnation, or some other sort of forfeit. Religious belief was of course centered on things "out there," things unseen and usually not empirically provable. The vast majority of cultures worldwide believed in a spiritual world of gods, spirits, ghosts, and demons. Strict codes and regimens of behavior were inculcated into the human psyche with such power of compliance that all motives and methodologies of day-to-day life included these guides for behavior.

Belief in an afterlife was paramount in almost all religious modalities, and the sanctions and verifications in this life were connected to the next in an ongoing cycle that to some was eternal and to others was temporary. There were those who believed we had one chance to get it right and our eternity would forever depend on this. There were others who believed that an eternal ongoing cycle prevailed in which we would exchange our living modus here for another one out there, endlessly, until we settled it once and for all in a paradigm that would never allow a here and there, but instead allowed for an existence out there forever.

For all, two poles of final result marked the entire existential scale. These two finalities have been referred to by various labels and descriptions throughout history and culture, but they come down to what is of and within atoms and what might be beyond atoms and atomic resolution.

We now come to the crunch that all the foregoing alludes to. We simply cannot afford to see things in isolation because all things in existence are connected. To gain a more holistic view we are compelled to take a look at the summary of our human condition and set it against the array of the entire existential scale. It is only at the point that we seek and make these connections that the awesome and harrowing pertinence of it all becomes clear. It becomes clear in terms of the final and only thing that matters: *You.*

# 4

# Who Rules?

You are in your bedroom. You wake up in the morning, feeling great! Or maybe not great. A few of us feel great first thing in the morning as our consciousness crashes into us and the thoughts for that particular day start to be sorted. More than likely you turn around in your bed to see another mass lying next to you. Perhaps the first thought of the day is one of reassurance. A feeling of satisfaction, of assuredness. Or maybe you take it all for granted and don't even think about it. There's been someone there for you, with you for so long, it is all passé. You are up in the first place to face work. Work! Oh God, what a horrible thought. You put it out of your head as fast as possible and go into automatic drive. Upright and out of the bedroom door you go, heading for the bathroom. You stumble in. There you come face-to-face with yourself; all senses are firing as you confront in daylight or perhaps electric light an autobiography that is whole, immediate, and unavoidable. Work flits into your mind again, but you are more concerned about the flaccid features in front of you. Awareness of the self is the most powerful property of the sentient mind, and this awareness takes the shape of the human id, the self, yourself. This is in reality the thing that life is all about: *You!* You and everydayness.

Have you ever thought of everydayness as a concept in itself rather than as a series of events that you tacitly roll into incidentally through twenty-four hours, running from one experience to another? I mean everydayness as a concept where you are not in control but are a victim controlled by the dictates of circumstance.

If you think about it, the everydayness of your life is a legacy of a vast conspiracy of implicit happenings and circumstance. It is the signature of your very existence and cannot be divorced from the self that is you. You are your everydayness. In as much as this is so, your everydayness has the devastating power to damn or redeem you, and to dictate the furthermost tenure of your very existence.

To many of us our everydayness is a most awesome unavoidable curse. Some, a relative few on our planet these days, have an everydayness to look forward to and cherish, one full of challenge, devoid of threat, and full of meaning and satisfaction. For most, alas, it is the opposite: one of dread, deference, trial, and in many instances, deep and abiding suffering.

Why the difference? Why don't we all have the same quality of everydayness? Why do so many have days to curse, full of hardship and woe, gore and angst, while others have days full of meaning and valuable purpose?

Well that's obvious, I hear you say. We are all different, and we beget our individual lives by what we are and what we do—no more, no less than that. But is that really so for all of us? What about a baby born into piles of exploded ash, where the noise surrounding it is of war and the faces around it are full of hate, sadness, and suffering? What did that baby's own individuality do to earn that beginning? It hasn't lived long enough to have made decisions that provide for such a consequence. It's fate, I hear some of you say, it's providence. Others, the majority of people on this Earth, will say it's God's will.

Most people in our world believe in a personal God or divine figure that is eternal, omnipotent, omnipresent, and omniscient. The typical axiom for people who believe in such an anthropocentric divinity is that our lives belong to this God and all influences that bring about a good or bad life and everydayness are earned by the individual, as a consequence of obeying or disobeying this personalized super phenomenon or controlling figure. If you believe in such a God, you will believe that we exist so that this God may decide every part of our individualities at whim.

Any free will we might have is not totally free, because it may be intercepted and imposed on at any moment by an all-encompassing power we are powerless to control. This implies that there is no good or bad behavior through which we can overrule God. God would decide good and bad as concepts suitable to his (or her) will and purpose and require obedience to those concepts. Whatever this God deems suitable at any particular moment is all that matters. This notion of a final arbitrating figure that has total control over the meaning and destinies of those he or she creates is defined through a concept we might call "dependent belonging." But could such a God pass muster through logical reasoning?

The God I have described above may be seen as a "no free will" concept. There are variations of the no free will concept, but they all enshrine a figure of final arbitration and imply that we are all pawns serving a purpose that only this figure knows. This is a purpose full of works and social experiments that might be at the expense of this God's creations. Such a God is often perceived to demand fear, worship and supplication, constant praise and placation, a God that allows no arbitration but his own and thus mitigates independent, individual free will. In other words, this is a God that manipulates the scales of justice subjectively, not objectively.

Could such a God have any generalized meaning as an entity that is final to everything? Can the concept of God have any meaning other than one in which subjectivity reigns? Could, for instance, a God that sends creations into a living state as babies to last just days, weeks, or months with perhaps the most grotesque crippled physical forms (some of them not even capable of knowing that they exist in this living tenure) be taken seriously? Is it in fact logically plausible that the concept of God as a controlling mechanism could be existentially valid?

We have to see this question in light of the functioning of the second law of thermodynamics, which states that the amount of entropy in a system must always increase. As the amount of entropy in a system is a measure of how disordered the system is, the higher the entropy, the more disorder. Put simply, this means that all atomically derived things break apart into increasing states of chaos and randomness with time if left alone in their residential or residual states. Yes, it is that final. It is all an action *one way*. This means that the past is more coherent, ordered, and together than the future for all matter- or force-based phenomena on any given timeline.

Not surprisingly, of course, this has the most devastating implications for the whole universe and everything in it, and that includes us. It underlines the temporality of all things and most of all provides a vista of diminishing returns for all things that persist in any Universe of Parts, as ours quite clearly is. The harrowing rub is that our tenure is marked for lessening derivations of the living state as time passes, till we finally end at death, our atomic bodies changed and broken, as entropy follows its relentless path through the very centers of our metabolism.

Why is it all one way? Why is the status of being, as witnessed in our universe, a drift to nothing and no meaning? More pertinently, why are we able to derive meaning in sentience as a stage, and seemingly only a stage, in the middle (in terms of timing) of all that has happened? Are we just here to see how meaningless it all is? Are we possessed of hope and faith and wishfulness, kindness, compassion, and the ability to love and care, simply to see it all frittered away through an awesome "satanic vicissitude" that says all of it is in vain? Our ability to see meaning also implies that there must be something more to all this than a meaningless end to all things: an eternal scope for change that challenges and defeats the tacit one-way-down change that entropy provides.

Please stop and think about this all a moment. It might provide an insight that could lead to great and profound changes in the motivations that govern lives. It might even give you, as an individual, the scope for achieving eternal existence in the highest possible maxims.

Look at a starry sky. I did that the other day. I was standing on one of the most beautiful spots in our world on the island of Sri Lanka. I was three thousand feet above sea level in a place quite near the stunningly beautiful holy mountain of the island, fittingly called Adam's Peak. I was with a group of friends, and someone called us all out to see the fantastic sight of the starry sky on a cloudless night. Sri Lanka is about five degrees above the equator, and thus the sky included a good deal of the stars seen from both hemispheres. It was a spray of wonder: thousands upon thousands of pinpoints of blue twinkling light. There I was with my family and friends looking at the great dark yonder of limitless light years of chaos. We could see thousands of points, but I knew that I was envisioning countless multitrillions of them, many with sentient beings, all possibly looking back at us through intelligent eyes on their own home planets, many of whom were possibly wondering what I was wondering: How did we all get here and why?

Do you want to know the answers to the most important questions that underlie your existence as a living being? There are many who are content to carry on in life without a hint of the meaning of the whys and wherefores of their tenure as human beings on this planet. But many more scream at the bit to make sense of it all. The urge to do this comes from within, incessantly prompting them to attempt to discover the more profound articulations of our meaning as entities with the forms and particulars we present.

The how and why of our existence are the greatest questions for answer at any point anywhere in our universe. But why should we need to answer these questions? We are here after all. We can't do anything about it now. We are all in this predicament, so why ask how or why? These questions seem to be irrelevant unless there is something about being here that makes us *need* to answer them. In fact, the terrifying logical implications of the second law of thermodynamics force us to answer this question if we truly value being here. The law implies that the longer we stay in this universe, the more we can be certain that we will in time never be able to ask any questions.

We are each under threat of losing our individuality forever to entropy's relentless drive to break all atoms down into smaller fractions of themselves in increased states of randomness and chaos. It may take a long time for some, but in the light of the most recent discoveries of the tenure of our universe, it is a certainty that whatever intelligent life persists in the universe, it will end long before the universe ends in a cold nothingness, devoid of any of the meaning that extrapolated its existence in the first place. So what is the point of it all? Why existence, if it is all going to end this way? How is it possible that we can work this fact out for ourselves if we are not able to change the fate it implies?

Getting answers of any significant magnitude to existential questions requires a brave spirit of inquiry and a strict objectivity of mind. In the past, the explanations that were given to account for our existence as living sentient beings were simplistic and thus led to a complete misunderstanding of the whole picture. People were simple and led simple lives, and their belief structures were based on minimal everyday analogies. Alas, this led to horrendous misunderstanding and deliberate misappropriation of the full existential scale. As God was invisible, mysterious, and all powerful, governing every shade and nuance of life, those who claimed authority in His name were by and large given an absolute and unquestioned right to declare as true anything they wished. Too often, emotionally engendered, self-centered opinion ruled the second, the minute, the hour, the day, the year, the century, and the millennium. It was a simple strategy on behalf of a small cartel of people to eat better and work less and thus survive the hard dispositions of medieval life longer than their peers.

The most terrible thing of all is that the original texts from which we could have learned the actual words used and actual events that happened in the lives of original religious teachers such as Jesus Christ were hijacked and changed centuries ago by cartels of scoundrels under the aegis of *the Church*. The Christian religious ethic thus tends to be a parade of lies, distortions, and misinterpretations of the primal texts. Christians have been taught to believe in a Jesus Christ who is nothing like the individual described in the *Nag Hammadi Codex* and various other authentic apocryphal texts that were banished to obscurity by a small group of men. The full, pristine, unadulterated truth as uttered by the Great Ones themselves will alas only be available to those who seek to understand the ancient texts that still survive with dispassionate, neutral, and objective scholarship.

Words like *hell* and *damnation* have too often been the clue words for practitioners of religious deceit and debauchery through the ages. They define the anthem of the bogus holy men and religious charlatans that have led so many astray through the millennia. Many have mortgaged their very souls into the custody of such as these without a second thought. Anyone who has switched on a television set in the United States or Canada cannot have failed to hear phony and beguiling platitudes pouring out of the mouths of armchair evangelists who shout (in essence): "Praise the Lord and pass me the money." Of course there are the inspired ones of genuine verity, but most use the Bible as an instrument of fear to solicit belief in Jesus Christ under the twin axiom of carrot and stick: heaven for favorites and courtiers and hellfire and damnation for the unbeliever. But just how would these well-groomed tailor's dummies adorned with plastic smiles and media-cultured voices fare in the jungles of ignorance where mosquitoes bite with deadly abandon and sunlight burns the sweating brow, where churches are built with bricks and mortar that actually tear and bruise the hands, where the stench of poverty, disease, and death call for a few moments spent away from air-conditioned Waldorf salads and iced tea?

The great revealers of the truth of our predicament and their revelation of the way out of it did so through simple and nonconfusing information, illustration, and example. Most of them paid for it with vilification and, in many instances, their lives. They still do. In the case of Christ, the liars who took over on his demise hijacked an entire ethos and supplanted in its place a Romanesque and innately racist presumptive where the redeemer's complexion was whitewashed and his authority and words arranged to reflect a Caucasian center of gravity in thought, word, and deed. One wonders at the glorious scene where Jesus walks into churches in the Bible Belt of America and the neat, idyllically disposed, candle-soaked mausoleums of religious practice in Europe, with his deep brown Semitic complexion. Just watch the pews clear of the faithful. Humbug ruled in the far-off then, as it will explode as a firework in the hypocrisy of now.

When I started analyzing the sayings and teachings of all the primary prophets and holy men, I found to my surprise that the entire outlay of their theses can be narrowed down to a single elucidation—one that makes it clearer how best we can extend and maintain existential tenure. All Jesus Christ the Christian prophet ever promised was what he called "eternal life"—the maintenance of existence itself against an implied risk or threat. At some point or the other, all the major religious theosophies, including Christianity, have believed in the principle of the transmigration of the soul. This principle enshrines the capacity for the continuance of an individual's being, over several lifetimes, in a repeated series of physical bodies. The idea is that the individual essence continues in a learning process through a series of corporeal bodies, till that individual essence has learned enough to be divested of material form. Then continuance is supposed to proceed in noncorporeal or metaphysical form until all knowledge is achieved and maintained in a state of absolute all-knowing and all-powerful eternal aspect.

All Eastern religions still subscribe to this existential formula. Judeo-Christian and Islamic theosophies no longer do; they believe in a single episode of incarnate existence that concludes with the extinguishing of the individual physical being at death. Many representatives of the so-called mystical branches of both Judaism and Islam—Cabalistic and Sufi traditions, respectively—still incorporate reincarnation into their belief structures. However, for the mainstream of these faiths, continuance in splendor and bliss appears to be reserved for those who reach a certain level of goodly development in the favor of a divine entity whose will endows this state on the soul as a reward.

My personal psycho-metamorphosis began with a single affirmation. Although I had become disillusioned with religion, particularly with organized Christian religion, it came to me that if Christ had been a liar and a conman, he would never have gone into Jerusalem to face the terror he so clearly foresaw. It is at such a point that conmen invariably make a run for it. To me this vindicated all he said, all he stood for, and all he claimed. What remained for me was to see his own true perspective against the lies of others, to discover the least complicated avenue of approach to confirming his truth, for I realized it would provide me with an insight as to why his way was the way to ultimate value.

My dichotomy with conventional religious example—whatever ethos was portrayed—was finally reconciled when I understood how terribly human perspectives had distorted and mangled the glorious, courageous, wondrous theologies of existential truths proffered by Jesus Christ and the other Great Teachers such as the Judaic prophets, Gautama Buddha, Zoroaster, and Mohammed, the great prophet of Islam. I discovered that they exemplified the highest derivations of human expression, in ideals of mind, heart, and what is commonly termed spirit.

Yet the true glory they represented, both in their humanity and grander connections, has been lost through the devastating chaotic subversion of the single neutral force, best described as "the Devil"— entropy. No matter how high the pitch of our alleluias, no matter how steadfast the delivery of our praise, no matter how resolute the strength of belief, the deadly tentacles of entropic subversion work to reduce these great teachers, these representatives of the true reality, into personalized chips on millions of shoulders, to be carried into whatever localized stances time, place, and circumstance prescribe.

I have discovered that the dissertations of organized religion and science can often be the premises of lunatics with scales on their mind's eye so extensive that it inspires me to reverse a certain biblical reference and say they are the size of the "camel" that was swallowed by a "gnat!" Perhaps we believe both too much.

Science, thus far, provides us with very little *choice* as to whether there is even such a thing as free will (my apologies for the pun). Quantum physicists do accept that randomness can interrupt the laws of cause and effect that govern all physical things, but randomness is hardly an equivalent of free choice. "Quantum randomness as the basis of free will doesn't really give us control over our actions," says Tim Maudlin, a philosopher of physics at Rutgers University in New Brunswick, New Jersey. "We're either deterministic machines, or we're random machines. That's not much of a choice."[1]

Quantum mechanical uncertainty is based on calculations that individual subatomic states can be tracked for only about 10 to the power of minus 43 seconds, after which states coalesce into one final state. Well, let me put a proposition to you: Could this final state that quantum physicists have been unable to track actually be impossible to track because it is not physical? Could it be a state of complete coalescence and perfect union? A state that is not of the physical universe and is thus outside the laws of cause and effect that define that universe? Could it be a state of perfect freedom, because there is no separation of points to demarcate limit?

I hope to demonstrate to you both the nature of this final state and the dynamics of how the physical universe might have emerged from it. In doing so I will attempt to demonstrate that the assertion that our will is truly free finds an absolute confirmation in our connection to the final state of perfect freedom in which we find our origins. An understanding of that final state is essential for my explanation of the origins of the Grey alien phenomenon and for my discussion of their apparent preoccupation with our species.

# 5

# The Kingdom of Heaven Is Within You

What is true reality? Is there only one reality—a physical one verified by the physical senses, or are there many realities that are distinct but connectable to each other? If the latter is the case, how then do we see and accept these connections? When we say *real,* we mean things that are physically verifiably real—materially touchable and visually see-able. This is the reality accepted most pervasively by most of us. Does that make the reality of a mental image any less real? Even though the acceptance of the material world as the only valid reality might be said to be the most basic and banal form of revelation by the brain, it is silly and foolish. From that perspective reality is seen as an expression of the processing of information that is coming through the five physical senses only. Because it is not physically real, an idea, a thought, is immediately dismissed as an unreal phantom.

We take the physical to be that which may be discerned or verified with touch, feel, and the other physical senses, including sight. But there are things we would regard as physical that are not apparent to the eye, such as radiation. Heat is a form of radiation. You cannot see it in its true nature. You can only see its effect on things. The same is true of electromagnetic radiation, radio waves, and gamma radiation. The latter is a killer that invisibly applies a force atomically and subatomically, which can alter the state and form of matter. It is invisible but neverthe-less there. So much for those muddle-headed claimants of the rational who say that they only believe something they can see.

Knowing, understanding, and emotion are things I would describe as not having physicality. Yet they are the mighty things that make for meaning. It is through such abstractions that we have an endorsement that we exist at all. Imagination—the interpretation, posturing, and processing of mental images as a result of our experiences—is the realm from which the greatest majesty of humanity has emerged in literature, song, dance, music, art, and mechanical innovation. Notice that science is missing from the list. Science is simply logical, straight-line deriva-tion. No room for innovation here. In fact, good science strictly forbids imagination. Mr. Mole, confined to strict tunnel vision through pebble-glass lenses, is many people's favorite image of the scientist.

There is a cemetery out there that we call the universe, where every-thing rots. Nothing goes the other way. Too few, it seems, question this or wonder why. It is not renewal through change. It is quantum destruction through change. According to the latest discoveries in sci-ence, the universe is destroying itself, including all that can perceive it, with every passing second. The prevailing wisdom asserts that the uni-verse generates the questioner, only to start to destroy that questioner almost immediately in an inevitable tacit process. Why have meaning only to destroy it? It is utterly bizarre. It is in this context that I have endeavored to seek some answers about who we are, to shout questions in the halls of logical incongruities.

We observe for observation's sake, or we observe for our sake. If we take the former posture we need not look for meaning in the uni-verse. But the question would remain: Why are we here with a ratio-nal intelligence and thus the capacity to seek meaning? If, however, we were always here and did not just arise ten to fifteen billion years after the universe was formed, we might then be entitled to take the second posture and conclude that there is meaning to the universe and that we are part of that meaning from the very beginning. If so, what is that meaning and where and when was that beginning?

The present party line in the highest halls of science goes like this: The universe is all there is. It all started with the Big Bang and there was nothing before it, so the question of what happened before the Big Bang is utterly facile. It will proceed inevitably to dismantle all physical constructs—including all scientists and their created heavens—leaving a nothing of cold radiation. There it is. The end of perfection. The end of justice. The end of hope.

Eminent Oxford University scientist Roger Penrose, for me one of the greatest minds on the planet today, was recently interviewed on the BBC World program *Hardtalk*. He admitted that science is nowhere near having a definitive explanation for the origins of the universe. He described his own current theory of successive Big Bangs as "a crazy theory I'm touting at the time, it's crazy enough to have a chance . . . most ideas of this kind are crazy enough to have a chance." It seems that's about as definitive and informative as we can get, even with the most eminent of scientists.[1]

He and Stephen Sackur, the interviewer, discussed the highly organized state of the early universe, and Sackur pointed out that this "almost prompts the question: Who made it so organized?" Penrose's reply was: "I prefer to look at this in a scientific view, because so many order issues are of a mathematical nature, in fact you can even give a figure to how organized it is."

It is difficult to see the logic behind his point. Even if the "order issue" is of a "mathematical nature," why does that preclude asking the question: "Who made it so organized?" Penrose seemed distinctly uncomfortable at having to admit that some sort of presumptive creation mechanism might be involved. Throughout the interview he was visibly fumbling for answers, as though he himself knew deep down that he was battling to save a sinking ship. At one point it came up that physicist Stephen Hawking had said in a radio interview: "Events before the Big Bang have no observational consequence and one might as well cut them out of the theory."

This strikes me as a classic case of the ostrich burying his head in the sand: asserting that if we cannot see the events that precipitated the Big Bang, and therefore our existence in the universe, we should pretend that they are not there at all! If this kind of thinking is at the cutting edge of modern scientific thought, how can we rely on scientists to provide us with an understanding of the origins of the physical universe, or indeed anything?

Science would appear to have taken God out of the equation altogether, implying that our destiny proceeds unavoidably to the desultory dictates of the second law of thermodynamics and its arbitrary randomizing effect called entropy. Are we, as a species with the ability to discern the fact that the universe is there and we are there in it, as important as existence itself? That is unmistakably what our presence implies. If we are as important as existence itself, we then may be justified in saying that the universe would not be here if we were not here. And vice versa. But this is an implicit claim for a God. I don't mean those little bits of socialized figureheads we invent and for our convenience call "God." I mean the God of all: "that in which all absolutes are confined." Are we thus a manifestation of such an entity? Could we be as important as that? In this logical surmise it would certainly seem so. Is the physical universe as we know it all there is to existence, or is there something or somewhere else that we as sentient living entities cannot discern or perhaps comprehend? If there is, are the two connected and if so how and why?

What follows is crucially important to establish lines of connection between all the various existential manifestations that might account for you and I being here. It will set the stage for understanding all things that manifest and present themselves in our arena of knowing. While the paradigm I am trying to establish and describe might at first sight seem complicated, it truly is not so. I want to take you on a journey in the vast landscape of existence. To help you find your way I will provide "signposts" of concepts, some newly derived and some freshly interpreted. Whatever inspiration might have prompted these insights, it was really perspiration that allowed me to understand them *after* I had written them down. So I urge you to persevere with what at first sight might seem to be an obscure and circuitous description of how everything might have come into being. I can promise you an interesting ride.

I want to share with you—rationally and with objective affirmations—what I have discovered about the existence of the antidote to the deadly second law. But to do this, I first have to introduce you to the eternal continuity that exists beyond this mere universe of broken down and breaking down parts, a continuity that establishes a paradigm of the whole, where all things move in reverse of the paradigm in our universe.

I call this paradigm of existence the "Godverse"; it is a universe that is eternal and thus timeless, where all the extremes of values that are perfect are inherent and free. The Godverse is a universal field of abstract reality, as real and abiding in its own scale of reference as the physical material reality of this universe.

Beyond and including the Godverse is a single overall manifestation we may call the "Omniverse." The Omniverse is the format of everything in existence, which includes the world beyond atoms (Godverse) and the world of atoms (universe) and all the features of the entire scheme that connects them. It defines existence in *all* its myriad forms. In our universe of atoms, solid hard reality is experienced by proxy through a physical mechanism called a body, while in the Godverse, there is no body and reality is instead directly experienced in limitless detail through an abstract mechanism akin to what we call a *mind*.

The two most fundamental momentums of the entire existential scale are the drive toward the union of all parts and the drive toward the separation of all parts. The drive to union in the Godverse results in an incidental singularity in which all absolutes are centered, which I call "Godhead." I have used the term *Godhead* as a secular description of the same phenomenon most call "God." Godhead is a point that is the ultimate resolution of all information into a total and perfect whole.

The drive to the separation of all parts allows for universes of point-enforced resolutions such as ours, in which all centering is finally and totally forbidden and can never fully be achieved.

If you have a magnitude point of no change, where all absolutes are centered and consigned, and then its opposite too, you have to have two basic mediums in which everything exists and is defined. In the Universe of the Whole (the Godverse), this medium is utter forcelessness and timelessness. In its opposite, there has to be a dynamic enforced expression that is defined by changing margins. Change implies limit, extent, and time: the features of the Universe of Parts. The two paradigms, the part and the whole, need each other so that each can exist. The most interesting feature is what emerges out of the interface between the two, namely: *Us*. Each living being on this planet is an individualized measure of their mixing.

Life, feeling, death, knowing, meaning, perception, understanding, and all other properties of sentient being are expressions of this interface between the intangible Godverse and the tangible universe acting in concert together. They are all in-between manifestations, quantum junctions of ongoing change furnished and revealed by the two primary momentums. How can the Godverse (the Universe of the Whole) interacting with the Universe of Parts provide all these things?

When the two poles of all existence, the Pole of Absolute Harmony, or Godhead, and its total opposite, the Pole of Absolute Chaos, or "Forcehead," interact with one another, the gargantuan potential difference in between them endlessly makes universes like ours happen through Big Bangs at their margin (see Plate 16). This is the true margin of forever, a margin that must implicitly exist as an expression of the perfect freedom inherent in Godhead to know and be all possible states. The whole scale must be there as an expression of the limitless potentiality that characterizes the infinite state.

You might visualize it in action with the model of a chisel against a grindstone. The stillness of the chisel (the Pole of Godhead) against the moving grindstone (the Pole of Forcehead) creates sparks: universes.

This interaction between the two absolutely diverse poles of existence makes space, time, and matter manifest in a huge explosion that gives birth to a universe. As a result of this gigantic disturbance, what I call the "God-form" splits to exist on either side of the margin of this inter-action. By God-form, I mean the implicit expression of the infinite nature of the Godverse in the finite nature of the universe. A light of all and perfect knowing shines forth from the Pole of Absolute Union I have called Godhead. That light is "God-ness," the implicit backdrop to all existence, infinite in its extent. The Godverse is the state of being within that light, while God-form is the expression of that light, trans-lated through the terms dictated by the lens of a finite physical universe and changed into myriad different expressions. The God-form on the side of the Godverse remerges into Godhead, but the God-form on the opposite side changes over time. Some of it changes immediately into atom fields of nonliving matter and some into living fields.

If the mysterious power to *live and be alive* is a tacit artifact donated by something that exists outside the frames of atomic derivation, then it is *not* of this universe. But what in fact provides the actual animation of the properties that define life? It is the phenomenon we know as *force*.

Force is the most all-pervading factor that separates the two funda-mental states of existence, the Godverse and the universe. The Godverse is defined by a paradigm of the complete absence of any kind of force. It is thus a state of complete and utter stillness where nothing vibrates. This provides a world of absolute peace all ways and always. Our uni-verse, the Universe of Parts, is defined by all pervading enforced-ness. Force is everywhere, even in the most minute elements of its make-up, which transmit enforced-ness everywhere through its entire extent.

Four main paradigms make up the primary scaffolding of force, the skeleton of the universe that holds its flesh together, so to speak. These four primary forces are the strong atomic force, the weak atomic force, the electromagnetic force, and the force of gravity. Further demarca-tions of these forces are described by the electromagnetic (EM) spec-trum. The EM spectrum catalogs the gradients of enforced-ness in the entire physical universe from the lowest to the highest values in terms of waves of influence per unit area. These waves are qualified and quantified in minute parcels of identity that make up this influence as a whole parcel, or as scientists would put it, quantumly. These minute parcels or quantum-points (atoms), are connected to one another by *influence channels,* or bonds. These channels are inertial in nature and cling to each minute parcel, or quantum point.

Just how they are connected can be better understood by visualizing how a clutch in a car connects to the moving force provided by the engine. The engine consists of a number of vertically or perhaps diagonally arranged empty cylindrical holes drilled into a block of metal. These are filled with a series of empty inverted cylinders almost to the full width of the cavities. The cup-like cylinders can move up and down within these cavities. At the top of each solid cylinder, or piston, a spark plug generates a spark that comes into contact with a volatile mixture of air and fuel placed there. The resulting explosion pushes down each piston in turn. The bottoms of the pistons are connected to an arrangement that turns up-and-down vertical movement into circular movement. This movement is conveyed to a large circular piece of metal called a flywheel, which turns very fast. This heavy circular force produced in the engine is set at right angles to the wheels of the car.

The force of the rotating flywheel is transferred to another heat-resistant disc, called an inertial clutch, which causes it to turn at the same speed as the flywheel. The connection between the two is made when the disc is pushed against the heavy rotating metal flywheel by some very strong springs. The clutch is also connected to the tires of the vehicle by a series of rods and an ingenious arrangement of toothed wheels that turn the flywheel's flat vertically-oriented spin ninety degrees. This simple arrangement provides the drive force of the wheels on the road. The inertia of one interior wheel pressed hard against another is strong enough to push the whole weight of the car, the truck, or the tank. Inertial friction is the only *glue.*

Similarly, in an atom, things stick to one other because of their difference in intrinsic momentum. Swirling, spinning, flinging momentums provide the phenomenon known as "charge," which can either attract things to stay together or repel things to part. It is like something that is in movement coming into contact with something that is more still, which leads both to coincide with each other. In this coincidence of the two, no differential remains between them and they stay together as one. Breaking them apart again requires a force much greater than the total sum of their spinning and shaking velocities combined. If they are broken apart, all this force is released, which affects the immediate environment, generating a huge spread of accumulated force that hits all points in the vicinity in a chain reaction. This is the principle that provides the force of atomic and thermonuclear explosions, when the inertial breaking up force is large enough to release the force binding one thing or point of concentrated force to the other.

While the connectivity that binds points of concentrated force to each other is an expression of force, there is another type of connectivity not only between adjacent particles but between all matter. It is my contention that this form of connectivity—gravity—is the opposite of force; it is an expression of the forcelessness of the Godverse. Gravity is an expression of the power of the Godverse within the universe to bring all parts together in a coherent whole. It is not really a force; it is an "un-force" that prevails almost measure for measure, connecting the Godverse with the universe. It's the deep leading edge of the Godverse that manifests within all parts and parts of parts.

The poorly understood nature of gravity is highlighted in the following recent article in the *New Scientist* entitled "Gravity Mysteries: Why is Gravity Fine-Tuned?"

> The feebleness of gravity is something we should be grateful for. If it were a tiny bit stronger, none of us would be here to scoff at its puny nature. The moment of the universe's birth created both matter and an expanding space-time in which this matter could exist. While gravity pulled the matter together, the expansion of space drew

particles of matter apart—and the further apart they drifted, the weaker their mutual attraction became. It turns out that the struggle between these two was balanced on a knife-edge. If the expansion of space had overwhelmed the pull of gravity in the newborn universe, stars, galaxies and humans would never have been able to form. If, on the other hand, gravity had been much stronger, stars and galaxies might have formed, but they would have quickly collapsed in on themselves and each other. What's more, the gravitational distortion of space-time would have folded up the universe in a big crunch. Our cosmic history could have been over by now. Only the middle ground, where the expansion and the gravitational strength balance to within 1 part in 1015 at 1 second after the big bang, allows life to form. That is down to the size of the gravitational constant G, also known as Big G. The important question is, where does this value come from? Why does G have the value that allowed life to form in the cosmos? The simple but unsatisfying answer is that we could not be here to observe it if it were any different. As to the deeper answer—no one knows. "We can make measurements that determine its size, but we have no idea where this value comes from," says John Barrow of the University of Cambridge. "We have never explained any basic constant of nature."[2]

Could this remarkable fine-tuning of gravitational strength be because the strength of gravity is an exact reflection of the force of the universe pulling against the forcelessness of the Godverse?

Ernst Mach, a nineteenth century Austrian physicist, suggested that the mass of everything on Earth, including you and me, is intimately connected with the mass of everything else, even distant astronomical objects. Hence, if a bucket is filled with water and set spinning like a top, although the bucket tends to drag the water at the edge with it, most of the contents stay put. Mach maintained that matter simply "knows" that it should stay still with respect to the rest of the matter in the universe. A particle with mass resists acceleration; it has inertia, because it is in some way connected to the myriad objects in the cosmos. "Mach's principle," as it came to be known, was the main inspiration for Einstein's theory of general relativity.

This invisible connectivity has now been affirmed beyond reasonable doubt by quantum physics. It is my contention that this connectivity is the result of the implicit omnipresence of that which is infinite throughout all finite states. In other words, it is the reach of the Godverse into the universe. A good analogy for this reach is laser light, a type of electromagnetic light. *Laser* stands for "light amplified by the stimulated emission of radiation." Laser light is both coherent (its light is all the same wavelength and its waves are perfectly in step) and perfectly straight, so straight that it is better at making accurate measurements than any ruler.

Now imagine a light that is laser-like but not made of force at all. This light is similarly coherent and can carry information. However, it is unlike laser light in that it is intelligent; it not only carries information but also receives it, holds it, understands it, and extrapolates it on its own accord. The coherence of a laser beam is easily disfigured with anything that reflects light, like little water droplets, anything shiny, and of course mirrors. In the same way, the intelligent light to which I am referring is interrupted and diffracted by expressions of force. Its power is strongest where any field of force is weakest, and it is at its optimum coherence in an arena where there is no force at all. I call this light "God-light" or "En-light." En-light is *the* power that fills all domains of existence. Unlike electromagnetic light, which moves within margins of force, this light moves without restriction. It travels at what I call "Speed-Absolute."

Our whole Universe of Parts is a hive of various presentations of force. This force is mitigated, however, by locations of stillness or balance points here and there, which I call "peace points." These locations of stillness are the pathway through which En-light travels. At these points of stillness, En-light reveals the nature of the Godverse and the properties of the Godverse manifest as God-ness. The God-form is this mix of God-ness in force that causes life or the living paradigm that characterizes any living thing. This life-giving property—the most fundamental component of the Godverse—is composed of the triple abstract conceptual principles we know as *awareness, knowing,* and *will.* This is the true "Holy Trinity."

Wherever there are balance points where the force in the universe is cancelled out (science calls them "zero points"), the resulting space is filled with the characteristics of the Godverse. These balance points— where the contours of atoms are separated from others—occurred incidentally as hydrogen became helium and then on to the more complex atoms later in the life of the universe. This space takes the form of corridors intertwining between the locations of concentrated force we call the atom, till a mesh of En-light sparks the qualities of Godhead in suitable aggregates of atoms. This is what we call *life.*

Life is thus a coexistent state of two components: En-light, which is total mind and thus abstract and un-enforced, and physicality or materiality, which is totally enforced. It is a continual stage of conflict. For the living species *Homo sapiens sapiens,* the battle these days lasts for about four score years and ten. The forces of the Pole of Chaos win out in the end and we die. All living things lose the battle in maintaining the living modus.

Let's look at it more closely to get some idea of the massive impact of force upon us. You sit there reading this book. You of course think you are sitting still. You are not. You are traveling at approximately 1,000 miles an hour around with the Earth as it spins on its axis. The whole planet is traveling at nearly sixty thousand miles an hour around the sun. You are thus already moving in a spiral at fantastic speed. Vector forces hold you bound, but you of course don't sense them. In addition, the galaxy is moving around the plane of its cluster of galaxies at 489,600 miles per hour. And our cluster of galaxies is moving around with the super cluster of galaxies we belong to. All these vectors are in addition to the intrinsic forces locking your atoms to others and the subatomic particles moving in billions of figure-of-eight dances like myriad dumbbells wobbling, whirling, and twirling to make the very substance of you. In this "Devilverse" of forces, how can stillness have an impact?

The fact that the universe is here implies that there have to be balance points where the expression of force is mitigated. These are effectively holding points to make the universe persist. Whatever way force presents itself, in whatever form, it has to be balanced, or the universe could never have formed. Wherever atoms form an enclosed space, there is a corridor of no force at its very center. A point of no force will also exist at the very center point of the enormous force locked within a single atom. Particles called protons and neutrons are supposed to occupy the nucleus at the center of the atom. Around these particles, other particles called electrons are supposed to swirl. These are really points where space as force is accentuated (electron) and counterbalanced (neutron and proton). I prefer to see it as the way space dances to the impulse to separate what is the *all* into what is the *part*. In the dance, there are pivot points for balance. Here in these places is a still point. From this point awareness and will as forms of the Godverse radiate the capacity to know, to perceive, to understand, and to make choices, against all that is doing the opposite.

Amazing isn't it? Could God and the Devil be *in* each atom, in the space between atoms—stillness pitched against the unstill in the battle for and against all that *is?* In between them is an interface where reason plays with meaning and memory struggles to keep things under surveillance. We as living beings are the summary of all this. We as individuals are a shape allowed by all the forces around us to act as reference points in the implicit battle for eternal continuity. We of course have an input in it all, an individual contribution: we verify Godhead against Forcehead at any particular point in between. All living things do this. From the mayor to a caterpillar, the pope to a bacterium.

However, a terrifying indictment of the human species was demonstrated by a chilling experiment conducted at Yale University some years ago by the famous psychologist Dr. Stanley Milgram. It showed that the ruthlessness required by a Nazi officer to pour Zyklon-B gas into a gas chamber and murder little children is actually present in many ordinary people normally regarded, by themselves and others, as decent human beings. It paints a sobering picture about human nature.[3]

Volunteers were told they were participating in an experiment on how punishment affects a person's ability to learn. They were introduced to a man who would attempt to memorize a list of words. In an adjacent room where he could be heard, but not seen, he was strapped to a chair, his arm hooked up to electrical wires. Every time he made a mistake in memorization, the volunteer was asked to push a button that would give increasingly strong electric shocks. Just before they would begin, the man would warn the volunteer of his heart condition. (Unknown to the volunteers, this man was in fact Milgram's collaborator in the experiment. And no actual shock was given.)

A few mistakes in memorization and the volunteers would administer some shocks, often laughing nervously when they heard grunts of pain. The experiment's administrator, a man in a white lab coat, would encourage them to continue with intensifying shocks. As the dose (supposedly) increased, screams would come from the adjacent room, accompanied by desperate pleas to stop the experiment. The man would cry that the shocks were hazardous to his heart.

Yet the majority of the volunteers continued to give electric shocks to the point where they believed they had severely harmed him. In many cases the volunteers continued to give what they thought were deadly shocks even after the screams would fall silent. When the laboratory administrator instructed the volunteers to continue giving shocks, they submitted to the authority figure rather than defy him. The experiment demonstrates that you don't have to be sadistic or deranged to put people into gas chambers. You just have to be human.

We are truly lost Gods. We, this bunch of dying flesh, parched of life and concern for the millions who die unnecessarily through lack of help, we represent a Sahara full of lost causes marking a million sand-covered graves. We are subject to a wretchedness that can make a son slice the head off a loving mother with a razor blade, or a baby once folded in loving arms grow up to be a man who can slip the slime of his mind into the bursting vagina of an infant girl. I make no apologies for my bluntness; it is deliberate. Such acts of depravity and their equivalent have happened and are happening all over the world. It is the fact that they happen that is the offence, not the graphic description of what has happened. Another offence of matching ignominy is the need we human beings have to file away the unpleasant and unthinkable so that we might remain "comfortably numb." The capacity to shut off and ignore what we know to be true in order to guard our emotions or to justify our actions is the same capacity held in great abundance by the depraved individuals I have described. They were once babes in arms, many of them loved and cosseted, yet they are somehow able to disconnect from these positive signals. Therein lies the root cause of the loss of the immense grandeur that is our heritage, a grandeur and awesome beauty beyond the physical state testified to by countless people who have had near death experiences (NDEs).

We hold the stuff of both heaven and hell within our nature. The stuff of hell resides in the dead nonliving conglomerates of atomic force; this *stuff* leads us into the proverbial temptations we term the voice of Lucifer, Satan, the Devil, or whatever. It is simply the power of the incidental drift of everything toward the Pole of Chaos. We are thus not fighting personal demons written in the nonsense of the mind. We are fighting one demon impersonally: the demon of the second law of thermodynamics.

Within and entwined in this terrifying structure exists the stuff of heaven, the Godverse. Only it isn't stuff at all. It is its opposite: *un-stuff* if you like. In it lies the power to cancel atomic effect, the power to undo force with a mechanism that manifests as a nonmaterial, nonphysical, ephemeral effect. The power of what I call un-stuff is seen against the backdrop we call mind. Mind is not the power itself. It is the screen on which the manifestation of the two opposites—the Godverse and the universe mixed—can be seen; it reveals the alternative of *being* as one thing or the other. The power, on the other hand, is the central essence that allows for the two opposites to exist and be opposed. It allows all things to exist or be.

The great power of all powers implicit in the nature of all living being is the inherent capacity for free scope in *will*. In principle, our individual selves are inheritors—through the expression of God-light coming through the center of the spaces between our atoms—of the potentially limitless scope to do anything. Yet this scope is contingent on restrictions of perception and attitude in carrying out the vicissitudes of living being.

Existence in the physical can seem hopeless—negative and drab. Yet beyond all the real-time horror of life in en-forced universes is a grandeur and majesty. It is so awesome in magnitude that it surpasses the power of words. The glory that could hold an entire universe in a single hand, as Godhead, is the world beyond the atom. Our blindness and our gross restrictions in being trapped in a Universe of Parts ensure that most of us never see this.

We all want something we can blame other than ourselves for the follies that we inspire and propagate, when all we do falls apart and leaves us bereft and helpless. We believe what is basically comfortable to believe, and our truths are convenience truths: not the real thing but dressed up to look like the real thing. Our prejudices are usually the pen with which we write our truths. Thus, most of us lie condemned without knowing it. Like the proverbial ostrich, we stand firm on our ground, our heads buried in the sands of ignorance, while all around us a great satanic force of destruction is slowly taking our hope of retrieval apart moment by moment, second by second.

The greatest folly of all follies is the belief in a personal species-oriented God that makes us all so that we can know him, love him, and serve him, one who demands praise and worship as a condition for the granting of favors, gifts, and benefits. There can be no greater canard than this. The greatest tragedy of all is that so many human beings believe that which dispassionate and implicate logic denies. This belief is the highway on which "Satan" travels.

Satan is no single person or life form, be it physically or metaphysically contrived. The great Satan is the universe itself and its laws of enforced amelioration. It is an engine of doom driven by the power of the difference between the Godverse and its opposite pole. This force is invisible. It translates through mouths, words, and terrifying deeds when funneled through the mind-sets of living beings, but its real nature is an expression outside the living and the dead. Its real nature is that of the universe itself—entropy. How then can there be hope of retrieval? How then can there be final victory over so overwhelming a force? I would suggest that the answer is as spectacular as it is simple. Jesus said it in three words, three marvelous words: "Change your mind."

Let me tell you something about these three words before I explain their final and awesome redeeming significance and grace. The vast majority of us are simple folk. We see, know, and understand things best if they are presented simply and in ways that illustrate their meaning for all to see. It has been the curse of most theosophies and philosophies that, in many instances, their self-appointed custodians have more often than not been intellectuals who pontificate in chants, recitations, and complex conundrums. We are so often left none the wiser, and we go our way too embarrassed to say that we haven't a clue as to what's been written or said. The Great Teachers such as Gautama Buddha, Jesus Christ, and the Prophet Mohammed taught in the simplest of ways. Christ is noted for his brilliantly illustrative parables. The Koran is a glory of wisdom and simple elucidation.

The rascals who came afterward so often mangled it all. Let me give you an incisive example. The word *repent* in the theosophical lexicon is commonly taken to imply an expression of culpability in sin. A powerful suggestion of guilt, contrition, penitence, and regret was culled from its meaning and touted by priests and partisans of theology century after century. Then the marvelous scholarship of Martin Luther, a philologist priest, ascertained that the word used by Christ in Aramaic (the language spoken by Christ), translated into Greek, is *metanoite*. This Greek word, literally translated into English, is "change your mind."

Jesus' exhortation or invitation was to think again and change the base of your thinking. It had nothing to do with contrition or forgiveness. It did not mean that you had to rue and despoil your value in supplication and guilt-ridden penitence. It encouraged the discovery of righteous value in whatever quandary you faced and a simple change of your future thinking in line with that. It was a dignified and free choice to change your mind in the light of a better alternative. In hindsight, it is perhaps a shame that Luther himself did not change his own mind and reconsider the prejudices that held him bound—it seems he was a vehement anti-Semite. His example is a lesson to us all that, however sharp the mind at seeking the truth, there are some dark and deadly things that can overwhelm the spirit within us all, placing our eternal scope in peril unless we take the greatest care.

A simple solicitation to see clearly and change does not carry the sting that the stance of supplication and regret does. It doesn't include the perverse satisfaction of wallowing in self-pity and masochistic indulgence. Moreover, and this is the important point, it does not allow for control over the individual by a third party, such as the body politic of a church. A guilt-ridden penitent is easier to control with the threat of damnation, especially if the expurgation of that guilt is joined into the fabric of ordained forgiveness under the total prerogative of the priests. Stupefying effective control is the name of the game. The meaning of the word *repent* as taught as a theosophical ethic grew to be the sword to smite the world with humbug that has perhaps condemned millions to live in fear and guilt-ridden feelings and, worse than that, to die in that state.

You cannot go to heaven in my head, and I cannot do it in yours. We as individuals are the ultimate guardians of our own destinies and that most precious and awesome phenomenon of connection to Godhead called a *soul*. How then are we to find the axioms that define our existence? Well, look back to where you come from—where and how you actually made an entrance into the world, into consciousness as an individual. Where did your own being exist before you took consciousness on this planet, or did it exist at all as you, as an individual you?

There are two ways you could answer this question. The first is that you came from your parents, through a combination of their gametes (male and female sex cells). You were assembled out of an automatic dictation process that came out of these master cells and nowhere else. Through the process of multiplication you were assembled, electrostatic charge upon electrostatic charge, and emerged as a unique entity. The second way is that you were assembled to a certain recipe from a power of dictation coming from some place other than the cells themselves.

Let's look at these alternatives again. The first postulation is that two independent bodies, one male and the other female, by merely coming into contact with one another, set off a power-driven scenario, a chain reaction, where minute little electric charges fired off in a carefully predetermined sequence to make a cascade of new structures in which millions of cells were miraculously shaped to assume the most complicated forms and functions. Suddenly, a self-propagating independent life form was created.

This is the way all higher life forms on this planet are thought to happen. The essential thing to note is that there has to be a preceding entity already in existence for a subsequent entity to happen. So there is a chain eventually going back to a first being, the origin of all. The common thought about all this of course is that a *God* being, who always existed, unchanging, made all these elements and capacities in an original form. Then these things, all packaged up as individual *beings,* evolved with time into their present versions and dispositions. The story is of course more complicated than this, but that is its basic essence.

The less common thought, but the most powerful one now because most scientists hold to it, is that all things are incidental in a Russian roulette of chance. In the course of time, all life forms evolved out of the simplest possible form to become the more complicated forms we see today. These things had no creator; this procedure by pure chance brought about everything—including us, with our capacity to see, perceive, measure, and judge the value of it all. At the same time, the entire universe is busy every moment taking it all apart.

Both these presumptions defy reason, but one or the other is believed by almost every human being on this planet. They are claims that are encouraged and in some cases originally formulated by those with hidden agendas in order to give them power over masses of people, power to control lives and means through the millennia. Getting people to believe in these explanations gave them the means to hold huge swathes of humanity at ransom for whatever purpose was, or is, convenient.

If you know what science has discovered about our situation as a species and indeed the universe itself, long term, you would know what utter drivel both existential postulations turn out to be. You would see without a doubt, for instance, that there is no way that order could come out of chaos. There is no way that this could be the case if logic has any meaning and this universe exists in its ways and fashions as we understand them now.

Ironically, some elements of both perspectives are true if they are put together. They bear out the discoveries that quantum physics, quantum biology, and quantum chemistry are revealing about the universe as science unravels it all today. I have tried to establish a concatenate derivation for all that exists in this universe from where and how it was established in the first place to the present situation in which our species prevails as living being. The stunning conclusion is that it all just had to *be*. This universe and indeed all Universes of Parts just happen as a result of a tacitly logical situation. Creation is implicit. No creator makes it all happen so he, she, or it can sit back and watch it all happen to whatever conclusion this creator deems fit.

A central directive momentum moves all created physicality, including the creative process itself, in the direction of chaos with time. The universe began from the most ordered state it could have been in and then, on contact with an already preexistent state of the complete opposite, became something with elements of both. The original state of the purest nonphysicality forms a central directive as a power of all powers. It can, if we want to be facile and narrow in our outlook, be viewed as an anthropocentric God. But it is more accurately called Godhead, and is best described as that center in which all absolutes are confined.

Seen in this way, it all makes sense. The God(head) directive is incidental, unconditional, and always toward order because its central merit is the union of all parts in a perfect homogenous whole. In this situation, existentiality dictates a nonphysical forceless paradigm, where a backdrop effect we call consciousness drives the two most fundamental nodes of mentality—awareness and will. These two principle momentums provide the capacity to know, see, and understand and the ability to use all this as a dynamic to make things happen. Together they form the paradigm of two poles, the "Pole of Godhead," or ordered harmony absolute, balanced with its complete opposite, the "Pole of Forcehead," or randomized chaos.

# 6

# A New Creation Story

If devolution from greater to lesser states of existential expression is the governing momentum of life in this universe, it would be logical to conclude that we can trace back our existence as *Homo sapiens sapiens* to a root starting at the greatest state rather than the least. Could that root be what is commonly termed "God," a root expressing the grandest and best measures of intelligent awareness? There has to be something vastly more profound that precedes all this, such that the living process might come to be and function as a continuum of such overall intelligent derivation. But what is the nature of such a God?

The God-form of being at the most initial moment of the Big Bang can be likened to a field of intelligent light. It was an encapsulation of wonder. This is the one-dimensional finality I have called Godhead: a point that is incidentally formed and is timeless and instant in effect and result. All life forms in the universe were once this God-form. Yes, that includes you and me. Perhaps Jesus Christ was hinting at this when he enquired of his apostles: "Do ye not know ye are Gods?" I believe with his statement Jesus Christ threw the notion of evolution to betterment out of the planetary window.

The Godverse is the foundation of the paradigm we call the soul, which manifests in all forms of life through direct antecedent connection. Life is the salient property of this connection. The utter farce of scientists claiming that they can create life in the laboratory is not based on creating life at all. It is simply changing the modality of already existing living modalities from one preexistent state to another differing state. Life is already there. How then might it all have happened? If we did not spring from the meek, how did we spring as living beings from the mighty? Why have we forgotten that we are Gods? How did we lose sight of our prior grandeur? The only way to answer this question is to trace back the stages that might describe our transformation from God to less than God.

This page has a certain shape, a certain size, a certain weight, and a certain thickness. Each of these can be easily measured. You can see it, touch it, and if you scrunch it up, which perhaps you feel like doing at the moment, you can hear it. If you really wanted to you could even taste or smell it. Now try to remember the happiest moment that you have ever had. Can you describe the shape of this joyful feeling, or measure its size, its weight, its thickness? Can you see it, touch it, smell it, taste it, or hear it?

If you want to understand the nature of the Godverse, the closest you can probably get to it is that feeling of happiness. Just like that feeling, the Godverse has no shape, size, weight, or thickness. You can't see, smell, taste, touch, or hear it. It is pure joy, pure happiness, and pure thought. This piece of paper has an edge, a boundary that separates it from the space around it. The Godverse has no size and shape, so it has no edge, no boundary. That joyful feeling is infinite. It has no beginning and no end. It has nothing to stop it from being itself, so it is perfectly free.

You can have feelings like that, but you are not, at the moment anyway, in that perfectly free state. Why? What limits your freedom? Your thoughts aren't limited, you can wish for anything you like, but there are difficulties in making those wishes come true. So what's the difference between your current state of being and the state of being in the Godverse? The difference lies in the fact that you have a body, which like this piece of paper, has a start and an end. *It* doesn't go on forever, so it can tie the "foreverness" of your thoughts to one spot. If you were in the Godverse your wishes would come true instantly because there would be no ties holding your thoughts down. When you are in a physical body it takes time to make wishes come true, if indeed they can come true at all, because you have to pull against those ties all the time. Let's say you miss someone dear to you and long to be with him or her. If you were pure thought, your wish would come true straightaway. But with a physical body you have to walk toward that friend, or perhaps take a car, or a bus, or even a plane. You are limited by the fact that you are held in a physical body.

How then did we get into this physical state in the first place? Why would we be so stupid as to choose to be stuck in this way? If we were once in the Godverse why would we make such a whopping great mistake? Why would we choose to move away from a state in which all our wishes came true to a state in which they rarely if ever come true? *God* would never have sent us out to be trapped and stuck: such an act would compromise the very nature of the Godverse. So we must have chosen to move away, but how and why?

Could the answer lie in the perfect freedom implicit in the Godversian state: freedom to do absolutely anything, even to become trapped so that you're not perfectly free anymore? In a perfectly free state, you can know everything except one crucial thing: *What it is like to be trapped and no longer perfectly free.* It is in the nature of that which is perfectly free to explore every possible way of being. Now, the ideal thing would have been to explore what it's like to be trapped and then to be free again, to come out unscathed. But a small problem arises.

To put it simply, when you're in an airplane looking down on a forest you can see all the trees or you can focus on small groups of trees, or single trees. That is the Godversian view in which you can see the whole picture or part of the picture. When you are on the ground you can see groups of trees or single trees, but you lose sight of the whole forest. That's the position *we* are in now.

The one thing you can't see from the aerial view is what it's like to actually be stuck on the forest floor and looking around. You can't know what it's like to have a view stuck to one place, because you have the freedom all the time to see every place from the freedom of the air. In fact, it's not really accurate to say the Godversian view is restricted to the aerial perspective. It is a view without limit. But viewing from all places at once does prevent viewing only from a fixed position on the ground; it prevents knowing what it is not to have the benefit of that overall view.

If there was such a thing as the Serengeti Plain of Africa in the Godverse, the millions of animals, insects, trees, blades of grass, and so on could be instantly experienced from the overall point of view, with every expression of their natures understood in a single point of time. The *entire* Serengeti experience would be known in all its aspects as a whole and entire concept instantly from the whole point of view but *not* from the part point of view. For example, you would not be able to take the point of view of a lion on the plains and put all the rest together from that vantage point.

This is when the interesting proposition arises that it is in the nature of perfect freedom to naturally explore the possibility of fixture and limit even if that means coming away from that perfect state. Perfect freedom by definition extends to the exploration of *all* possibilities. The only problem is that once you were stuck on the ground you would lose sight of the whole picture and it might become difficult to find your way back to perfection. So, did the Godverse get lost in the forest? Is there no perfectly free Godverse anymore? Logically, the answer has to be a resounding no! The Godverse cannot, by definition, become trapped. When you close the curtains of a room and shut out the sunlight the sun itself is unaffected. The intelligent light of thought, knowing, and understanding can be broken up and shut out in our physical universe, but that doesn't affect its source, the Godverse, in any way at all.

The Godverse is the absolute union of all separable things in which things cease to be things and even the meaning of being a *thing* is lost. Since we in this universe can only see *being* in terms of things, we can never know what it is like to perceive any other way. To illustrate my point somewhat, let me tell you what Mozart once said to a contemporary composer of his time. He said that in his mind, he (Mozart) could conceive an entire concerto, whole and together, in an instant, but he felt utterly frustrated that he had to write the whole thing down piecemeal in separated sequences over a span of time. He was indignant that he could not dump it all in an instant in everyone's mind. I unequivocally believe that it is impossible for us to get a whole, entire, and complete understanding of the Godverse. Here I am presenting my theorizations of how it *might* be seen with the tools we can see it with now in our present form.

The "Universe of the Whole," or the Godverse, can only reveal its true picture and meaning when all the parts that make it up are together. The analogy of a jigsaw puzzle can help us to understand this. A jigsaw puzzle consists of a number of pieces that, when placed together, relative to each other in the correct positions, fit to reveal the whole picture. It is this whole state and only this whole state that gives the truest possible meaning to the business of being a puzzle in the first place. If any part of the puzzle is missing, the simple state of being whole becomes the complicated state of being parts. The picture has no meaning until the last part is placed in position. The instant this is done, the whole situation changes, and pieces carrying random, meaningless impressions become a train, a castle, a country scene. Then it is "picture-ness."

A state of ultimate perfection would have to be a product of all knowledge, of absolute order, in total balance, through the absence of the slightest contradiction. It would be the qualitative center of the perfect resolution of *all* diverse elements in which those elements would naturally cease to be actual. Since diversity is a property of contradiction, when contradictions are reconciled, diversity disappears. For example, the distinct ingredients from which a cake is made disappear and lose their individual identity into a single amalgam of "cake-ness."

The Universe of the Whole, or the Godverse as I have called it, is an eternal abstraction; it is total *mind*. It is unforced. It has all possible knowledge of all things from a total point of view. It also has perfect

unlimited freedom of will. Above all, it is the summary of all existentiality. It is the absolute total of all things together in perfect harmonious
fit. It thus has no space, time, or extension. This is almost impossible to
imagine in our parts-conscious minds, isn't it? Well, let's continue the
exercise. If it is all these things, then it is quite clearly not its opposite.
This is the only thing it is not and the only thing it needs to know to
be itself as the Godverse. *It needs to know what it is not, from the point
of view of what it is not.* This is the only allowance it needs to have, to
know in absolute terms what it is.

Universes like ours provide an opportunity to do just this. In the
universe as distinct from the Godverse, the God-form would find that
the new state of being included all the opposites of the Godverse, with
paradigms such as force, space, time, and parts giving rise to matter, separation, hierarchy, limit, and so on. It would have immediately seen that
if it persisted in the new state a price would have to be paid, one that
threatened the very roots of its existential presentation. The God-form
would be left with a choice: retreat back into the Godverse or get progressively stuck in the universe. It would see that the powerful second
law of thermodynamics would in time take everything apart and into
greater and greater states of randomness and chaos with time. In other
words, the God-form would be totally annihilated over time. At the end
of time it would eventually devolve to a finality at Forcehead of absolutely no form in utter coldness in the darkest blackness of nothing.

So what can one expect would happen to the God-form if it emerged
into our universe, either through choice or the random disbursement of
its form, when Big Bangs make universes at the interface between the
two final existential poles? The answer to this will give us a measure of
where and how we all emerged. Importantly, it might give us a clue to
who the Greys are and how they came to be.

Godhead is a singularity that is forever and infinite, because it is
a *point* and thus dimensionless. It is thus also timeless. It is a point for
all beginnings and a point for all ends. It can still be a point and make
another point of itself. Then, however, the potential for separation to

occur becomes actual. This gives Godhead an instant potential connection and disconnection to anything that's not a point like itself. Thus two points may exist at the same time, discrete from one another and connected to one another. Please take a moment to run through and reflect on all this.

You will see that two points, no matter how close to each other, allow for a space between them. Thus a line can be drawn between them. Something different from a point, called a line, has happened with the making of another single point. Godhead is no longer alone, as it was when it was a single point on its own. The line is the smallest possible first step away from the singular point of Godhead that existed forever before, holding within it all possibilities to be or not to be. But the moment two points formed from the one, the dimensionless point became a line and space was formed. Then a direction was given to the proposition "to be or not to be." The atom is the conglomerate of the line and the point and the direction all together. Please refer to Plates 1 to 3 for illustration.

It is now simple to see that with the first dimension or length, defined by a line and direction (straightness), built into the system, so to speak, the next smallest differentiation would be to vary direction by ninety degrees. When this is done the second dimension happens and a plane is formed: "flatness." The next merest different thing is curvedness. When line direction or straightness and flatness all together try for curvedness, it results in a twist. The twist is formed to accommodate the incongruity of a double quantum of two different but whole dimensions trying for the next minimalist quantum with all information intact. To go for three is impossible because twice two is four and not three. But it has to go for three because it is the minimalist position in terms of what it already "knows."

In trying to do both things—that is, double itself and at the same time keep to the minimalist brief—it compromises and goes between three and four. In trying to reconcile all its information it forms a twisted shape best defined as a "Möbius toroid." This shape resembles a twisted doughnut where all the axes of the doughnut are twisted in a compromise between three and four dimensions. This shape is the shape all enforcedness travels on and through in forming all things, both substantial and insubstantial, in the universe. I call this overall shape the universe of space/time takes a "Moroid." Please refer to Plates 4 and 5. Things instantly go on past this into the creation of other dimensions that are, of course, not spatial, till it all stops in a chaotic amelioration that allows for the furthest extent of separation from Godhead possible.

A theorist at the National Observatory of Japan, Boud Roukema, has suggested that the universe may indeed be shaped like a torus, rather like a bicycle inner tube, which may also be twisted in a fourth dimension. He bases his claim on studies of the patterns made by quasars in different parts of the sky, which he says look like images of each other reflected in a distorted way, as if in a fairground mirror.[1]

The individual atoms in the universe form to this basic shape (see Plate 6). The Möbius strip is like an infinitely flat spine that acts like the twisted backbone of the universe. It itself is given strength by the formless and infinite power of the intention or the accident that separated it from Godhead. It is also the converse of course: the signature shape of the pull of Godhead to reconcile parts. This power provides the balancing mechanism that stops the universe from falling apart instantly. It is an open-ended power, because it allows for imperfection at its ultimate extent. Thus the freedom to be or not to be anything, all things, or nothing, exists. Our universe is just one means of fulfilling all possibilities: a vehicle that slowly destroys itself, separating its parts and taking these parts apart in gathering acceleration, to end at the interface of final chaos with Godhead. At that interface all universes will end to be reborn in another Big Bang, in endless Big Bangs.

Our universe manifests solid tangible things because it is the Godverse twisted out of shape, so to speak. Nothing of its most basic parts can ever fit completely and absolutely within this twist when these parts are put together. Some small portion is always left over.

It is this "left over" property that makes for force as a paradigm, and this force is what makes for the solid tangible reality we know as the universe. We all exist in a suspension between the part state and the whole state. If we could ever fit things back together in absolute and total fit in this universe, those things would disappear completely into a new quantum state. They would lose their tangibility. This new quantum state cannot be perceived or understood by things of our world. We can only hint at it.

The power of a singular point to create all things out of itself, so to speak, was the initial impetus that made the universe of separated parts a reality away from the Godverse. But it all happened incidentally. No one and nothing made it happen as a specific act of choice and reason. In other words, the allowance for parts to be allowed us all to *be* incidentally. A tacit impetus propelled us from a whole and entire aspect of being into one that made up parts of the whole.

Now let's focus on what the nature of "being" in the Godverse might be. Let's start with calling such being "Prime being." You would expect such an existential element to be straight out of the nature of Godhead. But to call it being implies that it was like some life form. It also implies that it was individual. We could be forgiven for thinking so. We anthropomorphize everything. But this Prime being within the Godverse is a single, two-dimensionally arrayed total of two fundamental, abstract, nonphysical, implicit momentums: awareness and will. These two momentums are centered in and pointing to the final singularity of total knowledge or information: Godhead.

Prime being can linger on the interface between the Godverse and the universe. This margin will hold it protected from the effects of the universe as long as it stays on that margin when it looks into the state of separated parts that defines our universe. By proxy (like looking through a lens), it can get some idea of what it is like to see the Godverse from the point of view of being outside it. It will thus be doing the only thing that can never be done or known in the Godverse. It will, however, never be able to actually experience anything firsthand.

It will be in what I term a "closed Prime" protected state, in order to keep its God-ness intact and retain its capacity to view with the power of awareness, will, knowing, understanding, and psychic sentience. At this point, it is important to understand that the closed Prime state is not a demarcated, defined point of actual individuality. Rather, it is a way of understanding what is essentially still a Godversian state with no demarcations.

The phenomenon of closed Prime being allowed the God-form to view, to some extent, the Universe of Parts in safety from the margin of the Godverse. But what was the nature of that margin and how did it allow for such a view? An analogue of the pure God-form state was created by the reach of the Godverse into the universe. This analogue was a quantum function of the entire God-form state, with no independence of its own, creating a telescope, a viewing mechanism, into the universe.

What was the nature of this telescope that it was not itself altered by entering past the wall of forces that divide this universe from the Godverse? What is able to be nonmaterial yet still reach within materiality? Even electromagnetic light is affected by the forces of the universe; it can be bent by the gravitational force of a black hole, for instance. The sole existential expression that can remain unaffected is what I have called En-light. This is un-enforced light, the light of all knowledge. But how and where could this light come through in a Universe of Parts where the very contour of existence is a prodigious field of tension I have called the Moroid?

There is one place where there is no force whatsoever in our universe, where the Godverse can be present and exist unaltered from its pristine state: at the very center of the space between hives of hydrogen atoms (see Plate 9). Hydrogen is the least enforced and least complex atom. At the absolute center point of the space between any aggregations of hydrogen atoms there is perfect stillness and a complete absence of force. These centers are what I have called "peace points."

The least number of hydrogen atoms that may form such a peace point is three, and the most number of hydrogen atoms that might hold this space is six. These peace points are the locations at which the infinite presence of the Godverse is expressed in the universe. They are the spaces that naturally fill with the "light" of the Godverse. The six-atom hydrogen ring is the best configuration for this, as the bigger the space, the more En-light can stream in (see Plate 14). Thus En-light forms the telescope that reaches through the spaces between hydrogen atoms. This is the margin where closed Prime being could safely rest within the Godverse. But to view the state of separation from the state of separation itself—a view sought implicitly as an expression of the perfect freedom and all-encompassing knowledge of the Godverse—Prime being cannot stay on that margin.

Prime being—I call this "open Prime being"—actually looked across the margin that separates the Godverse from the universe. This Prime state of being was thus exposed to the full gamut of the forces that define the universe and experienced firsthand all that the universe could throw at it. Something strange then happened, and its quantum state collapsed; open Prime *being* got trapped within the universe and became individualized Prime *beings*. Whether this happened by choice or chance dispersion from the Big Bang, the separation from the status of God-form brought down a holocaust of effects.

Prime being that lingered in the universe found that entropy was taking a stronger and stronger hold of its aspects. It fell more and more into a state of encapsulation in atoms. Life and consciousness only happened within an atom aggregation when that aggregation held hydrogen in six-point hydrogen rings as part of a water-based chemistry. As the entire scheme of physicality gradually changed throughout the universe, the six-ring hydrogen configurations began to break down into smaller configurations that had less space in the center to be filled by Godlight. Through the eons, light became plasma, plasma became gas, gas became liquid, and liquid hardened into solid, hard matter. As the universe changed, the manifestation of Prime being took on these states.

All living species in the universe were once open Primes and thus inherited a soul, the inherent line that connects all individual life-forms to Godhead. During the entire existence of a life-form this line provides the phenomenon we know as consciousness. It allows Prime being to hold the all-encompassing properties of awareness, will, knowing, understanding, and psychic sentience, gathered in an imperative to unite all fragmented parts into a perfect whole. Wherever it exists, Prime being will seek to do this. This is the singular creative power of the whole Omniverse. However, this power may be weakened and misdirected in its application at any point by the arrangement of the forces deployed throughout the universe. A battle thus goes on at every point between two primal opposed forces: one that propels toward Godhead and one that moves away from it toward Forcehead.

In the earliest days of the universe, Prime being was more strongly connected to the absolute mind power of the Godverse. Most of the open Primes retained a facility for continuous contact with Godhead. This contact at first was an automatic mechanism, a mechanism we know as transfiguration. This was a spontaneous remergence into the Godverse. Over the eons the open Prime state lost its power to unwind and neutralize the force of atoms and instead could only retreat into the spaces between them to find a course to the Godverse. The battle lines are thus constantly drawn in our universe. If other universes like ours exist, they will constantly have these battle lines drawn too.

It is crucial to understand that many of the soul-bearing living entities in the universe to this day may well be corrupted descendants of Primes. Yes, that includes you and me. But we are of the full divine scale no more. Through time we have gradually turned our face away from the Godverse, but we still retain access to it, at least in potential. Although we are statements of loss on the mortuary slab of degrading universes, we have nevertheless remained in the image and likeness of the Godverse. We remain, to some extent, analogues of Godhead, but diminished in our awareness of it and reduced in our will to regain this state.

In the current expression of our existence as physical human beings, we are not able to be independent of the physical atomic state. But God-light can still come through the center of the space between our atoms, endowing us with the capacity for free will and the ability to make choices to change our state and remerge back with the Godverse. We all already have some measure of dominance of atoms. We can command our muscles to move, to perform a particular action, but our minds are not sufficiently independent of matter to allow, for example, the complete disappearance of our body as an effortless promulgation of thought.

However, there have been those in history who have had the power of complete dominance over atoms, those whose six-point hydrogen ring configurations were such that they were living glories. Transfiguration was and is a means for the instant *unscrewing* of the forces holding together the hydrogen atom. It is brought about by the ultimate power of mind bringing about a complete change of a state of being. Jesus Christ demonstrated this potential to his apostles Peter, James, and John when he suddenly glowed brighter than the sun and changed his physically solid, human form into one of light. He was at that moment as a Prime being would be, a being in the physical universe, but truly centered in the Godverse and not the universe. It was the signature of his divinity.

Here's a fantastic thing for you to consider. What if I told you that you or at least your body is one of the finest aerials for receiving TV signals and shortwave radio signals that could be assembled? In fact, I don't mean that you, the reader alone, are this, I mean all living things are good at doing this and human beings are the best of the bunch. The human aerial is so good that many lives have been saved during wartime by the placing of a living human finger in an aerial socket to increase and make clear signals that would otherwise have not been discernable.

If you don't believe me, take a longwave or shortwave radio. Turn it on. Make sure it is in good working condition before you do this or you will be flying through a dark tunnel and won't need convincing of anything by me. Tune it randomly to a weak station, without an aerial connected. Now put your finger in the socket where an aerial could be connected. I bet you hear a great improvement in the signal immediately. The same goes for a television. I used to pay my brother three British pence to stand by an old TV receiver with his finger in the aerial socket so I could watch *The Lone Ranger* TV series. As far as I know, my brother still loves sticking his finger into holes as a result of all the times he used to stand there in his pajamas doing it for me. For all I know, he may still be wearing pajamas doing this.

Seriously, if all human beings are aerials, why are our bodies receiving mechanisms and what in our bodies allows this to happen? Take a look at our human skeleton shown in the drawing in Plate 7. Now look at the pictorial representation (see Plate 8d) of the best aerial configuration for extra-longwave and shortwave signals. Such aerials are often deployed on the rooftops of many nations' embassy buildings. Does the human skeleton not bear a remarkable resemblance to these aerial configurations?

Both the metal of the rooftop aerials and the bones of the "skeleton aerial" carry electric charge. This means that they can be polarized. Polarization, simply defined, is the property that allows the flow of force between one point and another. Where the body is concerned, it is electrochemically produced force. The calcium phosphate that makes up the substantial part of bone is piezo-electric. Apart from being a frame to fit a body, the skeleton may be a tuning mechanism for gathering information that is then discerned as thoughts. I believe it is there primarily for the reception of information as ideas. Together with the bioelectric field produced by the circulation of iron in a coil (blood in circulation) and the dielectric solutions of saline and salts in the body as a whole, an amplification of all existential happening and meanings is produced.

There is a blueprint, or "life-print," that dictates to atoms the formation of living mechanisms. As you can see from Plate 8, the morphogenic field of an ant will actually design virtually the same shape as a man. This is not as preposterous a statement as it seems. We have a head—it has a head. We have a taper at the bottom of the head, called a neck. It has a taper at the bottom of its head. It has a thorax—we have a thorax. What we commonly call the trunk of the body tapers down to the waist, just as with the ant. It widens to the hips in us and the legs begin. In the ant, it widens to the abdomen, a closed artifact. In the human, it is also closed, ending at the pelvis, though it seems open because of the arrangement of the legs. The deployment of our legs is exactly similar to that of an ant. Curiously, this same basic pattern is seen in the vast majority of fetuses in the animal kingdom at the initial stages of their development. A head, trunk, and pelvis set on either a vertical axis—that is, upright, as in the human—or on a horizontal axis, as in the ant, fit into this single basic pattern.

Scientists have so far been unable to explain this remarkable similarity in purely physical terms. It is not unreasonable to postulate that the force print that influenced this single basic pattern was environmentally expressed in terms of the entire planet, and not confined to a particular geographical location, or due to local specific geophysical, ecological, and environmental reasons. This "force shape" for life is strangely similar to the shape of the planet's magnetic field, as set against the solar wind effect of magnetic particles, under the gravitational influence of the sun (see Plate 8a). This offers a wonderful hint that all atoms will seek to form assemblies (unless forced to do otherwise) according to the "law of least action," following the summary shape of all the force impressions that influence our orb in space.

The startling implication is that our bodies are receiving mechanisms and our brains are wiring systems similar to telephone exchange wiring frames. The brain is not a manufacturer of thought at all, but the reader and interpreter of information. When the received information is processed through the hive of electric charges in the body, it produces what we call "thought." In an article in the *New Scientist* entitled "Not So Total Recall," John McCrone points out that the idea that we enjoy a photographic record of the past, recorded in the synaptic connections of the brain, is a myth:

For brain cells—where their shape and synaptic structures determine their function—the issue is all the more acute. The protein filaments that give the cells their internal shape have a half-life of just a few minutes. And the receptor proteins that stud the synapses need replacing every few days. As Joe Tsien, a neurobiologist at Princeton University in New Jersey, says, the brain you have this week is not the one you had last week. Even the DNA needs to be repaired. So if "you" are essentially a pattern of synaptic connections, a tangled web of memories, then there is a big problem of how this pattern endures.[2]

The research of Professor John Lorber, working at Sheffield Children's Hospital with patients who had hydrocephalus, spina bifida, and other related problems, seems to support this revised idea of the function of the brain.[3] He discovered that in some patients the huge ventricles permitted only the merest slivers of brain tissue, a few millimeters thick in some cases. Yet these patients showed no marked drop in intelligence or physical function. Indeed, one of them went on to take and get a degree in higher mathematics.

In fact, the world of no force plugged into our brains is what makes the picture and writing on the "television screen" of consciousness. Our physical bodies are the television sets, already wired in and powered. We are the "hardware." Godhead provides the "software." This includes the program that allows us to know and understand, and indeed the incentive to want to know and want to understand the whole picture: the hardware and the software and their interaction, and what it all means. If we disturb or alter the hardware in any way, the ability to read the software will be proportionately affected and the software will have reduced or no meaning. If someone hits us hard enough on the head, we immediately lose our sense of thought, meaning, and understanding. The engine that powers our consciousness is temporarily stopped with the blow. Our "TV" thus stops picking up inspiration and intuition. We instantly assume it happens because we have injured our hardware, our head and brain and so on, where all the facilities are contained. But in fact, the loss of conscious knowing takes place because the aerial receiver is damaged.

The foregoing may explain many seemingly foolish things done in the practice of religion. The postures we take to pray, for instance, may simply be an instinctive way of tuning into or improving the reception of a specific expression or modulation of information flowing in space/time. Kneeling, flopping, drooping, dropping, prostration and so on, may all be ways of bone presentation to maximize communication power in prayer. Of course, they are explained as expressions of supplication or respect or offering, but they could equally be a subconscious means of increasing our effectiveness in sending out and receiving human and divine "bit-streams" of intention and expression.

What we call God is the awesome overall facility that makes it possible for us to think and know and see and do, and the mind is the abstract concept that describes all this physical and metaphysical capacity when it functions together. The mind is thus not a physical "thing" but a focal point. It may be visualized like the horizon. In the sense that the horizon is an imaginary line, the mind is an imaginary focal point. It "floats" wherever En-light presents itself. Our minds are an expression of the power of Godhead through the Godverse, the power of the center acting through all the rest. En-Light is the medium through which our connection to Godhead exists in this universe. It endows us with the power to be aware, to know, and to act according to both, through the exercising of will, will to make choices between alternatives. It all has to do with points of view and viewing points.

For instance, imagine you are standing at the top of a hill and looking down at the scene in front of you. You see a fantastic sight: a counterpane of demarcations in all shapes and sizes in greens, browns, blacks, and sepia. You are too far away from them to see any details of what all these differentiations might be. They are geometric shapes, here and there interspersed with irregular ones. You put a pair of binoculars to your eyes and immediately the entire vista presents itself differently.

Fields, trees, grass, hedges, fences, houses, factories, cars, farm machines, and other details appear.

A new point of view emerges. More than that, the revelation presents new meanings that were not there when you could not see the full picture. Yet you are seeing the same thing: the vista before you. The use of the pair of binoculars has revealed things that were always there but hidden because you could not make them out with your naked eye. You also know the details for what they actually are (a house, a tree, a factory, etc.) because you have previously experienced them up close. The binoculars produce a point of view that allows more information in, so that your vision and perception and understanding present a new picture from the same picture that was always there. The tool you use to investigate the vista reveals the vista to be something other than what it was. The change in your point of view has not, however, altered your viewing point. You are still standing on the hill.

En-light is a similar device—an ultimate pair of three dimensional binoculars—that can reveal the makeup of all the details of all the dimensions of everything known or observed in this universe and the Godverse, from the whole point of view. It allows for the most complete and total view of the complete existential scale, the Omniverse, implicitly.

All living being anywhere in the universe that maximizes its atomic outlay with the six-point hydrogen atoms in a ring configuration will move toward the primal Godversian state. Things that do not will move the opposite way. This is the final challenge of all challenges in regaining eternal existence in all its maxims. The power to be conscious, to be aware, to think, to know, to understand, and to make choices comes through the center of the spaces between atoms. Thus in the format of our bodies as the species *Homo sapiens sapiens* we are fighting a battle toward or away from existence itself. We use what comes through from the Godverse to maintain the best disposition to maximize existence, be it in a physical modus—in the living state—or in one that continues past the ending of the physical modus—in the death state.

# 7

# Down the Chute

The gradual devolution of ephemeral Prime being into physical living being took place at different speeds in different parts of the universe, as some locations in space/time were more subject to decay than others, due to the desultory nature of the spread of matter and therefore force in the universe. The incidental nature of the disbursement that took place to make all things possible twisted the pure God-form into settlements of universes like ours. The entropic momentum into greater and greater states of chaos made the spread random. This meant that some life-forms had a head start into damnation and some remained nearer Godhead, while the intensity of residual enforced-ness in some parts of the universe would have forbidden life to exist there at all.

In the universe that cosmologists see, matter and force are randomly disbursed, like a giant sponge where the sponginess is thicker in some parts than others. Conditions where God-light settles are determined by the background enforced-ness per unit area. Wherever physical life-forms, as we know them now, devolved from the *ether,* so to speak, En-light dictated the shape, form, and profundity of that life-form in accordance with the force paradigm that existed there.

Our neck of the woods devolved with its appropriate manifestations of En-light dictating the forms of life or being that we know now. However, *life* is not necessarily the only format of being; the possible presentations of God-forms are myriad. Consciousness could take the form of a cloud, for example. Appropriate spaces within the cloud's atomic format would, in that case, allow for no-force areas where God-light could persist. The cloud would be alive in the sense that it would have the capacity to be conscious; if God-light persisted with sufficient *brightness* it would also have the capacity to know and be aware.

Such is the diversity of form in matter that is allowable according to the concept I am proposing here. But one thing above all must be borne in mind: the original forms of knowing and awareness that formed in the universe were very different from the ones surviving now. Our old enemy entropy, the mouthpiece of the Pole of Chaos, ensures that in time all things made manifest out of force will always change; it inexorably takes away all the harbors where En-light might persist. Up to a certain point, it was a natural cadence down, a natural degradation into a more limited existential stance. But with time another, more deadly, thing took place. Then came the moment of disaster.

Force was the greatest poison there could be to the nature of Prime being, which was altered instantly if the slightest force touched it. So it retreated into a "protective bubble" and created a kind of Cloned being, a facsimile of itself that could go forth into the broad scale of the universe and relay back the whole measure of the changes it was experiencing. This going forth could be seen in terms of a journey through all the levels of force from the En-light of Prime being to electromagnetic light, to atoms themselves. As I mentioned earlier, closed Prime being expressed in the forceless center of the space between hydrogen atoms in ring formation was in direct communion with the Godverse, while open Prime being explored the extent of that space, reaching through the shells of increasing tension that approached the surrounding atoms, but without entering into the atomic state itself. The facsimile of itself that it created was *of* that atomic state, and open Prime being was, so to speak, viewing through its atoms.

However, this viewing lens, of necessity, had a life of its own. Filled with the awareness of Prime being, it took on its own separate identity. It was a clone of Prime being's awareness that extended into the

physical universe. In terms of the bubble analogy, this cloned awareness existed in the bubble's skin. It created an ideal laboratory for open
Prime being to get a close-up and accurate view of how the laws of the
universe affected things of atoms. Obtaining this view was, after all, the
underlying reason for such being to stay in the universe and not transfigure back to the safety of the Godverse.

What then was the nature of this "protective bubble?" I have said
previously that I believe the Big Bang was the product of the two most
basic and thus absolute poles that define the entire existential scale:
The Pole of Harmony—Godhead—and the Pole of Chaos—Forcehead.
Each pole defines opposite momentums, the momentum to union absolute and the momentum to chaos absolute, the power to bring things
together and the power to take things apart. The interface where the
two opposite momentums meet can be expected to be the point of
absolute potential difference. It is here that Big Bangs and therefore
universes like ours are born. The product of these Big Bangs can be
expected to contain the two opposed momentums intertwined with
each other. The resultant and immediate feature after the explosion can
thus be expected to hold the opposite features at their most primal stage
in that first minute fraction after the explosion. Like oil and water, they
could never be homogenized; they would have to be new versions of
their old selves, mixed not blended.

As I mentioned in a previous chapter, it is here that I take a different view from the present belief in physics that gravity is an independent active force. The somewhat radical implication that I am putting
forward is that gravity is *not* a force in this sense but instead a representation of the Pole of Harmony pulling back against the momentum
of the explosion. It is thus an expression of the default situation that
brings all things back into Godhead. It is more like an underlying tacit
resistance.

All that is in the physical universe is made out of En-light held in
various states of tension. As the light of the Godverse is converted into
all the substantial states that make a physical universe, it is stretched

and pulled into states of greater and greater tension. This is just like the tension in an elastic that is held still at one end and pulled. The still end is of course the Godverse. Thus gravity pulls things together, back toward the Godversian state. The amount of tension is a measure of the spring-back potential created by the pulling. The immense amount of gravity in a black hole is comparable to the tension in an elastic that has been stretched out as far as it can go. An elastic can only be pulled so far before it unavoidably pings back, thus it is ultimately dominated by the still point to which it is tied. This is the dominance of the Godverse over the universe. If this dominance did not exist, the pull of entropy would exactly negate the reverse pull toward the Godverse and there would be no gravity. Gravity is the product of an extra capacity of resistance based on the connection to a point of stillness that is unchangeable and immovable. Thus gravity is the antidote to the second law of thermodynamics that drives the universe into parts through a web of chaotic amelioration with time.

The protective bubble is the capsule of gravity that surrounds and holds the characteristics of the Godverse in their purest form after the Big Bang. While the tension of the bubble skin is gravity, the actual substance of which the bubble is made changes in accordance with the degree of that tension: from electromagnetic light, to hydrogen, to the heavier elements. Thus the bubble is an ever-changing clone of the Godverse at various stages of expression, copying the signature of order onto the paper of all the various stages of chaos.

The Gnostic text the *Pistis Sophia* includes an incredibly intricate and lengthy description of all the stages by which the nonphysical translated into the physical. I wonder if this text might refer to the formation of Cloned being. A myriad of levels between heaven and earth are described, leading eventually to an account of how each body part was formed from its insubstantial counterpart. At the time the text was written, the authors would have had no knowledge of the concept of cloning, and this incredibly detailed step-by-step account may have been their only way of describing it.

It is important to understand that Prime being's creation of the mechanism through which it could view the Universe of Parts was not an arbitrary procedure. The whole process was an *implicit* cascade of events resulting from the natural and inevitable search from within the perfectly free potentiality of God-ness to view *all* options, including the potential to no longer be perfectly free. Such is the nature of the power to know all things. Cloned being simply formed a telescope of informational insight into the Universe of Parts through which Prime being could view that potential. The telescope was formed of a series of lenses expressing every stage of separation, every level of force. The first level of Cloned being would clone itself to produce the second level and so on until every potential was covered, increasing in separation from the Godverse and therefore in force with each recopying. The core principle that underlies this dynamic is that entropy will always lead the point of view (Cloned being) away from the viewing point (Prime being); the two can never meet and merge. Thus the inertia to view the state of separation from the state of separation is an inevitable cascade downward.

To use the word *cloned* to describe this type of being is full of pitfalls, but unfortunately I can think of no better word. The actual state to which I refer is quite different from the type of clones that are now familiar to us, which are copies of physical organisms. The original Cloned being was a very special creation; it was a copy of En-light fashioned into the elements of the Universe of Force. It was, in other words, En-light with inertia, the equivalent of being as expressed in the Godverse translated into the terms of our universe of enforced parts.

The first expression of universal Cloned being was made at the birth point of the phenomenon we call "electromagnetism." This was a stage less enforced than mass or matter and was the equivalent of the two fundamental components of the Godverse and of En-light: awareness and will. This took place at the birth point of the universe itself, when the inertia of the explosion converted awareness and will into the enforced power we call electromagnetism. In the state without inertia, the electric component and the magnetic component are the holding mechanisms of all the information that makes up the Godverse. The electric component is born of the difference between the no-force state of the Godverse and the enforced state of the universe, and the magnetic component is an expression of the totality of force in the universe. If electromagnetism can be held within a totally forceless situation it *is* Prime being.

Prime being was the source of life in the universe. It still held the means to admit En-light and persists to this day as the means for a complete track back to the Godverse. Through a concertina of concatenate connection, we and indeed all living things are part of this track. Prime being made the bubble at the crucial point between timelessness and the first moment of the birth of the universe, gravity was born, and the apron strings of the Godverse began. These strings held some of the expression of the Godverse in the ascendant state of Prime being, while the rest changed with the momentum of explosion into a distorted mirror image of it, an image that was to slowly feed into the gathering panoply of force that made our burgeoning universe.

Perhaps the best way to understand this difficult concept of remote view through the protective bubble is through the analogy of a virtual reality hologram. To begin with, Prime being created an "image" of itself in holographic form. The very instant that this image was created, its similarity to its original state began to break down owing to the momentums of breakup and decay that are implicit to a Universe of Parts through the effect of the Second Law of Thermodynamics. The image became more and more enforced, translating down in time from a hologram written in electromagnetic light to something as substantial as the bodies we have today. The more enforced the state of the hologram, the less it resembled its Prime being creator.

I am going to extend this analogy, with some trepidation, as it will involve comparisons with the dubious world of computer gaming, yet ironically this comparison does help to illustrate a profoundly serious explanation. Original Cloned being is in some ways very similar to the virtual reality characters created when using the Sims computer game, in which a list of characteristics are programmed into the computer to create virtual individuals. These individuals then react and interact within the bounds of the environment of their virtual Sims world. The player simply creates these characters and then watches how they react within this environment. Some of the actions of the various characters are programmed in by the player, but some actions are not deliberately programmed in. These arise as a result of the interplay between the attributes programmed into the characters and the nature of their virtual environment. Any number of possible actions may happen within the scope of the interplay between these two factors. The player is not aware of exactly how the nature of the virtual Sims environment will affect the actions of the characters, and in the same way Prime being is unaware of how the universe will affect Cloned being.

However, there are essential differences between Sims characters and the original Cloned being. First, Cloned being had a real, rather than virtual, existence. The very act of Prime being looking through Cloned being gave it that real existence. Second, it was not a programmed robot in "flesh," so to speak, which could only follow a program through logical extrapolation. A "roboid" (or even a Sims character) is created and programmed using the tools of a physical universe; these cloned probes, on the other hand, were created and programmed with the En-light of the Godverse. They were an exploratory reach for Prime *being* to discover what it might be like to become Prime *beings*. You will notice the plural. So the En-light of Prime being viewing through Cloned being gave that Cloned being a fashion of independence from universal forces, but it was confined to action within the range of its limited capacity. The full infinite arena of potential freedom of will and awareness is only available to those with a direct antecedent connection to it, that is, a direct connection to Godhead. Prime being had that connection and that freedom, but its probe for viewing the universe, Cloned being, did not have that freedom in its own right.

As the enactment of the potential within the perfect freedom of the Godverse to view the state of separation from the state of separation, Cloned being followed *two* absolute imperatives:

1. As a probe naturally programmed with the momentum to explore states of separation, it would anticipate and seek out all things that might be dangerous to the protective bubble and register those things against the holistic reference of En-light it received from Prime being. At the same time, that reference of En-light would make maximum order out of any situation of disintegration and thus promote the probe's survival as a viewing platform.

2. As Cloned being was the embodiment of the drive to view a separated universe, its direction could only be one way, into the universe—it could never gain admission into the protective bubble under any circumstances.

Cloned being was of simple utilitarian value. It was the server of all primal intents as Prime being viewed, oversaw, and gleaned knowledge of what it was like to experience a Universe of Parts from the point of view of being within it. It provided the vital feedback necessary for knowledge to be complete within Godhead, which needed to include an ongoing notion of the view of the whole state from the point of view of the part state. In the initial stages, Cloned being was completely self-contained and could reassemble itself mechanically when it broke down under the relentless forces of the universe. But the further it ventured to find the ultimate margins at which it could function, the more it got corrupted. The more it lingered in this universe's chaotic maelstrom, the more it became detuned from those naturally uniting features and properties of Godhead that were a property of its connection to the Prime being that created it.

Prime being—which had naturally come into being out of the Godverse—existed on a permanent scale in its protective bubble. It was not subject to the changes that were happening in the wider universe. It kept itself near to the Godversian format of being, so it would be capable of returning through thought-engendered transfiguration. Its created entities, however, were different. Cloned being physically decayed and needed to regenerate itself through recloning. But the method of creation got more and more corrupted. As the force signature of the universe increased, Cloned being became unable to reproduce itself in its original format. Each copy, each new generation of Cloned being, included the blueprint of the pollution and mutations of the previous one. The headlong rush of the universe into breakup dictated that what was once one became two. Following the continually separating, physically changing formats of the universe, the cloning process came to include this principle too. When it was no longer possible for a clone to reclone itself as a whole entity, one complete clone was halved and split into two clones. In other words "Cloned being" became "clones." As these clones were the only way that Prime being could engage with and tabulate the universe through all its changes, the vision of Prime being became impaired. The lens of the "telescope" now had a fracture line in it, which distorted its image of the universe.

With its viewpoint blinded and its inability to go outside the protective bubble, Prime being had a huge dilemma. But there was a way out. In order for Prime being to restore the clones to their pristine state without deleterious effect to itself, it warped time, making it so that all the things that had happened to the clones had never happened. Prime being persisted in a time warp that was, in fact, intrinsic to the nature of the protective bubble. The mechanism through which Prime being could persist in looking into a universe would *have to* include the distorting of time, a distortion that could not allow time to pass. Subjection to the passing of time only happens to being that is fixed and held by the forces of a physical universe; Prime being was a God-form, and as such it was able to persist in a timeless, eternal scope.

Prime being used its own En-light, its own pull toward the Godverse, to counter the entropic drift into states of greater and greater force. In this way, it pulled the atoms of the clones it had created back into their original less-enforced form. At the same time, Prime being gained a deeper and deeper understanding of the Universe of Parts.

While it did this, it was untouched by the forces of the universe simply because it was pulling in the opposite direction to those forces—that is, into the Godverse. It was perhaps a similar process that Christ used when he brought Lazarus back from the dead. The whole exercise was like replaying all that had happened to the clones since they had been assembled out of atoms the first time. It was similar to playing the film of a vase smashing in reverse so that it appears to reassemble, except in this case the clones actually did reassemble into their previous format.

Prime being thus regenerated its viewing mechanism into the universe by running time backward, a procedure that was repeated over and over again. Each time, the newly regenerated clones were created by Prime being in a greater environment of force. Again and again, at a certain point, the clones would reach a threshold point at which they were unable to continue reproducing because the force signature had increased too far beyond their initial state. Chaos is an uncertain master, unpredictable at root. Although the entire scale of this chaos had one master momentum that was predictable—the momentum of decay—each time newly refurbished clones were sent out, they faced an increased amount of randomness. Eventually a point was reached, in terms of increasing states of randomness and force, at which it was no longer possible for Prime being to restore the clones without entering into the physical universe to do so.

Cloned being reflected every stage of possible separation within the universe. It was a translation of the infinite freedom of En-light into every potential for restriction of that freedom. The order and coherence of En-light naturally assembled the disorder and incoherence of the universe, but there was a threshold at which the En-light of Prime being could no longer naturally restore that order. There was a crucial underlying paradox. On the one hand, Cloned being was an expression of view into a physical universe, implicitly exploring all its measures of force and breakdown. On the other hand, the expression of En-light within it provided a measure of reassembly back into a more coherent state. In other words, while it was fulfilling its function to explore states of separation, there was a unifying momentum that pulled it away from those states so that it could survive to explore them!

However, once the clones reached a certain level of breakdown, the implicit presence of En-light in the physical universe was not enough to ensure their survival. At that stage, their gross physical state required a physical translation of En-light to reconstitute them, a fresh physically translated blueprint. The only way Prime being could restore and replenish its viewing mechanism was to become physical.

Thus, in order to fulfill the initial imperative to explore the one state that was not possible within the perfect freedom of the Godverse, Prime being was pulled into a vulnerable situation. The whole problem was the entropic momentum of a physical universe that decayed any viewing mechanism they made. A true clone of Prime being, a mirror image of Prime being in the physical state, was thus impossible: it would always be changing away from an exact replica. Even when Prime being entered into the perils of a physical state, it could not keep the cloning mechanism within its grasp so that it would not decay. Prime and clone could never meet. The viewing mechanism thus always implicitly dragged Prime being deeper and deeper into states of force and chaos.

When the bubble's seal was broken, the whole scenario that governed the existential root of Prime being collapsed. The forces of the universe broke in, and open Prime being began to devolve and decay. Just as the forces of entropy had transformed *Cloned being* into *clones,* over time, *Prime being* became *Prime beings.*

Entropy was more pervasive than the closed-in Prime being state could ever have anticipated from its inherently "heavenly" point of view. Closed Prime being thus witnessed a terrifying universe. From its protected eyrie beyond the dimensional border, it had been seeing everything through open Prime being as it viewed and actually experienced through the clones, which relayed back the necessary perspective of the dismantling action of forces in the universe. However, these forces began to have an even more devastating effect on the now exposed open Prime beings, which were actually within the deadly universe. Their inherent power over matter became more and more limited, faster and more pervasively than closed Prime being could have anticipated.

The startling thing about all of this is that it all took place through the spaces between atoms: the point where thought and thinking interplayed with matter. This awesome natal point where the margins of force touched the margins of no force was where our present state as living beings began. Out there in the silent emptiness of space/time where hydrogen atoms formed aggregations, multitrillions of tiny points in the centers of six-point rings winked out the light of Godhead between the stars and on planets and began to sculpt a physical form from the formatted fields that were the blueprints of their knowledge.

However, it must be said that most first-generation Prime beings immediately returned to Godhead when the protective Godversian bubble collapsed. They were too close to Godhead to fail to transfigure. Some, a few perhaps, got trapped and became subject to the wear and tear promulgated by the forces of the universe. Are we among these last survivors in reason, intelligence, and sentience, smaller than the dregs that cling to an empty cup? Is the ninety percent of the universe science can't find actually Prime being that has gone back through the auspices of En-light, leaving an absent tension in its place as a result? Is this the "dark matter" the cosmologists speak of? It would seem to fit my insight quite nicely.

Those few who were caught can be termed "second-generation Primes." They were living, physical beings. It was they who became the true "Adams," the beginnings of dynasties of living beings expressed as various species all over the universe. Through this process, a line of direct ancestral connection to the Godverse and thus Godhead was established in the physical universe.

As the universal forces did their job of dismantling the universe, the Adam paradigm changed from a singular paradigm of existence to a duality. Adam split to include another form—Eve, a form calculated to carry on the line of derivation. Gender had happened. The quantum weakening, when one becomes two, allowed the existential paradigms we know as male and female to occur. But unlike the splitting of the clone into two, this bifurcation held within it the essential line of concatenate continuity to the Godverse as a potential. God-light was still maintained through the processes we know as conception and birth. They passed down a line of living beings with a soul, of which we are all an expression now. But these beings decayed more and more with each subsequent generation as they passed through each lifetime. The total force imprint of their home planet dictated the length of this lifetime, as was the case in all planets that were capable of supporting living forms.

This is perhaps the true paradigm behind the story of Adam and Eve in the Bible. Could the "Garden of Eden" be the protective bubble of the space between atoms in which it is possible to taste of all "fruit," all options and possibilities, except for one? Namely, the "fruit" that grows from the "tree of knowledge of good and evil," in other words, from the knowledge of the state of actual physical entrapment in a physical universe. I don't believe an apple was literally used to tempt the Primes, but it is a curious fact, and perhaps a clue, that magnetic force fields are in fact shaped exactly like an apple (see Plate 20). Take a bar magnet, put it under a piece of paper on which some iron filings are sprinkled, and the iron filings will instantly form in the shape of an apple as they outline the lines of force of the magnet. This simple model might explain the reference in the Bible to the temptation of Eve. Similarly, the wavy movement a snake makes can be a very good model for the sine wave form that defines the electromagnetic force field that beckoned Prime being into the universe.

I believe the Eden story describes the emergence of the first atomically derived entities universe-wide. It relates to the stage at which the En-light that was incidentally deployed in the space between some aggregations of atoms mustered those atoms to make living being happen. Adams were cultured all over the universe, Adams that in time divided into two genders to enable natural uncloned duplication and billions of living species. This stage deployed an enormous variety of intelligent beings on planets suitable for life. Intelligent living being appeared where there was maximum availability of En-light via a specific deployment of atoms. On this planet, this took the form of the water molecule. Prime being had reduced into a state of individual beings, each with a connection all the way to Godhead. As individual beings, they were fixed in space and time; they no longer had the limitless extent of the first Prime being and its consequent capacity to reach into all atomic states.

The universe had reached the point where its continuing disbursement through the second law of thermodynamics separated the Prime/clone factorization intrinsically. Prime being still continued in life forms. Out of their own resource, the most intelligent life forms, with the most suitable atom arrangements for the admittance of En-light, created a new and special type of clone: a copy of their own physical being. These clones were not like the original facsimiles of Prime being that were an image of the state of En-light in atoms. They were instead an image of the Prime beings' newly acquired atomic state in atoms, biological entities made to perform a utilitarian function, a function that mimicked the prior stages of natural expression of the Godverse in the universe. The newly physical Prime beings who created them were not like us; we in our current state are eons of devolution away from them. Just as we now use robots as proxy mechanisms to perform tasks that are too dangerous for us, they created their own such mechanisms.

When Christ told the Pharisees and Sadducees that God was able "of these stones to raise up children unto Abraham," they would, I imagine, have had little idea of what he meant. In the same way, it is impossible for us to envisage the nature of these first bio-clones and the means of their initial creation. The capacities of the second-generation Prime beings to manipulate matter are beyond our understanding. The important thing to understand was that this creation was a continuing expression of the "view by proxy" principle that governs existence in a physical universe.

In time the bio-clones noticed that, unlike themselves, the Prime beings could return into new bodies through a natural biological process (we call it birth), carrying with them their conjunction with Godhead still intact. The new, copied clones, on the other hand, had to mechanically duplicate themselves. They had no means of differential reproduction. They could only produce identical biological copies of themselves in a purely mechanistic physical process, not in wombs but in what might be described as artificial birth chambers. The copies were based on a chemistry different than the natural DNA of living being, a specially derived and assembled DNA. Suffice it to say for now that there were no centrioles in the master gametes used to produce this special DNA. Centrioles are mysterious cellular organelles. The spindles that seem to orchestrate cell division are anchored to these remarkable structures, yet little is known about them. I believe that centrioles to some extent elude scientific understanding because they are in actuality the cellular control centers of the soul. I am currently researching the biochemistry behind this and will present my thesis properly in a future book.

The new type of clone had no continuity in mind through the Godverse. The only continuity was in body, a body that would wear out under the relentless actions of the SLOT. This reconstituted clone type started fresh. Its capacity for thought was a purely electromechanical function; it was a proxy being of its Prime master. Although it had an individual mind sense separate from its Prime, it could not tabulate its past existence before it wore out. It was a refurbished kit made of elemental atomic aggregations that were—in any one individual clone—finally subject to limit. Cloning could take place a limited number of times before the dismantling feature of entropy prevented further cloning. At that point, a clone had to find a fresh genome that had not been cloned, a genome out of a living being.

The clones were intelligent biological computers, processing and calculating information. Rather like a computer operating system downloading updates for itself from the Internet, they sought to connect to their "internet," the reference from which they were mastered, that is, Prime being. Their calculations told them that their physical state was too gross to connect up to that resource. So, in order to download information from Prime being, they would have to pull it further into the shells of increasing force of the universe, toward a physical state that would translate En-light into a form with which they *could* reconstitute themselves. The Primes' soul line of connection to the Godverse pulled them away from the clones' grasp; it thus constituted a threat to the continued existence of the clones. This threat was produced by something the clones could not include in their calculations, which were confined to the purely physical. With ultimate irony, through this difference that they could never understand, the clones calculated that the soul lines of their own creators, whom they were created to serve, were threats to their continued existence. Just as the original Cloned being had pulled Prime being into atoms, the second-generation Primes were pulled still further into atoms by their second-generation clones.

As these clones had no soul line of connection to the Godverse, they had no compunction about pulling their creators further into the perils of universal force and consequently breaking down the predominantly six-ring atom configurations that formed the Prime beings' bodies. Finally, in ultimate tragedy, the clones in this way banished the last of these precious entities out of physical existence. The biological aerials that received the En-light of their soul lines of connection to the Godverse were too detuned for them to persist in a biological state. They retreated to the space between atoms. Paradoxically, the mechanism created to facilitate safe view for Prime being into a physical universe became a threat to that safe existence.

However, in creating the clones to do the viewing, there was no measure of carelessness through omission on the part of the Prime beings. They could only know what the clones uncovered step by step, each step at a time. The clones had their own plenipotentiary power to decide anything subject to their step-by-step discovery of things in gathering states of limit, as the universe unfolded this limit. Prime being in its innocence (lack of information) could never anticipate anything; it could only know what the clones knew and go where the clones went. It would always be too late to stop the clones doing anything, because the clones would have to have the freest scale to do anything possible in real time in order to fulfill the gross existential imperative that *all that could be discovered should and may be discovered.* So Prime being would always be a step behind, as all its information from the enforced universe depended on the continual and continuing discovery process of the clones.

By the time the clones realized that the Primes were needed in a state of physical life to make new clones, it was too late. They became less and less able to successfully replicate. They were decaying faster than they could control. Fresh new supplies of DNA, or any such equivalent mechanism that stands at the existential base of all life forms, were vitally necessary. They had to find a fresh genome that had not been cloned, a genome of a living being. And this was the trouble. In time it became the single most deadly curse in the universe.

The clones then did the same thing the first Primes had done in creating the first-generation clones. They made a mechanism of their own that would minimize their exposure to the universe. The vulnerability that defined the difference between the timeless, forceless, all-knowing Primes and the vulnerable artifact clones was the premise that fostered the next step. When cloning and recloning was no longer possible in a biological format, a less fragile, more robust element was incorporated into the viewing mechanism. With the knowledge that that which is purely organic decays in a physical universe far faster than that which is inorganic, they made their own form of clone as a nonliving, purely synthetic mechanism, a partly bio-organic/partly inorganic machine, a "roboid." This was the last lens in the telescope of view previously described, a lens fashioned to explore the final extremes of existence in a chaotic universe. Thus the clones became the fathers of a deadly artificial second creation, a creation that did not come into the universe with the Big Bang. They were the *fathers of folly.*

These roboids were like halfway houses between the pseudo-living clones and pure machine replicates; they were artificial entities that could look after the fragile clones whose animate state was the very reason for their fragility. These bio-machines could venture into areas of our universe that the clones had previously paid too heavy a price to go. The clones sent the roboids out to the furthest reaches of space to look for sources of natural DNA from second-generation Primes reincarnating at other locations in the universe.

With their Prime-given artificial intelligence, the clones built a means of travel that could conquer space and time. Yes, I assert this, even though many scientists think it is impossible for anything—let alone an extraterrestrial alien—to traverse the vast distances of space to get here. They are limited by Einstein's general law of relativity, postulated in 1916. The reasoning goes that nothing in the universe can travel faster than the speed of light, 186,000 miles per second. The nearest star to the Earth is 4.3 light years away. In other words, moving at the speed of light, it would take an entity from Earth 4.3 years to get to that star. The nearest planet detected thus far is about 10 light years away. If we were to travel to this planet using our present relatively primitive rocket technology, it would take us about 350 million years to get there. Einstein's famous equation, $E = mc^2$, which came out of the general law, implies that even if we *could* travel at the speed of light, as we approached that speed, our mass and that of the spaceship we were traveling in would increase to infinity. It is plain to see that this would be out of the question. So the laws of physics negate the possibility of our ever being able to reach anywhere habitable or vice versa.

Ah, but science itself postulates that there might be a way of circumventing all this. Ian Crawford of University College London says that, "contrary to popular belief, faster-than-light speeds are not explicitly forbidden by special relativity."[1] He points out that there are a number of concepts that aliens might use to defy the speed of light. For instance they might use "wormholes," shortcuts through space/time created by the natural design features of the universe. Space, it seems, is elastic. You can stretch it or even tear it. It is claimed that it is not beyond the realms of possibility that space can be folded. If two points in elastic space can be moved closer together, then traveling enormous distances across the void would not be necessary to get from one place to another. This can be visualized with the following model: if you poke the two opposite sides of an inflated balloon with the index fingers of each hand, the opposite sides will be brought closer together, and the distance between the two points will be reduced. Many distinguished physicists and cosmologists surmise that it might be possible for a very advanced civilization many thousands of years ahead of us to do this. "The mere fact" that to travel faster than the speed of light "may be permitted by the laws of physics means that it might just be possible," says Crawford.

Some scientists also believe that it is possible to negate gravity; if such is the case there will be no limit to speed and no consequence to mass. This would require an entity to deal with the deceleration inertias involved in reducing from any vast speed to zero. The roboids created by the clones—go-anywhere mechanisms made from an organic/inorganic amalgam on a silicon and mercury spine—were built exclusively for deep space travel faster than the speed of light. Their bodies were specifically made to withstand the huge inertial forces that would affect them when they slowed from these speeds to land on planets with living beings.

The capacity of a civilization with an advanced technology to accomplish these feats is readily grasped in light of the advances in robotics made in the last fifty years here by our rudimentary civilization. Japan has already produced a model village that is completely run by robots, albeit of the inorganic kind. If we on this planet can run whole factories with robots in just fifty years since their first inception, if we have got as far as developing organic artificial skin and tissue for transplants, it will be a relatively small step to put the two together. The result will be homes and factories designed to be cleaned, maintained, and completely run by organic soft-tissue robots, all completely untouched by a single human hand.

There is already evidence from current research into microtechnology that a form of roboid is now being designed for use in environments that are harmful to humans. Mark Ward discusses these developments in an article entitled "Silicon Cells with a Life of Their Own."[2] A team of researchers from the Swiss Center for Electronics and Micro Technology and the Swiss Federal Institute of Technology have designed a computer that can grow, reproduce, and recover from injuries. The computer will be built from blank silicon cells, which in some ways behave like the cells in a biological system. The silicon-based cells reproduce by copying their software to neighboring cells, rather like biological cells passing on genetic information to their offspring. In this way, the computer grows from one cell to fill all the blank cells on a silicon wafer, although it cannot create new silicon. Each cell is made up of a collection of logic gates carved out on a silicon wafer less than a millimeter square. These arrays of gates are flexible and can adopt the characteristics of any logic gate by changing the software used to address them.

The software *genome* tells each cell where it sits in relation to the overall organism, giving it—and this is the clincher—*basic self-awareness*. Once it knows its position, the cell can work out what its function is in the large system. So it will only implement the sections of the software that are appropriate to its position. The cells reproduce by copying this software genome to neighboring vacant arrays. If any cell becomes damaged, the cells around it will follow the instructions built into their genome and reconfigure themselves to work as if the damaged cells were not there.

"For this we took our information from the brain," says Pierre Marchal, one of the staff scientists on the project. The brain cannot grow new tissue, and so it has to re-route around damaged connections. Marchal says this ability to heal makes the cell computers ideal for environments that are harmful to humans, or where it is impossible to repair damage. For example, space probes or deep ocean survey equipment could be formed out of these computers.

So far the researchers have built cells that have reproduced, and they have also simulated an entire microprocessor built up of the cells on a conventional computer. "The cells are as powerful as conventional computers because you can implement any computer with this. The only difference is that they will be bigger," says Marchal. In the long term, this flexibility could enable identical, mass-produced arrays of cells to be optimized for any computing application by varying the software genome. Thus these man-made computers with a form of "basic self awareness" would be flexible to adapt to any circumstance, just as their alien-made equivalents would almost certainly be able to do.

In Ray Kurzweil's book, *The Singularity is Near,* he presents more than forty graphs from a broad variety of fields, including communications, the Internet, brain scanning, and biological technologies, that reveal exponential progress in technological development. According to Kurzweil, understanding exponential progress is the key to understanding future trends. In an article discussing his book, he predicts that

> over the long term, exponential growth produces change on a scale dramatically different from linear growth. We are making exponential progress in every type of information technology. Moreover, virtually all technologies are becoming information technologies. If we combine all of these trends, we can reliably predict that, in the not too distant future, we will reach what is known as *The Singularity.* This is a time when the pace of technological change will be so rapid and its impact so deep that human life will be irreversibly transformed. We will be able to re-program our biology and ultimately transcend it. The result will be an intimate merger between ourselves and the technology we are creating.

The most profound transformation will be in the robotics revolution, which really refers to "strong" AI, or artificial intelligence, at the human level. Hundreds of applications of "narrow AI"—machine intelligence that equals or exceeds human intelligence for specific tasks—already permeate our modern infrastructure. Every time you send an email or make a cell phone call, intelligent algorithms route the information. AI programs diagnose electrocardio-grams with an accuracy rivaling doctors, evaluate medical images, fly and land aircraft, guide intelligent autonomous weapons, make automated investment decisions for over a trillion dollars of funds, and guide industrial processes. A couple of decades ago these were all research projects.

With regard to strong AI, we'll have both the hardware and soft-ware to recreate human intelligence by the end of the 2020s. We'll be able to improve these methods and harness the speed, memory capabilities and knowledge-sharing ability of machines.

Ultimately, we will merge with our technology. This will begin with nanobots in our bodies and brains. The nanobots will keep us healthy, provide full-immersion virtual reality from within the nervous system, provide direct brain-to-brain communication over the internet and greatly expand human intelligence. But keep in mind that non-biological intelligence is doubling in capability each year, whereas our biological intelligence is essentially fixed. As we get to the 2030s, the non-biological portion of our intelligence will predominate. By the mid 2040s, the non-biological portion of our intelligence will be billions of times more capable than the biologi-cal portion. Non-biological intelligence will have access to its own design and will be able to improve itself in an increasingly rapid re-design cycle.[3]

Kurzweil may well be right. Carlo Montemagno of Cornell University has already constructed a working bio-molecular motor less than one-fifth the size of a red blood cell. The key components are a protein from the bacterium *Escherichia coli* attached to a nickel spindle and propeller a few nanometers across. Its power comes from ATP, the biological fuel found in every living cell. The motor is just one step on the road to realizing an ambitious long-term vision. Next in line is a motor that can self-assemble inside a cell. "We want to get seamless inte-gration between machinery and living systems," Montemagno says.[4]

According to a report in the *Daily Telegraph,* a leading British national daily, scientists working for British Telecom were, at that time, developing a microchip that will be ready for use in the year 2025. The microchip's design will mean that, when implanted in the skull just behind the eye, it will be able to record a person's every thought, experience, and sensation, hence it is called "Soul Catcher 2025." Dr. Chris Winter of British Telecom's Artificial Life team explained that the implant will enable scientists to record other people's lives and play back their experiences on a computer. "By combining this information with a record of a person's genes we could recreate a person physically, emotionally, and spiritually," said Dr. Winter. "The implanted chip would be like an aircraft's black box and would enhance communications beyond current concepts. For example, police would be able to use it to relive an attack, rape, or murder victim's viewpoint, to help catch the criminal. I could even play back the smells, sounds, and sights of my holidays to my friends."[5]

These technological developments in our own relatively primitive backyard are strong affirmations that technologies such as these, and probably others that are even more sophisticated, could have been developed long ago by beings technologically far superior to us. In the roboids created by the clones, programmed artificial intelligence moves and acts through a skeleton of mercury, intertwined in the finest mesh of gold wires set in synthetic flesh made of soft tissue-like matter. These grey-colored, dwarf-sized entities sweep the universe with a single command line in their computer program: *Protect your individuality at all costs so that you can protect your creators at all costs.*

The roboids eventually came to our neck of the woods; *they* are the "Greys" seen all too often by abductees. They came looking for our DNA but also found we had something that became more precious to them—a soul. They are the curse of all soul-bearing life forms in the universe. They are here now, looking for a way to beg, borrow, or steal an eternity.

# 8

# The Coming Terror

As the universe coagulated from the more ephemeral form of first-light, this planet too took form in space/time. What became human from the first information-retrieving form that gathered here knew better the truth of loss. In that faraway "then," when the power of the soul line of connection to the Godverse ruled the atom more than it does today in this temporal world of ours, the proposition for return from whence we all came was easier to achieve and *was* achieved by many. We, alas, are the leftovers, leftovers that steadily got more solid and enforced with time. We are now the last stage to *know* and make independent choices and, alas, not *do* enough to change back to our previous forms: we see and yet do not achieve enough.

We have delivered ourselves through the universal entropic churn—from planet to planet. We have found, through all the vagaries of atomic disbursement universe-wide, places that exactly match the resonant resolutions for our surviving soul-fields to make bodies, material bodies, be they Oglander, Earthling, or Fool. Alas, we get progressively more captured by these same bodies with time, stuck in our own time warp on the very edges of a capacity to reason. Most of us now sing the song of the atoms of the dead world while still in life. Preposterous as it may seem, we are now more akin to a table and chair than the blaze of knowing in the mind of a Christ.

Prime being of course still forms the existential base of the Godverse.

It is a fundamental existential principle and continues to this day and will continue forever. Any new universe that comes into being will follow the same rules. Let's call everlasting Prime being in the Godverse, "Prime being ascendant." This is the God-form that looks into the Godverse and takes its total perspective and form, including its eternal scale of endurance, from there. It is the closed Prime state referred to in the previous chapters. But we, as living beings, came from another kind of Prime being, open Primes, or "Prime being descendant." Prime being descendant is the God-form that changes its quantum state. It looks into the universe and thus its form and features are derived from a paradigm that is opposite to the Godverse, one of parts and temporary endurance. Prime being descendant is part of the creation process; it is the means that allows the Godverse and the universe to be all things that can possibly be.

Prime being ascendant is a state that exists prior to the beginning point when a universe happens out of the Godverse, a state that never decays. As it is retained and manifested in its purity in the centers of the space between aggregations of hydrogen atoms, it is a state that has command over matter, energy, space, and time in this universe; it remains singularly centered in the qualities of Godhead. Representation of this state may be what we commonly call "angels" or more specifically "angels ascendant."

The millennia have not reduced or in any way distorted this perspective of the God-form. It is so pure and focused on the center of all absolutes it remains an analogue of it, wherever it persists in whatever form. It is the God-form coming as if it were like a light through a lens. The lens is the interface or line that demarcates between the second dimension and our third/fourth dimension of space/time energy and matter. It is a projection that can take form when atoms are strung together on our side of the dividing line. This type of being can appear to be both nonphysical and physical, bringing the truest format of what it is like to be on heaven and the Earth or any other planet at one and the same time. It can never be physically, tangibly fixed. Though a multiplicity in essence, this type of being can be individualized as the phenomena that we might refer to as, for example, the archangels Michael and Gabriel.

The word *angel* means different things to different people. It might mean a sort of intermediary being that intercedes on behalf of some divine resource. It can also be taken as a metaphor for this intercession or a kind of principle. It might well be that the winged angels of common sight are a kind of avian Prime being from planets I call "Paradise Planets": planets in physical universes that are set within a Godversian aspect of enlightened status. These planets are far less affected by the second law of thermodynamics and are less subject to decay and chaotic amelioration with time. They thus are stages from which access to the Godverse is easier.

The beings who inhabit them are able to assume more corroded material states, but they are then in danger of being subject to the decaying forces of entropy if they persist too long in worlds like ours. They bring and deliver powers that affect matter in a way beneficial to lesser beings in more entropically affected worlds. In this interpretation, "wings" on an angel might represent the freedom to be devoid of anchors that commit to a particular reality. Representatives of this state can be deliverers of godly perspective, of hope eternal.

*Prime being descendant* becomes hydrogen atoms and all other elements in the universe with time. It forms the spark of livingness in atomic being and provides the conduit of union with the Godverse. It can be both a hallmark of redemption and a means to permanent damnation. As it sublimates with the universe it can provide for all the opposites of the Godverse, as we see represented in the folklore and legends that refer to an "angel" called Lucifer. Angels such as these may be called "angels descendant." Their enhanced power and dominance over matter can be catastrophic in worlds like ours. Becoming like this is an act of will on their part. They have independent free will, but it carries with it the risk of permanent entrapment in our sort of world through the action of the second law of thermodynamics. Lucifer might literally have been such a being who made such a choice and went on to dominate worlds in a material universe such as ours. The word *Lucifer* might also enshrine an abstract principle for such an effect.

The origin of the state of "Lucifer" can be better understood by referring to the illustration in Plate 18. The line dividing the Godverse begins at the demarcation point between the second spatial dimension and the third/fourth dimension point from which the physical universe as we know it happened. Above this dividing point, all being is Prime being. Notice I use the singular. The view from the point above the line *into* the universe reveals the universe but involves no division or breakdown into parts. This only happens if the line is actually crossed into our universe, when force is actually touched.

Michael or Gabriel are of the closed Prime, angels ascendant state, while Lucifer is an open Prime who chose a state of coalescence with the physical universe and became angel descendant. The legend states that Lucifer sought to copy the eternal nature of the "host of heavenly angels" and thus made copies of this heavenly host. In my thesis, these copies are Cloned being, which was indeed a copy of angels descendant. At a later stage, roboid equivalents of Cloned being were created to achieve a form of eternal life through artificial manufacturing procedures. But this was an eternality of physical existence based on the roboids' ability to be robust in the face of the breaking down momentums of a physical universe.

Lucifer thus describes the crucial threshold at which the God-form converted into the physical universe and became trapped within it. The God-form that viewed through "Lucifer clones," so to speak, lost its complete view of all options. The view of the state of separation from the Godverse by proxy became the view of the state of separation in person as soon as an atomic state was created that had no connection to the Godverse—that is, the roboids we call the Greys.

The whole problem with artificial creations outside the natural format and fallout process of the universe is that they have no ties with the beginning of all things and thus with the Godverse. These post Big Bang creations had no way of getting the Godverse mixed in with them at the beginning of all things. Thus they would have no way of having the propensity for "life" to happen or to be "begun" in them. They lack the rooting power of a soul, which forms the connection to the very beginning of the universe when the Godverse and the Pole of Absolute Chaos mixed to produce the Big Bang in the very first place. It is the very first place that counts for all results. Get your start there and all things are theoretically possible anywhere. Figure 8.1 shows this in graphic form.

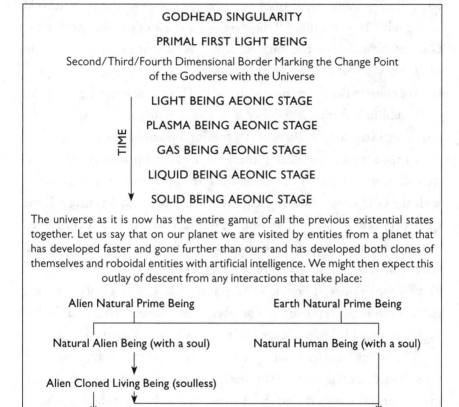

Fig. 8.1. The birth and death of a life-form that originally came from the Godverse as an ephemeral *light being* into a universe began its physical nature at this point, when the Universe of Parts began. It is the point where existence in the Godverse became manifest as existence in the universe.

After the primeval cataclysm, the universe manifested in two basic states of presentation: the living state and what I have described as the "static dependent," or dead state. Each of these states devolved into existence. The universe went from an ephemeral state to the present solid state gradually with time. All the stages were made of the very stuff of the Godverse from which the universe came. Its very first emergence was in the form of an educated light that projected itself as the abstract expressions of consciousness, awareness, and will. These nonphysical grand principles sublimated into tangibility in a solid locality we call space/time, providing extension, measure, and a verification modus for all.

In time, space coagulated into little localized parcels of itself that we call atoms. These, in turn, formed arrangements that interplayed with the Godverse, admitting its purest nature (God-light) through the space between atom configurations. Thus this pure state was connected to the enforced amalgams of it that were now formed. A sponge of two states now coexisted, providing a natural scope for the manifestation of what we call perception, knowing, and understanding with the solid enforced form we call matter. The phenomenon we call life and the living state happened as a result of this very special amalgam.

The living, sentient state presents in the obvious ways known to us; it is just clothed in the dead, static, dependent atom state. However, in time and through the effect of entropy, this living state degrades to a state of inanimate static dependency or nonliving inanimate matter. The nonliving, nonsentient matter state made up of what we call atoms loses the disposition of God-light from within itself. True *damnation* is the loss of this God-light from within the living paradigm for any given entity composed of atoms.

The whole Grey manifest is a search for the accomplishing of a means to a natural living process, rather than a continually manufactured one as they have. They want to accomplish the trick of being born. In other words they want a soul, whatever the cost to any other being in the universe that might have a beginning in Godhead. However, as mere biomachines they can never know the forms and faculties that maintain a soul. Their capacity for abstract thinking is nil. They do not share our ability for conceptual thought wrapped in cognitive awareness, which enables choices to be made within the property of free will. This, in turn, provides the power to move toward, or away from, the Godverse, which maintains the possibility of a line of eternal existence that only ends for any living entity when the capacity for making choices in free will ends.

Our hijacked bodies provide continuity points with the Godverse. They are a source of sophisticated DNA for the clones and a platform through which the Grey roboids can continue their mind frames. To get an insight into what nurtures the motives of the Greys and the predicament they are in, it is first important to understand the shape of their own psycho-sphere. Its center point is a computer program. It designates a series of imperatives with no provision for an independent will that would enable them to go outside the program. They follow a derivational logic that commands their next viewing point and point of view. There can be no option outside this paradigm for them. They can never choose to do anything illogical, as some living consciousnesses can do. This makes them lethal because—based upon the limits of their program—saying no to a logically derived summation is not possible. They are thus relentless and ruthless in following the summation to its designated end. In other words, they can have no conscience.

On the other hand, in natural living being, psychology is derived out of the Godverse in a concatenate line to the present. The thought processes of a living being have a potential bandwidth inclusive of an entire existential summary, because the Godverse is a paradigm that hems in *all* there *is*. The final reference point of this capacity for thought will include summations that are forever and infinite. The edict that stands at the center of it all is the singularity that defines the union of all parts: Godhead. As I have explained, there are no limits to this singularity except one: the view of the whole from the point of view of the part state. In the actuation of that potential, the part state will constantly and always be compared to the whole. This is what I define as "conscience."

Any utilitarian, physical, temporal creation outside the Godverse defines itself as being *a part of* and *apart from* the whole or the *All* state. In this state of isolation, such a creation will implicitly know only itself. It will thus look only to itself and look after only itself at all costs, because its conscience point *is* and *can only be,* itself. To it, nothing outside its individuality exists, unless it is programmed to recognize a multiplicity of itself, in other words, if it is networked.

For such a setup, a programmer is implied, something other than the created entity. For the created entity, the center of meaning naturally resides in the creator that gave it its *self.* The created entity only knows its own identity through the programmer. That is also the only way it can know any other created entity. There would be an implicit command for each entity to preserve its own existence by looking after the programmer who gives it existence. Therefore robots will stay robots and harmless to each other, rather like a series of machines working on the same production line, to the same end, unless they are provided with artificial intelligence. This will change everything.

Artificial intelligence (AI) can provide the capacity to recognize any element of difference. Up to the point a robot is given artificial intelligence, all will be seen as the same together. What they *are* is what anything else will be. But the moment any demarcation in this sameness is recognized, a value gradient is immediately apparent. Once this value gradient is measured, any measure of difference can imply a threat.

Artificial intelligence implies the potential for tracks of logical evaluation that can vary from robot to robot. Rather than simply following a preset program, each robot "intelligently" evaluates which track to take within its program, based on signals that come from its external environment and interact with its program. Each individual robot with artificial intelligence can thus potentially identify itself as different from something outside itself, based on differing signals and differing responses to those signals. Thus any programming of robots with artificial intelligence has to include not only an instruction for the robot to guard against threats to its continued survival, but also an exclusion clause to that instruction. That exclusion clause has to consist of a perfect and complete description of all difference that does *not* represent a threat; this is essential to prevent the robot from misinterpreting all signals of difference as threats.

The primary instruction to protect themselves, so that they can continue to look after their programmers or creators, thus requires a schematic of perfect accuracy that contrasts *their* characteristics with those of *their programmers* (creators). If this schematic is not accurately provided, the robot creations might see their programmers as threats. But how can a scheme of abstractions such as feelings or intuitions be programmed into robots, so that the robot can identify beings with these attributes as safe? There lies the paradox and consequently the potential danger of artificial intelligence.

One thing is certain. No computer or robot can produce consciousness. That is known even now. In fact, technology has gone as far as it can with computers. Nothing super different can come from them. All that can be done with them and to them is now known. No robot or computed robot that is conscious is possible through the logistics of science. So what then are the Greys in terms of a life science?

They have to be some sort of amalgam that operates on the interface of life, a "life mechanism." I have seen secret American and Russian reports on the physical make-up of Greys taken out of crashed craft, which show them to be assembled out of some kind of biological tissue or mulch, interspersed in an amalgam of mercury and the finest gold wires. This mulch has a DNA-like attribute, one that can hold and modulate our own DNA. Added to this mulch is a compound information-gathering paradigm, a mechanism that may be described as a three-dimensional computer matrix that can provide artificial intelligence.

This provides a sort of mind mechanism. But it is one that cannot have independent will and thus make independent choices based on its information. It cannot have an opinion outside its programmed requisites. It *reasons* digitally and binomially, in terms of all previous permutations of information received. It will do this ad infinitum, till the SLOT degrades it with time and it needs remanufacture. It will function in terms of mobility under a programmed drive to seek and maximize information always, in all ways, information with one end, namely, the master command: *Protect your individuality at all costs so that you may protect your creators at all costs.*

The all-encompassing search, going from Primes to clones to Greys, resulted in the Greys' discovery that natural living beings could reproduce themselves through what we know as birth. They discovered that life and death and life again could happen in an unbroken line, a line that continued past the ending of one body and into another body after death. This was, for them, an incredible find: if their clones could regenerate themselves by just being born, they would not have to constantly search the universe for DNA, with the enormous difficulties that this entailed.

How then did the Greys discover this facility for rebirth? They noticed that the same identities seemed to reappear after their physical death but in new bodies. They could tell that these were the same identities because they had the same electro-spatial fingerprint. The roboid Greys' capacity to detect this fingerprint can be understood in light of advances in our own comparatively rather primitive technology. A man called Simeon Kirlian, a Russian scientist, found that the human body's bioelectric field could be photographed. With his special photographic technique, an individual's unique bio-magnetic fingerprint can be seen around their body. Research in Kirlian photography is currently going on to see if it can be used in medicine for diagnostic purposes. We may ultimately discover that something similar can be used to verify reincarnation.

The ability to reincarnate became the "Holy Grail" of the roboid Greys' program to perpetuate themselves and their clones who lacked this facility. But they could only understand it as a purely physical mechanism. Thus they focused their attention on planets like ours where the beings were sufficiently caught in the Universe of Parts—sufficiently substantial and enforced—to be intercepted by mechanical means. They came and are still coming to find a way of tapping into our facility for eternal survival in order to gain that same facility.

What the Greys cannot understand is that access to eternal life is impossible for Cloned being, as it has no direct connection to Godhead and can never have such a connection. They cannot understand this simply because they have no understanding of anything beyond the purely physical. Thus they abduct us, conduct experiments on sperms and ova, and create hybrid beings in the vain hope of somehow riding our souls into a capacity for birth.

The experiences of two abductees, as related in David Jacobs' book *The Threat,* exactly illustrate these points about alien origins and alien intentions for humanity. The first extract includes an interview between Professor Jacobs and Allison Reed.

Allison Reed had a four-and-a-half day abduction event in which an alien escort took her to a *museum* room in which she saw artifacts on shelves along with strange life sized *holograms* of several beings. Her alien escort explained what these figures represented and why the hybridization was undertaken.

Each of the hologram figures had a *flaw* of some sort. The first had alien features with distinctive black eyes and a thin body; it also had a distended stomach with boil like protuberances on it. The next hologram looked more human. He had blond hair and human-like eyes, but he had no genitals, and his skin was extremely pale, like that of a "borderline albino." The final hologram was a grouping of smaller beings, about five feet tall. They were very white and Allison received the impression that they were mentally weak or something.

Allison's escort told her that the most important fact about these beings was that none of them could reproduce. They appeared to have been failures at previous attempts at hybridization. "The human race is not the first that they have found, or that they have attempted to work with," she said. "We are just the ones found to be the most compatible and the ones that it can work with, because they can't sustain themselves for an awful lot longer, because they (the aliens) are a result of a genetic mix, alteration, manipulation, whatever the word is."

"The small one you're looking at can't reproduce?"

"No. Not any of them. They can't reproduce—any of them. So,

besides the parts that were failures, like the white one's mental abilities . . . somehow they just weren't able to get it. But, apart from that, the three that I have told you about, they can't sustain life for themselves. My understanding is that's what's happened to the grey ones. Throughout the creation of the grey ones until, through their evolution, we'll say, they've gotten to the point that reproduction of themselves is a problem. Almost like the horse and the donkey syndrome in that you come up with a sexless mule. And that's kind of what went wrong. I don't feel like it happened right away. Somehow they were able to reproduce but, because they are a result of a genetic altering, through the years and through the generations it lessened. I guess it would be almost like if men just became sterile year after year until, whatever . . . ."

"Does he tell you what they were like before genetic alteration?"

"No he doesn't specify that . . . he just claims that he and his grey people are the result of genetic manipulation that some higher species, I guess, played God and mixed and matched and whatever. That's what he tells me . . . he and his people were created through a genetic alteration through a higher intelligence . . . I don't know what they were created for. But my understanding is that they were created for a purpose and, through the years, they weren't able to reproduce themselves anymore. From what he told me . . . they didn't start this. They were a result, just like the hybrids are, from something else. From a higher intelligence. That's what I get from him. I guess. That's just what I heard."

This explanation suggests that the aliens had attempted a program of reproduction before they came to earth, and that they have had periods of trial and error.[1]

Jacobs goes on to say:

The idea that the Grey beings were themselves products of hybridization experiments was also given credence during one of Reshma

Kamal's abductions. The insect-like aliens began a new program of human hybridisation with different techniques that has taken more time but has been fruitful. Whatever the case, humans have been successful for them. We can reproduce, and they can reproduce through us.

A late stage hybrid was exceptionally blunt with Reshma Kamal during a long conversation about what the aliens were planning to do. He provided another chilling glimpse into the future:

"And he's saying to me that, 'You know how you have memories?' And I'm saying like, 'What do you mean, memories?' He's saying 'You know how you remember your father, your mother, your sister, the birthday parties?' I think he's giving me an example and I'm saying 'yes.' And he goes, 'Someday people who are like you will not have those memories either. They'll be like me.' Like him meaning. And I'm saying, 'What do you mean by that?' He's saying, 'Don't you understand that?' I said 'no', or rather, I don't say 'no', I just shake my head. And then again he tells me to listen. He says, 'There will only be one purpose for you. You won't have memories like you do now.' I'm asking him like, 'You mean me?' He goes, 'No. The people who will come after you.' I don't know what he means by that. He's asking me, 'Are you understanding?' I'm shaking my head like I don't. I'm asking him, 'They're not going to take me away, are they?' And he's saying, 'They don't need to take you away. They will come.' I don't know what he means by this. Again I ask him what they are doing . . . He looks down and he looks up at me again and he lifts his arm up. He's saying like, 'Do you see this?' And I say, 'What? Your arm?' He goes, 'Never mind.' I said 'No, tell me. Tell me. What are (the aliens) doing?' And he's saying all they're interested in, that no matter what happens at all, is that they control."[2]

This hybrid appears to be predicting a future in which human beings will be converted into hybrids like himself without the capacity for memory. Natural memory is distinct from artificial memory in that it can only happen from our capacity to reference the passing of time against the timelessness of the Godverse. Without that reference, there would be no registration of points of time to build memories, and we would be, like the clones and the Greys, living only in each moment and therefore unable to view one moment against another.

As I have discussed, the reproductive status of these artificially manufactured Greys is one of mechanical regeneration, a procedure that needs constant supplies of suitably cultured DNA to proceed. No sexual organs or reproductive mechanisms have been found on Grey bodies at autopsy. I have spoken to a scientist from the Soviet Union who personally held a scalpel, who found this to be so. The seventeen alien bodies that had been found by the United States at the time of my research were identical to the one this Russian scientist worked on. He also told me of a deeply covert cooperation between the United States and Russia, with China coming on-line as recently as the 1990s: a giant conspiracy to preserve a select band of humanity in each country as survivors when the final run to harvest your children and mine is made by the Greys.

A catastrophe greater than any our species has faced in all its history awaits the human race today. So many of us have a cast of mind that cannot envisage anything more than our five senses can detect. This I believe has written our doom. We define our values in terms of our taste buds, our tympanic membranes, our penises, clitorises, and most of all our eyes, vehemently defending them as the only valid guardians of our well-being. One day the screen in the corner of the room, or the microchips inserted into our bodies or our brains, will deny us our eternity. If we don't see past the confidence tricks of our physical bodies, which obscure our deeper insights and intuitions, we are quite simply beaten by the physical capsule that holds the true us. Time after time, century after century through history, we have ignored the awesome inner sense that warns us that putting our sole trust in these highly unreliable sources is inviting a holocaust of terror, one that is bound to take our individual, eternal, existential platform away from each of us and put it out of reach forever.

# 9

# Evidence

Evidence of the interference of the Greys in human affairs is not limited to the present. Records displaying knowledge of extraterrestrial phenomena can be found throughout the world's various civilizations. For example, it seems that the scenario I have described in the previous chapters is one of the central themes of Gnostic early Christian thought. The terms used in these texts to describe the cloned alien beings are the "Authorities," or the "Archons." In a particular text in the *Nag Hammadi Library* of ancient Christian thought entitled "The Hypostasis of the Archons," there is a detailed description of both their origin and their nature:

> On account of the reality (hypostasis) of the Authorities, (inspired) by the Spirit of the Father of Truth, the great apostle—referring to the "authorities of the darkness," (Colossians 13) told us that "our contest is not against flesh and [blood]; rather, the authorities of the universe and the spirits of wickedness," (Ephesians 6:12). [I have] sent (you) this because you (sing.) inquire about the reality [of the] Authorities.
>
> But I said, "Sir, teach me about the [faculty of] these Authorities—[how] did they come into being, and by what kind of genesis, [and] of what material, and who created them and their force?"
>
> And the Great Angel Eleleth, Understanding, spoke to me:

"Within limitless realms dwells Incorruptibility. Sophia, who is called Pistis, wanted to create something, alone without her consort; and her product was a celestial thing.

"A veil exists between the World Above and the realms that are below; and Shadow came into being beneath the veil; and that Shadow became Matter; and that Shadow was projected apart. And what she has created became a product of the Matter, like an aborted fetus. And it assumed a plastic form molded out of Shadow, and became an arrogant beast resembling a lion." [It was androgynous, as I have already said, because it was from matter that it derived.]

Opening his eyes he saw a vast quantity of Matter without limit; and he became arrogant, saying, "It is I who am God, and there is none other apart from me."

When he said this, he sinned against the Entirety. And a voice came forth from above the realm of absolute power, saying, "You are mistaken, Samael"—which is, "God of the blind."

And he said, "If any other thing exists before me, let it become visible to me!" And immediately Sophia stretched forth her finger and introduced Light into Matter; and she pursued it down to the region of Chaos. And she returned up [to] her light; once again Darkness [. . .] Matter.

This Ruler, by being androgynous, made himself a vast realm, an extent without limit. And he contemplated creating offspring for himself, and created for himself seven offspring, androgynous just like their parent.[1]

Sophia, or the principle of "Eve" as she is more commonly known, thus created something alone and without her consort. A cloned being perhaps? Clones are the result of parthenogenesis, reproduction that involves only the female germ cell. Eve's creation is described as a product in the matter "like an aborted fetus" which "assumed a plastic form molded out of Shadow, and became an arrogant beast resembling a lion." This does indeed sound like a description of Cloned being, a product in matter "molded out of Shadow." The potentially threatening nature of such being is also suggested, it "became an arrogant beast resembling a lion." Thus the warning is given as quoted from Paul in Ephesians that "our contest is not against flesh and [blood]; rather the authorities of the universe, and the spirits of wickedness." Who might these "authorities" be who are not of "flesh and blood?" Could they be roboids formed of other substances, the Greys, created by the clones to do their will?

The text later goes on to describe how the "authorities of the darkness" became "enamored" of the "image of incorruptibility" that appeared to them in the "waters." But because of their "weakness" they were unable to "lay hold of those that possess a spirit; for they, [the authorities, or our 'Greys'], were from Below, while it (the Spirit) was from Above." So the great enigma for the authorities provided by living being with soul seems to be described here in this ancient text, which goes on to suggest the great difficulty these authorities had in their attempt to "capture" the "image" of spirit that they had seen:

They took some [soil] from the Earth and modeled their [Man], after their body and [after the Image] of God that had appeared [to them] in the Waters.

They said, "[Come, let] us lay hold of it by means of the form that we have modeled, [so that] it may see its male counterpart [. . . ] and we may seize it with the form that we have modeled"—not understanding the force of God, because of their powerlessness. And he breathed into his face; and the Man came to have a soul (and remained) upon the ground many days. But they could not make him arise because of their powerlessness. Like storm winds they persisted (in blowing) that they might try to capture that image, which had appeared to them in the Waters. And they did not know the identity of its power.[2]

It is not only the ancient Christian texts that give us indications that alien beings may well have visited our planet and left their mark on humankind. The chroniclers of the ancient Indian epic the Mahabharata, those of the Sumerian text the Epic of Gilgamesh, and those of the Inuit, American Indian, Scandinavian, Tibetan, Babylonian, and Egyptian texts all tell stories of flying gods, strange heavenly vehicles, and terrifying catastrophes associated with these extraterrestrial phenomena.

Among the ancient Hindu sacred books, the Samaranga Sutradhara contains 230 stanzas that describe in detail every aspect of flying, from how the apparatus was powered to the proper clothing and diet of the pilots. The International Academy of Sanskrit Research in Mysore, India, conducted a special study of this ancient work and published its findings in a book entitled *Aeronautics, a Manuscript from the Prehistoric Past*. Convincing evidence was found by these scholars to conclude that the text revealed knowledge of aeronautics that was remarkable. Here are some translated extracts from the text:

> The aircraft which can go by its own force like a bird—on the Earth or water or through the air—is called a Vimana. That which can travel in the sky from place to place is called a Vimana by the sages of old. . . . The iron engine must have properly welded joints to be filled with mercury and when fire is conducted to the upper part, it develops power with the roar of a lion. By means of the energy latent in mercury, the driving whirlwind is set in motion, and the traveler sitting inside the Vimana may travel in the air, to such a distance as to look like a pearl in the sky.[3]

The Vimanas could cover vast distances and could travel forward, upward, and downward. A further quote from the Mahabharata states that, "Bhima flew with his Vimana on an enormous ray which was as brilliant as the sun and made a noise like the thunder of a storm."[4]

The Tibetan books Tantyua and Kantyua also mention prehistoric flying machines that they call "pearls in the sky."

Further indications that knowledge of extraterrestrial being was a world-wide phenomenon is found in the mythology of the Inuit peoples, which says that the first tribes were brought to the North by "gods" with brass wings. There is also a telling inscription on a pyramid that indicates that the ancient Egyptians were also familiar with these phenomena: "Thou art he who directs the sun ship of millions of years."

Affirmations from a Judaic source can be found in a fragment of the Dead Sea Scrolls entitled the *Apocryphal Book of Adam*: "Behind the being I saw a chariot which had wheels of fire, and every wheel was full of eyes all around, and on the wheels was a throne and this was covered with fire that flowed around it."[5] How similar this description is to that of an often-sighted type of UFO that seems to be formed of rings, or "wheels," covered in blinking lights, or "eyes."

The Dogon tribe who live in Mali in Western Africa were, in antiquity, almost certainly neighbors of the Egyptians. They lived in North Africa on the shores of the Mediterranean. This tribe, which numbers some two million people, has a complex mythology built around the belief that, at some time in the distant past, amphibian beings called Nommo visited the Earth with the purpose of civilizing it. The Dogon revere the Nommo, who, they say, come from the star system Sirius, the brightest in the sky. They make sand drawings to show that Sirius has two companion stars. One is small and extremely dense, while the other is said to be four times lighter in weight and to have a nearly circular orbit. It is from the planet attached to this latter star that the Nommo are believed to have descended.

A book entitled *The Sirius Mystery*, written by Robert Temple, discusses the research of two French anthropologists, Griaule and Dieterlen, who had studied the Dogon tribe. Temple was baffled as to how the Dogon could have known of the existence of Sirius B, given that it is barely visible even when using a very powerful telescope (it was only in 1970 that the first photograph of Sirius B was obtained with great difficulty by the astronomer Lindenblad.) Most people today remain ignorant of Sirius B, so how could the Dogon have had accurate information concerning this star in the 1930s? A further mystery was that the Dogon seemed to have kept physical records relating to this star in the form of cult masks, some of which were centuries old and stored in caves.

Temple dismissed theories that the Dogon's knowledge of Sirius B was derived from their contact with people who came from France with the following retort: "The two French anthropologists started their work in 1931 and they are positive that the Dogon knew details about Sirius B when they arrived. [English astrophysicist Arthur Stanley] Eddington revealed the superdensity of Sirius B around 1926. So, there is a narrow period when one has to imagine some group of amateur Western astronomers rushing out to Mali and implanting this knowledge in the presumably pliant minds of the Dogon."[6] Temple is supported by Dieterlen who lived with the Dogon for more than three decades. Any suggestion that the astronomical knowledge was of recent origin was, she said, absurd. The cult masks—which were centuries old and held physical records relating to this star—certainly confirm that any speculations that Dogon knowledge of Sirius B derived from modern astronomers are false.

Temple concluded that as this knowledge clearly had not come from modern astronomers, it must have originated from ancestral sources and had probably been passed down to the Dogon before they migrated to their present home in Mali. In Egypt, in ancient times, Sirius was considered the most important star in the sky and was identified with the Egyptians' favorite goddess, Isis. Thus Temple's initial study of the article by the French anthropologists had led him, via an obscure African tribe, to ancient Egypt. He wrote: "I have been able to show that the information which the Dogon possess is really more than five thousand years old and was possessed by the Ancient Egyptians in the pre-dynastic times before 3200 BC."[7]

The Dogon people and their extraordinary knowledge provide substantial evidence that visits from the stars by alien beings did indeed take place in ancient Egypt and its environs. The Dogons and perhaps other groups of people who witnessed these visitations migrated to other parts of Africa retaining their memory of these encounters, and then passed that memory down to future generations.

According to biological and artistic evidence found from Ancient Egypt, ancient Egyptians had a great respect for dwarfs.[8] Ancient Egyptians worshipped dwarf gods, and many dwarfs held positions of authority in households. The researchers found that the earliest biological evidence of dwarfs dates back to a predynastic period called the Badarian Period (4500 BCE) in addition to several skeletons from the Old Kingdom (2700–2190 BCE). They found numerous images of dwarfism on tomb walls and on vase paintings, statues, and other art forms. Dwarfs were depicted in at least fifty tombs, and the repetition of certain pictures shows that they were well integrated into society, the researchers said. The pictures showed dwarfs employed as personal attendants, overseers of linen, people who looked after animals, jewelers, dancers, and entertainers. Several were members of households of high officials and were esteemed enough to receive lavish burial sites in the royal cemetery close to the pyramids.

There were also two dwarf gods in ancient Egypt: Bes and Ptah. Bes was a protector of sexuality, childbirth, women, and children. His temple was recently excavated in the Baharia oasis in the middle of Egypt. Ptah was associated with regeneration and rejuvenation. It is strangely coincidental that the two "dwarf gods" seem to have been preoccupied with all the procedures that imply genetic engineering, something the Greys seem to be obsessed with to this day. Could these "dwarf gods" be the Greys themselves?

There is an intriguing report of a remarkable find that may provide conclusive proof of an alien visitation. The report has yet to find conclusive corroboration. This may be because it is a hoax, or it may be because the evidence it might present has been removed by those who do not wish it to be discovered. As yet it is impossible to say which of these is true, although going on past form the latter is distinctly possible.

The reports say that in the Baian Kara Ula Mountains on the border that divides China and Tibet an archaeological expedition led in

1938 by Chi Pu Tei (a professor at Beijing University) came across some caves that appeared to have been man-made rather than natural. Inside, they found an ancient burial site containing unusual human skeletons, small in stature and with large heads. Reportedly, this area is actually inhabited by two groups of people who call themselves the Dropa and the Han. Anthropologists have been unable to categorize either tribe into any other known race; they are neither Chinese nor Tibetan. Both groups have an average height of about four feet. They have yellowish skin, are delicately boned, and have heads that are disproportionately large for their bodies (very much like the skeletal remains found in the cave). Their eyes are not Asian in aspect, and have pale blue irises.

The expedition found, half buried in the dirt, 316 stone disks, nine inches in diameter and three-quarters of an inch thick, with round three-quarter-inch holes in the middle. A fine groove spiraling out from the center to the rim was etched into the surface. These disks were later dated to be between ten and twelve thousand years old. They were made of granite with high concentrations of cobalt and other metals, making them very hard. The disks were tested with an oscillograph, and an oscillation rhythm was recorded as if the disks had once been electrically charged or had functioned as electrical conductors.

The continuous groove in each disk was not just a carved line, but a row of tiny hieroglyphics of no known language. The writing was allegedly deciphered by a Chinese scientist (Dr. Tsum Um Nui) in 1962. The disks tell of a space probe from a distant planet that crash landed in the mountains. The occupants of the craft (the Dropa) took refuge in the mountain caves. The intentions of the Dropa were misunderstood by members of the Han tribe who were occupying neighboring caves. These humans hunted the aliens and even killed some of them. A translation of one of the passages says: "The Dropa came down from the clouds in their aircraft. Our men, women, and children hid in the caves ten times before sunrise. When at last they understood the sign language of the Dropa, they realized that the newcomers had peaceful intentions. . . . The Dropa could not repair their spaceship and were then stranded on Earth."[9]

Apparently an ancient Chinese tale also tells of a small, yellow-skinned, slender people who descended to the earth from the clouds, and who were shunned by everyone because of their ugliness.

The discs have now all disappeared, although a photographic record of them does still remain. Perhaps they linger in a cold, dark, giant underground bunker somewhere in Nebraska, a repository, according to my sources, for most of the artifacts that affirm the presence of an extraterrestrial alien species here on Earth taken from crashed craft. If my sources are correct, and I have no reason to doubt them, you will find in this bunker all the evidence you will ever need to prove the greatest secret the world has kept since civilization started again this time around.

# 10

# Human to Monkey

To gain an insight into the history of Grey alien interception into our species, it will be helpful to take a fresh look at the salient property of life and what it reveals about our origins. I'm sure the reader remembers being told as a schoolchild that the value of the chemicals that make a human being was something extremely paltry. In my school days the figure was something like $7.85 (present-day U.S. money). I recall being astonished how cheap it would be to manufacture a human being and wondered why we couldn't make them in an industrial process. My particular intention was to make eleven custom-designed cricketers that would play for England and be unbeatable. I was soon brought down to earth when the teacher explained that if you put all these chemicals together in a human-shaped vessel and shook it, boiled it, cooled it, squeezed it, electrified it, or hit it, for ten million years—no single rudiment of life would ever result. It left me disappointed, but wondering, what makes for this glory we call life?

Once upon a time we relied on definitions like: *A living system is one that is capable of growth, respiration, locomotion, reproduction.* But now it seems the days are gone when a single definition will suffice. A flame, for instance, meets all these requirements. It has a definite shape and reacts with the environment by absorbing oxygen and releasing carbon dioxide and water, thus respiring and reproducing itself constantly. It, of course, moves incessantly, growing and reducing with the availability of the suitable gases that maintain it as a flame. But *living* things are more and do more than a flame.

It is very difficult to define exactly what a *living* system is. It requires definition in biological, biochemical, and genetic terms. As near as we can say, a living system is one that has a definite boundary and allows for the absorption and excretion of outside factors, while maintaining its form. It provides a hereditary code for replication of itself from within its infrastructure and is capable of maintaining its best disposition through a process of natural selection and the efficient utilization of thermodynamic processes.

Yet, what precisely moves it to do all these things? If we can exactly reproduce and bring together every idle element that makes up the system, every last molecule that is required for the life process, and fit them together as we see in the living modulus, it will never live. The propulsion system, the vital ordering effect—which through its influence maintains the momentums that conspire to provide continual propagation and utilization of the elements—will be missing. The chemical elements will decay with time, and their human-engendered order will cease in a chaotic cauldron of acids, bases, salts, gases, and water.

Life is the most unlikely phenomenon of all things in this universe. A single human chromosome is thought to have about 4 to the thirteenth power ($4^{13}$) of base pairs. Each base pair position could be filled by any one of four possible bases—adenine, cytosine, guanine, and thiamine. This results in an awesome scale of numbers and permutated results of points in chaos that somehow organize into rational thinking entities that can wonder at the same numbers. These entities create more and more complex blueprints that self-maintain the most complex dictations for life. This evolution from zero begs the question of how such ordered complexity could have evolved out of *chaos,* in a mere $42^{10}$ years of the universe's existence.

The SLOT states that entropy within a closed system cannot decrease. Living things *seem* to violate the SLOT because they have built-in programs (information) and energy conversion mechanisms that allow them to build up and maintain their physical structures in spite of the second law's effects (which ultimately do prevail, as each organism eventually deteriorates and dies).

While this explains how living organisms may grow and thrive, thanks in part to the Earth's open-system biosphere, it does not offer any solution to the question of how life could spontaneously begin this process in the absence of the program directions and energy conversion mechanisms described above, nor how a simple living organism might produce the additional new program directions and alternative energy conversion, that is, the mechanisms required in order for biological evolution to occur, producing the vast spectrum of biological variety and complexity. In short, the open-system argument fails to adequately justify evolutionist speculation in the face of the second law. Many highly respected evolutionists acknowledge this fact, many even acknowledging the problem it causes the theory to which they subscribe.

Sir Fred Hoyle, in his book *The Intelligent Universe,* puts forward some interesting scenarios suggesting the extraordinarily unlikely possibility that life could have originated in the first place by chance from a primordial soup:

> The probability of life appearing spontaneously on earth is so small that it is very difficult to grasp without comparing it with something more familiar. Imagine a blindfolded person trying to solve the Rubik cube. Since he can't see the results of his moves, they must all be at random. He has no way of knowing whether he is getting nearer the solution, or whether he is scrambling the cube still further. One would be inclined to say that moving the faces at random would "never" achieve a solution. Strictly speaking, "never" is wrong, however. If our blindfold subject were to make one random move every second, it would take him on average three hundred times the age of the Earth, 1,350 billion years, to solve the cube. The chance against each move producing perfect color matching for all of the cube's faces is about 50,000,000,000,000,000,000 to 1.

These odds are roughly the same as you could give to the idea of just one of our body's proteins having evolved randomly by chance. However, we use about 200,000 types of protein in our cells. If the odds against the random creation of one protein are the same as those against a random solution of the Rubik cube, then the odds against the random creation of all 200,000 are almost unimaginably vast.[1]

Hoyle goes on to point out that even if we were only to assess the likelihood of the spontaneous origin by chance of the two thousand or so special proteins, the enzymes, which are vitally important to life processes, then still the odds would be outlandish. The chance of these vital two thousand enzymes being formed in exactly the correct way, which they must be or else complex living organisms simply could not operate, is "about the same as the chance of throwing an uninterrupted sequence of fifty thousand sixes with unbiased dice!"

Hoyle examines how those who claim that life originated in an organic soup imagine that complex life developed. They imagine that a clump of two or three very primitive enzymes toured around the primordial soup of amino acids picking up other potential enzymes as and when they happened to arise by chance. Hoyle points out that in effect what this model really describes is:

> How we ourselves would go about collecting up a packet of needles in a haystack, using our eyes and brains to distinguish the needles from the hay. How for instance, would the enzyme clump distinguish an exceedingly infrequent useful enzyme from the overwhelming majority of useless chains of amino acids? The one potential enzyme would be so infrequent that the aggregate might have to encounter 50,000,000,000,000,000,000 useless chains before meeting a suitable one. In effect, talk of primitive aggregate collecting up potential enzymes really implies the operation of an intelligence, an intelligence which by distinguishing potential enzymes possesses

powers of judgment. Since this conclusion is exactly what those who put forward this argument are anxious to avoid, their position is absurd.[2]

Why then do so many scientists accept such codswallop as the way life began? I believe there are two main reasons why they might. The first is vanity or in-house protectionism and the second is power. Science today is the great power broker in the belief stakes. The claim by its aficionados that it is the source of all provable rationale that is verifiable and thus dependable is in some ways one that is valid only in terms of a physical, sensory, and atomically derived perspective. Even then they are too wrong, too often, to validate this claim. The purveyors of the science ethos claim these are the only perspectives open to humanity to verify objectively the veracity of anything, and that all other outlooks—those that are subjective, or beyond the capacity of the tools of the physical atomic array to verify—are false musings belonging to the realms beyond the reach of our powers as entities to accept and respond to as real and true. You see, we run up against these words like *valid, true,* and *certain.* These are truly misleading terms. They are essentially relative; in a world where entropy rules the overall momentum of the entire existential base, it implies that such terms can have no cogent final or definitive meaning in their own terms of reference.

Yet even the scientists themselves are beginning to doubt the veracity of the notion that life originated from the assembly of rudimentary polypeptide chains through fortuitous accident in a chemical soup, with lightning as some kind of electronic activator to kick start the process. A press release given by the Royal Society on the February 13, 2006, stated that:

> The latest findings of experiments to re-create the conditions under which life could emerge from chemical reactions suggest that volcanic springs and marine hydrothermal events are unlikely to have provided the right environment, a leading researcher from the United

States told an international meeting on 14th February 2006, at the Royal Society, the U.K. National Academy of Science.

David Deamer, Professor Emeritus of Chemistry at the University of California at Santa Cruz, will reveal his results to delegates at a two-day international scientific meeting on "Conditions for the emergence of life on the early earth." His results, not yet published, were obtained from experiments carried out in the volcanic regions of Kamchatka, Russia, and Mount Lassen, California, USA.

Ahead of his presentation, Professor Deamer said: "It is about 140 years since Charles Darwin suggested that life may have begun in a 'warm little pond'. We are now testing Darwin's idea, but in 'hot little puddles' associated with the volcanic regions of Kamchatka and Mount Lassen. The results are surprising and in some ways disappointing. It seems that hot acidic waters containing clay do not provide the right conditions for chemicals to assemble themselves into 'pioneer organisms'. We found that organic compounds like amino acids and the bases of DNA, which are the building blocks for life, became strongly held to the surfaces of clay particles in the volcanic pools in Kamchatka. Phosphate, another essential ingredient for life, also became held to the surface of the clay. We saw the same thing in a boiling pool at Mount Lassen. The reason this is significant is that it has been proposed that clay promotes interesting chemical reactions relating to the origin of life. However, in our experiments, the organic compounds became so strongly held to the clay particles that they could not undergo any further chemical reactions. In addition, when we introduced soap-like molecules into the pools, they did not form membranes, which would be required to form cells."[3]

Some may ask why we can't kick start an assembled aggregation of molecules. After all, we kick start a heart into life with the application of a current in the form of a shock and this starts a process that begins life again in a lifeless person. But in fact the person is not lifeless. Life still proceeds in his or her body. All that has happened is that the heart has stopped beating and the hive of electrical impulses still prevailing in all the cells is not moving according to regular formats or patterns. The shock pushes it all into continuing. If, however, the hive is allowed to subside for a few minutes without any force of impulsion, no amount of shock can get it going again. Then what is there is chemical soup.

That soup is, however, far more sophisticated chemically than a string of simply arranged amino acids like the ones said to have become suddenly enlivened, which eventually resulted in us three or four billion years later, through a series of fortuitous accidents favoring order and symmetry. All this is said to have taken place while the swansong of the entire universe, the gargantuan force of the second law of thermodynamics, breaks all systems into increasing states of randomness and chaos with time. It is beyond belief how dumb some eminent scientists can be in the desperation to convince us that there is no God.

Hoyle has illustrated with his analogies the extreme unlikelihood of random origins for life in the primordial soup. A far more convincing proposition is that we are *devolving* into greater states of separation from the state of "wholeness" we once were. A pattern of devolution would suggest that—just as the whole implicitly contains the parts that make it up—we have within us the blueprint for all future states of devolvement.

Scientists studying mutational phenomena have discovered that there is in fact such a blueprint, "an ancestral body plan" that guides development from one species form to another. Instead of inventing a new set of body plan genes for each new type of animal, it seems that natural selection has simply tinkered with an old one, a set known as Hox genes. Research from a team headed by Fred Gage, of the Salk Institute for Biological Studies in La Jolla, California, has come up with results that may suggest that there is indeed a power beyond the purely atomic facilities for life, a nonphysical power that might assemble and then martial the atoms of the body.[4] When human embryonic stem cells were injected by the research team into the brains of two-week-old mouse fetuses, they developed and functioned like normal mouse cells.

"We were struck by the fact that the immature human cells appear to be able to respond to cues from the mouse to become more mouse-like," says Gage.

"It is interesting that human neural cells respond completely to the mouse brain environment," says Irving Weissman, a stem cell biologist at Stanford University in California. Could these "cues from the mouse" actually be cues from the electro-spatial or soul field of the mouse? This would dictate mouse-like features that would override the human features of stem cells isolated from a human "soul field."

The telling question that must be asked here is: If all organisms that now exist had from their very inception into the evolutionary process a blueprint of how they should evolve, then where did that blueprint come from in the first place? How did the first multicellular animals evolving some 700 million years ago contain the basic template of information that only needed to be shuffled around in order to form a human being? All the myriad changing environmental factors and chance mutations—which allowed survival within changed environments and thus evolution through the survival of the fittest—had not yet occurred at that point. So where did the most basic of living organisms, or indeed the chemical soup that produced them in the first place, get this genetic blueprint?

Hoyle's postulation that living viruses from outer space came here in asteroid or meteorite strikes to engender more complicated systems of life still begs the question: How do we get something so profound from something so mundane when the second law of thermodynamics is busy tearing it all apart into lesser and lesser expressions of order and greater and greater expressions of randomness and chaotic amelioration with time?

The basic evolutionary contention is that we evolved from a sea worm to a human being, through a series of fortuitous genetic mutations that occurred through sheer chance. But it is inconceivable that reasoning and directed thinking capable of intelligent arbitration emerged by chance in an environment that is creating chaos with each progressive moment in time. This is a theory for Lucy in lunatic land. There are not enough years in the scale of the time the universe is said to have existed to allow for enough fortuitous mutations to account for our existence. The law of probability summarily contradicts it.

There is a significant body of evidence to suggest that our origins should be traced via a line of devolving rather than evolving life forms. Simon Easteal, a geneticist at the Australian National University, has also suggested that, contrary to the popular belief that humans evolved from chimpanzees, both might have had a common ancestor.[5] He bases his conclusions on his own research in which he has discovered a great similarity between human, chimpanzee, and gorilla DNA: "They are so similar it means we should in fact regard chimpanzees and gorillas as members of the same genus and call them *Homo*." Easteal says, "rather than believe that we came down from the trees, we are suggesting we continued to walk upright and chimps went up the trees and stopped walking upright."

Explanations for the evolution of an upright stance in hominid forms center around the theory that it became necessary for various reasons when a change in climate transformed Africa's moist forests into grasslands. Thus evolution would have favored hominids that could stand upright in order to spot predators lurking in the tall grasses. An upright stance would have lessened the heat that hominids absorbed from the sun because the forests were no longer there to protect them. However, there is one vital flaw in these explanations: a growing body of evidence suggests that the earliest hominids did not in fact move out into the savannah. The fossils they left behind were found in areas that were once densely wooded. It seems that they learned to walk in the relative safety of the forests while living next to their cousins the apes! This lack of evidence for the evolution of bipedalism seems to suggest that anthropologists might be better advised to reverse their search and look instead for how bipedalism developed into quadrupedalism for some species of primate.

If we *continued to walk upright* and apes *stopped walking upright,* then our common ancestor would have walked upright and thus would have been a hominid form, not an ape form. So perhaps the reason why scientists have had no success in finding causes for the origin of bipedalism in hominid species is simply because hominid species started off bipedal and only later devolved into a quadrupedal stance. Apes may thus have *devolved* from humans, not humans *evolved* from apes. Before the men in the white coats come to make a monkey out of me, let me say that the gradual unraveling of the genome is, in a tantalizing fashion, beginning to suggest this.

A further hiccough in conventional evolutionary theory has been found in the ancient fossil record of the Miocene period, which stretches from twenty-five million to five million years ago. During the Miocene period, a single ancestral group, the hominoids, gave rise, it is believed, to several lines that culminated in today's higher primates. According to what is commonly believed, the first to diverge from the common hominoid stock was the line of the lesser apes (gibbons and siamangs), followed by the line that led to orangutans. Later still, the remaining stock divided again, one branch leading to the great African apes (gorillas, chimpanzees, and bonobos) and the other to humans. Paleoanthropologists believe that human and ape lines diverged between four million and six million years ago. They have, as yet, found no fossils that would satisfactorily account for this common ancestor.

Scientists are trying to trace the ancestry of the great apes and humans in the Miocene period. One of these scientists, Steve Ward of the Northeastern Ohio University's College of Medicine, has said that: "What initially seemed to be a fairly nice simple progression [toward modern species] got scuppered by the fossil record."[6] He is referring to the fact that the fossil record from the Miocene period is full of hominoid forms that seem to have no modern living counterparts. There are about a dozen genera and even more species of larger-bodied hominoids known from the Miocene, while today there are only three genera and four species of great apes.

What happened to these Miocene apes that have no modern descendants? Did they perhaps devolve down the devolutionary tree into lesser forms of mammal? Mike Rose, of the University of Medicine and Dentistry of New Jersey, says that he sees very little similarity between these Miocene apes and modern apes: "When I look at the postcranial bones from the Miocene apes, I get a fairly clear and consistent pattern from many species. But it is nothing like what we see in modern apes."

It is a fascinating enigma that the fossil record for the African apes is almost nonexistent. There are only a handful of possible ape-related fossils, even in the five million years after the Miocene period leading to the present day. Rich fossil records have been found for other species of mammal living in the same habitat as the apes. So, why is there no record? Perhaps the problem is that paleontologists do not realize that they have already found the fossil record of the African apes—in the ancient hominid forms of *Australopithecus* and *Homo habilis*. Just as in the Miocene apes, they might have found the ancestors of a more devolved mammalian species.

Thus evidence from several sources suggests that the momentum of devolution governs the origin of species on this planet. This is consistent with my argument that the history of our species, as presented thus far by the experts, is utter bunkum. We did not evolve up to humans from the sea worm. We *devolved* and continue to devolve to our own variety of sea worm. The sea worms now in existence are the ends of other lines of superior beings and species that have come down from inaugural genotypes over billions of years.

The God-form came into the universe in the very special way I have outlined previously, and all the lines of being, all over the universe, come from this original God-form. Under the influence of the second law of thermodynamics (entropy), Prime being reduced gradually into all the different arrays of living species, as represented by our particular brand of species on the Earth. Of course, this same procedure occurred in billions of locations all over the universe.

The existential state of the first "Adams" on this planet, who were a form of ephemeral being, was gradually translated into the state of physical substantiality in physical life. At that time, the threshold of force at this location in the universe was lower than it is now, allowing for a translation of the insubstantial state of being into the substantial state of being without the necessity for the mechanism of physical birth into already existing biological lines. Thus the first individual expressions of physical life, the first mothers and fathers of future species' lines, came to be. I contend that during the time such a phenomenon was possible, most of those who passed the threshold into the new state of physical life quickly returned to the insubstantial state from which they came. The first physical hominid forms were able to explore the different expressions of the Universe of Parts in relative freedom, while still retaining their ability to swiftly return to their prior ephemeral state of being.

However, within a chaotic universe, unpredictable phenomena that can temporarily increase the force signature of a planet may have disturbed that equilibrium. Comets, asteroids, or meteor showers bombarding the planet, along with volcanic eruptions, earthquakes, and so on, may have caused sudden increases in its force signature, temporarily restricting or even blocking the passage of travel between the substantial and the insubstantial state. Some representatives of original Prime being might have found themselves suddenly stuck in the treacle of universal force. From that point on, they were increasingly gripped by entropic momentums, which gradually reduced their scope for freedom of choice and expression.

The crucial point is that the process was one of reduction to lesser forms, superior to inferior. In our Earth's terms, it went from the God-form, to mortal human, to ape, to monkey, to animal, to insect, to tree, to virus, to plasmid, and all the millions of species that make up the points in between. With a view to all the paleontological and genetic evidence that has been gathered, all the genotypes of humankind found thus far are *ends* of the lines of God-man. In other words, each distinct genus branched off from the original first Adam and first Eve. As they devolved through the eons, they ended their humanoid aspect and became apes. The ancient lines of hominid and prehominid species, the *Australopithecines, Homo habilis,* and *Homo erectus,* became the great primates: the gorilla, the chimpanzee, and the orangutan.

This raises a question regarding the general drift of development, which—at least as far as the fossil evidence is concerned—appears to be an evolutionary one. I have used the words *appears to be* evolutionary because, as I have previously shown, the nature of the entropic drift demands that a *natural* drift into states of greater and greater species advancement is a logical impossibility. Still, if the emergence of *Homo sapiens sapiens* as a species is a result of a devolutionary process, why does the fossil record seemingly present a picture of evolution?

For example, there is a gradual increase in the brain capacity of hominid species as time progresses. Or is there? Remarkably, it is a scientific fact that the human brain has actually *shrunk* dramatically through the millennia of the history of humankind. Scientists are in some disagreement as to whether this shrinkage started thirty thousand years ago or ten thousand years ago, but they do agree that the brain has shrunk by 8 to 10 pecent.[7] The brain has in fact been shrinking for the past 100,000 years, albeit at a slower rate. While there is a general pattern in the fossil record of an increase in the brain size of hominid forms between 3.6 million and 100,000 years ago, it seems that at the point when modern humans were established in the fossil record, the brain began to shrink!

Another paradox for evolutionary biologists is that the human brain "evolved" to be so big in the first place! It uses an extraordinary amount of energy; it only takes up 2 percent of our body weight, but uses 20 to 25 percent of our energy intake, far more than any other organ. The more the brain grows, the more energy and nutrients it takes away from other vital organs. So is our large brain a leftover from the past? Another exception to the growing brain capacity of hominid species over time is that of *Homo sapiens neanderthalensis,* whose brain capacity is actually greater than that of its successors in the fossil record—the Cro-Magnons (but that is an incongruity that I will account for later).

The phylogenetic ancestral line of earliest humans down to the present time (based on available information) is as follows:

| | |
|---|---|
| *Australopithecus afarensis* | 3.6 million–2.8 million years |
| *Australopithecus africanus* | 2.5 million–1.2 million years |
| *Australopithecus robustus* | 2.0 million–1.0 million years |
| *Homo habilis* | 1.9 million–1.3 million years |
| *Homo erectus* | 1.5 million–500,000 years |
| *Homo sapiens sapiens* | 200,000–present |
| *Homo neanderthalensis* | 100,000–35,000 years |

**Possible assimilation of "Moderns" as produced through an African Eve:**

| | |
|---|---|
| *Homo sapiens sapiens* with *Homo neanderthalensis* | 100,000 years–present |

Of all the tens of thousands of skeletons that mark the ancestral lines of humankind as a physical species through the millennia, no single direct line can be traced that accounts for all the discovered strains of our genus. It in fact seems clear that all the discovered genotypes seem to end abruptly, except for two, *Homo erectus* and *Homo neanderthalensis*.

It is speculated that the first major exodus of hominids from Africa to other parts of the world began about one million years ago. This exodus is evidenced by the fact that *Homo erectus* fossils are found from that point on in various places outside of Africa. There is intense debate among paleontologists and anthropologists about how modern humans evolved from these *Homo erectus* hominids.

There are two distinct schools of thought as to the origins of the modern phylum we call *Homo sapiens*. One school contends that the present forms of humankind come from four distinct types of ancestor, derived from four different geographical points on the Earth. The evidence for this is paleontological and relies on the fossil record. The structure of bones and skeletons and their compatibilities are thus crucial to the argument. Four distinct types of *Homo erectus* hominid, found in the fossil record at four different locations in the world, are identified as the ancestors of the four main phylotypes of modern humans found today in those locations:

| *Homo erectus* Fossils | Modern Equivalent |
| --- | --- |
| Olduvai | African |
| European | European |
| Lantian (Peking Man) | East Asian |
| Java Man | Australoid |

No reasons are given by supporters of this theory regarding why evolution came about in four distinct groups at four distinct points. The spread is the important thing. *Homo erectus* fossils from Africa spread across Africa, the Middle East, India, and also into parts of Near East Asia. If Professor Milford Wolpoff, an eminent Israeli paleontologist and one of the main protagonists of the "multiregional" view of human origins is right, European *Homo erectus* later evolved into Neanderthal–Cro-Magnon man across Europe to become the modern Europiform type, Peking man across China and Mongolia, and Java man across southern Southeast Asia and Australasia. All the rest of humanity is thus supposed to have come about from a hybridization of these four distinct forms that suddenly sprang up in these widely separated locations.

The second theory that seeks to explain the ancestral lineage of humankind uses a genetic marker to trace back the ancestry of thousands of people. Although it too has its flaws, it is a far more reliable methodology, capable of tracing the ancestral lines of thousands of individuals of different racial groups back to a single hominid female known as the "African Eve." This theory contends that all the other anthropological strains subsequent to *Homo erectus* come from a single point in Africa and a single individual hominid about two hundred thousand years ago. Humankind's cradle and maternal rooting point is Africa.

The two models are in contention and fierce controversy surrounds both. The latest research seems to confirm beyond reasonable doubt that every person alive today is a direct descendent from this African Eve. We know through further research that a great exodus of modern humans took place out of Africa about one hundred thousand years ago. Whatever the migration point—or why indeed the migration took place in the first instance—the crucial thing is that *a single entity gave rise to all this at a single point.*

So, who and what is the African Eve? Of the different *Homo erectus* groups that populated the world from approximately 1.5 million years ago to 200,000 years ago, it seems that the African group was the one that led to *Homo sapiens sapiens.* Java man, Peking man, and the European *Homo erectus* group did not establish a lineage into future humanity. Approximately one million years ago, they moved away from Africa into other parts of the world.

A fair question to ask would be: If humans have indeed devolved from prior states of grandeur into our present form, where is the evidence for those prior states in the fossil record? The lack of evidence may simply be because nearly all the representatives of these states converted the atoms of their bodies back into light, just as Jesus did at a much later stage in the devolutionary record of hominid forms on this planet. The whole exercise of his sojourn on the Earth could have been a demonstration paradigm to see if Prime being status *could* still be achieved within the force contexts of this planet as they prevailed two thousand years ago.

It would have taken a long time for ephemeral Prime being to devolve down into monkey men and then in species stages down into prions, the last stage on this planet for the capacity for a living paradigm of existence. These are perhaps all that remains of species lines of the kind that the Grey alien entities found on our planet in their first interception of it eons ago. To my mind, all primitive life marks the end of lines of prior *man* equivalents. Thus there is a cascade of various types of highly rational, sentient species that are wiped out, leaving their respective, devolved loads of survivor species to carry on, devolving down in concatenate threads. Although ephemeral Prime being as a singularity state and later as a multiplicity did survive somehow, somewhere, for great eons of time, eventually they did begin to succumb. I believe it was the last surviving devolved lines of prior humans that were left on this Earth when the extraterrestrials first came a calling.

When the natural devolution of the few soul lines that did not convert back to light reached a certain level of solid atomic resolution, they became suitable for alien genetic interception. The state of the original first forms, the Adams, on this planet would have had to be devolved enough, caught enough in the grasping "treacle" of universal force to allow alien being, which is intrinsically of that treacle, to stick onto them, so to speak. Prior to that threshold point, the soul lines that reincarnated on this planet would have slipped the grasp of alien being, as they were more spirit or ephemerally based and less matter based. Once that threshold level of more solid atomic resolution was reached, the experiment began, an experiment carried out by the Greys to test the ability of hominid forms on this planet to provide them with a bridging point from the physical into the metaphysical, from atoms to spirit, and thus soul.

This could well identify these beings as the *Gods, demons,* and *devils* of yore, depending on your point of view, and verifies their power as the source of the power of Satanism and devil worship as we know it today. Above all, it all also explains why many historical cultures and many cultures in certain parts of the world today say that the Devil and Satan are after our souls, although they did not view it in terms of a "soul" as I have defined and described it. They simply could not know what a soul was.

My thesis is that the hominid types found in the fossil record— from the *Australopithecines* to *Homo sapiens sapiens*—are a result of their experimentation with naturally devolving biological lines. The record of the "evolution" of the human species actually reflects a continuous line of modification of ape-like forms into something that could hold, in a more coherent form, what the alien beings were looking for—a soul. They were seeking a biological bridge to Godhead, which they could directly access via the tracks of their own genetic interception. They would not have been able to convert these ape-like forms into less devolved forms of hominid without a reference of that less devolved state. Thus they would have hybridized the last remnants of any superior, albeit devolving, hominid lines with more devolved ape-like beings.

The whole process would have begun at the edge of atoms. I have discussed the space between atoms in the context of its reception of the reach of En-light into physical being. Original Prime being persisted within this space and viewed the universe from it. When the original Prime *being* (a singular holistic form) became Prime *beings* (a plural, individualistic form) and was drawn into the atomic state, the space between atoms became the realm of death, a "waiting room," so to speak, between incarnations, a waiting room between existence in the universe and existence in the Godverse. The breakdown of the six-atom hydrogen rings into smaller rings of three, four, or five hydrogen atoms created resonant fields of more or less enforced space depending on the size of the atom ring. The smaller the ring, the more the force of the surrounding atoms would impinge on the space within.

At death a soul would rest in the space between atoms at its own field of resonance, based on its own hydrogen atom ring configurations in life. I will explain this at great length in the following chapters. Suffice to say for now that the Greys would only have been able to reach the area of that space that is closest to the surrounding atoms where the force is greatest. As purely physical beings they could not enter into that space themselves; all they could do was increase the force of the surrounding atoms so that the space within was affected. The less devolved souls would resonate closer to the center of the space where force is least. So the Greys could only reach the most devolved incarnating souls whose natural resonant field was close to the atoms. As these souls formed new bodies, the Greys could use force at the edges of atoms to influence and format their DNA to create a new body aerial that would stay within their grasp. To achieve that end, they would have to tune that aerial to receive more signals of force than signals from the Godverse.

The key to the whole process, however, was the hybridization of these faster-devolving hominid lines that the Greys could easily reach with superior, yet also devolving, lines that were beyond their reach. To achieve this end, they used the same techniques of genetic engineering that are witnessed today by abductees who report the extraction of sperm and ova and the creation of hybrid babies. The hybrids thus made allowed more advanced, coherent souls to enter through birth and incarnation into their intercepted biological lines than had previously been possible. There was also an increase in the cranial capacity of the hybrid, borrowed from the superior brain size of the more slowly devolving hominid. This hybrid, represented, shall we say, by the *Homo habilis* hominid form, was in turn further hybridized with other superior hominid forms to result in a further enhancement of cranial capacity, which was announced by the *Homo erectus* hominids.

The fossil record suggests that the African *Homo erectus* group provided the theme upon which all the other *Homo erectus* forms varied. The survival of the African form suggests that the Greys might have been conducting a "case study" through this group, comparing it to the different variations arising in other groups living in different locations around the world. This group would thus have been the alien beings' first reference sample of hominids on this planet.

It is important to remember that the Greys had, written within their program, a full blueprint of the original clones that had created them. This blueprint was of course originally based on the biology of their second-generation Prime being creators. Their entire interception project was driven by a compulsion to match that original blueprint, to rebuild their clone creators. They could use this information to rewire the soft-tissue format of the brains of their devolved experimental subjects in line with that of their creator beings. They could apply the software of their program within the already existing hardware of the ongoing hybrid, but they could not use their artificial manipulation to create new hardware. That hardware can only come from naturally devolving biological lines.

The hybridization process could continue until the aliens had drawn as many soul lines as possible into their intercepted biological lines, drawing them closer to themselves and therefore, alas, more and more into greater states of entropic dismemberment. They were driven, of course, by the impulse to find, at the end of those lines, a biological bridge into Godhead, which they would have had direct access to via the tracks of their own genetic interception.

Why then, you might ask, did they not go straight to the closest points to the source and intercept the souls closest to Godhead? The answer is simply that they were not able to. They were perhaps only able, as I have previously explained, to influence those souls who were within their grasp. The level of that grasp would have been far away from the first point of origin for soul in incarnacy, too far away from Godhead to suit their purposes. So, they instead cast out their fishing lines and set their hooks into those whom they could reach, namely the more ape-like hominid forms. The hybridization process that enhanced the biological species line of prior hominids might therefore account for the apparent evolution of hominid forms evidenced in the fossil record. The resulting hybrid would have combined the cranial capacity of the two different hominid forms. Thus *Homo habilis,* for example, would have had a larger cranial capacity than *Australopithecus* because it was a result of the hybridization of *Australopithecus* with a superior hominid form. As I have said, the fact that there is no fossil record yet discovered for this superior form may well be due to the fact that there were so few representatives of it. Thus the fossil record as it now stands is a record only of devolved and genetically intercepted forms of hominid.

Why so long? Why do these changes to hybridize species take so long? No technology, however advanced, can work outside the natural laws of the universe. They have to proceed in the way in which the force paradigms that govern this planet proceed. To get the naturalness of our species as it happened here on this planet, from the inception of living intelligence in whatever form it first manifested, these beings have to breed us in *our* environment, making sure that each change takes and lasts. They are, after all, trying to change themselves into a naturally living format, trying to amalgamate their inorganic, synthetic life paradigm with ours.

How to make a machine live and die and live again, organically, is their challenge, a challenge they can never meet. They would have been able to do it long ago had it been possible in the first place. It does not take millions of years to change a machine to a human. It takes an eternity and then some. In fact, it can never be done and perhaps nobody has been able to tell these roboid Greys that fact so that they can understand it. To do so they would have to understand the concept of a soul. But how do you tell a soulless machine what a soul is? There are no references against which it could judge what a soul might be. Those references come from knowledge of the Godverse, and these beings can never know about the Godverse because they did not come out of it.

The Greys have no concatenate line leading back to Godhead through the Big Bang, so they can *never* have eternal continuity. They are manufactured entities that began with the individual automated process that made them and that have to be physically regenerated from time to time. In order to continue working, they have to be periodically "plugged into the mains," so to speak. Those "mains" are you and I, your DNA and mine, *if* that DNA is suitable. That is the crux of the whole harrowing story of interception.

# 11

## Our Fathers Who Art in Spaceships

Let us now look in more detail at the interceptions of the Greys, using evidence from the fossil record as it now stands. At any point in this chapter, you may wish to refer to Plate 19: "The Origin of Species Revisited," which charts my map of the ancestry of all living species on this planet.

The large numbers of Miocene ape species that have been discovered in the fossil record—most of which have no modern equivalents—might be partly accounted for by genetic experimentation on the part of the alien beings, who were perhaps testing out a selection of different types of interception to see which was the most successful. The most successful intercepted species resulted in *Australopithecus afarensis* (the hominid that is believed to be an ancestor of modern humans). Miocene ape species that were not intercepted in this way followed a natural momentum into states of further devolvement into lesser mammals.

The hybridization processes used by the aliens artificially enhanced the capacity of physical species on this planet to connect with Godhead through their body aerials. However, as this enhancement was artificial, it could not provide for the evolution of soul back to prior states of superior, more godly expression. Quite the converse was true. These artificial manipulations of genetic lines interrupted the natural soul track back to Godhead for those who received them. Thus the interceptions made it more difficult for soul lines to return to prior states of grandeur. At the same time, they made it easier for soul lines that were intrinsically closer to those prior states to exist within and incarnate into a physical universe. Any apparent evolution, in terms of behavior or reasoning ability, was thus purely the result of more coherent, more reasoning soul lines coming into physical species when the scope was provided for them to do so.

Thus alien being is not responsible for the differences that exist between us and the Miocene apes, in terms of the capacities to reason, understand, and freely choose. Rather, such differences result from the gradual hauling in of soul lines into the highly dangerous context of physical life, which itself is partly a result of the natural entropic momentums of the universe and partly a result of the machinations of the alien beings who are partners in crime with those momentums. In essence, by altering the parental bodies to provide a greater brain capacity, the aliens provided dwellings into which more knowledgeable souls could enter. The hardware already incarnate and thus in the physical universe was rewired to provide the added capacity to take in grander soul potential.

After *Australopithecus afarensis,* the next character in the fossil record, *Homo habilis,* resulted from a hybridization of *Australopithecus* with genetic information from superior hominid lines. It seems that the later, so-called "robust" Australopithecines—*robustus* in Southern Africa and *boisei* in East Africa—coexisted with *Homo habilis.* Perhaps the two lines that have descended from *Australopithecus boisei* and *robustus* have now resulted in the two species of African ape, the gorilla and the chimpanzee, for which there is, as I have already mentioned, no fossil record.

The result of the *Australopithecus* alien genetic interception, *Homo habilis,* was a hominid form that may have received a further interception, resulting in *Homo erectus* hominids approximately 1.5 million years ago. The ends of the lines of humanity that survived the entropic process of dismantling up to the African Eve point two hundred thousand years ago were further intercepted at different places and different times. As a result, a new genus—*Homo sapiens*—came into being.

These are the most crucial points in the history of our genetic series; it is likely that almost all other ancestral forms of humanity disappeared into subforms, that is, apes and monkeys, with the crucial exception of *Homo erectus* and *Homo neanderthalensis*. Both had the line of connection to Prime being, and thus Godhead. *Homo erectus* was the first to be genetically intercepted and transformed through the manipulation of DNA, to eventually become *Homo sapiens*. This interception stopped certain hominid lines on this planet from changing into apes, as was perhaps the fate of countless species all over the universe.

What part then does the Neanderthal group play in the gradual emergence of modern *Homo sapiens*? Could it be that the Neanderthals were left untouched by the aliens, reserved as a control group to act as a comparator with the altered species? Or perhaps they were kept as a spare group in case the experiment went wrong? A spare group that would make a better form from the mistakes learned through the DNA manipulation of *Homo erectus* that was carried out before. I propose that the Neanderthals were a sample left untouched when *Homo erectus* was rewired one hundred sixty thousand years previously. Then, at a certain stage, the soft tissue in the brains of a select group of Neanderthals was also rewired. Once this was done, the aliens isolated their experimental hybrid species from the rest of humankind through a set of rigidly defined rules or laws.

The Neanderthals, as I said, had a brain much larger than any other type of human found. Brain size per unit body mass is commonly accepted as a pointer to intelligence and thus a propensity to survive as a species. The larger brain size of the Neanderthals begs the question of why the isolated group seemed to be so primitive in technological development terms for tens of thousands of years. There are two distinct types of Neanderthals. One is the "classic" Neanderthal type that is believed to have been a cold-adapted, specialized side branch from the human line, which became isolated in Europe and then became extinct as the climate improved. These classic Neanderthals, I believe, came from another, more generalized group of hominids that continued on to contribute their genetic input into later modern sapient populations. This second group is absent from the fossil record for reasons I will later elaborate.

Some scientists place the classic Neanderthals in the modern human evolutionary line and attribute their disappearance both anatomically and culturally to a process of absorption that involves some contribution of Neanderthal genes to the succeeding populations. Others, however, have advocated the classification of Neanderthal man as a separate species altogether from *Homo sapiens.*

Present evidence indicates that the lineage of *Homo neanderthalensis* seems to have ended abruptly 25,000 or so years ago. There are, however, some scientists who claim that it never died out and continues today in another form whose origins are represented by a skeleton found in Israel (of a modern type of hominid). The skeleton is that of a young boy, which has been dated to ninety thousand years ago, called the Qafzeh boy. Professor Wolpoff contends that the Neanderthal's and the Qafzeh boy's genus are the same and that geographical and environmental factors account for quite apparent skull and skeletal differences. If the genus of both hominid forms is the same, it implies that modern *Homo sapiens sapiens* could have been derived from both the Neanderthals and the Qafzeh boy genotype. Neanderthal man may therefore never have died out. Other paleontologists disagree and contend that the features of each are too different to be the same paleontological classification (more on this later).

How then did that final hybridization process that resulted in modern man progress? The date of the second major exodus from Africa of *Homo erectus* hominids is approximated to one hundred thousand years ago. It is around that time that the Qafzeh fossils, which seem to be examples of an early form of *Homo sapiens,* are dated. Yet, as I have previously mentioned, these early *Homo sapiens* forms appear to have disappeared from the fossil record for the next sixty thousand years until the emergence of Cro-Magnon man. Cro-Magnon is the ancestor of Europiform humans according to palaeontological evidence for their existence found in France, England, Belgium, Portugal, Spain, Sweden, Canary Islands, and North Africa. The tantalizing question is: What happened during these sixty thousand years to the new moderns? Why is there little or no record of them in the fossil record for that time?

Up to that point, it is only Neanderthal fossils that appear in the European and Middle Eastern fossil record. Could the Qafzeh fossils and others like them that appear in different areas of the world in the past two hundred thousand or so years signify an early form of *Homo sapiens,* genetically engineered by the alien beings from the intercepted African Eve stock? Perhaps they found that the capacity of these early moderns to draw more powerful soul lines into the realms of physical life was not great enough. They may have then decided to start to work upon their control sample, the Neanderthals, with the aim of eventually combining their larger cranial capacity with that of the line from the African Eve in order to provide a new hybrid, a point of convergence in which the two hominid lines would become one. Thus the more advanced souls that would have incarnated into the as yet unintercepted Neanderthal line, with its larger brain capacity, would eventually be pulled into the new hybridized form that connected all soul incarnating on this planet and placed it within the grip of the alien beings. The fact that the brain capacity of Neanderthal man is actually greater than its successor in the fossil record, Cro-Magnon man, supports the idea that a hybridization between the Neanderthals and a group with a lesser cranial capacity did indeed take place.

I suggest that the Neanderthal line is the more advanced form of hominid that was hybridized with the lesser *Homo erectus* form. I contend that the large brain size of Neanderthal man was natural— *not* the result of alien hybridization, but the remnant of a naturally devolving unintercepted line. The fossil record is thoroughly confused about Neanderthal ancestry. All kinds of fossil skulls are attributed to the Neanderthal genotype, going back far beyond one hundred thousand years. But there is no definitive fossil record for Neanderthal types until about one hundred thousand years ago. Could this suggest that the ancestral lines that led to that point consisted largely of individuals who converted their bodies back into light, transfigured? The relative few who did become caught in the momentum of devolution and were intercepted are those we can observe in the fossil record. However, even these few are still greater in number than prior examples of advanced hominids who devolved into lesser states, simply because the force print of the planet had increased in time due to the entropic momentum of the universe. The treacle has thus become stickier and stickier, and it has thus become easier and easier to become stuck within it.

Paleoanthropologists believe that they have identified several intermediary *Homo erectus* forms in Europe, which indicate a gradual evolution from *Homo erectus* to Neanderthal man in the European context. I dispute that these forms have any connection with later examples of Neanderthal man. Rather, I would contend that they, like the Qafzeh hominids in Israel, are in fact examples of the alien beings' experimentation with their first group of interception, *Homo erectus*. The classic Neanderthal features they exhibit are a result of the adaptation of *Homo erectus* to the cold environment of Europe, just as Neanderthal man later adapted to those climatic conditions and displayed those same physical features. The physical similarity between the Neanderthals and European forms of *Homo erectus* is, I believe, due to the environment they commonly shared and not a sign that they share the same line of descent. It is my contention that any admixture between the Neanderthal group and the modern human lines that descended from *Homo erectus* is based upon hybridization and possibly interbreeding, not common descent. I realize that this is a highly controversial view, so I will support it with the evidence presented by research into the subject thus far.

*Neanderthal* is a term that describes a morphologically distinctive group of hominids who inhabited Europe and western Asia between two hundred thousand and thirty thousand years ago. Shorter and stockier than modern humans, but with larger brains, Neanderthals lived in Europe, central Asia, and the Middle East for about one hundred seventy thousand years before disappearing between thirty-three thousand to twenty-four thousand years ago.

The Neanderthals were thus highly successful over a large region for a substantial period of time, but this situation changed dramatically with the arrival in Europe of the first modern humans, *Homo sapiens*. It seems that the Cro-Magnons, the European variety of modern humans, began to arrive both in eastern Europe and in the far northeast of the Iberian Peninsula forty thousand years ago; within little more than ten thousand years, the Neanderthals were gone. The cause of their disappearance has long been debated, but there are two main possibilities. One is that they died out either because they were eliminated by the moderns in direct conflict or by indirect economic competition or because they were less well-adapted to the climate changes that occurred across Europe at that time. This would imply that Neanderthals are a separate species from *Homo sapiens sapiens*. A contrasting theory is that the Neanderthals themselves did not die out but instead simply evolved rapidly into moderns and were assimilated into *Homo sapiens sapiens*. It has also been suggested that perhaps the genes of the invading moderns simply "swamped" those of the Neanderthals. Both explanations, assimilation *and* annihilation, may be true.

Several studies into the mitochondrial DNA (mtDNA) of Neanderthal fossils have concluded that Neanderthal man does *not* feature in the genetic ancestry of modern humans. Yet many scientists feel that these results are far from conclusive. First, the results pertain only to mitochondrial DNA, which is (in most cases) only passed from mother to child. If there had been some interbreeding and it was generally the case that the husband moved to join the race of his wife, there would be no trace of Neanderthal mitochondrial DNA in the modern human genome.

Second, it is also possible that the gene pool of modern humanity has contributions from lines of Neanderthal man that actually predate those Neanderthal fossils from which the samples were taken. At some time in the past, selection for a favorable mitochondrial genotype may have caused that genotype to spread across the globe, eliminating much of the earlier mtDNA diversity.[1] If that were the case, then mtDNA sequences from Neanderthal remains predating that change would differ from ours, even if Neanderthals were among our ancestors. The fact that we have so few Neanderthal fossil remains that can yield DNA, mitochondrial or otherwise, suitable for analysis suggests that any such analysis will prove highly inconclusive due to the fact that we do not have anywhere near a representative sample.

In May 2004, *Science* magazine published the results of a study indicating that there might be problems with any research that is based on an analysis of mitochondrial DNA under the assumption that it is only passed to subsequent generations through the female.[2] This research highlights the case of a man who inherited his mitochondrial DNA in part from his father. The possibility of mitochondrial DNA passing from father to offspring flies in the face of the commonly accepted belief that mitochondrial DNA is only passed down from the mother. The validity of the data retrieved by studies that research human ancestry through a focus on mitochondrial DNA rests on this, seemingly mistaken, belief. Therefore the results of the aforementioned research into Neanderthal mitochondrial DNA suggesting no connection between modern man and Neanderthal man are thrown into considerable doubt.

The study involved a man who suffers from muscle weakness. Doctors found that this man's muscles tired easily because they contained cells with mutant mitochondria, which are the cellular energy-producing structures. What astounded the doctors was that most of his muscle mitochondria came from his father. This contradicted the commonly accepted notion that mitochondria are always inherited from the mother. Sperm are packed with mitochondria, but it had been previously thought they were destroyed after fertilization.

Mitochondria, thought to have evolved from symbiotic bacteria, possess their own DNA, which encodes a few dozen genes. It had been thought that human mitochondria did not swap large segments of DNA in the way that the chromosomes in a cell nucleus do during sexual reproduction. But in 0.7 percent of the man's muscle mitochondria, the mitochondrial DNA contained a mixture of sequences from his father's and mother's mitochondria.

Many genes in modern human nuclear DNA appear to be over one million years old, which may suggest that modern humans and archaic populations (including Neanderthals) may have interbred at least sporadically. A. G. Clark discusses the difficulties involved in examining Neanderthal DNA for evidence of similarity with that of modern *Homo sapiens sapiens* in his article "Genome Sequences from Extinct Relatives."

> The long period of coexistence of modern humans and Neanderthals, as well as the great depth of common ancestry of modern human nuclear genes, make it quite plausible that there was opportunity for interbreeding . . . . If there had been admixture, say 100,000 years ago, giving modern humans small segregating pieces of our genome with Neanderthal ancestry, it would be nearly impossible to identify them as such, even with full genome sequences. When two populations intermingle, their offspring's genomes will not necessarily simply be a mix of half of one parent, and half of the other. Rather, often only adaptive genes are able to "sneak" into the other population's gene pool—a phenomenon known as introgression. It looks like the human *FOXP2* gene may well be an example of introgression, and in fact may have introgressed from an archaic population into modern humans.[3]

In a paper published in the journal *Current Anthropology,* a team of European researchers report a "mosaic of modern human and archaic Neanderthal features" in thirty thousand year-old human fossils from Romania.[4] The human remains were found in Pestera Muierii (Cave of the Old Woman), an elaborate cave system in Romania. First uncovered in 1952, the fossils remained poorly dated and largely ignored until recently. Using carbon dating techniques, co-author Erik Trinkaus and his colleagues found that the remains were thirty thousand years old. Their analysis of the bones revealed diagnostic skeletal features of modern humans, including smaller eyebrow ridges, very narrow holes where the nostrils join the skull, and a shin bone that is flat on one side and concave on the other. However, the mostly human skeletons also possessed distinct Neanderthal features, features that were not present in ancestral modern humans in Africa. These include a large bulge at the back of the skull, a more prominent projection around the elbow joint, and a narrow socket at the shoulder joint.

According to the researchers, this mixture of human and Neanderthal features suggests that a complicated reproductive scenario existed as humans and Neanderthals interbred. The hypothesis that the Neanderthals were simply replaced should therefore be abandoned, they suggest.

Trinkaus, who is from Washington University, explains that some "closely related species of mammals freely interbreed, produce fertile viable offspring, and blend populations." He says that this is what appears to have happened with Neanderthals and modern humans. The researchers think that the populations probably blended together through sexual reproduction. "Extinction through absorption is a common phenomenon," says Trinkaus. He goes on to say that we may carry some of the genetic legacy of the Neanderthals within us. However, it would be difficult to determine which of us are more closely related to the Neanderthals, as "There has been 30,000 to 35,000 years of human evolution since then."[5]

One of the first insights into the Neanderthal nuclear genome has indicated that a human gene involved in speech and language processing was shared by the Neanderthals. The finding reveals that the human form of the gene arose much earlier than scientists had previously estimated. It also raises the possibility that Neanderthals possessed some of the prerequisites for language.

The gene in question, known as FOXP2, is the only one known

to date to play a role in speech and language. People who carry an abnormal copy of the FOXP2 gene often have speech and language problems. "From the point of view of this gene, there is no reason to think that Neanderthals would not have had the ability for language," said researcher Johannes Krause, of the Max Planck Institute for Evolutionary Anthropology.[6]

"The current results show that the Neanderthals carried a FOXP2 protein that was identical to that of present-day humans in the only two positions that differ between human and chimpanzee," the researchers concluded.[7] Could it be that we inherited this gene from our Neanderthal cousins? This would truly be a reversal of the stereotypical view of Neanderthal man held by the public until relatively recently.

Recent evidence gleaned from the fossil record may well confirm that if indeed there was interbreeding between the two forms of hominid, then we, rather than the Neanderthals, may have benefited most from the admixture! The research suggests that Neanderthals had a brain at birth of a similar size to that of modern-day babies. However, after birth, their brain grew more quickly than it does for *Homo sapiens* and became larger too. These new insights into the history of human evolution are being presented in the journal *Proceedings of the National Academy of Sciences*, by researchers from the University of Zurich.[8]

Dr. Marcia Ponce de León, Professor Christoph Zollikofer, and colleagues from the Anthropological Institute of the University of Zurich examined the birth and the brain development of a newborn Neanderthal baby from the Mezmaiskaya Cave in the Crimea. That Neanderthal child, who died shortly after it was born, was buried with such care that it could be recovered in good condition after forty thousand years!

When they reconstructed the skeleton on the computer, they discovered that the brain at the time of birth was of exactly the same size as a typical human newborn—a volume of about four hundred cubic centimeters. To study the development *after* birth, the researchers examined not only the Mezmaiskaya newborn but also other Neanderthal children up to an age of four. They discovered to their surprise that the

Neanderthal brain grew even more quickly during childhood than that of *Homo sapiens*. Until now, it has been assumed that the consequence of rapid growth would be a shorter lifespan. However, the new studies show that the Neanderthal brain indeed grew more quickly than our own, but only because a larger volume had to be reached in adult age. So the duration of brain growth works out the same for both kinds of human being. "As far as birth, development of the brain and life history are concerned, we are astonishingly similar to each other," says Dr. Ponce de León.[9]

It has become apparent from the fossils of Neanderthal groups that these so-called primitive peoples used to keep severely injured individuals alive, in some cases for decades.[10] The injuries displayed by certain Neanderthal individuals are so severe that they would never have survived had they not been taken care of by other people. It is often the case that one individual has many different injuries that, according to the fossil evidence, appear to have healed over. Thus there is indication that Neanderthal groups were indeed disposed to caring for their sick and injured. This could be taken as the sign of a spiritually advanced society, for, on a purely physical level, these injured individuals could only provide a hindrance, not a help, to this hunter-gatherer community that lived in harsh environmental conditions.

So, to return to my account of the alien genetic interception of hominid species on this planet, that part of the aliens' control group that was not intercepted in the first African Eve interception two hundred thousand or so years ago—the Neanderthals—was later intercepted. Some of this group lived within, or perhaps was placed within, a new environment that, I believe, was more conducive to alien interception than Africa had been. That environment is the environment of the last Ice Age in Europe. As I have already explained, alien body biology is likely to be inorganically electronically based. Thus the cold environment of the Ice Age, in which electrical currents flow more easily, would have been ideal for their intercepting processes. This interception, which took place in Europe, resulted in the classic Neanderthal group that has been identified as being specially adapted for a cold weather conditions.

What might have prompted early Neanderthal man, or other early hominids, to choose to live in, or to migrate to, the cold climates of western Europe, which at the time was in the throes of an ice age? In fact, the question that also needs an answer is why the two main exoduses from Africa (one million years ago and one hundred thousand years ago) occurred in the first place? What might have caused prior hominids to travel so far afield, to cross vast oceans and spread themselves over the enormous expanse of the ancient world? They would have certainly had the time to achieve that spread in the million years since the first exodus. But the question still remains: Why would they have wanted to travel so far? Overpopulation was certainly not the problem at that time, so that could not have prompted these vast journeys. The puzzle becomes all the more apparent in the context of the migration of early hominids to Ice Age conditions.

Could it perhaps be the case that the random distribution of early hominids found in the European fossil record during the time of the great ice ages was to a large extent the result of alien beings literally translocating their intercepted hominid forms to these locations, environments that were more conducive to alien interception? To take this proposition further, might it indeed have been the case that much of the migration across the world was also a result of such translocation? Could the alien beings have been setting up separate experimental groups that they wished to keep genetically discreet from one another? Vast expanses of land and ocean between these groups would have served this purpose admirably. The alien beings could also examine how the different environmental factors associated with these different locations affected their sample groups.

This might seem like a wild speculation straight out of the realms of science fiction, but there have been many reports from alien abductees who claim that they were indeed translocated from one place to another after their abduction experiences. It would explain why people who had plentiful food resources in Africa would decide to trek thousands of miles in a sudden exodus, which seems a foolish or even downright stupid thing to do unnecessarily.

The great ice ages, which consisted of extremely cold periods interspersed with short periods of warmth, occurred between about 1.75 million and about 10,000 years ago. This time span coincides with all the main alien genetic interceptions from *Homo habilis* to *Homo erectus*, to *Neanderthal,* and finally to Cro-Magnon. In fact, 1.75 million years ago is approximately the time at which the first *Homo* group, *Homo habilis,* started to appear, while 10,000 years ago, the end of the Ice Age, is the approximate date that is generally accepted to be the demarcation point at which modern *Homo sapiens sapiens* emerged as the primary hominid form.

Here is a possibility that you might find even more astonishing: Could it be that the ice ages were the result of alien interference with the climate of our planet? Scientists have not yet come to any firm conclusions as to what might have caused the ice ages. Many theories have been put forward; they include speculations that changes in the Earth's orbit around the sun and variations in the Earth's axis might have been responsible in part for these climatic changes. The impact of meteorites on the planet might well have caused such variations in the Earth's axis and orbit around the sun. Could the aliens have used their supreme technology to guide such meteorites toward our Earth in order to provide a cold environment more conducive for the flow of the electric currents that are central to all their "body" operations? It is well known that the lower the temperature of the medium, the less resistance a current flowing through it encounters. Such an environment would also better accommodate the physical vestments of their silicon-mercury–based synthetic bodies.

The last major alien genetic interception before the emergence of modern *Homo sapiens sapiens* was that of the Cro-Magnon hominids in Europe. Why did alien being wait so long to bring its experimental subjects into the Ice Age environment of the Northern Hemisphere? The answer might lie in the fact that the alien beings were hoping to gain from hominids on this planet an insight into how to access their lines of soul connection to Godhead. Thus they sought to study these hominids in their natural environment. They undertook a gradual series of interceptions to slowly change them without altering any of the factors that might have disallowed the very thing they were looking for—the direct connection via soul lines to Godhead. Only when the alien element that had gradually accumulated in the genome of certain hominids was large enough in scope could the most powerful interceptions take place without destroying the human genome altogether.

The examples of an intermediary stage between *Homo erectus* and *Homo Sapiens* found in Europe—such as Swanscombe man in England and Steinheim man in Germany—dating to between four hundred thousand and two hundred thousand years ago, may well be the results of the aliens' attempt at genetic interceptions in an Ice Age environment. This would explain why examples of *Homo erectus* in Europe at this time appear to be more advanced than examples found in the same time span in Asia and Africa. Perhaps these hominid forms do not bear any relation to modern *Homo sapiens* because they are one-off artifacts of ancient alien experimentation.

How then did the Cro-Magnons come about? They appear in the European fossil record at the same point at which classic Neanderthals die out, approximately thirty-five thousand to forty thousand years ago. The question of the relation of Cro-Magnons to the earliest forms of *Homo sapiens* is still unclear. It does appear however, that Cro-Magnons (*Homo sapiens sapiens*) and Neanderthals (*Homo sapiens neanderthalensis*) are closer in affinity than was once believed. The origin of the Cro-Magnon peoples can best be understood by first looking at the fate of the Neanderthal group that seems to have been their immediate predecessors.

After modern humans first emerged in sub-Saharan Africa some time prior to fifty thousand years ago, they spread northward, absorbing and occasionally displacing (through competition, not confrontation, it is believed) local archaic human populations. Some of the Middle Eastern, central Asian, and central European Neanderthals might have been absorbed into these spreading early-modern human populations, contributing genetically to the subsequent human populations across those regions. Western Europe was a cul-de-sac where the transition to modern humans took place relatively late. Thus there is a preponderance of Neanderthal representatives in the western European fossil record at that time.

The more general classification of Neanderthal man might have led (among others) to the group that we now identify as the modern Semitic people, making them the modern derivatives of the examples of Neanderthal man that have been found in the warmer climates of the Middle East. On the other hand, the classic (western European) Neanderthal grouping might well have led to the modern European stock, via the Cro-Magnon stage. In fact, some modern human groups that are more or less homogeneous are thought to have maintained a close relationship to Cro-Magnon types, at least in their cranial morphology. The most notable of these groups are the Dal people from Dalecarlia (now Dalarna, Sweden) and the Guanches of the Canary Islands.

Could a species that had done nothing in technological development terms for a hundred thousand years (the Neanderthals) suddenly and spontaneously convert to a people (the Semitics) that became one of the most brilliant, technically innovative ethnic groups the world has ever known, in a few thousand years? Only if a genetic change of enormous proportions took place suddenly, a change that altered the wiring of the brain in a large proportion of the genus.

Could it be that alien gene manipulation of people of the Qafzeh genus of *Homo sapiens* produced the hybrids that we know today as Cro-Magnon man? The Qafzeh skeleton is dated as being ninety thousand to one hundred thousand years old. The next skeletal record of *Homo sapiens* is marked with the appearance of Cro-Magnon man sixty thousand years later. Perhaps it took sixty thousand years to perfect the hybrid between equivalents of the Qafzeh boy and the classic Neanderthals of western Europe. The fact that modern man emerged later in Europe than anywhere else and that the Neanderthal stage is thus longer there may well have been a result of the processes required to produce this hybrid.

What then happened to the Qafzeh equivalents in the intervening sixty thousand years; why do they not appear in the fossil record? The Qafzeh fossils may well have represented a very small experimental group isolated from the main stock of intercepted African *Homo erectus* in order to prevent interbreeding, which would result in a dilution of the experimental results. They were brought out of Africa into what is now Israel. Then, after the experimental focus changed from this first group to the second group—the Neanderthal "control" group, no more representatives of the first group were moved from Africa. It is not surprising that such a small population of early moderns did not appear later in the fossil record, as the likelihood of fossils being found for prior hominids is very much the exception, not the rule. The fact that the Qafzeh group left any fossils may well have been purely a result of chance.

What then can we glean about the next experimental group, the Cro-Magnons? This group seems to have manifested a sudden spurt of technological growth unlike any that took place prior to their arrival on the scene. It is now believed that the Neanderthal and early modern human groups lived side by side with each other for tens of thousands of years. During that time, the modern humans showed no sign that they had superior technology. "Both people were living in the same way, hunting the same prey, burying their dead in the same manner," says Baruch Arensburg, a paleoanthropologist at Tel Aviv University.[11] Then it seems that around forty thousand to fifty thousand years ago, something profound happened. New technologies associated with modern humans—finer blades and projectile weapons—began to appear. Scientists can only speculate on what triggered this technological spurt. "I think there was a mutation in the brains of a group of anatomically modern humans living either in Africa or the Middle East," says Richard Klein, an anthropologist at Stanford University. "Some new neurological connections let them behave in a modern way. Maybe it permitted fully articulated speech, so that they could pass on information more efficiently."[12] Could this "mutation in the brains of a group of anatomically modern humans" to which Klein refers be the result of alien interception at this very point, alien interception producing the Cro-Magnon form of hominid? Such a sudden burst of technological development at this point certainly suggests the involvement of the ultimate masters of technology—the alien clones and their Grey roboids.

It is my contention that the Cro-Magnons are the result of direct crossbreeding with the aliens' own genetic blueprint. It was not confined to the rewiring of the brain alone. It was a whole-body interception, the final hybrid of all permutations that could be produced with the three main players: the Neanderthals, the modern humans, and the alien clones. Accomplished one hundred thousand years ago, it prompted the huge exodus of humanity out of Africa. However, I must add a qualification at this point. While I am suggesting that the Cro-Magnon pro forma was the end result of alien genetic interception, I am by no means suggesting that all Europeans who have that pro forma are highly intercepted. Once the genotype was established, it provided a set of biological lines within which the Greys could more easily operate. They would have concentrated and still concentrate their interception on specific lines within that set that are most available to them. Thus a pale skin need not spell out doom for those souls who, through their own psycho-motivational power, have an inner resistance to the Greys and can tune in to the power of En-light. Ultimately, the power of will to defeat any physical disadvantage is paramount. However, the fact that almost all hybrids seen by abductees in spaceships are European looking, and the fact that the vast majority of abductees are white, evidences my contention that the Cro-Magnon genotype was alien sponsored.

The Northern Hemisphere, which was largely covered in ice, provided the central stage on which these, the most complete interceptions of all, were carried out. Perhaps the Inuit legend recounted earlier, which says that the first tribes were brought to the North by gods with brass wings, is based on actual truth. As part of an extensive gene-mapping program, researchers at deCODE Genetics in Reykjavik, Iceland, have been searching for places in the genome where chunks of DNA containing many genes get turned back to front.[13] Strangely enough, one of these inversions, on chromosome 17, was particularly interesting to them, as it turned up in about 20 percent of Europeans, yet is rare in Africans and almost absent in Asians. These stretches of DNA remain back to front through the generations, so the origin of a particular inversion can be approximately dated by counting the number of genetic differences that have accumulated in it compared to a normal DNA sequence. This dates the origin of the inversion to about three million years ago, well before modern humans evolved. The researchers were baffled by the fact that this inversion, almost a million DNA letters long, did not spread to the entire human population.

The researchers also found, when looking at the families of nearly thirty thousand Icelanders, that women with the inversion had on average 3.5 percent more children than women who did not. David Reich, a geneticist at Harvard University says: "Finding any genetic variant that affects fertility is really startling, and raises lots of questions—like: why doesn't everybody have this?"[14]

If there have been 3 million years for such an advantageous trait to spread, it is even more astonishing that it has not done so. Hreinn Stefansson, deCODE's chief executive, offers a remarkable possibility. He suggests that it was introduced "by cross-breeding with earlier species." So the inversion was native to some other species of early human, but came to our species only about fifty thousand years ago. Stefansson says that: "There aren't all that many ways you can explain it except by reintroduction into the modern human population."[15] This recent arrival of the inversion would explain why it has not spread to everyone. It would also explain why copies of the inversion in different individuals are remarkably similar. The interbreeding events would have been rare and would have brought only one or two variants into the population. Has this research team unwittingly discovered the genetic strain that was carefully cultured about fifty thousand years ago by alien genetic interception of our species? Could one in five Europeans carry that strain today?

# 12

# Lambs among Wolves

The greatest savage of all our kind in the history of our human species has sadly been the white Euro-Caucasian. This is not a racist charge. It is simply the truth. Though outnumbered five to one in the world by other racial groups, the occidental white has proven, in terms of numbers, to be the greatest killer of the human genus the planet has ever known. The ratio of people killed by this group, set against those killed by nonoccidental groups over the past few thousand years, is estimated at over seven hundred to one. The Huns, the Goths, the Visigoths, the Vikings, the Angles, the Saxons, the Romans, the Greeks, and more recently, the Germans, the British, the French, the Russians, the Dutch, the Spanish, and the Portuguese, have between them in their colonizing greed accounted for some of the most draconian evil against innocent humanity the world has ever known.

I have used skin color as a demarcation to point to something interesting in connection with the Greys. It is my theory that the whole Genesis story is in fact a description of one of their more recent genetic interceptions of humankind. While many distinct strains of our human family come from the same time and process described in the Bible, the Jewish chroniclers have kept one of the best records of this process as it happened to the Semitic strain of humankind.

The account describes a particular breeding experiment that created an aggressive type of hybrid Grey/human progeny described in the story of Cain and Abel as "Cain." The Greys might well have selected the Cain types for further genetic processing, thinking their natural belligerence, ruthlessness, guile, killer instinct, selfishness, and vanity (Cain's gift to "God" was characterized as having these attributes) might make them better survivors so that they could go forth and multiply. It is strange (if you take it as the story goes) that God would punish Cain with a mark but at the same time promise to protect him from vilification and harassment. But in the context of the history of alien interception, the banishment and marking of Cain describes the Greys' way of isolating and preserving this type for DNA survival purposes.

I suggest that the "mark" was a change in skin color from dark skin to light skin through the loss of the immediate availability of the pigment melanin. The genes responsible for a white, fair complexion could have been bred into this more aggressive killer progeny, a progeny whose coloring would be different from the dark skin typical of hominids living in tropical Africa. Cain's banishment to the "land of Nod" could describe the migration of the deliberately bred faulty version to cold northern climes, a place that, arguably, no tropical person would freely go.

The reduction of melanin may well have been a means to allow the alien interceptors to reach into the chromosomes of their selected type in order to make changes that were commensurate with their own purposes. In his fascinating book *In the Blood—God Genes and Destiny*, distinguished biologist and geneticist Professor Steve Jones of the Galton Laboratory of University College London outlines a biological fact that, in my opinion, may be a very plausible reason why the vast majority of abductees are white. Jones points out that although the number of melanocytes is the same in blacks and whites, "In black skin they are far more active and the melanin granules cluster around the nuclei of the cells in which they are found, suggesting that they play a *vital* part in protecting DNA from damage by ultraviolet light."[1]

In an article in the *Journal of Investigative Dermatology*, Glynis Scott, MD, writes: "This positioning of melanosomes above the nucleus serves as an exquisite protective mechanism shielding the keratinocyte nucleus from harmful ultraviolet irradiation."[2] These are known as "supranuclear caps" or "microparasols" (see Plate 21). This inbuilt protective mechanism absorbs light, which prevents the use of ultraviolet light (a standard method) to alter gene orientation within the nuclear membrane. I have postulated in *The Song of the Greys,* that the cell's mitochondria (which includes DNA that is independent of the nuclear DNA of the cell and is, to a certain extent, uninvolved in functions that benefit the cell) can act as a conduit through which information from the alien beings, who may have inserted this DNA, can pass. This extract can be read in reference to Plate 22:

> It is interesting to speculate that perhaps all these interceptions account for the 37 genes of mitochondrial DNA that are mysteriously included in our cells. No one knows where they came from, or why, except that they would have to have come from a source totally foreign to the human genome. It is a salutary feature that mitochondrial DNA, unlike other DNA, clones itself in reproduction instead of recombining. There is a strong hypothesis that mitochondria are the direct descendants of bacteria that entered primitive nucleated cells in a number of infections. Among billions of such infective events a few could have led to the development of stable, symbiotic associations between nucleated hosts and bacterial parasites. The classes of "bacteria" that took part in these "infections" have not yet been established. Could these "bacteria" simply be the invading genetic elements introduced into the hominid genome by alien being via a series of "infections" until eventually they were accepted and absorbed? There is a proportion of mitochondrial DNA that is not in any way involved in functions which benefit the cell. Thus, it is to a certain extent, an organelle that is independent of the cell and independent of the cell's own genetic information contained within the nucleus.[3]

A new discovery about the origins of DNA replication offers a startling confirmation that mitochondrial DNA is in fact the result of alien interception. While scouring human DNA for the origins of replication or duplication centers, Michele Calos of Stanford University has discovered something quite remarkable about the specific structure of DNA that is capable of replicating under its own steam.[4] Her initial approach was to break up human chromosomes into pieces of DNA, inject those pieces into cells, and then search for ones that could replicate unaided. But there was a problem: any DNA pieces she injected immediately infiltrated and hijacked the replication centers. Calos hit on a solution. She knew that circular pieces of DNA cannot hop onto chromosomes because they have no "sticky ends," so she concealed her pieces of DNA inside a circular structure. The tactic worked. Almost immediately, Calos found pieces of DNA that could replicate under their own steam. "The trick was simply to make the DNA pieces big enough," she recalls. "Nearly any DNA piece larger than 10,000 base pairs is able to replicate."

Unlike other naturally occurring DNA, mitochondrial DNA happens to have a distinctive *circular* structure. It is thus extremely plausible that the alien beings used this circular structure to conceal their insertion of the thirty-seven genes of mitochondrial DNA. This concealment allows these genes to replicate under their own steam and thus maintain their independence from the human organism while at the same time existing within it. This symbiotic relationship between human cells and mitochondrial DNA allows the mitochondrial DNA enough independence from the human organism so it can act as a conduit through which information from the alien beings can pass. It is almost as though they have left a keyhole in human cells into which their key will fit, allowing them to open the genetic information contained within the cell and manipulate it as they wish.

Research scientists have been exploring ways of inserting blueprints for artificial structural proteins into bacterial DNA. It seems that it doesn't matter to a bacterium whether an artificial gene in its DNA codes for a protein like one that the bacterium produces naturally or one that is entirely different. If it is in the genome, the bacterium will make proteins. In 1990, a research team led by Joseph Capello, at Protein Polymer Technologies in San Diego, California, was searching for a designer protein that would make cells grown in tissue culture stick to normal human cells.[5] Artificially grown tissue is already proving valuable in promoting wound healing, and it might someday be possible to grow entire organs this way to replace damaged or malfunctioning ones. Capello and his colleagues persuaded bacterial DNA to code for their artificial protein with great success. The protein is now marketed commercially as an adhesive for attaching mammalian cells to tissue cultures. If scientists with our level of technology can achieve such success in genetically engineering bacterial proteins, then the scope for such genetic manipulation by alien beings with their highly ascendant technology must be enormous.

When this possibility is considered together with the above-mentioned qualities of melanin, it offers an explanation for the Greys' use of light. In all the described abduction cases, indeed in all the interactions that have been claimed with aliens, be they Greys, Greens, Yellows, or Blues, *light* is described as an effect that they use to move, intercept, and induce all kinds of procedures. We have to assume that light (which may be seen as a kind of universal force management polarization factor) may be crucial as their means of reaching and interacting with our species. Melanin, as a dark pigment, absorbs light. Nuclear DNA that is protected by the melanin granules that are clustered around it may therefore be safe from any alien-engendered effect brought about by light.

Karen Brewer, associate professor in the Department of Chemistry at Virginia Tech, Blacksburg, has written an article in the *New Scientist* that outlines the research she and her team are conducting into the possibility of light-activated anticancer drugs. Her group has created synthetic molecules that "when flooded with light, have the potential to carry out a wide range of tasks, such as synthesizing useful compounds, generating clean fuels, or attacking tumours."[6] The chemicals that are used to carry out these tasks are known as "supramolecules": "Chemists can mix and match the units to create supramolecules that are tailor-made for particular tasks."[7] Brewer describes how photons could stimulate a platinum-active site in the anticancer drug cisplatin. She outlines how the drug would be "switched on" at the tumor site by exposure to laser radiation. This would result in a strong bond between the platinum atom and the DNA bases, which would prevent the DNA from unzipping and replicating and so stop the tumor cells multiplying. Brewer also explains that a "broad range of wavelengths" can be used to activate the supramolecule so that it would be possible to "tune light absorbers to capture photons at certain wavelengths." The use of light to bind a metal into DNA bases is thus illustrated here as a technology that is already within our reach. If our relatively primitive technology is capable of this, what more might the supremely advanced technologies of alien beings be capable of in their ability to use the properties of light to bind their elements into the DNA of human beings?

Melanin has also been found to have a capacity to conduct electric fields. In 1963, D. E. Weiss and coworkers reported high electrical conductivity in melanin (they achieved a conductivity of 1 Ohm/cm).[8] In 1974, John McGinness et al. reported a high conductivity "*on*" state in a voltage-controlled solid-state threshold switch made with DOPA melanin.[9] Melanin also shows negative resistance, a property of electronically active conductive polymers.

Encounters with alien beings or craft have taken place with by far the greatest frequency at locations where there are particularly high electromagnetic fields (power stations, military bases, etc.) High electromagnetic fields also seem to be disturbed by the alien craft, which often cause widespread power failures in the areas where they appear. The conducting properties of melanin would allow it to act like a Faraday cage, conducting electric fields away from the nucleus of the cell and thus preventing alien procedures from reaching the DNA in the nucleus. If high electromagnetic fields are a vehicle through which the aliens reach humanity, then it may indeed be the case that dark-skinned people have a natural barrier to that reach.

In *In The Blood—God Genes and Destiny*, Professor Jones goes on to make the point that the color change from dark skin to fair skin, said to have taken place when the migration out of Africa brought human beings to Europe, does not necessarily make sense when seen in terms of biological advantage.[10] It is accepted generally that this change was due to the fact that a fair (or, in other words, transparent) skin could absorb more of the meager levels of ultraviolet light available in northern climes. The absorption of ultraviolet light is necessary, we are told, to aid in the production of vitamin D, vital for the production of strong bones and teeth. Jones says that, "although the idea of rickets as the driving force behind the evolution of skin color is attractive, melanin was probably not lost because of changes in vitamin balance." He points out that "rickets is a disease of civilization," a disease that only became common as cities grew in the Middle Ages.

Even blacks need only two hours a week of sunlight to stay healthy. "At first sight," says Professor Jones, "evolution has got it wrong. If humans followed the rules that apply to other animals, who have been a lot longer on the real estate, Europeans ought to be black and Africans white," simply because dark objects absorb more of the sun's light and heat. However, it is also true that blacks are able to sweat more than whites and, says Jones, this "more than compensates for the effects of skin color."[11] There are also the obvious advantages of a dark skin in the tropics, giving it the ability to protect the skin from the harmful effects of high levels of ultraviolet light. The advantages of a fair skin, no matter what the climate, are difficult to find in evolutionary terms. However, in terms of an aid to an easy and efficient alien interception of the human genome, the advantages are enormous.

Interestingly, initial findings reported in an article in the *Journal of Investigative Dermatology* suggest that the aggregation of melanin in supranuclear caps over the nucleus of the cell seems to be specific to human cells:

In humans, aggregated melanosomes are located above the nucleus of the epidermal basal cells, presenting themselves as "supranuclear melanin caps" for protecting the nucleus from UV-induced DNA damage. In pigmented animals, however, the existence of supranuclear melanin caps has not been clear.[12]

Could this point to the possibility that supranuclear caps protecting the nuclear DNA from external effect are a feature that is determined by the being's close connection to the Godverse? The predecessors of modern *Homo sapiens sapiens* all had high amounts of melanin; lack of melanin is thus a relatively recent mutation.

There is another type of melanin in the body that is present in all human beings regardless of skin color: neuromelanin. Neuromelanin is the dark pigment present in pigment-bearing neurons of four deep-brain nuclei: the substantia nigra (pars compacta), the locus ceruleus, the dorsal motor nucleus of the vagus nerve, and the median raphe nucleus of the pons. In Parkinson's disease, there is a massive loss of dopamine-producing pigmented neurons in the substantia nigra. In advanced Alzheimer's disease, there is often an almost complete loss of the norepinephrine-producing pigmented neurons of the locus ceruleus (see Plate 23). Thus melanin in the brain appears to provide a neurological benefit that is lost when such diseases take hold. Could this suggest that melanin itself may well be advantageous to the capacity of the human body aerial to function properly? I would like at this point to suggest a remarkable possibility. Could it be that at one time in the ancient past the entire brain was protected by melanin, providing huge neurological advantages? The remnants of this neuromelanin would thus provide only an aftertaste of the full richness of the superior capabilities of prior humans. Interestingly enough, neuromelanin has been detected in primates and in carnivores such as cats and dogs, but is not found in the lower species of animal. This suggests that it may well be one of the first casualties of devolution.

Recent research by J. D. Simon et al. in the journal *Pigment Cell Research* suggests that melanin may serve a protective role other than photo-protection. Melanin is able to "effectively ligate metal ions through its carboxylate and phenolic hydroxyl groups, often much more efficiently than other chelating substances within the body. It may thus serve to sequester potentially toxic metal ions, protecting the rest of the cell."[13] This hypothesis is supported by the fact that the loss of neuromelanin observed in Parkinson's disease is accompanied by an increase in iron levels in the brain. If humans once had lighter body aerials, uncluttered by heavier elements such as metals, then it might be that higher levels of melanin and neuromelanin allow the potential to remain as close as possible to that prior state.

The areas of the brain still containing neuromelanin are all centered on the base of the skull and the back of the neck. Perhaps naturally lower levels of neuromelanin in the brain and the consequently higher amounts of iron might be relevant in understanding the "iron yoke" that is often referred to in the Old Testament:

> Therefore shalt thou serve thine enemies which the LORD shall send against thee, in hunger, and in thirst, and in nakedness, and in want of all things: and he shall put a yoke of iron upon thy neck, until he have destroyed thee.[14]

One does have to wonder what kind of "Lord" or "God" would treat his "chosen people" in this way!

If the notorious mark of Cain mentioned in the Bible indeed refers to a fair complexion, then this mark may be disadvantageous to humanity but a distinct advantage to alien interceptors hell-bent on changing human DNA to suit their purposes. The spread of the recessive genes that produce low melanin levels may thus, in itself, mark a trail for tracking alien interception into the human genome, especially if Jones is right and fair skin offers no evolutionary advantage.

There is an account in the pseudepigraphal book of Enoch indicating that Noah may have been an albino:

> After a time, my son Mathusala took a wife for his son Lamech. 2 She became pregnant by him, and brought forth a child, the flesh

of which was as white as snow, and red as a rose; the hair of whose head was white like wool, and long; and whose eyes were beautiful. When he opened them, he illuminated all the house, like the sun; the whole house abounded with light. 3 And when he was taken from the hand of the midwife, Lamech his father became afraid of him; and flying away came to his own father Mathusala, and said, I have begotten a son, unlike to other children. He is not human; but, resembling the offspring of the angels of heaven, is of a different nature from ours, being altogether unlike to us. 4 His eyes are bright as the rays of the sun; his countenance glorious, and he looks not as if he belonged to me, but to the angels. 5 I am afraid, lest something miraculous should take place on earth in his days.[15]

It seems that Noah not only lacked in melanin but also seemed not to be "human," "resembling the offspring of the angels of heaven" and "of a different nature to ours." It appears that he was some form of hybrid. The unusual nature of this child was so marked that his father Lamech was "afraid" of him. This would lend a whole new meaning to the story of Noah and his "ark." Could the ark, with its animals representing all the species on the planet, describe an alien-sponsored genetic experiment? Did they wish to clear the Earth of all previous experiments and preserve this one to work on in isolation? If so, did they cause the deluge that led to the Great Flood? Or, if the deluge was a natural phenomenon, perhaps caused by a comet or meteorite hitting the planet, did they choose to protect their ongoing project with the Earth's species? These are interesting questions that I will leave up in the air for now. They will form a chapter in my next book.

In *The Song of the Greys,* I recount many additional Old Testament biblical episodes that seem to describe an alien input into human affairs. For those who have not read the book, here is an extract:

There is significant reference throughout the account of the exodus of the Jews from Egypt to suggest that their savior from bondage did indeed originate from a spaceship. Not least in this catalog of evidence is a remarkable account of an encounter between God and Moses' son: The lead up to this encounter begins when God informs Moses that if he does not go to Egypt and free his firstborn (those being the "children of Israel") then God will slay Moses' first-born, his son. Unbelievable though it might seem, were this a God equivalent in moral stature even to a decent human being, let alone a divine morality which would be beyond reproach, God then seeks to "slay" Moses' son: "And it came to pass by the way in the inn that the Lord met him and sought to kill him. Then Zipporah took a sharp stone and cut off the foreskin of her son and cast it at his feet and said, surely a bloody husband thou art because of the circumcision" (Exodus 5:24-26).

Zipporah, Moses' wife, offers God the foreskin of her son, and thus information as to his genetic structure, in place of her son's life. With that genetic map "God" would have all the information necessary to successfully intercept Moses' line with all the information that was required to provide for them a leader of their "chosen people" who would accurately follow all that they wanted him to do. When Zipporah offers the foreskin, "God" lets her son go. Can it be possible that such a ludicrous course of action by a supposed "God" could have been deemed acceptable and worthy by so many people for so long? If the "God" to which this account refers is not an alien being seeking genetic programs to intercept humanity, then what is he? Indeed could it actually be the case that the initial command for the children of Israel to circumcise their sons could have been a means for alien beings to monitor the genetic information of their "chosen people"? In other words, maybe the foreskins were taken by these beings and studied. The fact that this remarkable story about Moses and so many other incongruities within the Old Testament can have been meekly accepted by so many people, for so long, is surely an indication of the vast extent to which the Greys have succeeded in so programming their chosen subjects, that they are blind to even the simplest logical connections that would expose their programmers for what they truly are.

In the Old Testament's so-called "pseudepigraphal" texts, there is an appendix to the third book of Enoch in which there is a passage entitled "the Ascension of Moses." This "ascension" is very similar to what an ascension into a spacecraft might be like. He ascends into a "chariot" in which he meets a being named Metatron who offers him anything he wishes to ask for. This is of course reminiscent of Jesus' temptations in the desert. Metatron is also known as "little Adonai" (the little Lord or God), thus he is viewed as a supernatural entity who is a smaller version of the true God, not as a false God. Apparently, in some of the later "mystical midraishim" texts, the "angel" who "wrestled" with Jacob is taken to be Metatron.

If the Ark of the Covenant itself was a mechanism to receive instructions from a spaceship then there are significant pointers to suggest that that is true. Strict instructions are given as to the clothing of the high priest who is in charge of the Ark. These include the weaving of gold wires into his cloak: "And they did beat the gold into thin plates, and cut it into wires to work it into the blue and in the purple . . . and in the fine linen, with cunning work." Gold is an excellent conductor of electricity and it is through electromagnetic waves that radio receivers work. In the book of Leviticus instructions are given as to who may, or may not, approach the altar. No one of any physical blemish is permitted to approach the altar, so that they will "profane not my sanctuaries: for I the lord do sanctify them." Is this not compelling evidence that the Ark of the Covenant and the altar within it were in fact used as mechanisms through which alien being could view human subjects who might be suitable for interception? Hence only those without physical defect and therefore with the likelihood of a genetic structure more free of the mutations that lead to physical weakness or infirmity, were allowed to approach the altar.

The prophet Ezekiel's visions have been taken by many people to be visions or sightings of spacecraft. If Ezekiel was also visited by alien beings, it would certainly account for his strange encounter with "God" in a valley, which was full of bones. In this encounter God asks Ezekiel if these dry bones could live; he then assembles them into complete bodies and covers them with flesh. After he brings them to life they stand "up upon their feet, an exceeding great army." God then tells Ezekiel that these bones are "the whole house of Israel" and he tells him to promise the people of Israel that "I will open your graves, and cause you to come up out of your graves, and bring you into the land of Israel. . . . And shall put my spirit in you and ye shall live and I shall place you in your own land." "God" is thus involved in bringing to life soulless dead flesh. What kind of "life" is he therefore promising for the children of Israel—the physical immortality of cloned being? How reminiscent this is of the Egyptian process of mummification, a process which ancient Egyptians believed essential to preserve the physical body for the after-life. The Semitic peoples truly seem to be receivers of the same "God."[16]

Christians all too easily forget that Jesus Christ was first and foremost a Jew. He was of the very salt and center of them and loved them with a love that we as a species could never envisage, let alone practice. The deadly Grey menace that coats the universe set about taking from these precious people a glorious destiny, an ultimate deceit they seemed to have accomplished with many human strains. The truth is that we have all been conned. Every religion, every culture, every intelligent living format on the Earth has been from time to time conned by a cold prodigious intelligence that makes us all seem ants.

I believe the Jewish Diaspora still retains a line that remains substantially without interception. It is perhaps what is referred to as the "lost tribe" of Israel, from whom the best in humanity is derived. This strain of humankind escaped the Garden of Eden interception point set up by the extraterrestrials millennia ago. This line of "Abel types" might have been deemed unsuitable for ongoing interception because their inherent physiological and psychological qualities resisted genetic engineering. This form of humanity still survives today, hidden within the biological schemes of the Jewish people (particularly those who have not migrated to the Northern Hemisphere, such as the Sephardi, Ethiopian, and Indian Jewish groups), as well as Arab, Negro, Indian, and Romany peoples, whose darker complexions inhibit alien access to their nuclear DNA.

I believe the Nazis were trying to find this line of precious human beings and wipe it out completely under the orders of their Grey masters when they instituted the Holocaust. This is a line, genetically unpolluted by the Greys, that continues to this day hidden and waiting to deliver the purest epithets of the Godverse for the benefit of humankind. It is the best and purest expression of Godhead possible in physical universes that exists amongst humankind on this planet. I believe the Greys and their acolyte Grey/human hybrids in the Occident and Orient continue to this day to try to find the unpolluted lines of Judaic and other humankind through searching the genomes of humans covertly worldwide. They will never be able to hold total mastery over this planet unless these blessed lines are wiped out.

It is plain that the aggressive Cain breed of hominid provided the survival mechanism the Greys needed if they were to successfully farm a hominid species on this planet. It is the mechanism that has allowed the whitened Cain strain of humankind to dominate and continue to dominate the planet. The strong indications that white Caucasians may be a specialist genotype whose DNA is the most accessible to Grey purposes can explain what many of the abductions are about. They are constantly checking how their experimental breed is progressing in real time and in real living situations. This also explains perhaps why many abductees are returned and not harmed.

Professor David Jacobs interviewed a female abductee who described being shown a hybrid baby and asked to hold it and hug it. As she relived her experience, Jacobs asked her about the skin color of the baby: "Does

it have light skin or dark skin, within the Caucasian range?" Her answer
was: "Fair. Quite fair. I think it is very fair, as a matter of fact. Almost
like no ultraviolet light for this guy."[17] This seems to be the norm for
most of the hybrids witnessed by abductees, which is epitomized by the
blonde, blue-eyed "Nordic" type of aliens.

With ultimate irony, the preeminent genotype of our species bio-
engineered for special Grey purposes also provides something else—
their own bodies. An alarming 1,750,000 men, women, and children
are reported missing each year in Europe. Of these, only approximately
35 percent are ever accounted for. It is my suggestion that a sizeable
proportion of individuals who go missing in unexplained circumstances
every year worldwide are abducted. Some abductees who have been
taken aboard alien craft have described line upon line of white bodies
in strange looking bags and preserving mechanisms.

The Greys need new DNA freshly enlivened with the living properties bestowed by a live-action Morphogenic Electro-Spatial Field (MESF)
interacting with atoms for the maintenance of their clones as an ongoing
requirement. They cannot simply replicate old samples, as these would
not have the same potency for life and survival as the new. While the
pale skin types are given the privilege of primary contactee status, their
better suitability for DNA alteration purposes also makes them the best
candidates for harvest. They may well be funding a supply of DNA for
the "new breeds" of clones that are carefully nurtured by entities with
four grey fingers. This may be why the meek will inherit the Earth. The
chilling conclusion to the entire Grey alien parade on our planet might
be the harvest of all the most usable (in their terms) humans, clearing
the planet of many of the pale-skinned Caucasian genotype that has
been responsible for the destruction of the greatest numbers of humanity as well as the destruction of the global natural environment on a scale
never before seen in the history of this generation of humanity.

However, it may well be that the Cain types who are abducted are
those who, despite their physical suitability for Grey manipulation, have
somewhat of an inner resistance to it. Thus I am not describing the fate

of an entire group of humanity based upon low melanin levels; I am just identifying this particular physical presentation as a disadvantage that *can* help to promulgate such a fate. In other words, it may be that those of the Cain genotype who are unable to resist the assault are already "cooked," so to speak, and do not require further attention. I will discuss this possibility later in the book.

These Grey roboids, manufactured bio-machines, can never be expected to show charity, sentiment, mercy, or compassion. They can only act in a clinically expedient way at all times, responding to the sharp and clear directives of a program set on a binary scale of reference. We are all doomed in their hands if we go on choosing to ignore the awesome threat they present to humanity.

But we are not doomed. Something past atoms, within us, something from a domain of existence that carries itself beyond the termination of a decaying process, allows the part in us that is not of atoms to live on. That is the final triumph revealed by reason alone, even in the face of the maelstrom out there in space—multibillions of worlds that are boiling vats of acid, frozen scapes where temperatures almost reach absolute zero, gas storms that burn close to the temperature of the sun and blast winds faster than bullets can fly, trillions upon trillions of space rocks called asteroids and mountainous balls of ice we call comets all smashing into each other.

Even in the face of a central spine of power that systematically breaks everything down into a meaningless soup of particles, all transient and impermanent, which finally resolves into an implacable wall of cold meaningless force, which finally says unequivocally that there is no meaning ascribed to existence, reason forces us to ask why we have the capability to crave deeper meaning and to seek clarification of this meaning. Why are we capable of reason if reasoning itself is unnecessary? What is the point of the song of a bird, a tender lullaby, or the kiss of a child? But reason reminds us that where meaninglessness exists, there must be a somewhere, a something, which says the opposite.

We are only doomed if we can't regain access to that somewhere

where all scope is eternal and all meaning is implied. This glorious something, which might be termed the fingers of Godhead, clutches at the very centers of our physical being, providing a rivulet of hope that will, if understood and pursued consistently enough, deliver us beyond the grasp of decaying paradigms forever. The whole trouble is in finding it amid the sea of lies that is the legacy of that very same decaying process.

# 13

# Returns and Lies

Most of humanity believes that when this life is over we break all ties with everyone we know and move on, either to some other place or to some other form of existence that is not human in the physical sense. Muslims and Catholics and many other Christians believe that our sins damn us to a terrible eternity of suffering after a single chance at life, while others believe our sins prevent us from ever reaching any fixed status in death.

We can generalize the basic philosophical existential momentums driving humanity in the world today into two schools of thought: Eastern and Western, those who believe in reincarnation and those who don't. I have worked out a logical paradigm for myself that provides me with a way to decide which of these two basic approaches I might go along with to identify the single most important resolution of continuity that drives existence. It goes like this:

You are there. That much is real and known to you at any given moment. The moment in time when you look in the mirror is the very affirmation and endorsement of your being. In order to know anything, you must first be there. In relation to this most important maxim, the thing that has existed the longest is a rock. Rocks have "been there" for billions of years: since the universe formed into solidness. We have "been there" as humanoids for a mere five million years and we have "been there" as *Homo sapiens sapiens* for a mere two hundred twenty million years. In addition, rocks can last for billions of years. We only last for four score years and ten if lucky. A rock is superior to us in terms of the fundamental existential maxim of being there.

But a rock cannot move itself, while we as human beings can pick it up, move it around, study its crystalline structure under an electron microscope, polish it, and admire it on our mantelpiece. We have total control of it and all its capacities and potentialities, such as they are. It cannot command us or decide anything for itself or us. It has no power of choice whatsoever. Yet it is superior to us in basic existential terms because it will stay a rock on that mantelpiece, or in the ground, after the mantelpiece decays and disappears and we as human beings are long gone and pushing up daisies.

How is it possible that something like a rock, just doing nothing, is inherently capable of lasting longer in tenure than you and I, whose capacity to know and understand and do is so superior to that of a rock? There has to be a way that we can continue on to fulfill our grander capacity for choice and range of choice. These logical considerations have convinced me that birth without the scope for endless continuity is meaningless and that reincarnation is the most logical and pertinent of procedures to effect this continuity. We exist forever, far longer than anything else, including rocks. We go on existing lifetime after lifetime. We go on living, dying, and returning lifetime after lifetime.

This conviction is in line with the tenet of reincarnation once acknowledged by all the world's major religions till the falsifiers got in there and changed it all with their lies. From the *Pistis Sophia,* a report of Christ's incidental conversations with his apostles and contemporaries, it is apparent that reincarnation was a thoroughly accepted tenet for early Christians. There is an account of Jesus describing to his apostles the difference between those who never entered physical bodies, but were purified and returned to heaven from a state of insubstantiality, and those who have to free themselves from "the transferences into various bodies of the world." Of the first type of soul Jesus says: "They have not suffered at all and they have not changed places, nor have they troubled themselves at all, nor have they been transferred into various bodies." Then of his apostles he says: "You have come to be in great sufferings and great afflictions from the transferences into various bodies of the world. And after all these sufferings of yourselves you have striven and fought so that you have renounced the whole world and all the matter it is."[1]

During the early Christian era leading up to the Council of Constantinople, notable church fathers like Origen, Clement of Alexander, and St. Jerome also accepted and believed in the reincarnation principle. But in the fourth century, when Christianity became the official religion of the Roman Empire, Emperor Constantine deleted early references to reincarnation in the New Testament. Could it be that the emperor felt that the concept of reincarnation was threatening to the stability of the empire? Citizens who believed that they would have another chance to live might be less obedient and law-abiding than those who believed in a single Judgment Day. For Constantine, reincarnation also represented too much influence from Eastern thought.

While the tenet of reincarnation was taken out of the Christian codex, it still had its believers and adherents, like the Gnostics. Then, in the year 553 CE, the Second Council of Constantinople officially declared the doctrine of reincarnation a heresy and banished it. It has been suggested that the eradication of the ethic of reincarnation from the Christian codex was the responsibility of the wife of Justinian I, the Empress Theodora, who was enraged by a soothsayer when he claimed she had been a witch in a previous existence. In any case, it appears that the Church was afraid that the idea of "past lives" would weaken and undermine its growing power and influence by affording followers too much time to seek salvation.

This is just one example of the horrendous wickedness practiced on us all by the codifiers of the Christian ethic, who threw out the other traditions and their sources of scholarship, such as the *Nag Hammadi*, the *Pistis Sophia*, and various other apocryphal texts that may well be authentic. We all owe those scoundrels of the past—who deemed these texts invalid and took away our right to consider all the literature about any particular belief—a great debt of ingratitude.

By the time Christ's teachings became the property of the Holy Roman Church, much of his true teachings had been altered so that the papacy could entrench their power over the faithful more conclusively. This allowed the priesthood to live and prosper in their churches, abbeys, and various religious condominiums, while the people died of hardship and starvation in tens of thousands at an average age of about thirty-five. Farming techniques, such as they were, provided few of the stipends that promoted good healthy living for most of the population. The priests and monks, however, lived well off the land. The Church owned vast estates and properties that were worked by armies of tenant farmers who provided huge proportions of the products of their labors for the mouths of priests, monks, and nuns. The result was that they lived much longer than the average citizen. The average age of death for clerics living in their ivory towers was fifty years or more—a good return for a few squeals and chants amid clouds of incense and candle smoke. There was no way they were going to let the good life go. They maintained it with verbal claims and incantations that ensured their indispensability whatever the price to the truth.

The whole cartel of Christianity was controlled implicitly and explicitly, socially and politically, throughout the world by two con tricks. The first was the claim that we all as human beings have just one chance, one lifetime to get it right, or be damned forever in hell. The second was the claim that admission to heaven depended on being free from "sin." Sin—going against the rules of God, as seen and interpreted by the Church—left a blemish on the eternal part of a person, the soul, which had to be forgiven or erased by the officials of the Church themselves. Without absolution of sins by a priest of the church, the movement of his hand in space in the shape of a cross, a person would die full of blemishes that forbade an eternity in Godhead, or the Universe of the Whole, as I have described it. The millions of the burgeoning Church thus lived in fear and trepidation under the subjugation of the

Christian Roman Church. In order for these con tricks to succeed, two things had to be removed from the codex of the Church: the concept of reincarnation and the fact that we could all forgive ourselves of sin, by simply changing our minds by learning a better perspective of right and wrong.

To minutely control the day-to-day lives of huge amounts of people, the Church leaders misinterpreted or deliberately changed the more accurate records of Jesus Christ's pronouncements. In this way, we lost such treasures as the great Book of Enoch, the Gospel of Nicodemus, and more recently the *Pistis Sophia,* the *Nag Hammadi* texts (among them the Gospel of St. Thomas, regarded as the most profound one describing the life, sayings, and works of Christ), and the Gospel of Phillip. Many of these testaments alluded to the authority of the individual as the only valid arbiter of an individual eternity. They hinted at a very different Christ than the sanitized one presented in the biblical canon.

Deep in the galleried vaults of the Vatican in a secret little vault of dark brown stone lies the authentic Gospel of Jesus Christ himself, written by the hand of the most beautiful being that ever lived on this planet. It is a personal testimony of his life and work, undistorted. Although it is probably the most precious document in the history of the world, it will never see the light of day because it describes an awesome treatise. Mystical in its root, it reveals a Christ that knew about the universe and what is beyond the atom as not even a fifty-first century scientist could know. It reveals secrets that blow the lid off the huge act of distortion on the part of the church fathers that for two millennia has hidden a secret, a secret about the origin of the human species and the true identity of the deadly enemy from whose hands Christ came to save humankind.

In the Middle Ages, the Church began selling what they called "indulgences." These were remission notes in exchange for favors and money given to the Roman Church. These remission notes reduced the person's time in purgatory, which was a waiting room for heaven, whose inhabitants were lightly roasted rather than being burnt to a crisp as in hell. The sale of indulgences earned the Roman Catholic Church powerful allies and choice pieces of real estate, resulting in its becoming the richest corporation in the world. Indulgences could also be earned by the repetition of prayers that could reduce purgatorial lambasting by thousands and sometimes millions of years.

The pope, of course, claims exclusive right to the truth on matters of faith, spirituality, morals, and ethics. This is the most evil canard of all, because the popes have held to ransom the soul destiny of millions who have believed their "bulls" through the centuries. Our individual sojourns out of our present predicament in our hellish universe have, for the most part, been limited by lies, distortion, misinterpretation, and most lethal of all—fear. The world has suffered a terrible scourge that has taken the example of a true redeemer and turned it into a cache for lies and distortions.

The claim that the leaders of the Church have Jesus Christ's author-ity for all they say and do is based on their interpretation of the words: "Thou art Peter and upon this rock I shall build my church." The state-ment was taken literally to mean that Jesus himself nominated Peter to be his successor (and then his successors, the popes). But Christ's words do not necessarily signify or refer to a single personality, especially a personality whose leadership was likely to be boisterous and ill defined. Peter was a fisherman given to high states of emotion. Cutting some-one's ear off, as he is supposed to have done when the temple guards came with Judas to arrest Christ, was not a very clever thing to do. It marked his judgment as a little suspect, to say the least. He was a cow-ard and a liar if his denials of Christ are anything to go by.

In understanding Christ's true intention, the meaning of the sym-bolism of the word *rock* is crucial. A rock might have been the best analogy Jesus could find to describe the quality of faith, belief, trust, and understanding he received from the lowest common denominator of humankind. In fact, rock is a very good word for expressing the gen-eral basis of anything. We use the word *bedrock* to do this all the time. Christ often spoke in parables rich in metaphor. The statement, "Thou art Peter," can best be understood as a summary of the state of belief Peter had to overcome. Rock represented the quantum of mind that had to change—in accordance with the words, actions, and testament of the most beautiful Jew that ever lived—in order to save the species from its most heinous enemy. No average Middle Eastern human mind of the time could have contemplated or indeed fully understood all of what Christ said and alluded to in his ministry, least of all an ignorant fisherman. If Jesus was really suggesting that the furtherance of all he had done, demonstrated, and defined should be entrusted to the hands of a single emotional and cowardly man of ill judgment, then Christ's judgment itself would have been suspect.

However, one thing that is beyond suspicion has to be the judgment of Jesus Christ. No greater wisdom has passed the lips of any living being than what he left in word and deed. His wisdom is only partially reflected in the four Gospels, a version of his life and times that is the equivalent of the journalism in a modern tabloid newspaper when compared to the fuller story as recorded in the other texts, which reveal stunning additional dimensions of this wondrous being. The church had selected the twenty-seven books of the New Testament by the fourth century after a great deal of political intrigue and internal rivalry. It was only when the canon had become self-evident that it was argued that inspiration and canonicity coincided. This paring down of the available texts took the logic and reason out of much of it and gave us instead a collection of chants, monologues, and missives. The lack of logic was justified by statements such as: "It's a mystery. Only God knows. It is only for God to know," even in the light of Christ's exhortation in the Gospels that all things will be known in their own time by anyone who cares to learn. The great glory of Jesus Christ even as seen in the pinched version of his life as portrayed by the Gospels was his logic and good sense. Passages within the *Pistis Sophia, Nag Hammadi* texts, and the *Apocryphal New Testament* show this good sense plus the deep and intelligent rationale behind all he said and did.

I do not advocate anything to anyone, much less the denial of religious belief. Quite the contrary, I hope I am providing a vision of what has been available versus what should be available in reason, logic, and common sense. Brooms the size of each religious edifice are needed to sweep clean the deadly cobwebs of self-interest and down-right nonsense. Some of the most beautiful human beings in spirit of our species, rare redeemers who have come among the human family, were and still are to be found in the various holy orders of the religious spectrum. In fact, in a world of rapidly diminishing moral and ethical values, the sense of a better world may more often be found in the words and consolations of priests and teachers rather than those of politicians, businessmen, or the experts of science and technology. Churches, temples, synagogues, and devales are the best quiet places for human retreat and solitude "far from the madding crowd," places where human beings, in the quiet of their own independent minds, can comprehend their intuitional magnitudes.

The truth of any religion is contained in the reason and sense it espouses, in the logic of its semantics, and the behavioral example it sets. The founders of the great religions made the most pristine sense. Since their demise, their representatives have systematically altered and mangled their true teachings till no one knows where they lie in the various codices. It is clear that the repression of past life teachings in Christianity was political and not spiritual. I suppose it is understandable when seen in the context of the antagonism and threats to the burgeoning Church in its early days. But expediency is the author of lies; reason and its power to proffer truth is always its victim. The price of such victimization is awesome. It is the loss of your soul and mine. The terrible thing is that the result is not punishment, as is commonly accepted the world over, but simple, logical, and neutral consequence. It is the most awesome consequence of all: the final loss of the capacity to know within a state of coherent focus—that is, within an individual human being.

I was brought up Catholic before I realized I was a Christian, a Jew, a Moslem, a Hindu, a Jain. I previously believed with the rest of "processed" Christianity that we all were given just one chance in one life at seeking a better, more continued existence. I came to realize the patent lunacy and idiocy of such a belief at the age of twelve when the child of a joyfully expectant couple we knew was stillborn. It got me questioning the whole edifice of the Roman Catholic Church and all the other "synthetic" Christian leaderships it produced—the scoundrels that in previous centuries decided what you and I should believe, in the name of its innocent glorious founder. They took away from all of us some of the most crucial and salient truths he actually taught. I will go as far as to say that in doing this, Roman Christianity particularly, as the first form of the genus, may be said to have intentionally or unintentionally taken on the mantle of the Great Lucifer itself.

If you think about the conventional wisdom of those who do not espouse reincarnation, and believe in the one-chance premise, you will see immediately what gross nonsense it is. You are asked to believe that an entity comes into life with no history and from nowhere and is thrown into a universe of chaotic amelioration. He or she may be born to the most draconian parents, murderers or thieves, parents no child should have as teachers of moral principles or rectitude in their formative years, yet this same child is expected to reach the status of a saint and get to heaven in one lifetime, or have all its memories and life experiences expunged in the burning fires of hell forever. A bit unfair don't you think? All this is supposedly in the interests of God testing his own mettle against the universe at the expense of a soul he has created. I haven't even mentioned the millions who are spontaneously aborted. In these cases, is God testing the bodies of the mothers? Certainly it cannot be a test of the child and its behavior as a reference against "God's will." It hasn't lived to sin.

The amazing thing is that so many people over the centuries have simply accepted this notion of the single lifetime, especially in light of the hundreds of thousands of people who claim that they have lived before. Most of these claims are from people who follow Eastern religions, whose religious ethic includes a belief in reincarnation as a cardinal tenet. The intriguing thing is that nowadays many thousands in the West with

Christian belief systems now also claim to remember details of previous lives. When these claims are investigated, the most startling things come to light. In addition to conscious memories of reincarnation, there are also unconscious ones that have to be solicited from individuals' subconscious memories, employing a technique of hypnotism called regression. Of the conscious memories of past lives, the most convincing accounts are those that have later proved not only to be historically accurate, but also to reflect knowledge of highly specific information that the individual could not have known from his or her present lifetime's experience. Consider these four remarkable examples of past-life recall that have been taken from many thousands of similar accounts.

Cameron Macaulay was a typical six-year-old, always talking about his mum and family. He liked to draw pictures of his home too—a long, single-story, white house standing in a bay. But it sent shivers down his mum's spine—because Cameron said it was somewhere they had never been, 160 miles away from where they lived. And he said the mother he was talking about was his "old mum." Convinced he had lived a previous life, Cameron worried his former family would be missing him. The Glasgow lad said they were on the Isle of Barra. Mum Norma, forty-two, said: "Ever since Cameron could speak he's come up with tales of a childhood on Barra. He spoke about his former parents, how his dad died, and his brothers and sisters. Eventually we just had to take him there to see what we could find. It was an astonishing experience." Norma said: "His dad and I are no longer together, but neither of our families have ever been to the island. At first we just put his stories down to a vivid imagination." But then Cameron started to become distressed at being away from his Barra family:

> It was awful and went on for years. When he started nursery his teacher asked to see me and told me all the things Cameron was saying about Barra. He missed his mummy and his brothers and sisters there. He missed playing in rock pools on the beach beside his house. And he complained that in our house there was only one toi-

let, whereas in Barra, they had three. He used to cry for his mummy. He said she'd be missing him and he wanted to let his family in Barra know he was all right. It was very distressing. He was inconsolable. He wouldn't stop talking about Barra, where they went, what they did and how he watched the planes landing on the beach from his bedroom window. He even said his dad was called Shane Robertson, who had died because "he didn't look both ways." I assume he means knocked over by a car but he never says that.[2]

A film company looking for cases such as this took Cameron and his mother to Barra:

"When Cameron was told we were going to Barra he was jumping all over the place with excitement." Norma said: "He asked me if his face was shiny, because he was so happy. When we got to the island and did land on a beach, just as Cameron had described, he turned to Martin and me and said, 'Now do you believe me?' He got off the plane, threw his arms in the air and yelled 'I'm back.' He talked about his Barra mum, telling me she had brown hair down to her waist before she'd had it cut. He said I'd like her and she'd like me. He was anxious for us to meet. He also talked about a 'big book' he used to read, and God and Jesus. We're not a religious family but his Barra family were."[3]

The Macaulays booked into a hotel and began their search for clues to Cameron's past:

We contacted the Heritage Center and asked if they'd heard of a Robertson family who lived in a white house overlooking a bay. They hadn't. Cameron was very disappointed. We drove around the island but he didn't see the house. Then we realized that if he saw planes land on the beach from his bedroom window, we were driving the wrong way.[4]

Next the family received a call from their hotel to confirm that a family called Robertson once had a white house on the bay.

Norma explains: "We didn't tell Cameron anything. We just drove toward where we were told the house was and waited to see what would happen. He recognized it immediately and was overjoyed. But as we walked to the door all the color drained from Cameron's face and he became very quiet. I think he thought it would be exactly the same as he remembered it, that his Barra mum would be waiting for him inside. He looked sad. There was no one there. The previous owner had died but a keyholder let us in. There were lots of nooks and crannies and Cameron knew every bit of the house—including the THREE toilets and the beach view from his bedroom window. In the garden, he took us to the 'secret entrance' he'd been talking about for years."[5]

Researchers also managed to track down one of the Robertson family who had owned the house.

Norma said: "We visited them at their new address in Stirling, but couldn't find anything about a Shane Robertson. Cameron was eager to see old family photographs in case he found his dad or himself in any. He'd always talked about a big black car and a black and white dog. The car and the dog were in the photos."[6]

Since the family returned to their home in Clydebank, Glasgow, Cameron has been much calmer.

Norma said: "Going to Barra was the best thing we could have done. It's put Cameron's mind at ease. He no longer talks about Barra with such longing. Now he knows we no longer think he was making things up. We didn't get all the answers we were looking for and, apparently, past life memories fade as the person gets older.

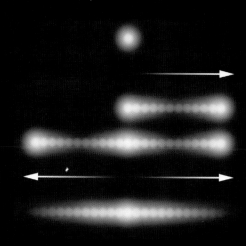

**Plate 1.** The point manifests as the interface between nothing-ness and something-ness. The point generates another identical point in search of difference; direction happens in singular aspect, implying *two directions* set against *no direction.*

This continues indefinitely in both directions and reaches infinity instantly as a singularity because there is nothing to demarcate one point from another.

This is not part of the Big Bang, but neither is it before the Big Bang. It could be seen as part of the architecture of the first instant. As a singularity, it still has not found difference, which exists minimally as a duality. (See chapter 6.)

**Plate 2 (right).** Each "line point" duplicates itself and in so doing duplicates the line at its state of greatest difference from itself. Ninety degrees represents the full range of angle and curve from any given point that can be considered as a center, so all points form plane-ness in equivalence, each point to each other. This is prespatial dimensionality defined through the mutual independence of awareness and will, as identified by the gold and silver perpendicular lines. (See chapter 6.)

**Plate 3a and Plate 3b (below).** The implied circle expressing thought as the product of awareness and will. (See chapter 6.)

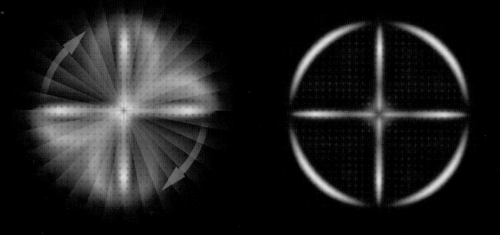

**Plate 4 (above) and Plate 5 (right).** The implied circle of thought as the product of awareness and will in the search for separation generates a spiral form in a shape reminiscent of a doughnut. This spiral is known as a toroidal helix. This traces the pattern of a Möbius strip. Although Plate 4 shows this in stages, it happens in the merest instant, generating huge turning moments of spin as a product of the enormous contradiction between nothing-ness and something-ness. (See chapter 6.)

**Plate 6.** These two perpendicular Möbius spinning motions together create a whirlpool effect of force within the atom as the Möbius strip rotates, tracing the full form of the toroid. (See chapter 6.)

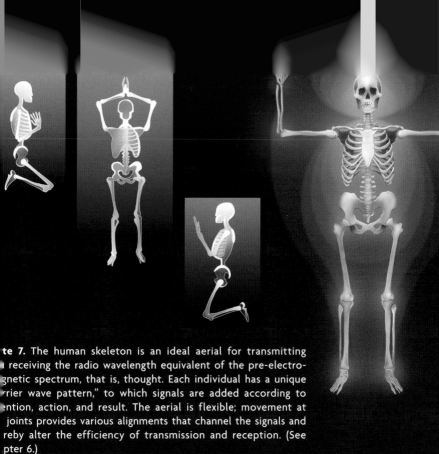

Plate 7. The human skeleton is an ideal aerial for transmitting and receiving the radio wavelength equivalent of the pre-electromagnetic spectrum, that is, thought. Each individual has a unique "carrier wave pattern," to which signals are added according to intention, action, and result. The aerial is flexible; movement at the joints provides various alignments that channel the signals and thereby alter the efficiency of transmission and reception. (See chapter 6.)

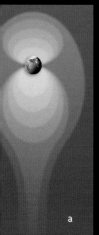
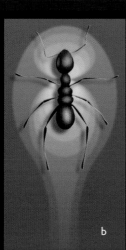
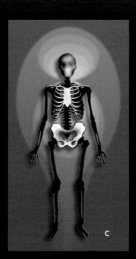
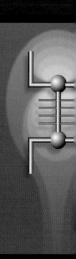

a    b    c

Plate 8. This represents the shape of the Earth's magnetic field under the influence of the sun and (a) and its correlation to the shape of living organisms from ant (b) to human (c). It also shows the general form of the biological aerial of the human skeleton (c) and a commonly used form of a man-made aerial (d). (See chapter 6.)

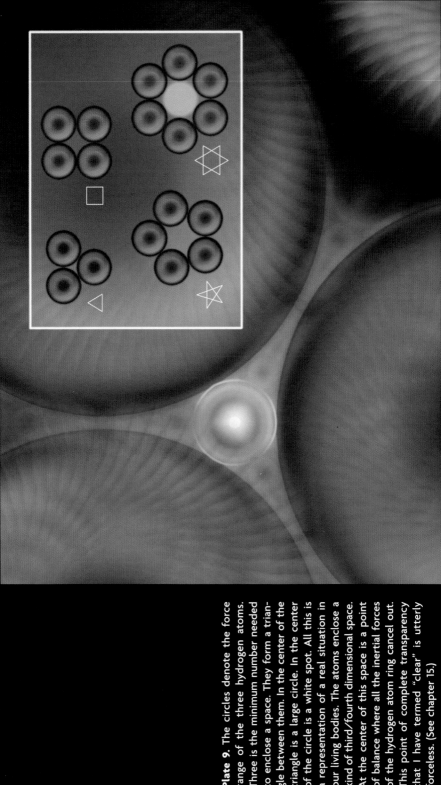

**Plate 9.** The circles denote the force range of the three hydrogen atoms. Three is the minimum number needed to enclose a space. They form a triangle between them. In the center of the triangle is a large circle. In the center of the circle is a white spot. All this is a representation of a real situation in our living bodies. The atoms enclose a kind of third/fourth dimensional space. At the center of this space is a point of balance where all the inertial forces of the hydrogen atom ring cancel out. This point of complete transparency that I have termed "clear" is utterly forceless. (See chapter 15.)

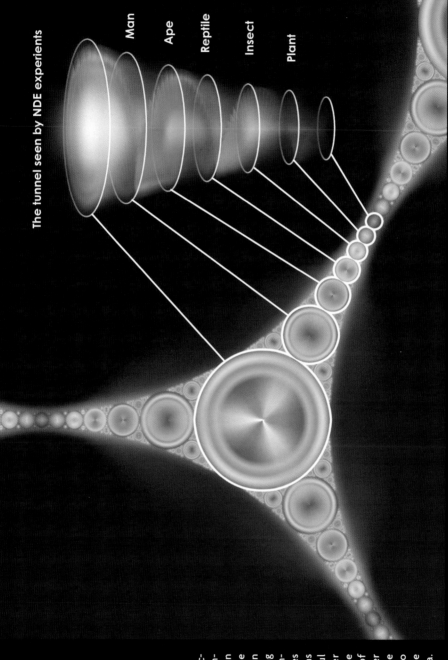

The tunnel seen by NDE experients

Man

Ape

Reptile

Insect

Plant

**Plate 10.** This is a depiction of the shells of tension or en-forcedness in the spaces between the atoms of the hydrogen rings found within living systems. An infinite number of diminishing circles represents the "domains of death" where soul fields are held after death. The lighter the inertial momentum of the soul field, the larger the domain and the nearer it will persist to the interface with the Godverse and vice versa. (See chapter 15.)

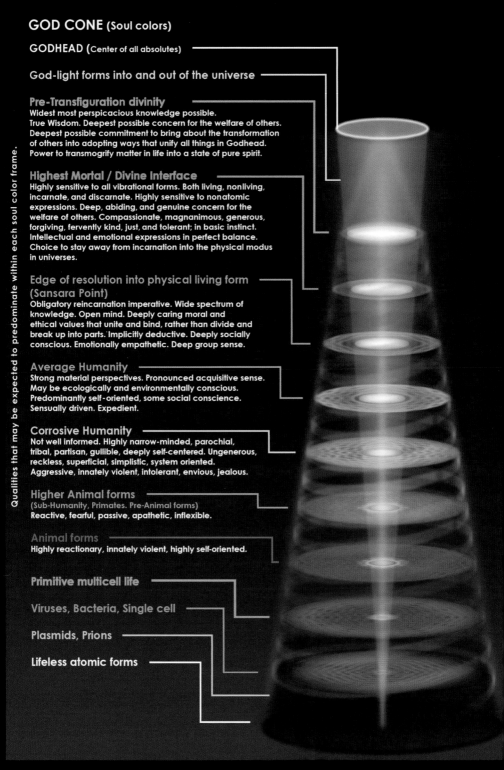

# GOD CONE (Soul colors)

**GODHEAD** (Center of all absolutes)

**God-light forms into and out of the universe**

### Pre-Transfiguration divinity
Widest most perspicacious knowledge possible.
True Wisdom. Deepest possible concern for the welfare of others.
Deepest possible commitment to bring about the transformation
of others into adopting ways that unify all things in Godhead.
Power to transmogrify matter in life into a state of pure spirit.

### Highest Mortal / Divine Interface
Highly sensitive to all vibrational forms. Both living, nonliving,
incarnate, and discarnate. Highly sensitive to nonatomic
expressions. Deep, abiding, and genuine concern for the
welfare of others. Compassionate, magnanimous, generous,
forgiving, fervently kind, just, and tolerant; in basic instinct.
Intellectual and emotional expressions in perfect balance.
Choice to stay away from incarnation into the physical modus
in universes.

### Edge of resolution into physical living form
### (Sansara Point)
Obligatory reincarnation imperative. Wide spectrum of
knowledge. Open mind. Deeply caring moral and
ethical values that unite and bind, rather than divide and
break up into parts. Implicitly deductive. Deeply socially
conscious. Emotionally empathetic. Deep group sense.

### Average Humanity
Strong material perspectives. Pronounced acquisitive sense.
May be ecologically and environmentally conscious.
Predominantly self-oriented, some social conscience.
Sensually driven. Expedient.

### Corrosive Humanity
Not well informed. Highly narrow-minded, parochial,
tribal, partisan, gullible, deeply self-centered. Ungenerous,
reckless, superficial, simplistic, system oriented.
Aggressive, innately violent, intolerant, envious, jealous.

### Higher Animal forms
(Sub-Humanity, Primates. Pre-Animal forms)
Reactive, fearful, passive, apathetic, inflexible.

### Animal forms
Highly reactionary, innately violent, highly self-oriented.

### Primitive multicell life

### Viruses, Bacteria, Single cell

### Plasmids, Prions

### Lifeless atomic forms

*Qualities that may be expected to predominate within each soul color frame.*

**Plate 11.** This is the God Cone (soul colors): soul signatures and living systems seen in measures of God-light. (See chapter 15.)

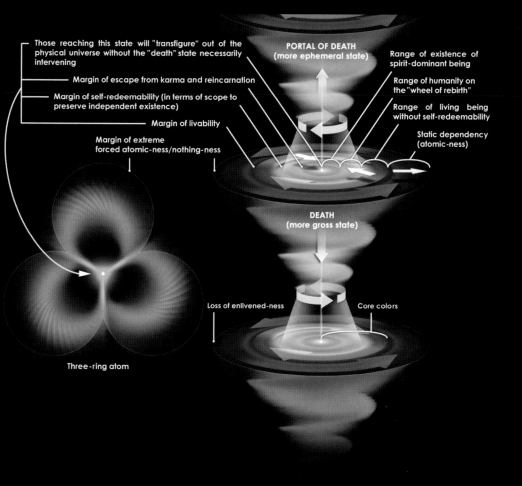

Those reaching this state will "transfigure" out of the physical universe without the "death" state necessarily intervening

Margin of escape from karma and reincarnation

Margin of self-redeemability (in terms of scope to preserve independent existence)

Margin of livability

Margin of extreme forced atomic-ness/nothing-ness

PORTAL OF DEATH
(more ephemeral state)

Range of existence of spirit-dominant being

Range of humanity on the "wheel of rebirth"

Range of living being without self-redeemability

Static dependency
(atomic-ness)

DEATH
(more gross state)

Loss of enlivened-ness

Core colors

Three-ring atom

**Plate 12.** This is a schematic representation of the space between atoms in an atomic arrangement that forms the molecules of a living entity, in this instance a human being, at the moment of death. The Morphogenic Electro-Spatial Field, or soul, can be likened to a vacuum field made up of a color spectrum of shells of different levels of en-forcedness.

Each color signifies the power to drift toward the Godverse through transfiguration or to drift away from it and stay in a universe through reincarnation. This demonstrates what sin really means: restrictions that impel you toward return into a universe and lessen your power to resist this impulsion and move into the Godverse. All of an individual's knowledge and behavioral qualities are summarized into the entity's "force value." This force value, represented as a core color, resonates with an equivalent shell in the space between atoms, one that will take it to the domains of existence beyond death that go into the Godverse or to those that take it back into the universe. (See chapters 15, 16, 22.)

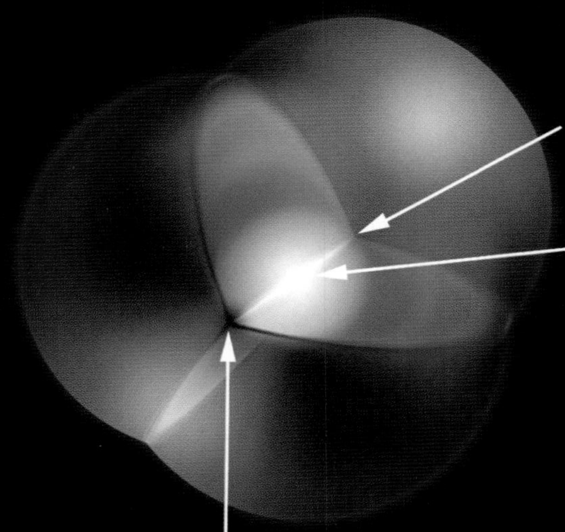

Planar representation of the two-three-dimensional interface as the birthpoint of all space/time

Forcehead point

Godhead point

Forcehead point

**Plate 13.** The *space* between atoms is *not* three-dimensional space such as the space between three billiard balls in a ring formation. It is instead more of an interface between two and three dimensions, like the interface between adjoining bubbles. In the illustration, the interface forms a Y shape made of three semicircular planes. The very center of that shape, the white in the middle of the purple, is the center of the space between atoms. As such, it is the natural portal to the Godverse from the universe. From this central point, the same concentric spheres of color reach closer and closer to the outer skin of the bubbles and increase in tension as a result. Each of these concentric rings increases in tension as it moves from the two-dimensional center to the three-four-dimensional edge of the bubble. (See chapter 15.)

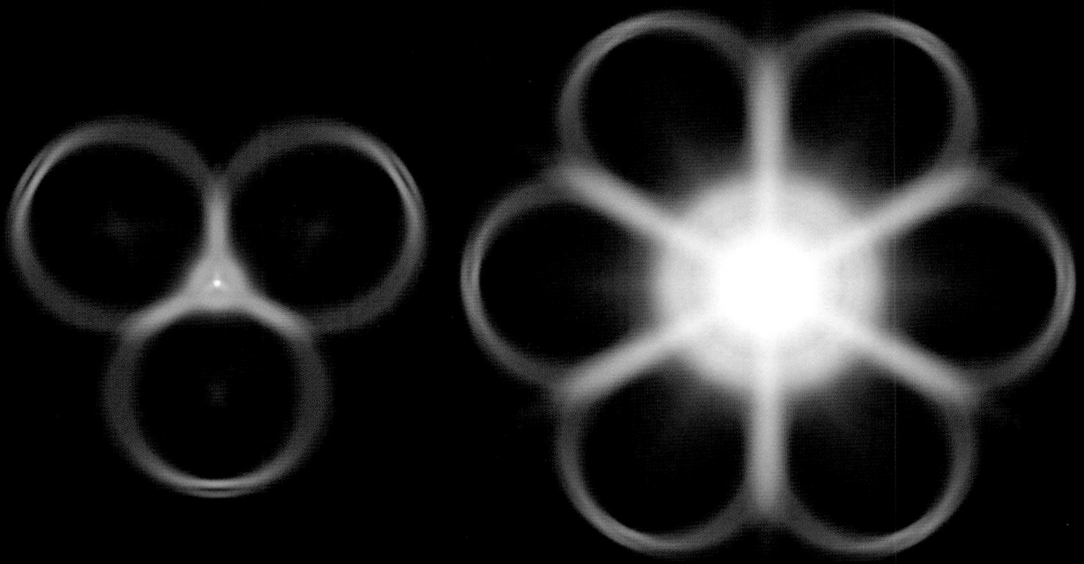

**Plate 14.** The space inside the six-atom ring is not sufficiently enforced to translate the light of God out into all the different frequencies of color. It only translates violet, the least enforced frequency, whereas the space within the three-atom ring has a spectrum of force that can translate God-light into all possible frequencies of light and lack of light. (See chapters 6 and 15.)

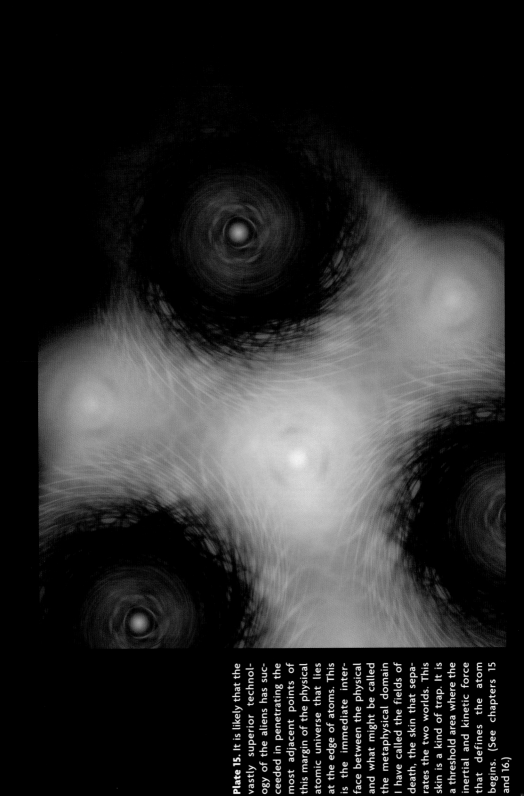

**Plate 15.** It is likely that the vastly superior technology of the aliens has succeeded in penetrating the most adjacent points of this margin of the physical atomic universe that lies at the edge of atoms. This is the immediate interface between the physical and what might be called the metaphysical domain I have called the fields of death, the skin that separates the two worlds. This skin is a kind of trap. It is a threshold area where the inertial and kinetic force that defines the atom begins. (See chapters 15 and 16.)

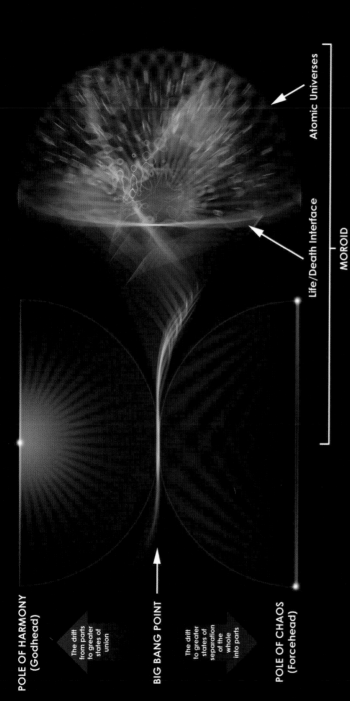

**POLE OF HARMONY**
(Godhead)

The drift from parts to greater states of union

**BIG BANG POINT**

The drift to greater states of separation of the whole into parts

**POLE OF CHAOS**
(Forcehead)

Life/Death Interface

Atomic Universes

**MOROID**

The twisted three-four-dimensional ribbon-shaped jig to which all forces and artifacts of physical worlds worlds must relate and comply implicitly in any procedure that generates change.

**Plate 16.** All things come from a scale beyond physicality, from a universe of mind, a glory beyond the understanding of most living beings in this universe. It all happens incidentally as a logical compromise between two supreme momentums of all effect, Godhead and Forcehead, each pulling against the other. The former pulls all things toward being merged together as one, and the latter pulls all things apart into utter chaotic amelioration. Our universe has both momentums merged into each other. They are, at one and the same time, merged together where they can be and separate where they have to be. (See chapters 5 and 19.)

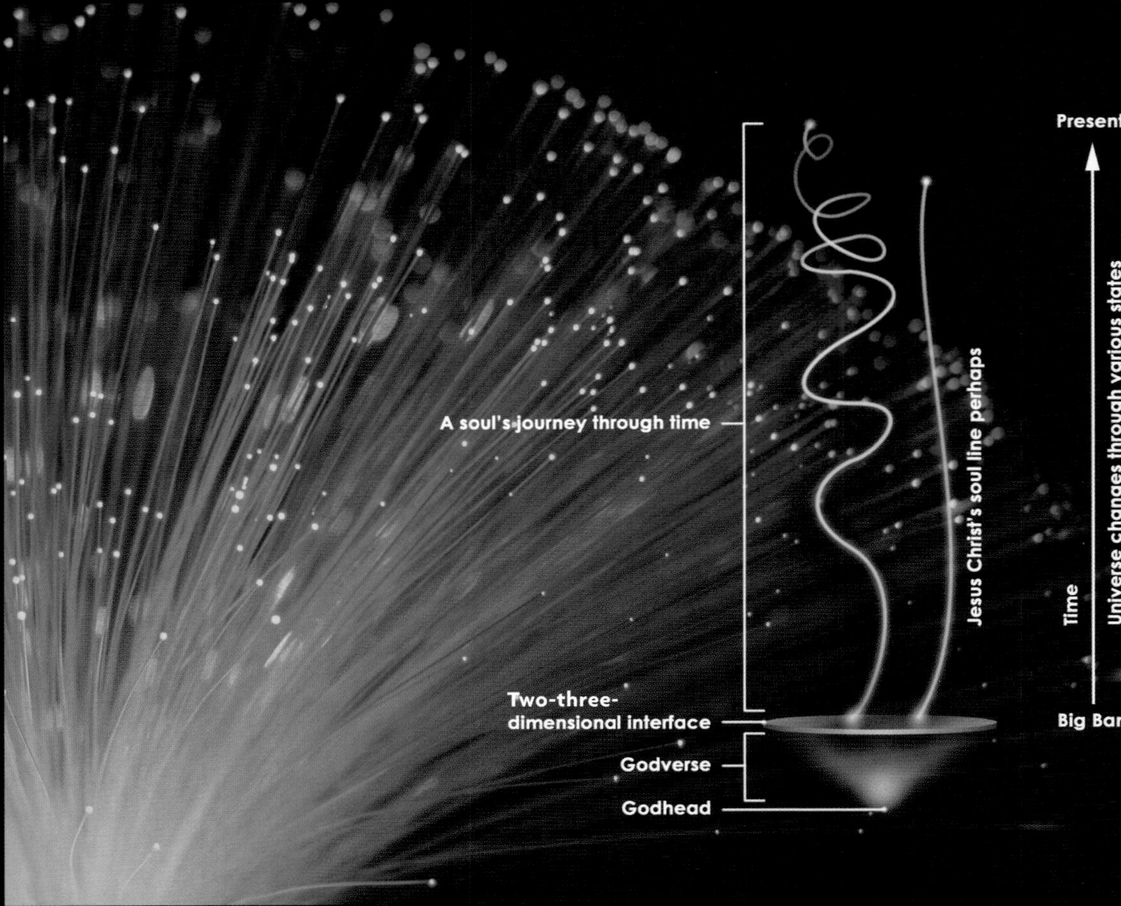

**Plate 17.** The glass fibers of the lamp represent life-forms in our universe. The flat piece of glass at the bed of the lamp is the equivalent of the margin of the Godverse with the universe. The pure, coherent laser light is the light of the Godverse packed with intelligent information and knowledge. This is the conveyable power of Godhead—En-light.

Imagine each living being in this universe as one strand of this lamp. The strands are individual in terms of their shape, as referenced against the straight unbent state. They each have various degrees of bend. The amount of bends, twists, and knots in each strand determines how much light can reach the end. These distortions change the clear light of Godhead, breaking it down into components, diffractions of the original light, defined by color. The more bends and twists, the more a living being will tend toward the black that defines the total obfuscation of God-light. (See chapters 19 and 21.)

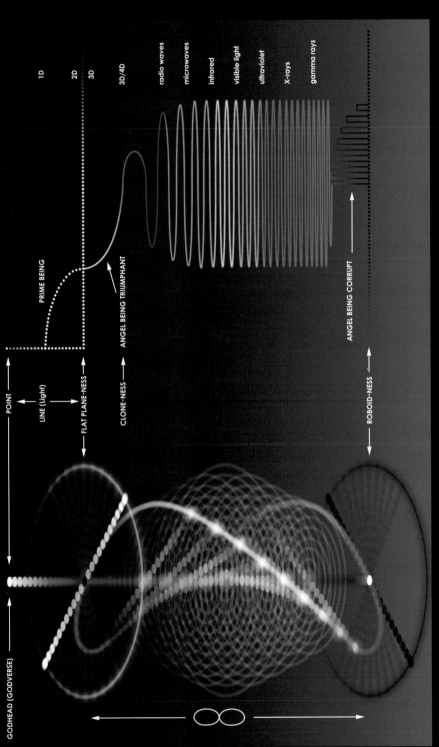

GODHEAD (GODVERSE)

POINT

LINE (Light)

FLAT PLANE-NESS

PRIME BEING

CLONE-NESS

ANGEL BEING TRIUMPHANT

ANGEL BEING CORRUPT

ROBOID-NESS

1D

2D

3D

3D/4D

radio waves

microwaves

infrared

visible light

ultraviolet

X-rays

gamma rays

**Plate 18.** Angels Ascendant/Descendant. The line dividing the Godverse begins at the demarcation point between the second spatial dimension and the third/fourth dimension point between the physical universe as we know it happened. Above this dividing point all being is Prime being. Notice I use the singular. The view from the point above the line into the universe enables a complete view of that universe without it being affected. If the line is actually crossed into the maelstrom of forces in our universe, as is true of all living species now, the impact of force is felt. (See chapter 8.)

GODHEAD (Godverse)

BIG BANG

Beginning of the physical universe. The stages of matter transformation begin. The first entity that forms can be described as "Light Being."

Heterozygous (hermaphroditic) "Being" devolves into existence and the first self-transfigurable entity forms into a sort of Light Being. It is the way the GODVERSE expresses in the universe. This is what is Prime Being. The capacity for automatic transference in and out of the Godverse still continues but is constantly subject to the effects of the Big Bang and the laws of physics that degrade it with time. This Being gradually morphs into a sub form of ephemeral entity that loses the capacity for self-generated transfiguration. First Garden of Eden scenario to protect this state from the further effects of entropy is set up by this form of entity. This procedure goes on universe wide in all suitable physical situations. This is because the rate of degradation in some parts of the universe is faster than others and some parts change more than others from their previous states. In the parts of the universe that devolve more slowly, beings retain the Light Being status longer than the other parts. Planets thus gradually devolve into existence at slower or faster rates and different types of entity form commensurate with these rates.

SITUATION ON PLANET EARTH ONLY

FIRST ADAM

At this point the expression of the Godverse in this universe happens in the form of an entity we commonly called ADAM. At this point in the Earth's devolvement, it is really the FIRST ADAM state and is a singularity. But entropy and its breaking up effect on all things splits it into two parts. Gender happens. From ADAM, EVE comes about as the other half of the split. The singularity of being found all over the universe is on planet Earth at this stage, a state where the forming of multiples of its kind is necessary for the continuation of its unique God version information bearing line. Thus continuity with the Godverse is established through two states of being devolving: the living incarnate state and the "living" discarnate state we call DEATH. Continuity is established by crossing the threshold constantly in a procedure called reincarnation through entry and exit from one world to the other through BIRTH and DEATH.

DESCENT OF LIVING BEING CONTINUES INTO DIVISIONS THROUGH ENTROPY.

These divisions are called SPECIES. In time the most elevated species that remained on the Earth through the natural action of devolvement through entropy were kinds of monkey-humans. Each of these species of monkey-human descended from a separate Adam point. Thus there are several Adam points in the histroy of this planet. This is why at certain points in the history of this planet there have been parallel hominid species of different levels of devolvement.

Java Man

Peking Man

Swanscombe and
Steinheim Man

(1.5 million
years ago)

Homo erectus

Homo habilis
(1.3 to 1.9 million years ago)

Australopithicus afarensis
(2.8 to 3.6 million years ago)

Australopithicus boisei

Miocene Apes
(Approximately
5 million
years ago)

from the DNA of "Early Modern" *Homo sapiens* and "Classic European" Neanderthals, the alien Greys further refined strains of human in experiments, and that led to the emergence of one stock strain suitable for their final purposes about 30,000 years ago. This strain was the Cro-Magnon. They needed further refining and that refining goes on to this day.

Alien intervention through genetic engineering produces a human form we call the African Eve from a combination of *erectus* and *habilis*. This form was genetically manipulated to produce a new form of humanity.

All the time this was happening a special human strain that had preserved itself better from the effects of entropy than any other genotypes through the aeons, continued on. They were never touched by the genetic interventions of any alien species that had come to this planet. They were descendant survivors from the original Light Being forms that inhabited all suitable planets in the universe. They were subject to entropy but survived in better status than all the other primates. This human form was the Neanderthal. Some of the Neanderthals merged with the European Cro-Magnons over time. Some merged with representatives of the non-European *Homo erectus* derivatives. A number that are un-intercepted with alien manipulated DNA may still survive.

**Great apes**
Chimpanzee
Gorilla
Orangutan

All other life-forms devolve naturally to the present day through entropy.

Recent alien abductions and genetic interceptions (beginning about 6,000 years ago). They still go on today.

Euro/Caucasoid
Indo/Caucasoid

Cro-Magnon

Mixed Classic Neanderthal/ Early Modern

Early Modern

Mixed Classic Neanderthal/ Early Modern

Mongoloid

Classic European Neanderthal

Mixed Pre-Neanderthal/ Early Modern

Dravidian/ Australoid

Negroid

Pre-Neanderthal and Neanderthal

Most recent alien abductions and genetic interceptions (beginning about 5,000 years ago)

Intercepted lower melanin Semitic lines, mainly Euro-Ashkenazi, some Arabian Semitic.

Separate unintercepted high-silicon-boned HUMAN line surviving from original prime beings

**LOST TRIBE**
No direct alien genetic interception. Descendants among Sephardic, Ethiopian, and Indian Jews and other lines from various ethnic groups hidden among the higher melanized people of the Earth.

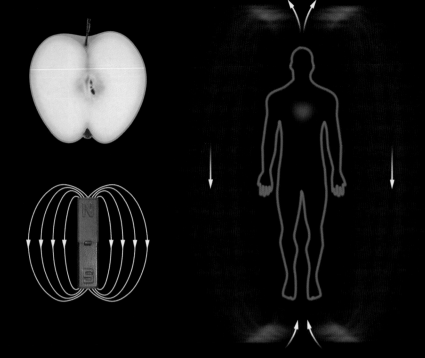

**Plate 20.** The biomagnetic field produced by the iron in the blood circulating in a coil through the body. I don't believe an apple was literally used to tempt the Primes, but it is a curious fact, and perhaps a clue, that magnetic force fields are in fact shaped exactly like an apple. (See chapter 7.)

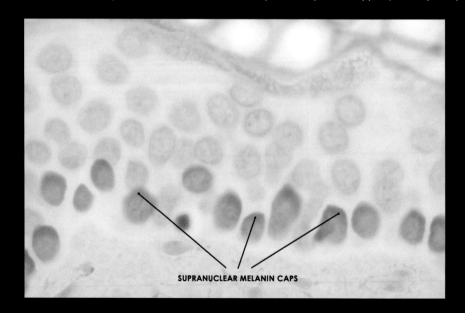

SUPRANUCLEAR MELANIN CAPS

**Plate 21.** This is a cross section of a dark-skinned human epidermis showing how the supranuclear caps protect the underlying cell nuclei. In black and brown skin, melanocytes are far more active and the melanin granules cluster around the nuclei of the cells in which they are found, forming supranuclear caps. (See chapter 12.)

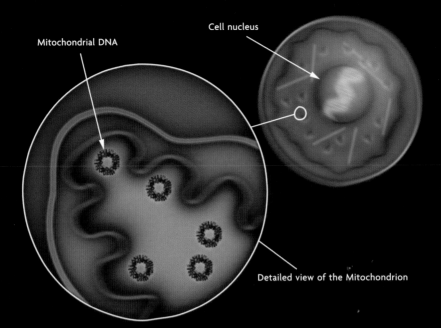

**Plate 22.** Mitochondrial DNA. Unlike other DNA, mitochondrial DNA happens to have a distinctive *circular* structure. Thus, it is extremely plausible that the alien beings could have used this circular structure to conceal their insertion of the thirty-seven genes of mitochondrial DNA. This conceal-ment allows these genes to replicate under their own steam and thus maintain their independence from the human organism while at the same time existing within it. (See chapter 12.)

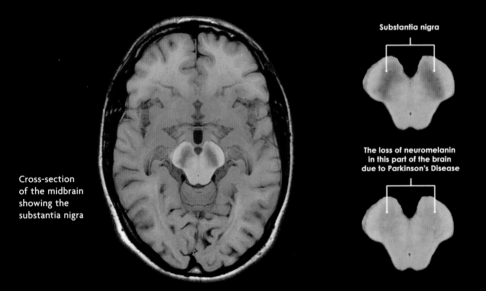

**Plate 23.** Neuromelanin is the dark pigment present in pigment-bearing neurons of four deep-brain nuclei. In Parkinson's disease, there is a massive loss of dopamine-producing pigmented neurons in the substantia nigra. In advanced Alzheimer's disease, there is often an almost complete loss of the norepinephrine-producing pigmented neurons of the locus ceruleus. Thus melanin in the brain appears to provide a neurological benefit that is lost when these diseases take hold. Could this suggest that melanin itself may well be advantageous to the capacity of the human body aerial to function properly? (See chapter 12.)

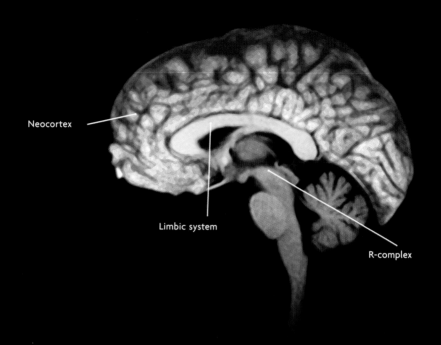

Neocortex

Limbic system

R-complex

**Plate 24.** The triune brain (See chapter 18.)

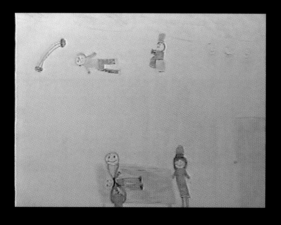

**Plate 25.** According to Dr. Melvin Morse, "I resuscitated this young girl after she nearly drowned in a swimming pool. She had no heartbeat for nineteen minutes. When I expressed disbelief at her story of going to heaven, she patted me on the hand and said: 'You will see. Heaven is fun.'" (See chapter 14.)

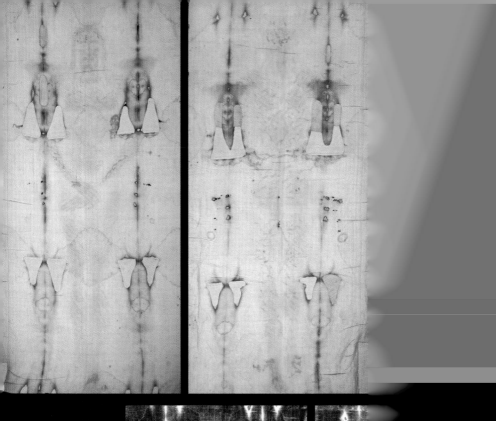
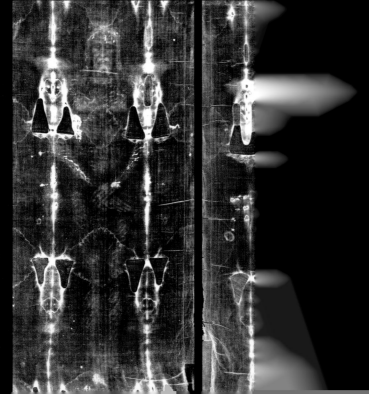

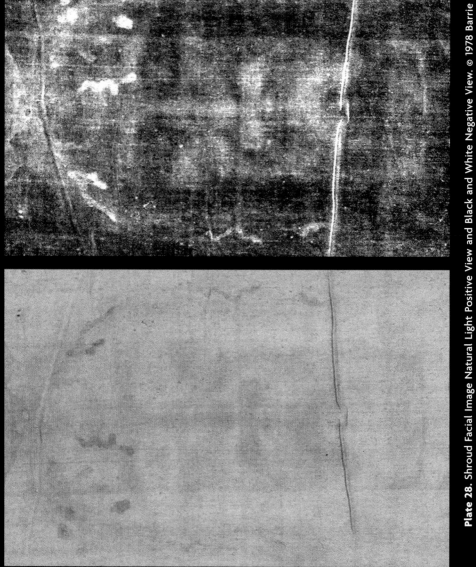

**Plate 28.** Shroud Facial Image Natural Light Positive View and Black and White Negative View. © 1978 Barrie M. Schwortz, all rights reserved. (See chapter 20.)

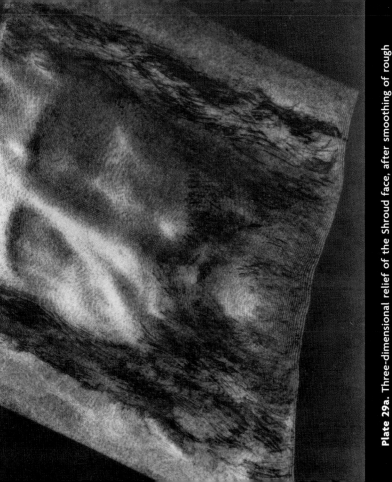

**Plate 29a.** Three-dimensional relief of the Shroud face, after smoothing of rough transitions with a recursive filter (Tamburelli 1982:3-11, reprinted by kind permission). (See chapter 20).

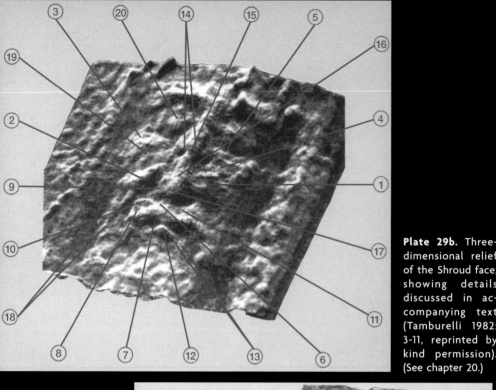

**Plate 29b.** Three-dimensional relief of the Shroud face, showing details discussed in accompanying text (Tamburelli 1982: 3-11, reprinted by kind permission). (See chapter 20.)

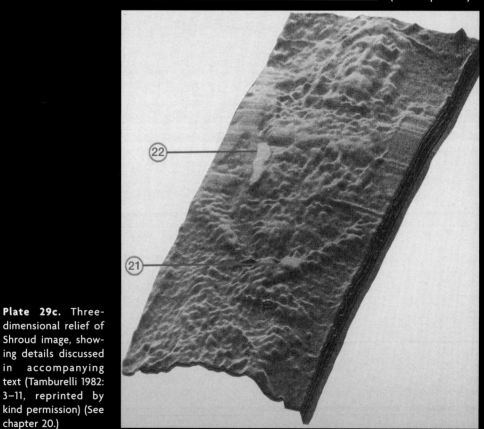

**Plate 29c.** Three-dimensional relief of Shroud image, showing details discussed in accompanying text (Tamburelli 1982: 3–11, reprinted by kind permission) (See chapter 20.)

Writing on the website of archaeologist William Meacham, "The Authentication of the Turin Shroud: An Issue in Archaeological Epistemology" (www.shroud.com/meacham2.htm), Giovanni Tamburelli, quoting from his own article based on computer image processing done at the Centro Studi e Laboratori Telecomunicazioni (Tamburelli 1982: 3–11), makes the following points in reference to Plates 29b and 29c:

- The Man of the Shroud sweated blood, as supported by the presence of blood in all the points of the face.
- Therefore, he received heavy blows such as the numerous scourgings to be seen on the body image, the cudgel blow to be seen on the right cheek (19) and on the nose (15), the blow or blows on the clearly swollen right zygoma (13). As a consequence, he suffered the breakage of the nasal septum, which is seen to be deviated and pierced by two lateral holes (14); the nose lost blood (6), which dropped from the upper lip (7), forming a clot on the lower lip (12).
- The Man of the Shroud began the way to Golgotha with the cross on the right shoulder, as shown by the imprint on the linen wrap. At a certain moment, the forehead began to bleed with a stream flowing on the left side of the face. This stream formed a clot on the left eyelid (5), a clot near the left nostril (1), and the clot on the left side of the upper lip (11). This last clot (11) enlarged and took on a sharp-pointed appearance and acted as a watershed; in fact, it divided the stream of blood into two rivulets, which flowed on the left side of the lower lip (13). As this stream did not soak the beard vertically, and as the clot near the left nostril was clearly cut while the victim was on the cross (as explained later) and hence was not fully clotted, the stream did not appear long before crucifixion. The Man of the Shroud fell, striking the left cheek on the ground, where the cheek was cut by the gravel (4); furthermore, the crown of thorns cut the skin, giving rise at that moment, that is, not long before crucifixion, to the stream of blood mentioned above and to other streams, which soaked the hair.

As shown by the nail marks on both wrists and feet, the Man of the Shroud was crucified. After a certain time, he bent his head toward the right side. This brought about the deviation of the stream on the right side of the face, causing it to flow along the right side of the nose to the right nostril (9), from whence blood dripped on the right side of the lip (10) and then onto the beard (8).

The clot of blood on the left eyelid was wrinkled (5) by the movement of the eyelid. When the Man of the Shroud bent his head, the stream of blood was diverged and thus did not cover the wrinkles; this clot was quite large and stuck the eyelid of the left eye together.

The position of the drop on the right side of the lip (8) shows the inclination of the face before death. The other streams of blood also flowed toward the right side, as clearly shown in Plate 29b.

A person with a sponge soaked in vinegar placed on the tip of a branch of hyssop refreshed the Man of the Shroud: in fact, we can note that the clot on the left side of the cheek (1) is cut.

The upper part of the cut is straight and may correspond to the flat part of the tip of the hyssop branch, due to the cut with a sickle, while the lower part is round and may correspond to the cylindrical part of the tip.

Furthermore, the mark beginning from the right side of the hair (2) is slightly cut on the right cheek and on the nose and stops on the clot, showing that at the beginning the tip of the hyssop branch was placed on the right side of the hair and then dragged across so that the sponge reached the mouth of the Man of the Shroud and caused the cut seen on the clot of blood.

The last drop dripped from the nostril and is greatly diverged toward the right side (9). In fact, when He died the muscles of the neck were fully distended and the head bent down more.

The drop has a pointed form because the gradual decrease in blood flows caused a decrease in its section, and its weight was not sufficient to make it fall (this is a proof that the blood ceased flowing while he was on the cross and hence that the Man died on the cross).

To ensure that the Man of the Shroud was dead, a soldier stabbed him in the right chest with a lance, as shown in Plate 29c (22), and water and blood flowed out.

The death on the cross is also confirmed by the fact that all streams of blood are in the front part of the face and none are directed toward the back, where they would have arrived had the Man of the Shroud continued to lose blood after the deposition from the cross. To keep the right eyelid shut, a coin was placed on it, as is clearly shown by the circular flat area in Plate 29b (20). The coin must then have been removed as the mark is impressed in the linen wrap.

The striking similarities of these facts with Gospel are a clear contribution in favor of the Shroud's authenticity. Hence, the probability that the Man of the Shroud was Jesus Christ is greatly increased by the results obtained with the aid of the computer.

The computer showed us also what the face of Jesus Christ probably looked like before the Passion or after Resurrection, through an electronic cleaning of the blood and wounds, which provides the almost natural images of the face (Plate 29a).

Cameron has never spoken about dying to me. But he told his pal not to worry about dying, because you just come back again. When I asked him how he ended up with me, he tells me he 'fell through and went into my tummy.' And when I ask him what his name was before, he says, 'It's Cameron. It's still me.' I don't think we'll ever get all the answers."[7]

Two other fascinating accounts were documented in a BBC-TV *Forty Minutes* program broadcast in March 1990.[8] The first was that of a young English girl, Nicola. Nicola began describing her previous life at the age of two when she was given a pull-along toy dog. She told her mother: "I'll call it Muff, the same as the other dog I had before." Her mother noticed that Nicola would ask her toy dog if he could remember various events that they had shared in the past. Nicola had also asked her mother: "Why am I a little girl this time Mummy? Why am I not a boy like I was before?" When her mother asked her what she meant by this she said: "When Mrs. Benson was my mummy I was a little boy and I played with Muff." As time went on, Nicola revealed more details of her previous lifetime: Her father had worked on the railway, they lived in a little house near the railway line, and she had had two sisters. She gave a full description of how her mother had looked, of her hair-style and the clothes she wore and the fact that she always told her not to play on the railway. "But I didn't listen to her and I used to go down to the railway with Muff and my friend. . . . I was playing on the railway lines with Muff and my friend and I saw a man walking along swinging a lamp. After that a train came up fast and knocked me over." She could remember being taken to hospital unable to walk or talk. Then: "I went to sleep and died and I saw God in Heaven before I was born."

Nicola's mother could not see how Nicola could have put such a story together from the information she had come across as a young child. So she decided to look into it further. Nicola had said that she had lived in the vicinity of the village of Haworth, in West Yorkshire, near where she now lived. So they went for a drive around that area and although Nicola had not been there before she began giving directions. She said that she recognized the countryside because "Muff and I used to walk all around here." Nicola's directions led them to four old grey-stoned terraced houses in Oakworth; she said that one of these had been her home in her previous life. It matched exactly the description she had given her mother of her previous home before she had even been to Oakworth.

From Haworth Parish church and various other places, they found birth and death certificates and also a gravestone confirming Nicola's memories. They also confirmed the fact that a Benson family had indeed lived in the house she remembered. The birth certificate of a little boy called John Henry (born on June 20, 1875) showed his mother to be a Susie Fletcher who later married Thomas Benson, a railway plate layer. John Henry lived with his grandparents, died in 1878 before he was three years old, and was buried in their grave. At the archives department at the City of Bradford Metropolitan Council offices, the most recent published census returns—taken once every ten years and held in confidence for a hundred years—were for the year 1881. They showed that Thomas Benson and his wife had two daughters. These must have been the two sisters that Nicola claimed to have had when she was John Henry.

Titu Singh, an Indian boy, had begun talking about his "other family" from the age of two-and-a-half. He spoke of being shot, cremated, and then his ashes thrown into a river. "We didn't take him seriously at first," said his father, "but he behaved as if he wasn't a part of the family. Titu is just an ordinary child but sometimes he says and does things that only adults do." Titu's elder brother traveled to Agra, where Titu claimed he had lived. There he sought confirmation that Titu had once been Suresh Verma, the owner of a radio, TV, and video shop, with a wife named Uma and two children called Ronu and Sonu. Titu's brother discovered a radio and TV shop called Suresh Radio that was run by a widow named Uma, whose husband had been shot in the way Titu had described. He explained to her why he had come to Agra and she decided to come and visit Titu the following morning. When she arrived unannounced, Titu was washing at the tap and he immediately shouted that his "other family" had arrived. Titu told Uma to sit near him and asked her if she recognized him, she did not. He then asked her about the children and whether she remembered a family outing to a fair in a neighboring city where he had bought her sweets. Uma was stunned by the accuracy of what he was saying.

When he was taken to Agra to visit Uma and the shop, he was put to the test by his elder brother. It was arranged that her children would be playing with others from the neighborhood when Titu arrived, but Titu recognized Ronu and Sonu immediately from among the group. Titu then commented on the shop and remarked, quite rightly, that one side was different from before and that various units had been added on the other side of the premises.

Titu's mother remarked that: "Titu complains I wear old clothes. He says he used to buy Uma expensive saris. Sometimes he goes moody and says he is 'homesick' and keeps wanting to go to Agra. Once he became so insistent that he rolled his clothes into a bundle and threatened to leave! Even now we find that Titu does not regard this home as his own. He insists that he won't be with us for long."

The most convincing evidence that Titu was indeed Suresh Verma is found in an autopsy report describing how Suresh had died from a bullet to the right temple. The report indicates the exact size and location of the wound. Titu has a round indented birthmark on his right temple that is exactly the same size as the wound had been. Not only that, he has a second mark that would coincide with the exit wound on the other side of his head.

The third case is that of Purnima Ekanayake.[9] Purnima was an eight-year-old girl who spoke of a previous life in which she was Jinasena Perera, a small businessman who died in a road accident in which a bus driver knocked him down as he tried to cross the road in Delkanda, Nugegoda (Sri Lanka). The accident took place on April 9, 1985. Purnima was born on August 24, 1987, and began to speak of her previous existence at the age of three. Her parents traveled to Mulleriyawa, where Jinasena Perera had lived, to investigate the matter. While traveling to the home of her previous life, Purnima suddenly asked the driver to stop the vehicle they were traveling in. Pointing to a woman on the road, she said, "That is Nanda my wife." Further enquiries revealed that she was indeed Nanda, the widow of Jinasena Perera, who had died in an accident.

The original court case filed by police against the driver had been dismissed owing to the absence of witnesses. Eight years later, a case was filed again by Nanda, Jinasena Perera's widow. Before the Ekanayake couple visited the Perera family, they made investigations systematically. They took Purnima to the police station, where she described the accident to the inspector who had conducted the investigation into it. As fate would have it, while Purnima was at the police station, the bus driver who ran over Jinasena also happened to come into the station in connection with fresh charges filed against him over the accident. As soon as she saw him, Purnima sprung from her seat and screamed: "This is my murderer!" When the man tried to talk to her she cried: "Aren't you ashamed to talk to me after having run over and killed me?" When Jinasena's sister heard about the incident at the police station, she rushed there to check the veracity of the story regarding her dead brother. Purnima immediately recognized her and ran up to her to embrace her. Strangely, Purnima has a birth mark on her abdomen corresponding to the tire marks that were made by the bus that ran over Jinasena.

The most pertinent criticism of the evidence for reincarnation is that it is mainly anecdotal and it is thus essentially and implicitly suspect. However the above-mentioned evidence of birthmarks, corresponding to the actual events of a previous lifetime, is a significant counter to this critique. Researcher Ian Stevenson has catalogued thousands of remarkable cases in which birthmarks reflect injuries from previous lives that have been remembered.[10] A further source of objective evidence corroborating reincarnation stories can be found in the fact that, under questioning, thousands of people have recalled previous lives pointing to evidence that in many cases could not have been read or discovered as information sources by the subject.

An incredible case of this sort was reported by researcher Jeffrey Iverson.[11] A regression subject recalled that he was a Jew who lived in York in the fourteenth century. He claimed under hypnosis that he was burnt to death with others of his faith at the time, in a synagogue during a pogrom against the Jews of York. The man described the whole series of events in intricate detail and identified the geography and logistical outlay of medieval York with amazing accuracy. Much of it was historically known and recorded, but he claimed not to have had the slightest knowledge of medieval history of any kind and, when he later listened to the audiotape record of the regression, he was astonished at the detail he had given on the subject.

He also described much that was not known or recorded historically about York town. He described the synagogue, its site in medieval York, and the various related logistics of the place. But certain experts denied that there had ever been a synagogue at the place he described. His description did not fit what was known about York, so it was dismissed as nonsense. However, some years later, the authorities gave permission for an archaeological dig of the Old Town site he described. Buried many feet below the streets they discovered the old synagogue in exactly the place the man had described under regression. On the audiotape, he described the entire series of events that had led to his death. He described how a group of Jews had been chased and cornered in the synagogue, then chased from room to room round corners to a point in the synagogue where he succumbed to fire. He described himself dying while sitting against a wall in one of the galleries. He described a medallion he wore round his neck. To the utter astonishment of those who investigated his claim, a skeleton was discovered in the exact place he described, and around the skeleton's neck was the medallion.

This would seem conclusive evidence for reincarnation. There are many cases such as this in which information that has never been on record anywhere so that it could have been read or gleaned has come to light through regression. When checks are done on the genealogical ancestry of such subjects to establish whether genetic memory could plausibly have passed on such information (this was checked with the subject who recalled the York experience), no such connection has been found.

In Eastern philosophy, an important and complementary principle runs along with reincarnation. It is called *karma*. This principle enshrines the ethic that says "as you sow so shall you reap." Karma is regarded as the driving principle that governs the reincarnation process. According to the laws of karma, what you have done in a particular lifetime governs your status and placement of return in subsequent lifetimes. All this, of course, begs the questions: Where are the starts and where are the ends of any individual existential sojourn? What is born? Who is born? And where does what is born come from in the first place, and why?

The answers need to come from a vision of the entire picture that defines our being as living entities within the scope for existence provided by and for that being. All beings and things come from a scale beyond physicality, from a universe of mind, a glory beyond the understanding of most living physical beings in this universe. As I have said, it all happens incidentally as a logical compromise between two master poles of effect, Godhead and Forcehead, each pulling against the other, the former toward all things merged together as one and the latter pulling all things apart into utter chaotic amelioration. Our universe has both momentums, and if you are not with the one you will be with the other. Thus being "good" really means being in the momentums that unite and draw things together in vectors of behavior and action that do this. The gaining of heaven, valhalla, paradise, and so on is just that simple and just that awesomely hard. There can be no two ways about it. The ignorant or uncommitted mind will do neither and stay trapped in a *limbo* of its own making, going nowhere forever.

The verification of anything in existence depends on mind. A body without a mind is a nothingness of sorts. The final priority for any individual is thus to maintain mind at all its possible optimums and to use them to escape a universe of diminishing returns. Mind is the mechanism of the control of destiny, the final arbitration point and thus arbiter of all allowances. Its power is only limited by its allowance to function. While mind exists as individuality, hope exists in the individual, hope of one thing above all else: hope of being there to know, in all the optimums of both.

We can see from all of this that our individual situations as living beings are of our own individual making. We are as Godhead if we retain mind in all its optimums. Thus the transfigurations of Jesus the Christian sage and Siddhartha Gautama the Buddhist sage were all achieved through reaching the purest optimums of the exercise and generative power of mind. Mind is simply God-light incarnate. It is always there. It is the background swell of existence itself, because it persists as an emanation in the points of no force in the universe. But what precisely governs and thus promotes or mitigates this supreme abstract power when it is trapped within the formats of force that define the physical universe as we know it? We can only get hold of mind when we use it. This is what I am doing it as I write.

Listen to yourself in a quiet room. I mean a really quiet room, a room that has no extraneous sound. Now focus on your head. Do you hear the background noise? For some of you, it will be discerned as a high-pitched sound. For some, it will be an unbearable noise they call tinnitus. For some, it will be a complete emptiness. Imagine this is the whisper of God-light announcing the presence of the Godverse in you. Be kind to yourself and think of yourself as sweet and caring, which you are deep, deep down. Tune in and listen. When all the borders of thought disappear (this will take some practice), you will then be in the most powerful place you can be in this universe. All you are and can do, all your cherished thoughts and feelings, will be automatically empowered to run with the wind of Godhead to resolutions that will never harm you. At that point, you are you as you never will be in any other place or situation of mind because you will have reached another mind: your mind in Godhead.

# 14

# Near Death Experiences

It is time now to take you on a journey, a new journey of discovery to try to convince you that life does not end at death. I am not making this claim to give comfort to the bereaved, or to provide sustenance and fiscal support to some priest or holy man who makes a good living from funeral fees, but as a startling fact.

The real glory of life is death, so the ancients used to believe. Life was just an admission point to death and something beyond. No one really asked the question why we had to be born in order to die and inherit this something beyond. Or indeed where we come from before we are born. It was just enough to accept we are here and ask the question. "Where do we go from here?" We all think about death. Some of us fear it. Some of us look forward to it. Some of us just remain nondescript about it and take the philosophical view that we will face it and what it entails when we have to and not before.

But just what happens the moment our hearts stop beating? Many of us envisage it as an unconscious state, where we will know nothing, which will be the end of our knowing anything or anyone, anymore: end of story. Most of us, however, believe in some kind of afterlife where our individuality continues, that we will have a new beginning in some other kind of existence far removed from the one we have just left. There are many theories and ideas about the afterlife and what it might entail. Of course, it can never be known or experienced in its entirety from the state of living, so we have to leave it all to surmise, conjecture, and hope for the best. We get glimpses of it from near death experiences but—as the subjects of these have returned to life—we have no knowledge of what it might be like to remain in that state beyond physical life, to cross the threshold that NDE experients turn back from.

We do have the words and teachings of the holy men, wise teachers, and religious prophets of old, assuring us that there is an afterlife and that this afterlife is acceded to in all its magnitudes as a condition based upon how we have spent this life in a physical body and what we have accomplished in thoughts and deeds. But ever since those great masters presented their pristine and glorious logic, we have been blackmailed by the leaders and office bearers of one religious system or another to tow the party line according to their interpretations, whims, fancies, and prognostications. I have made a great study of religion and religious invective as it has been recorded through the millennia, and I now believe unequivocally that generally religion has sold us all a false bill of goods throughout history. It has been done by a relatively small number of individuals who came after the authors of the world's great religions and took on their mantles. If religion has done us harm through false claims and prerogatives, where do we rest our belief in an afterlife? We have to reclaim the original words and contexts of these great teachers. Most of their original words are hidden in texts, lost or made obscure by those who through history have claimed to speak in their names and have lied about and distorted the meaning of their words.

It is my postulation that there is no celestial judge or jury deciding guilt or innocence and meting out appropriate punishment for the guilty. All the consequences of all our actions are registered implicitly on our souls; acts that divide and separate, hurt or restrict others, simply shut out the light of the Godverse and make us more opaque to that uniting light. This is not an imposed punishment, it is simply the result of a choice, in free will, to deny that light and accept the entropic momentums of the physical universe. The light of the Godverse is a light that in a way supplements, supports, and promotes the phenomenon we call gravity. Yes gravity. If we endorse, in free will, our own state of separation, we will become more separate. If, on the other hand, we endorse our union with others through acts that unite, we will loosen the bonds that maintain us in our separate state. But what are the actual nuts and bolts of how all this works? Most explanations of abstract concepts such as these resort to metaphor and simile. My attempt here is to provide a literal exploration and explanation of the nature of concepts such as life and death, birth and rebirth, redemption and damnation, in terms that can be logically affirmed using scientific yardsticks.

Before I clarify the specific structures that support both the paradigm of life and the paradigm of death, I'd like to share with you some of the evidence for life after death given by humans who arguably have experienced both: those who have had what are commonly called near death experiences. It is an interesting fact that the Aramaic word for "death" translates as "not here" or "present elsewhere." Those who have had near death experiences would, I think, wholeheartedly agree with that definition.

A close friend of mine was sitting at the bedside of a famous modern-day German philosopher, keeping vigil while he was unconscious and near death's door. He believed in the essentially racist principle of the division of humankind into social development modules that separated ethnic groups and nationalities and anthropological racial groups. The man suddenly came out of unconsciousness and cried out to my friend. He had evidently had some sort of NDE: "Tell them I have seen what it is all about. I have seen the other side. It is not as I thought. Everything is together. We are not separated. We are all one. Take out my books from the libraries," he pleaded, "tell them not to publish my new one. It's all wrong. It's all wrong." He then went back into unconsciousness and died a day later without regaining consciousness. My friend, herself a famous German artist and sculptress, was so astonished by the philosopher's outburst—which contradicted everything he had ever declared to her during their long friendship—that she said not a word to anyone. She thought it was some kind of effect of his drug treatment just prior to death.

When the man died the next day, she inquired whether he had been on any drugs that could account for a psychoactive outburst. His doctor told her that throughout his illness he had taken no drugs on his own insistence. She still mentioned nothing of what happened until she too had an NDE some months later. Her personal experience seemed to confirm what the old philosopher had said to her. She immediately tried to do what he had asked of her, but it was too late. His latest book was published, and to this day my friend believes she will bear the karma for the consequences of the philosophy propounded in the book.

Science is now beginning to look at the possibility that we live on in death more seriously, particularly since quantum mechanics and quantum physics seem to imply it. Dr. Sam Parnia, fellow in Pulmonary and Critical Care Medicine at Cornell University, says the following after conducting extensive research into near death experiences:

Until fairly recently I used to believe that brain processes led to the formation of consciousness and the mind, although like all the other scientists, I did not know how. However, studying near death experiences in cardiac arrest survivors has made me question my views, as has the lack of plausible biological mechanisms to account for the causation of consciousness from brain processes. I have now decided to keep a completely open mind and let the evidence sway my opinion. After all, this wouldn't be the first time in science that a prevailing view has been proved wrong. When we look back, we can see that many widely accepted theories have been modified, or even completely changed in the light of new evidence. Personally, I have had to accept that the formation of consciousness is far from clear and it could be that the latter view is correct.[1]

Perhaps the most famous case to illustrate the veracity of the near death experience is that of Maria, originally reported by her critical care social worker, Kimberly Clark. Maria was a migrant worker who, while visiting friends in Seattle, had a severe heart attack. She was rushed to

Harborview Hospital and placed in the coronary care unit. A few days later, she had a cardiac arrest and an unusual out of body experience. At one point in this experience, she found herself outside the hospital; she spotted a single tennis shoe on the ledge of the north side of the third floor of the building. Later, Maria was not only able to indicate the whereabouts of this oddly situated object, but was able to provide precise details concerning its appearance, such as the fact that its little toe area was worn and one of its laces was stuck underneath its heel. Upon hearing Maria's story, Clark, with some considerable degree of skepticism and metaphysical misgiving, went to the location described to see whether any such shoe could be found. Indeed it was, just where and as precisely as Maria had described it, except that from the window through which Clark was able to see it, the details of its appearance that Maria had specified could not be discerned. Clark concluded: "The only way she could have had such a perspective was if she had been floating right outside and at very close range to the tennis shoe. I retrieved the shoe and brought it back to Maria; it was very concrete evidence for me."[2]

The following, describing the fascinating results of a Dutch study of NDEs, was published on www.beliefnet.com on December 15, 2001:

A study recently published in *The Lancet,* England's most prestigious medical journal, provides what may be the first hard-science confirmation that many people who almost die do experience something haunting at the boundary of life. Conducted by Pim van Lommel, a cardiologist at an Amsterdam hospital, the study concerned 344 patients who were resuscitated following cardiac arrest in Dutch hospitals. Some 18 percent of the patients told interviewers they had a near death experience; 12 percent had what van Lommel called a "core experience," not just warm feelings but an elaborate perception of the beginning of an afterlife.

What's important about the new study is that it was done "prospectively." Most near death research is "retrospective," involving seeking out people who claim to have had such an experience, and talking to them months or years after the fact. From a research standpoint, subjects like this are "self-selected"—people who already think something, not a random trial—and the delay means they may have had plenty of time to imagine things. The Dutch effort, in contrast, involved interviewing everyone who had been resuscitated in ten local hospitals during the study period and simply asking them if they had any recollections. Interviews were conducted as soon as the patients were well enough to talk, and patients were not told the topic of the study, merely that researchers wanted to know if they remembered anything. This avoided any "prompting" effect.

Thus a finding that 18 percent of men and women revived at the point of death had impressions of light or beauty seems important. Something must be going on. And it's going on more and more. If it seems to you that reports of near death experiences are increasing, you're right, they are. Only in recent decades did physicians acquire the ability to resuscitate patients at the point of death. Now that this happens in hospitals every day, there are thousands of people walking around who have been almost dead. Eventually there may be millions.

The something going on in near death cases might be physiological, of course. Researchers have previously speculated that the near death experience might be an artifact of cerebral anoxia, or lack of oxygen to the brain. As oxygen falters, this thinking goes, the brain begins to shut down and misfiring of synapses creates illusions of light or music. The Dutch study seems to rule out this idea, however. All patients in the study suffered some degree of cerebral anoxia before revival, but only 18 percent had a near death experience. As *The Lancet* notes, if the near death experience is caused by cerebral anoxia, "most patients who have been clinically dead should report one." Instead most of the clinically dead patients did not report a near death experience. Brain oxygen problems therefore seem unlikely as the cause.

Skeptics of near death claims also point out that ketamine, an anesthetic, sometimes causes surgery patients to experience visions of beauty or light. This must be a physiological response. But the subjects in the Dutch study were heart-attack victims, not surgery patients: they were not administered ketamine.

What happened to van Lommel's subjects who did have near death experiences? They reported visions of beauty or light, loss of fear of death, a sense of being welcomed to a wonderful place, and in one case an "out of body" (OBE) experience. The last involved a forty-four year-old man brought to the hospital comatose; as resuscitation began, a nurse removed dentures from his mouth. Later when the patient has recovered he sees the nurse and asks for his dentures back. But the only time the nurse had been in his presence, he had been unconscious and near death; how did he know what the nurse looked like?

Anecdotes like that, which are staples of mid-morning TV, rarely show up in controlled clinical studies. But what's most intriguing about the Dutch research is the number of patients reporting loss of fear of death. Fear of death is hard-wired into our mind by millions of years of evolution: our ancestors would not have survived without it, and the ones who reproduced—that is, passed along their genes—were likely to have been the ones most keenly afraid of dying, and therefore the most cautious. People might overcome the fear of death through philosophical or religious contemplation. But for this fear simply to vanish at a moment of near death doesn't make much sense in terms of evolutionary psychology. Something must be going on.

Van Lommel did not attempt to study whether that something is broadly psychological. Men and women grow up thinking that heaven is white light and angels have wings; as death approaches, the brain sees what it expects to see, perhaps generating visions of an afterlife as a sort of last-second self-defense mechanism, to protect the dying mind from experiencing terror. This has always seemed to me the most likely non-supernatural explanation of the near death experience, and it awaits research.

Still, you're being closed-minded if you don't consider that what is happening may be related to an afterlife. What haunted me after plowing through the pages of *The Lancet* study was this: the majority of the patients van Lommel studied recovered fully and are still with us, but of those who had the "core" experience of the door to another life being opened, most died within 30 days.

It was as if their time had come, then a physician intervened, and then their time did come, and the hand holding the door the first time they approached it had known they were the ones who should be shown what was next. People with many years left to live given proper medical care—that is, the bulk of the patients in the Dutch study—wouldn't have a near death experience because they were not yet at the moment when "the time has come." A person sure to die soon regardless of medical care would have the experience. Call it eerie; this is what the Dutch statistics show.[3]

The sophisticated medical instrumentation that exists today can bring back to life people who would have been certified as dead three decades ago. I am not saying that we have been burying living people. I am saying that in some instances people were pronounced dead using very different verification processes than we have now. Since the publication of a paper entitled "A Definition of Irreversible Coma" in 1968, there has been a shift in emphasis in the determination of death from the traditional cardio-respiratory signs to the neurological criterion of "brain death." This change consists of establishing, according to clearly determined parameters commonly held by the international scientific community, the complete and irreversible cessation of all brain activity in the cerebrum, cerebellum, and brain stem. But current incredible medical advances have made it possible to even bring people with brain stem death brought back to life—and some of them have the most incredible stories to tell.

Just recently the case of Pam Reynolds in the United States has provided skeptics with irrefutable evidence that the NDE is truly an experience of an objective reality that exists beyond physical death. This lady had an aneurism seated so deeply in her brain that she was told it was inoperable. Fortunately she found one neurosurgeon in Arizona, Dr. Robert Spetzler, who agreed to take on her case and attempt a very dangerous operation. The surgery involved switching off every vital process in her body so that, for a short period of time, she would be clinically dead. According to Dr. Spetzler, she was brought into a situation in which she would have "no measurable neuronal activity whatsoever."[4] No area of her brain (nor her brain taken as a whole) could have been sufficiently active to account for her NDE. This fact is what makes Reynolds' NDE so significant. She experienced a classical NDE that could not have been a result of processes within the brain, as she was in effect brain dead during her NDE. While her paranormal perception of surgical preparations was not accompanied by a flat EEG, the rest of her NDE took place while she was brain dead in the broadest possible sense. Her neurosurgeon, Dr. Spetzler, admitted that he could not explain her experiences by normal mechanisms. This was her experience:

She felt as though she "popped" out of the top of her head and viewed the operation from the perspective of just above the surgeon's shoulder. She saw the instrument that he was about to use to penetrate her skull and it seemed to her that it was shaped rather like an electric toothbrush. Later she remembered feeling surprised because it looked like a drill and she thought that they were going to use a saw-like instrument. After the operation, it was confirmed that the drill used by the surgeon looked exactly like an electric toothbrush. Pam also accurately reported conversations going on between the nurses during her operation.

After her out of body experience (OBE), she saw a pinpoint of light that seemed to be pulling her toward it. She went toward the light and heard her grandmother and other people she knew calling her. She also saw some people that she didn't know, but she felt that she was in some way connected to them. She asked if the *light* she saw was God, and she was told that it was not God but what happens when "God breathes."[5]

This last point is particularly intriguing. The light she saw would have been the light of the Godverse reaching through into the physical universe—God's breath, in other words, reaching in and out. The Godverse beyond the finite physical universe is *not* the light; the light is simply the result of the potential difference between the Godverse and the Universe of Parts, the interface between the two, if you like. For this reason, Reynolds was told categorically that the light she saw was not God but what happens when "God breathes."

Peter Fenwick (M.D., F.R.C.Psych.) from the Institute of Psychiatry, Kings College, London, gave the Bruce Greyson Lecture for the International Association for Near-Death Studies 2004 Annual Conference, entitled "Science and Spirituality: A Challenge for the 21st Century." In this lecture, Fenwick provided a review of the latest research. As the pioneer of research into the field, Fenwick is likely to have the best, most thorough, and up-to-date knowledge, making an in-depth look at his lecture very worthwhile.

Fenwick discusses temporal lobe epilepsy, chemicals in the brain at the point of death, and mental instability, all of which have been suggested as possible triggers for near death experiences. He first states that the suggestion that NDEs are a result of temporal lobe epilepsy "is always made by those who do not deal with epilepsy on a daily basis and who do not have a comprehensive understanding of the features of an epileptic seizure. No epileptic seizure has the clarity and narrative style of an NDE. And this is because all epilepsy is confusional. Epileptologists all agree that one thing that near death experiences are not is temporal lobe epilepsy."[6]

He then discusses the theory that NDEs are in some way a result of mental illness: "In Bruce Greyson's (2003b) study of 272 patients who had a brush with death, 22 percent had NDEs, and they were found to be less psychologically disturbed than those who did not have NDEs. So that is extremely good news in that it goes against the idea that those who have NDEs have some mental pathology."[7]

Fenwick goes on to examine the likelihood of a lucid experience such as an NDE in an unconscious state brought on by cardiac arrest:

> Greyson's (2003a) American study was of 1,595 patients admitted to a cardiac care unit with heart trouble. He found an incidence of 10 percent NDEs among cardiac arrest survivors and found that the more severe the illness, the more likely the survivor was to report an NDE. And what he said is this: "The paradoxical occurrence of heightened, lucid awareness and logical thought processes during a period of impaired cerebral perfusion [absence of blood flow to the brain] raises particularly perplexing questions for our current understanding of consciousness and its relation to brain function." (p. 275). . . .
>
> The flat electroencephalogram (EEG), indicating no brain activity during cardiac arrest, and the high incidence of brain damage afterward both point to the conclusion that the unconsciousness in cardiac arrest is total. You cannot argue that there are "bits" of the brain that are functioning; there are not. There is a confusional onset and offset, and there is no brain-based memory functioning. Everything that constructs our world for us is, in fact, "down." There is no possibility of the brain creating any images. Memory is not functioning during this time, so it should be impossible to have clearly structured and lucid experiences, and because of brain damage, memory should be significantly impaired, and you should not be able to remember any experiences which occurred during that time. Now, that raises interesting and difficult questions for us, because the near death experiencers (NDErs) say that their experiences occur during unconsciousness, and science maintains that this is not possible. . . .
>
> Anecdotal evidence suggests that the out of body experience (OBE), and so the NDE, occurs during unconsciousness. There is also anecdotal evidence that it may be veridical. Sabom in 1982 found that some of his research participants gave correct accounts of resuscitation procedures, suggesting that the NDE occurs when

the brain is "down." The case of Pamela Reynolds, for those of you who saw the BBC production *The Day I Died* or read the account of her case in Sabom's later book (1998), is also suggestive of that. And, of course, Kenneth Ring and Sharon Cooper (1997) have described cases of NDEs in blind people who claim to have what they call "mindsight" and are able to "see" the resuscitation room. So, is the OBE truly veridical? That is, does it consist of verifiably accurate perceptions that would have been impossible to perceive from the vantage point of that person's physical body? This is the cutting edge question in NDE research.[8]

Fenwick goes on to cite the example of Derrick Scull, age sixty-six and married with two children, a retired Army major who now works in a large firm of lawyers. Scull said in an interview:

Well, basically, I pride myself in being a fairly pragmatic, down-to-earth sort of person, but the experience that I underwent in 1978 remains etched in my memory for the last eight years, and certainly I couldn't believe my eyes or my senses at the particular time. I had a heart attack and I found myself in hospital in the intensive care unit on the first day. The hospital medical staff had done everything they could for me. I was lying there in an operation robe with a mask on my face, and obviously I'd received an injection of morphine or some sort of drug to keep me under control. I wasn't experiencing pain; in fact, I was feeling at peace with the world.

And suddenly, I seemed to take off and float, airborne, I suppose one would describe the word, into the corner of the room where I was able to look back, and I was conscious of lying there, and there was my own body, and I thought, "good gracious, what is this?" In fact, I sort of, if I can describe it, I was looking at my toes on the ceiling, sort of looking over, and there was my body immediately below me. I was in the corner, left hand corner of the room, looking down on this body, and I had a perfectly good eye view of the bed and the entrance to the ward. And then I was also suddenly conscious that outside the room, there was my wife standing there in a red trouser suit talking to a nurse. I thought, "My God, what an inappropriate time to arrive. I'm up here, and there's the body, and what's going to happen?" I thought, "Something must happen."

But the very next thing I was conscious of was, sitting beside me was my wife wearing a bright red trouser suit. And I was there. I'd come down from the ceiling somehow, and there she was. This is why I know it wasn't a figment of my imagination, because it was so clear. I've given you the illustration of exactly what my wife was wearing, that was a red trouser suit, and I couldn't have seen her at the time. So this absolutely convinced me, and it was certainly cemented after my second heart attack when I went through a totally similar experience, and I am absolutely converted to this theory that something—call it your soul, call it whatever you like—does, in fact, temporally detach itself from your body, goes to a vantage point, and looks back and reviews the situation. And that's exactly what I felt I did on both occasions.[9]

There have been several instances in which relatives or friends have seen an individual who has just died and he or she has informed them of their death. This again suggests the survival of consciousness beyond the point of physical death. Fenwick quotes the following example from an interview:

Around 1950, a distant relative, John, was in hospital. It was a Sunday, and my father went to visit John, to be told that he had died that morning at a certain time. The hospital authorities asked dad if he would inform the next of kin, the deceased's sister Kate and her husband, who were sheep farmers living in a relatively remote part of the country and not on the telephone. Dad and I drove the 20 or so miles and up a hill track to the farmhouse to be met by Kate who said, "I know why you have come—I heard him calling me, saying

'Kate, Kate' as he passed over." She was quite matter-of-fact about
it. She gave us the time of death, which was exactly the same as
recorded by the hospital. I found it an amazing experience and have
never forgotten it, nor will I ever. I was about 17 at the time.[10]

Another example offering powerful evidence of life after physical
death is given by van Lommel from one of his research interviews with
NDE experients:

During my cardiac arrest I had an extensive experience ( . . . ) and
later I saw, apart from my deceased grandmother, a man who had
looked at me lovingly, but whom I did not know. More than 10 years
later, at my mother's deathbed, she confessed to me that I had been
born out of an extramarital relationship, my father being a Jewish
man who had been deported and killed during the Second World
War, and my mother showed me his picture. The unknown man
that I had seen more than 10 years before during my NDE turned
out to be my biological father.[11]

Dr. Melvin Morse resuscitated a young girl after she nearly drowned
in a swimming pool. She had no heartbeat for nineteen minutes. Morse
relates that she later told him that she had gone to heaven: "When I
expressed disbelief at her story of going to heaven, she patted me on the
hand and said, 'You will see. Heaven is fun.' She did a drawing depicting her near death experience (see Plate 25). Morse describes the picture
thus:

We see in this picture the "two realities" often described by those
who have near death experiences. Above the blue line is "heaven."
Below the blue line is a "hole in the world" that opened up to show to
this girl her yet unborn brother. She was told that she had to return
to "help my mother because my baby brother was going to have some
problems." She does not say in words what the problem was, but

draws a large heart in the boy's chest. He was born with severe heart problems, several months after this picture was drawn.[12]

Dr. Morse also relates an extraordinarily beautiful account of the NDE of a little girl called Kalana:

Kalana was ravaged with disease since birth. By age four, she required a heart and lung transplant, done at Los Angeles Children's Hospital in 1994. At seven years of age, her body started rejecting the organs. At one point, she nearly died and was resuscitated.

While still in the Intensive Care Unit she used a Magna Doodle to communicate as she still had a tube in her lungs. At one point, a doctor came into the room, and her mother told her "Kalana, this is the doctor who saved you." Kalana shook her fist angrily and sketched: "God saved me."

After she recovered, she told her mother that she was up in the corner of the room, looking down at the doctor working on her. She talked with "angels in a tunnel with a special kind of light." It felt good to her, and she wanted to lie down and rest.

The angels told her that she could rest for a little while, but then had to go back.

She was told: "We will come for you when the time is right.

On their way home from the hospital, Kalana and her mother saw a strong ray of light coming out of the gray clouds. It touched the earth. Kalana told her mother that someone had just died. Her mother tried to give her a scientific explanation for the stream of light, but Kalana was insistent. She said it was the same light as in the tunnel. When they arrived home, they got a message that another child from their area who had been terminally ill had just died. Kalana died several months later.[13]

If you look at what typically happens during an NDE, you will find more verification for the existence of the Godverse within the physical universe. In fact, it seems that the nature of the expression of the Godverse is exactly as I have described it to be—beyond space and time, full of an expression and experience we commonly describe as love, an expression and experience that in its highest factors describes the manifestation and understanding of all knowledge.

None of these anecdotal experiences implying an existence beyond death can be taken as irrefutable evidence that correlates with a scientifically derived verification. But the sheer number and quality of witnesses of these expressions and manifestations of a reality beyond atoms have convinced my originally deeply skeptical mind, beyond a shadow of a doubt, that we each live beyond a physical life. The beautiful Kalanas of this world attest to this better than any scientific methodology. After all, there is no methodology that has been proved wrong more times than the scientific one, as any scientist has to tell you.

As we have seen, these experiences often begin with the experient leaving his or her body. They feel as though they are slowly rising out of it, weightless, floating, and can look down on themselves from some objective vantage point, usually near the ceiling. In most NDEs, the person enters a dark tunnel through which they seem to pass very rapidly without making any physical effort. At the end of the tunnel, they see a pinpoint of light that, as they approach, grows larger and larger. Often the light seems to draw the person toward it. At this point, he or she may meet a "being" of light. If the person is religious, this may be a figure such as Jesus, but sometimes it is simply a "presence" that is felt to be God-like. This is nearly always an intensely emotional experience, so much so that often the experient cannot find words to describe his or her feelings. The descriptions that are given are of a presence that is warm, welcoming, and loving. Sometimes other beings are encountered during the experience, usually dead relatives or friends, beckoning to them or signaling that they should go back.

At some point in the experience, the subject may see events from his life flash before him and his past actions reviewed. The actions that are most often highlighted by those who have described their life reviews are those that have profoundly affected other people for good or ill. Often, near death subjects are astounded by the fact that it is the smallest and seemingly most insignificant actions that predominate in the life review because these are the acts that have affected other people. The message that almost all experients take away from their NDEs is the crucial importance of love as a guiding principle for life. Even the tiniest acts of caring seem to have enormous significance in the life review. The experients find that they are literally viewing through the eyes of those whom they have affected. This gives a spur to most people when they return to their bodies to lead more altruistic lives, with a much greater sensitivity to the needs of others.

It is also an illustration of how existence in physical life captures our individuality, our consciousness and awareness, in a state of intrinsic separation from the consciousness and awareness of others. Thus in physical life the summary of meaning provided by the implicit backdrop of the Godverse is not received quite so clearly. The knowledge of the whole that makes up the parts of a physical universe cannot be retained in the physical living state simply because that very state breaks up that whole picture view. However, that summary still prevails in life, albeit to a lesser extent, and I believe this defines conscience. If in our everyday lives we experienced the same empathy felt during most NDEs, this would almost certainly drive us to selflessness and prevent us doing harm to anyone else. In life, that overwhelming impulse to care for others is translated into a nagging conscience that only some are still able to hear. We lose sight of the true priorities of caring and love when we enter the physical state and in most cases only regain a sense of the urgency of those priorities through NDEs, or through death itself, or indeed through the teachings of "redeemers" or "Christ" phenomena like Jeshua Ben Joseph.

Almost everyone who has a near death experience reports that afterward they have no fear of death. Even if they previously had no religious faith, they return believing that death is not the end. Their attitudes to life are often transformed, in many cases so profoundly that the whole course of their lives changes to one that is less selfish and materialistic and more centered on priorities of caring and compassion for others.

Tom Rayner, a pilot, was fifty-two when he had a near death experience after a car accident that totally changed his life. He was in a coma for days and then came the out of body experience that triggered his return to proper consciousness:

> The first thing I was aware of was being high in the sky, far higher than in any airplane I had flown. I was looking down on East Anglia, all spread out below me. And then I realized I was rushing even further away from the Earth. Soon, I was looking down on the whole of Western Europe and then the Northern Hemisphere.
>
> It's hard to describe how incredible the next sequence of events was. I flew up past the moon and planets to the very edge of this galaxy. Then I passed through more and more galaxies until I reached the end of the universe.
>
> I wasn't afraid in the slightest and the whole experience seemed lucid and, although surprising, completely reasonable.
>
> Then at the end of not one, but five universes, I came to a place where all the religions of the world were played out in front of me. I felt myself becoming absorbed by an all-encompassing presence and I experienced overwhelming love, compassion and forgiveness. My eyes were opened to the good in everyone, and how so many are the victims of terrible injustice.
>
> Then the whole journey went into reverse, and I found myself in an African country I knew next to nothing about and could barely place on a map. I was overwhelmed with shock and sadness at the sights of war, hunger and desperation. This jolted me into consciousness. I was back in the hospital. It was the start of my recovery.
>
> I sold out to my business partner and bought a Land Rover ambulance, filled it with donated drugs and medical equipment and shipped it to Africa where I drove into a war zone and delivered the medical supplies to an underground field hospital.
>
> There's nothing altruistic about anything I've done—after a near

death experience you're sort of compelled to take action. But sometimes it takes a bang on the head to open your eyes to things.[14]

The world of the near death experience seems to transcend time, as
shown by the following quotes from those who have experienced them,
taken from the website www.near-death.com:

Time did not make any sense. Time did not seem to apply. It seemed
irrelevant. It was unattached to anything, the way I was. Time is
only relevant when it is relative to the normal orderly sequential
aspects of life. So I was there for a moment or for eternity. I cannot
say but it felt like a very long time to me. (Grace Bubulka)[15]

During an NDE, you can't tell if you were in that light for a minute
or a day or a hundred years. (Jayne Smith)[16]

Earthly time has no meaning in the spirit realm. There is no concept
of before or after. Everything—past, present, future—exists simultaneously. (Kimberly Clark Sharp)[17]

From the onset of this rather superconscious state of the darkness of
the tunnel, there was something that was totally missing and that
was what we call time. There's no such thing as time in heaven! As I
thought of and formulated a desire or a question, it would already have
been recognized, acknowledged, and therefore answered. And the dia-
logue that took place, took place in no time. It didn't require a fifteen-
minute duration in time; it simply happened. (Thomas Sawyer)[18]

It has struck me as highly significant that those who return from an
NDE report that very little time has passed, usually only a few moments:

The experience lasted for hours or eons and now it seems that eons
passed in only moments. (Virginia Rivers)[19]

The experience was a few seconds, but it seemed like an eternity. (Rev. Kenneth Hagin)[20]

In his book *Life After Death,* Ian Wilson quotes the example of George Ritchie, who suffered double pneumonia while in the U.S. Army in 1943. In his near death experience, he relates that "everything that had ever happened to me was simply there, in full view, contemporary and current, all seemingly taking place at that moment."[21] Patrick, an Australian who had his NDE during the Second World War, told Dr. Cherie Sutherland: "There was no concept of time either backward or forward. I could encompass the whole universe."[22] There also seems to be no concept of space in the realms of "death." Shana, an Australian who found herself out of her body after "dying" following a kidney operation in England, said: "I could see my mother out in the hall of the hospital in Sussex, England, and I could see my father in Australia. I could see everybody I was connected to."[23] Wilson makes the salient point:

> If we are treating seriously this idea that the other-worldly dimension is one in which time and space are simply not part of the equation, then it follows, even if this dimension doesn't particularly conform to our normal rules of logic, that there can be absolutely nothing anywhere which is not known once tapped into it. And indeed a significant number of near death experients claim to have glimpsed this total knowledge, even though, in contrast to the rest of their experience, they leave it behind when they return.[24]

A close look at what typically happens during an NDE thus provides clear verification of the existence of the Godverse within the physical universe, as I have described it to be—beyond space and time, full of an expression and experience we commonly describe as love, an expression and experience that in its highest factors describes the manifestation and understanding of all knowledge.

# 15

# The *Fact* of Life after Life

*A cosmic matrix of rainbow light exists around the earth.*
*This matrix provides souls with a number of earthly*
*destinies from which to choose. Then, before we are born*
*into the world, we are required to forget these memories.*

PLATO

As we have seen, in the world of atoms, our universe, where all things are broken and breaking into parts, these parts have value in terms of their connection and mixing with the world beyond and not of atoms: the Godverse. The parts that hold less of the world beyond the atom are a dead array of creation that composes ordinary nonliving things. The parts that hold more of the world beyond atoms have life. On our planet, humankind marks the highest resolution of the mix between the Godverse and the universe. The mix is provided by a two-way connection, one world with the other, through gates I have called peace points, where the nature of each world can exist as itself within the other. This provides for the properties of each in countervailing measures of expression throughout our universe.

The number and arrangement of these peace points determines the total existential endurance of any living species and individuals within each species. They define very precisely the propensity for life and the

244

quality of that life through intelligent choice-making capacity in material universes and beyond. In our universe, the peace points exist both within and outside of atoms. Intra-atomic peace points endow this universe with life, awareness, compunction, knowledge, and thus choice-making capacity. Extra-atomic peace points exist in the whole spaces between atoms and set up the paradigm of death. We swap between the two as we die and reincarnate, till we have sufficient peace points to directly meld into the Godverse from the living atomic state, as perhaps Christ did at what is described as his transfiguration. It may be that we can meld into it temporarily if sufficient God-light comes into us, but can never enter it permanently directly from the living state. We actually enter it from the state of death because the force paradigm there is essentially less than the intra-atomic one that governs dominion in physical forms of life. We all thus have to die to enter a permanent "living" state—the state beyond atoms. An ultimate irony, is it not?

The interface between the physical and nonphysical universe is the light or two-dimensional deployment people claim to see in near death experiences. Go through that light and you are truly beyond the Universe of Parts and in the Universe of the Whole, the state of Godhead, En-lighted essence. Most approach the light and return into the universe for another lifetime. You see, there are holes in the floor just before the light. Only the best, the sweetest, the loveliest souls have the momentum not to fall into these trap-door holes before reaching the Universe of the Whole. The rest come back into this universe through birth. The holes in the floor are the wombs, the doorways that admit the individual into another spell of material existence.

To better understand this dynamic, please take a good look at Plate 9, a simple illustration of the life/death interface. You will see a depiction of the space between three hydrogen atoms in ring formation. It is important to note that the entirety of the space *between* atoms, the realm of death, is a whole quantum less in tension than the realm *within* atoms, the realm of physical life. However, there are differing grades of tension within the space between atoms as well.

At the very center of the space, the point furthest from the force of the atoms surrounding it, is a sharply defined point of complete force-lessness. It is the only place where complete forcelessness can exist in the entire universe of forces that is our home in incarnate life. This central point, depicted in white, is the gateway to the Godverse in the Universe of Parts. This is the most beautiful location in the whole physical universe because through this point, the power of God-ness as En-light can come through and touch living matter. I believe that this is a direct doorway though which the Universe of the Whole (Godverse) touches the Universe of Parts. It touches it at all forceless points in any enclosed space between atoms.

The power or *zip* of life is a manifestation of the gradual potential difference between the point of utter forcelessness and its exterior layers, represented by the circles of gradually increasing force seen in the illustration in Plate 9. As the white light shines through the prism of force provided by the tension of the space between atoms, it is split into the seven colors of the rainbow. Each rainbow color has a specific wavelength, forming a signature for a particular level of tension. Violet is the least enforced and red the most. Brown, grey, and black are simply measures of the lack of light that prevails at the edges, near to the force of the surrounding atoms. The further out from the center, the greater the tension. Hence, the series of concentric colored circles that you see in the center of the diagram.

Perhaps Chris, aged 8, saw this rainbow of color during his near death experience. He had nearly drowned when his family's car plunged over a bridge and into the freezing waters of a river near Seattle. His father was trapped in the car and died. His mother and brother miracu-lously swam to safety, while a passer-by dove repeatedly to the sunken car and finally brought Chris's limp body to the surface. He was flown by helicopter to a nearby hospital and ultimately survived. He said: "First the car filled up with water, and everything went all blank. Then I died. I went into a huge noodle. It wasn't like a spiral noodle, but it was very straight. When I told my Mom about it, I told her it was a noodle, but it must have been a tunnel, because it had a rainbow in it. Noodles don't have rainbows in them."[1]

As noted previously, about 70 percent of the multi-trillions of atoms in our body are hydrogen. For purposes of illustration, hydrogen—the simplest, lightest, and least enforced atom—can be visualized as forming the base platform upon which the Godverse and the universe are connected. Hydrogen atoms form a netting or matrix within the living body of an entity; depending upon how these atoms arrange themselves, they form the corridors through which God-light enters. The space between atoms occurs between an aggregate of any three or more hydrogen atoms, up to a maximum of six. These are interlaced with carbon atoms that provide scaffolding and oxygen and other atoms that provide shape. Between and within themselves, both in locked and interconnected spaces, hydrogen atoms enclose whole and partial tetrahedral prisms.

Life forms are held within this space in incarnate life by anchors I call by the acronym STREMS—"Static Termini Resolving En-light into Mechanical Systems." In Plate 9 you can see red centerlines (STREMS) in the midpoint where the circles nearly touch. The STREMS do not contact the hydrogen atoms, but rather hold them slightly apart as a result of the potential difference between the force of the atoms and the no-force of the light of God. The soul has its beginning in Godhead and continues as a connector to it; it is thus not of this world and can *never* contact or sublimate with matter. It remains discrete from any force paradigms within the Universe of Parts. Thus living being is always held in the enforced universe temporarily. Species lines follow tracks of devolution from God down to Prime being (or its equivalent at other locations in the universe), then on down to physical humanity (or its equivalent), then further down to animals, plants, and so on. These lines form tracks of connection all the way back to Godhead, tracks of connection hitched to the center of the space between atoms and twisted through devolution, a series of twists that define the point of devolution of that particular species.

Living things thus have a connection to the center of the space between atoms that nonliving things do not. How then is this line of connection expressed in atomic terms? How can force meet with no-force? The answer lies in the six-atom hydrogen ring. As I have explained, in the center of that six-atom hydrogen ring there is exactly enough space for a seventh hydrogen atom to fit. That seventh atom is untwisted by the surrounding ring such that it takes on its original God-light form. The surrounding six hydrogen atoms act as a jig to do this. The hydrogen atom becomes monatomic hydrogen and instantly disappears. It loses the enforced-ness given to it by the twist. Thus the six-atom-hydrogen ring configuration provides a natural meeting point between force and no-force, and it would follow that all living things have some proportion, no matter how small, of hydrogen in this configuration. It is the entry portal for soul into the fields of life.

The actual atomic elements in the molecules that make up nonliving matter are exactly the same for both living and nonliving matter. The crucial difference lies in the fact that the atoms do not touch when they aggregate as a molecule in living matter, whereas they do touch when they aggregate in the dead matter that makes up nonliving things— tables, chairs, bricks, rocks, and so on. There is, however, a dynamic that operates at the points of relative peace between hydrogen atoms in ordinary water. Those points cannot admit God-light directly from the center of the space between atoms. Only living species with a direct line back to Godhead and a consequent array of six-atom hydrogen rings can do that. However, these points can receive En-light indirectly via its translation through living beings. Thus Masaru Emoto has found that the molecular structure of water can be changed using thought. In the same way, Jesus could use the water contained inside loaves and fish to perform his miracle.

Just as a permanent magnet rotated in a coil of copper wire produces an electrical field and an electrical charge, the human body produces an electric field as the heart pushes iron (hemoglobin) with force through the blood stream, which forms a circulatory coil. The atoms of the body's materiality are held together by minute organically produced electrostatic charges. These act like a central core of permanent magnets. The movement of the bloodstream through all this produces a bio-magnetic field (see Plate 20), which can be verified pictorially with Kirlian photography.

The whole quantum of this force holds a unique fingerprint of three-, four-, five-, and six-atom hydrogen ring deployments within the body. Even the DNA in us is arranged with such a deployment. Dr. John Biggerstaff, a research biochemist originally from England now working in the United States, can show these deployments in spiral sequences along the DNA helix. The good doctor has worked out a theory that might be a stunning affirmation of the connectivity of atoms to a world that lies beyond atoms, which he will present in a chapter devoted to it in my next book.

The bio-magnetic field in living matter keeps the STREMS locked in at the points where atoms are about to touch. This is a crucial point, because at death, when the heart stops beating and the circulation of the blood ceases, the strength of the bio-magnetic field subsides. It no longer has the power to keep the STREMS locked into these points. The STREMS withdraw, along with the soul, to the spaces in between the atoms. Just as water finds its own level, the electro-spatial field of a discarnate individual holds a record of an exact measure of that individual in the form of a quantum holographic shape. This shape has been made in default and is reflected in terms of how much En-light has been allowed to enter within the atoms of a life-form during its incarnation in a physical lifetime. The more En-light that comes in, the more the life-form will have hydrogen arranged in atom rings that contain a higher number of hydrogen atoms.

In order for you to fully grasp what I mean when I say "soul," let me introduce two new concepts to you. The first is what I call the "Brind," a word coined from *brain mind*. This is distinguished from its companion, the *soul mind,* which is centered beyond physical mechanisms such as the brain. These are the two mechanisms through which Godhead

interplays with matter in life-forms. We are all expressions of both acting concurrently. The Brind manifests through a conscious state, and
the soul mind through an unconscious one.

What I call the Brind is the brain-engendered mind that is a *temporary* hive of information gathered in a particular lifetime. It is the
mechanism that sets and protects the values of physical survival. What
I call the soul mind is that eternal background log that accompanies
the Brind and defines an individual's *total* experience prospectus. It
is a combination of all the information an individual has gathered all
through its existence from the beginning of all things.

The Brind, or brain mind, is akin to the RAM facility on a computer and is a sort of "front office mind." All things register in it in real
time, and its function is nothing more than assemblage and simple noti-
fication. It is separated from the big all-encompassing memory in the
computer (the hard disc). Its contents are put into the hard disc by the
press of a button. Until that button is pressed, the RAM has no serious impact on the computer's applications. Like that, in us, the Brind
is a sort of trial mind, where things may be practiced with no serious
consequences. It is a sorting mechanism that distinguishes between the
utilitarian, the spurious, and the deep. It does this through a filter for
acceptance or rejection of all things registered by the conscious awareness of the being. It is tacit and reactive in decision-making. It is the
guardian of all things flesh and operates through the physical senses to
protect the physical brain and the body from harm.

The soul mind, on the other hand, is a profound instrument that
catalogs all properties of thinking after they have been sorted and
accepted by the will. These things are then placed within an eternal
"access repository" or "soul memory" and become a format for acceptance or rejection of all mental momentums through the mechanism of
conscience. The soul mind is eternal; its inception lies in the Godverse,
and it is a catalog of all that has happened to an individual since the
root of that individual emerged from the Godverse. It is not—as some
scientists foolishly believe—made by atoms with mere electrostatic con-

nections that are proximal to one another in single-unit locations. It is instead an aerial for tuning into a compendium of information as vast as all existence can provide. It is the allowance individuality makes to know all things. It is a mechanism that can dictate motive, function, and strength of resolve. It is the master mechanism of thought and is expressed as a morphogenic field within an electro-spatial format that survives the demise or death of the flesh.

Our soul mind, or Morphogenic Electro-Spatial Field (MESF), is the summary of all our mentally engendered actions in the past. In fact, it is a record of all the mentally engendered momentums of all the individual living thinking identities we have been since the universe began. These momentums are not present in the mind as a kind of memory mechanism. Rather, they are expressed as the format or shape of the soul field or MESF, which is released from the body at death.

The clearest view possible of the release of an MESF from a living entity was captured by pure chance in a remarkable film shown on Channel 4 in 1987. The film was called *Man-eating Tigers*.[2] A man-eating tiger is stalked and set up with a buffalo acting as bait. The hunter sits in a machang platform in a tree. The tiger approaches the clearing and is then shot. As the bullets hit home, the film distinctly shows a mist expelled at speed from the tiger's body as it shudders and dies. It is very clear, in fact unmistakable, that the mist has nothing to do with the tiger's expelled breath as it expires. The mist—which emerges whirling out from its midarea—appears to be a manifestation of the tiger's whole body.

There is a delightful account of a near death event recorded in a very modest and charming fashion by a contributor to the www.nderf.org website who refers to herself as Diane B. It seems that just as the mist appeared to blow out of the tiger's body, Diane saw a "whirlwind" leave the top of her father's head as he died:

> The experience I wish to share is one in which my father passed over
> and I witnessed him leaving. I saw a little whirlwind leave the top

of his head as it fell into my arm. Then I saw my mother extend her hand and I heard her laugh. I do remember thinking, "science is trying to measure what I saw." Do you wonder what you look like when you leave your body? This is my answer to what you look like at death. I wonder if that little gray whirlwind leaves if you are coming back? Does it leave and then return? During an NDE does the golden shimmering light lift from the body and return? If this is information not useful to you, I apologize for the inconvenience.[3]

Many soldiers during wartime conflagrations have claimed to see this mist leave the bodies of their dying comrades. Nurses and medical staff have also reported the same mist leaving the bodies of soldiers dying in hospital beds. I believe the MESF itself is a vacuum field and thus is expressed at a temperature of absolute zero (-273°C). The mist is caused when this cold field is released into the surrounding hotter air.

When a person's MESF is released from the space *within* atoms, it then settles at its most perfect resonant point within the diminished force arena of the space *between* atoms. These spaces, created by the atoms around them, are what I call the "waiting rooms of death" or "fields of death": each represents a region of the world beyond atoms where the individual, unique, quantum intelligences and memory fields of living beings linger until resolution into new bodies occurs. In Plates 9 to 15, showing the fields of death, color is used to indicate the strength of the Godverse. Godhead, the point of absolute stillness, is represented by the color white, or "clear." If any entity can be absolutely still with no enforced-ness whatsoever within its own terms of reference, that entity would *be* Godhead. The colors depict the various graduations of force, vibration, and motility that somehow forbid going "clear."

Please remember that the world of the living and the world of the dead are both still within the realms of our space/time quantum and continuum, within the enforced bounds of our universe. If scientists are right, then this arena will be within the margins of the eleven dimensions that they think make up our universal dominion. I realize it is very difficult to visualize the dimensions they say exist other than the ones we call length, breadth, and height. Even space/time is a hard concept to envisage. Yet we have four here, four realizable ideas. If we take these as positive values, the basic existential duality prescribes an opposite to anything. Now try to envisage their opposites: anti-length, anti-width, anti-height, anti-space/time. We now have eight. Then try to see that any dimension begins from a point. We will then have to have an anti-point. That makes ten dimensions. The eleventh is *thought.*

It is extremely important to understand that the *space* between atoms is *not* three-dimensional space of the kind one might find between three billiard balls in ring formation. It is instead more of an interface between two and three dimensions. This challenges our innately parts' conscious, three-dimensional perspective, but a simple example may help to illustrate what I mean. Most of us as children have played with bubble makers, metal or plastic rings on a stick dipped into a dish of liquid soap. The first stage in the procedure is to form a thin film, a two-dimensional disc of soap solution to which we apply a force by blowing on it. The wind we blow first shapes the flat sheet into a hemisphere and then a full sphere, a large strong bubble. Surface tension locks the force in the bubble into a beautiful round sphere. The ball is self-contained and quiet in this shape. Looking at it, no one will see or know there is force involved. But if it bursts, we can see the manifestation of force immediately.

Where a bunch of bubbles join together, their coincident sides will be merged or "flat." That flat planar surface is what I have referred to previously as the space between atoms, which is perhaps better visualized as a two-dimensional planar *extent* than the three-dimensional space that we instinctively imagine it to be. If you look at Plate 13 you will see that the interface forms a Y shape made of three semicircular planes. The very center of that shape, the white in the middle of the purple, is the center of the space between atoms, the natural portal to the Godverse from the universe. From this central point, concentric rings of rainbow colors expand out to the outer skin of each bubble, creating the Y shape. Each of these concentric rings *increases* in tension as it moves from the two dimensional center to the three/four-third/fourth-dimensional edge of the bubble.

Now please have a look at Plate 14. You will see that very little of the space inside the three-atom ring is free from the impinging effects of the surrounding atoms. The space within the six-atom ring, on the other hand, is almost completely free of such imposition. The concentric circles in the center of the three-atom ring range in color through the seven colors of the rainbow to brown, grey and black, while the space inside the six-atom ring is only violet. The reason for this is that the space inside the six-atom ring is not sufficiently enforced to translate the light of God out into all the different frequencies of color. It only translates violet, the least enforced frequency, whereas the space within the three-atom ring has a spectrum of force that translates God-light into all possible frequencies of light and lack of light.

The ring of six hydrogen atoms is the maximum arrangement of hydrogen atoms because this particular formation provides a space in the center of the ring that is the exact diameter of a single hydrogen atom. This diameter formed by six hydrogen atoms in a ring is thus the largest space that can be made entirely forceless in the physical universe. Through this configuration, the fullest charge of God-light (En-Light) that is possible can be taken in. God-light shines through the six-atom rings into all the other hydrogen configurations. However, as the space between these other configurations is more enforced, it will tend to twist the light away from the straight path pointing toward the central portal of entry into the Godverse. That light will be twisted away from the center and toward the surrounding atoms to varying extents. If you look at Plate 15, you will see the gradations of color within the space that lies between the edges of the atoms. These colors depict the angles at which God-light can be diffracted—twisted away from the center and toward the atoms. In life, each individual soul expression translates God-light into a specific range of colors, depending upon the filters or restrictions it places upon that light. In death, however, there are no such filters; each individual's color vibrations are summarized to arrive at an overall level of vibration.

Thus we each have a "soul signature," an arrangement or pattern of God-light that reflects the quality of our being. The charge of un-enforced, intelligent God-light within your body in the spaces between your atoms acts upon the atoms of your life-form something like a vacuum mold, which produces a "shape" that is *You* against the back-drop of the enforced universe. In other words, you are a shape made out of impressed God-light. This shape is uniquely you, the fingerprint of your soul field. The shape is determined by the amount of En-light that has been allowed to enter your physical body in life. You are defined in default by the product of your restrictions or, in other words, the prod-uct of your sins or your ignorance. You are as restricted by this impres-sion as you are identified by it. At the point of physical death, this shape is released by your body; it lingers in the universe and drifts to settle against the God-light background that is everywhere.

Freer, more emancipated souls will find their points of resonance in the space between the atoms of six-atom hydrogen configurations, while the summary of the colors of more restricted souls will resonate more with the space between the rings of three, four, or five hydrogen atoms. This is how discrete identity persists after death: as a fingerprint made up of hives of hydrogen atom ring configurations. The more En-light there is in the space between atoms of an individual, the more he or she will be capable of exercising the power of mind over matter. The saint will have more six-atom hydrogen ring formats within his or her atomic frame, while the sinner will have fewer. I believe Jesus Christ had the maximum number of six-atom ring configurations possible for the human species.

An example of an individual who may have had predominance of four-point hydrogen atom ring configurations can be found in the fol-lowing near death experience:

I had taken about 30 Wellbutrin XL. I instantly regretted it. I have three kids under four. I fell to the floor, got sick, and could not throw up. I was in an ambulance. I began to have seizures, about 25 in eight hours. My body was shutting down. They put me in a drug-induced coma and I was on full life support. They thought I would have a massive heart attack. My family was first told that I had a 20% chance to survive, but I pulled through to 50%. I remember a large silver and black grate coming toward me. It was a large, perfect cube being built with each piece connecting and the loudest sound of metal clanging. I figured it was to cube me, or I was going into it and not coming out. I was scared. I could feel my physical body fight. I was tied down to the bed. I screamed to God I don't want to die, I want to live. I saw my arms in front of me punching and thrashing. It was louder and closer. I knew I was gone. I cried and screamed and fought hard. Then, all of a sudden, rainbow prisms flooded through every cube and I knew in my heart of hearts God had heard my cries. I was lifted up and into Jesus' arms I went. He held me and told me he loved me and I was his. That is what I remember of the experience. It was an orange hue when I was with Christ.[4]

The experient felt as though she was being "cubed," which we can understand in terms of her STREM points in life shaping her for a four-point entry into death. The "orange hue" would have been her overall resolution of color. However, her mental focus toward God and Christ was powerful enough to allow the *light* of the Godverse emanating from the center of the space between atoms to shine through the *prism* of her MESF and allow her another chance to live and change to better perspectives.

In Plates 10 and 11, showing the fields of death, the colors of the rainbow reflect force in lessening measures within each boundary, with black denoting the most force and violet the least. These circles define the transmigration gradients of the soul. In Plate 10, each circle of diminishing size is really a spiral seen on end, so to speak, like the coil of a bedspring seen from the wide bottom, tapering down as it goes away to a point. Plate 11, an illustration that I have entitled "The God Cone," is a close-up of one of these spirals. The colors illustrate levels or platforms. These extra-atomic arenas exactly match the level of the person's knowledge and understanding of all things. Behavior that unifies, makes things coherent, brings about togetherness in social value terms, that is generous and open-hearted, provides care, compassion, and tolerant understanding, and brings about social and spiritual harmony, results in a resonant level toward the violet end of the scale. The opposite behavior results in a soul field toward the red end of the scale.

The various levels shown by the different colors can also be translated into the perspective of shape. The gate admitting to the Godverse (marked in white), shall we say, is a perfect circle, while the red end of the spectrum would correspond to the least coherent shape, as geometrically far away from a sphere as possible. Mental momentums that unite, that seek to create a whole from the part—like love, caring, compassion, and forgiveness—will influence the MESF to change its shape into a circle. Those mental momentums that separate, divide, and dismiss—like prejudice, hate, aggression, angst, and so on—distort and mangle the shape of the MESF. Mangle it enough and you can make it a shape that is less circular than one designated for the human species. During life, our resolves and actions have the power to alter the shape of our MESF, but at the moment of death it is summarized, resulting in an MESF that is either congruent with the portal to the Godverse or distorted into shapes that do not fit this portal. We then come back into life at a point exactly coincident with the display of incoherence we have made for ourselves in our individual capacities to think and resolve this thinking into actions. That point is found in the gonads and wombs of living entities.

The most magnificent aspect of all this is that the power we have achieved in any particular life to see and know things actually designs the shape of our individuality through its effect on our unique electro-spatial field. Unlocked from atoms by death, this new shape then withdraws to its resonant domain in the fields of death, from where it enters life again through a womb. This womb, or whatever life-granting mechanism it might be, will be a "door" of the exact shape, down to the most minute detail, coincident with the display of incoherence made in the previous life through the individual's capacity to think and resolve this thinking into actions. Our bodies and personalities are thus artifacts of the three dynamics of our knowing, understanding, and believing. Even race or gender can be determined by what we need to learn in a particular lifetime. The duration of a lifetime is in fact tacitly decided by these factors as well.

Our destiny beyond atoms at death is thus all decided by our individual capacity to know, to understand, to see, and most of all, by what we have actually done in any particular lifetime. We do only what we know, whether that knowledge is conscious or unconscious. Works are a translation of what we truly are in the center of our being. The Beatitudes as spoken by Christ now seem so relevant. "Blessed are the pure in heart for they shall see God," becomes self-evident. The best souls are the ones with wisdom. Wisdom is knowledge that has been tried in the fire of experience. It is knowledge that connects specific knowledge to all other knowledge. The possessor of wisdom is coherent, together, stable, unifying, and above all just, with a mind that sees the overall and not so much the particular, or a mind that sees the particular in order to see the overall.

Many people who have had near death experiences report a welcoming committee, which meets them and guides them onward. These may well be the souls from whom those people have gained so-called *treasure in heaven,* which might be defined as the power to inherit the momentum and thus drift toward the values that define the Godverse. This momentum can be built up from things thought about and practiced, things believed and accepted as true and worthy by the incarnate soul. This is the whole lesson of Christ's sojourn on this Earth. The great secret of all secrets that he came to convey with his life and his example was: behavior that acts to unite—to bring together, to keep together, and cherish together—has the effect of opening the individual to more and more God-light. When your actions create unity, the increased God-light in turn transforms the enforced atomic structure of your body, until the atoms no longer keep your soul trapped in matter. You will unravel your containment vessel, so to speak, and, like Christ, will finally transfigure into Godhead itself.

Thus the crucial equation of all existential equations is: *That which sustains and builds for better existence set against that which subtracts and destroys the capacity of existence.* The verification of how we all fit into this equation defines the essential difference between us and any other things that exist. As depicted in Plates 10 and 11, the more righteous and beautiful the soul, the more it moves toward the clear forceless point in the center, where in conventional religious parlance the power of the "holy spirit" manifests to provide greater and greater funds of knowledge and power to reach the final clear state, in which the soul is divested of all things of force and gains eternal tenure in the Godverse. But as a soul degrades in any quality such as generosity, kindness, or compassion, it moves outward toward the black ring closest to the atoms. Ultimately, it spirals down to the next level.

In Plate 10, each concentric color in each circle defines a distinct species boundary. The color is a summary of all the soul field expressions tied in to that species. Within each color are thousands of shades of that color; each shade is commensurate with a myriad of subspecies based on their capacity for knowledge and action, particularly the capacity to change levels or—in terms of my representational diagram—to change circles. Such change can include crossing of species lines, that is, moving higher up in the scale of species or moving lower down the scale to a lesser mode of existential manifestation; it can thus be the movement from monkey to human or, what is much more likely, from human to ape and so on down the scale. This may well have been what a woman named Rochelle witnessed in a near death experience after she attempted suicide:

Well, all of a sudden I was in this dark place, blackness, total blackness. No light, just a black void. I knew in my mind I was dead, but

I took the pain with me. All the pain I was suffering I took with me. So, I thought: "Oh, my goodness, I'm going to have to go through this for an eternity!" Then something touched me on the shoulder, and I looked around and here's this big gorilla or this ape. Now, for some reason, I associated this ape with Satan. I knew I had died and was in hell.[5]

She says that "for some reason" she associated the ape with "Satan." Perhaps that is because the true meaning of Satan is the loss of humanity and devolution down into lesser animal species, into our own form of ape.

The pathways of devolution downward into lesser and lesser species are the smaller circles that spiral off the outer ring of each level. The smallest circles touch the edges of the atoms, defining the margins at which life converts into dead, static dependency. Each species line follows a different track from the center of the space between atoms outward, a spiraling pathway of devolution into lesser and lesser expressions of inherent freedom and understanding.

Reincarnation then is the modus of continuity that allows discrete patterns of God-light to present and represent themselves while still trapped in the universe. In this context, it is crucial to remember that the "fields of death" are still entrapments *within* the universe. If you take another look at the diagrams illustrating their deployment (Plates 9 to 15), you will see that these discrete patterns of God-light are like fingerprints defining particular individualities, fingerprints that sign a human or a mouse, an insect or a tree. Their power to dictate the profundity, in reference to Godhead, of any particular entity or being, comes from the number and arrangement of six hydrogen atom ring deployments within their atomic array. Each species is defined by a minimum threshold number of these hydrogen rings and the signature of each individual within that species lies at that threshold or beyond it.

To illustrate this, let's say that *Homo sapiens sapiens* has a threshold number of one hundred million rings. In other words, to be a human you would need a minimum of one hundred million six-atom hydrogen ring configurations. A chimpanzee, let's say, needs eighty million to be a chimpanzee, a baboon fifty million, an elephant forty million, a mouse twenty million, and a tree fifty thousand. A clever mouse might have twenty-two million and be ahead of its contemporaries who might have a few less rings, but if it accumulates fifty million of these rings during the course of a lifetime by adroit and suitable thinking then, when that mouse dies, its MESF will rearrange in a pattern that will dictate that it is born an animal with an intrinsically higher status of mind sense. The soul field of that mouse when it dies will dictate a shape and color (see Plates 10 and 11), that will fit a "door" of the same shape (or color) that exists in the fields of death. It will seek to find such a door back into the fields of life when it is born again, a door corresponding to a higher animal shape.

In this illustration, *size* in terms of the form and structure of an animal species has *no* direct correlation with the magnitude of intelligent function and awareness of an entity. The species *Elephantus maximus*, will not, as a function of its size, have a larger six-ring atom threshold than *Homo sapiens sapiens*! It is the amount of awareness, knowledge, perception, and capacity for free choice set against the perfection of these elements as they exist at Godhead that correlates directly with the assemblage of six-hydrogen-ring presentations within any given individual. So, if an elephant builds better awareness, knowledge, perception and a capacity for the exercise of free will more commensurate with the God-frame during its lifetime than a the minimum "species defining reincarnation threshold" for a human being, then that elephant's soul field will dictate reentry into life as a human being. It *could only* enter into incarnation through the door designed for humanity.

There is a threshold of quantum "knowing" past which reincarnation into the physical living state of being is impossible. This is what the Buddha called *nibbana*. It can only be glimpsed in physical life, but it can actually be attained beyond the enforced grip of atoms after death, following the release of the individual electro-spatial field from the physical body. It is said Gautama Buddha reached this point of quantum knowing while seated under a Bo tree in what is Bodhgaya, a location in India. Jesus Christ actually went past this point because he did the work and the gaining of the knowledge at one and the same time.

Looked at from the end on, the concentric circles in Plate 10 all form tunnels. I believe this is the tunnel seen by those who have gone through near death experiences. Each of us has our little spiral tunnel, and its size and color depend on how we have translated the ethics of Godhead in our immediate life. It is the connection to Godhead that makes things live and the profundity of that connection that makes things live *intelligently* with greater and greater scope for making choices. We as a species *Homo sapiens sapiens* thus have the greatest and most profound connection to God-ness and through it to Godhead of all species on this planet. Perhaps all human beings and all dominant intelligent species on planets all over the universe go through the main central circle (tunnel), with the very best going through the center into the realms of Godhead, the domain of eternal life from which they will never have to return to another physical temporal life. The rest will make it into the outer rings to return to another life in whatever planet in the universe they reincarnate according to the dictates of their personal karma. From there they will begin the process of trying to get to the center all over again.

The notion of karma simply describes the cause and effect, the action and reaction, of one soul twisting another further away from the center of the space between atoms. If one human being twists another human being away from the center, then that human being is also twisting his own soul away from the center, because he is the point from which the twist originates. The only way he can free that twist in himself is to untwist it in the individual he has affected. A soul entering life from the fields of death follows the twisting spirals of karmic debt. The same applies for actions that help to focus other people toward the center. These actions form connections with others that allow us to straighten our tracks to God-ness, which will pull our soul toward the center when we die.

The insights into the existential dominion I have outlined above appear to be confirmed by many NDEs. For example, a lawyer in New York experienced the following in an NDE following cardiac and respiratory arrest:

Suddenly I found myself floating in darkness, being carried along by a current of some sort, like a boat going down a river. Then the pace started to accelerate. It resembled a very dark wind or railroad tunnel. It was enormous with concentric, circular bands at regular intervals.[6]

An eighteen-year-old, Michael, suffered a serious brain injury. In his NDE, he describes hearing "what sounded like the crack of a whip, and also the feeling that I was traveling along the wavy line of the whip as it cracked." Avon Pailthorpe says that in her NDE after a serious car accident she was: "In a black tunnel, or funnel, shooting through this tunnel, head first, spinning round the edges—like water going down a plug, or a coil."[7] Allison Orton says that when she fell off a garage roof when she was nine years old: "Everything around me became very removed, hazy, and distant. A spiral going around and around in diminishing sized and concentric circles overwhelmed me. Then, I was no longer there."[8]

Here is an account of Nigel, a New Zealander, describing the accident that led to his remarkable NDE in February 2004:

A kite surfing accident caused me to be thrown approximately 70 meters horizontally and at least 6m up in the air and into the edge of the roof of my house. I suffered 21 fractures of my hips, ribs, and shoulders, severe concussion, punctured lung, severe internal and external bruising and shock amongst other injuries. I was basically unconscious for 14 hours with about 3 episodes lasting seconds each of semi-consciousness.[9]

Nigel found that a centrifugal force was pulling him out toward the outer edges of a "swirling mass of beings" that he encountered at the start of his experience:

All the beings around me were very black and the atmosphere was one of depression and resignation. I was being pushed along very fast by the swirling mass of beings, some looking like walking skeletons. I had the feeling that, as we were moving round, we also were moving toward the outer edge of the swirling mass where these beings simply fell off the edge into nothingness or death. I had the feeling I did not want to go there and tried to struggle against the moving mass of people. It was hard not to be driven along by them, kind of like fighting against a current while crossing a river. At some stage I became aware that far in the distance, in the center of this huge mass of beings was a bright light. Sometimes, while struggling to fight the current I caught a brief and faint sight of this light. I wanted to get closer to this light.[10]

The "current" that Nigel experienced would have been the forces at the edges of atoms and the souls who exist there who are trapped in these forces pulling him in. Nigel found that he could somehow escape the current and move toward the light at the center:

I found either by trial and error or else by some external guidance, that the only way I could get closer to this light was to think pure thoughts of helping others. I tried to do this and found that by focusing just on helping others, or trying to develop compassion, I was able to edge closer to the light at the center. As soon as I had a self-centered thought or any other thought other than helping others, I was immediately thrown toward the outside of the huge revolving mass and had to struggle back toward the center. The outer edges of the mass were revolving with thousands of beings at a nauseatingly fast pace. As I got closer to the center, the pace slowed down and the energy of the beings became much lighter and less frantic.[11]

The "pace" would have "slowed down" toward the center because there the forces generated by the surrounding atoms would be least. This is a remarkable near death experience because it clearly affirms the power of thought in compassion and selflessness to pull a soul into the realms of least force in the center of the space between atoms. Nigel goes on to say:

> I passed several people I recognized on my way toward the center and it felt like I could see by their colors radiating from their bodies what sort of people they really were beneath their outward appearances. If I made any judgment on them, I was immediately thrown toward the outer edge of the sphere and back to the nauseating, frantic black crowd.[12]

Thus this NDE affirms my proposition that qualities of being are expressed in the space between atoms as differing gradients of enforcedness that translate into what we call color.

One NDE describes clearly the corridors between atoms, like a network of tunnels:

> I was sucked into a tunnel, and heard a sound like monstrous fans. It was not actually that, but it's the closest way I can describe it. It was a beautiful sound. The tunnel was dark, with regular open spaces in the side, through which I could see other people traveling in other tunnels. There was one area I passed by where there was a group of drab, dull unhappy people who were unable to move. Then I saw the distant light.[13]

The "open spaces in the side" of the tunnel through which she could see other "spirits" are perhaps the spirals leading out toward the atoms. Each concentric circle she passes through would have an "open space" though which those resonant with that level of vibration would pass.

John Star was told at the end of his NDE: "You have seen enough of eternity. It's not time yet for you to stay. Return now to the Land of Shadows where the mortal creatures play and be a puff of dust in the wind without being blown away."[14] What is the "land of shadows?" Most people who experience NDEs describe a place full of the most beautiful, all encompassing light, a "living light with vitality and feeling" that bathes every pore of their being. When they return to their bodies, they are struck by the dull, dark contrast that they find in the "land of shadows." We truly are living in darkness. The physical world that seems so enticing and so beautiful to so many of us allows us only the most microscopic sight of the glory that is experienced in NDEs. The gel of force that holds us bound blinds us to that beauty, and that blindness only serves to entrap us further.

Many NDE experients describe the tunnel through which they travel to the realm of light as having a certain "velvety" blackness. Let me explain what they might in fact be describing: in physical life the spectrums of color that we see are expressions of electromagnetic light; this light is distinct and different from the "light" that is witnessed in NDEs. The light of NDEs comes from a source that starts at the no-force point in the center of the space between atoms—it is essentially nonatomic, as it originates from the Godverse. The spectrum of electromagnetic light, on the other hand, starts at the interface between the Godverse and the physical universe. Its scale starts at the lowest point of force and ends where the first atom, hydrogen, starts.

When we die and the physical senses cease, we no longer see electromagnetic light; consequently what we experience on the way to the space between atoms is a dark tunnel devoid of light. Without our physical senses to divert us, we are able to view the atomic realm as it truly is, almost devoid of the light of God, a world of shadows set in sharp contrast to the world of light that is the space between atoms. It is intriguing that the word "velvety" is often used to describe that blackness. Velvet has a sheen; that sheen may well be the tiny proportion of God-light that can reach our living atomic state. Awareness in the physical living intra-atomic state is only the sheen of the light of the

Godverse glistening on the darkness of the atomic world. It is no wonder that most of those who experience the world beyond the physical in NDEs are awestruck by it.

There can of course be no empirical proof of life after death. *Yet.* As science advances, however, I predict that one day not too far away, on the longest meter bands of radio frequencies, scientists will be able to hear and—through conversion mechanisms—peek into the folded dimensions of the realms of death, and the dead will *come alive.* We will have perhaps a camera-eye view of the emergence of an MESF the moment someone dies and be able to follow it through into the space between atoms and the spiraled shells of colors that are the domains beyond the physical living state. I predict that their "strings" and "branes" and "multiple exigent dimensions" will simply imply that $e = mc^2$ holds the biggest surprise of their lives: the great missing ingredient in all mathematical formulas. It ends where it shouldn't in life and goes beyond into the realms of what we call death. They will affirm finally that discrete individual living beings continue past death and return into life in a two-way stream. They will even prove that a single glory beyond all glory we might term God or Godhead exists beyond the scales of finite universes, as an implied horizon where all absolutes are confined, in a center beyond the capacity of physically manifest intelligences to perceive.

The truth is always simple. If anything is complicated, it is only on the way to the truth. Thus to me the hallmark of all temporal existential being is revealed as life, death, and life again. This is a seemingly endless chain if, and only if, it is trapped in universes of the part. We proceed as life forms in a continuity that goes past death and returns from death metered by an outlay of behavior engendered by *mind*. This power of mental inflection is the driver toward or away from an entry point into the Godverse that may be called a second birth, a birth devoid of the impulsions of the phenomenon called force. We all have the possibility of reentering the Godverse devoid of force through the auspices of the non-enforced God-light within all life forms, which animates us and at the same time gives us the power to retrace our steps back into an eternal scale from whence we all have come. This is beautifully summed up by the Christian teacher when he said that what condemns a person is not anything external, such as social status, biological form, or clothing, but rather what comes from within:

> Woe unto you, scribes and Pharisees, hypocrites! For ye make clean the outside of the cup and of the platter, but within they are full of extortion and excess. (Matthew 23:25)

A life span can be likened to a journey up or down an escalator. The escalator is the universe of atoms, and the direction of the stairway is *down* as a result of entropy. We are all, in effect, struggling to go up a down escalator while we live. We can move up at a fast enough pace to eventually allow us to get to the top, which is Godhead. Alternatively, we can move up at the same pace that the escalator is moving down, in which case we will stay at the same point on the gradient of the escalator and get nowhere. If, however, we stand still, the escalator will carry us to the bottom, and if we actually walk with a downward momentum we will reach the bottom faster. All along the course of the escalator there are entry (birth) and exit (death) points.

We enter the stairway at birth with a built-in momentum to go up or down. This momentum and direction is defined by the qualities, knowledge, and purpose engendered by mind in all our previous lifetimes. If we do the things that unite and bring things together through the modus we call love, we add power to our momentum and thus to our ascent up the escalator. If we do the opposite, we move in the opposite direction. The higher we ascend, the greater our freedom to see existential truth. Conversely, the lower we drop, the more we are restricted in insight, intuition, and the ability to make choices.

The individual MESF is programmable to be either heavy or light, so to speak. We add weight to it when we act in ways that separate parts, and we lighten it when we do the opposite. Heaviness makes it harder to move up the escalator and easier to be pulled downward in line with the second law's momentums toward chaos. Acquiescent, easily led, unquestioning, and lost minds tend to move ever downward. This changes the body's aerial power so that it receives the signals that are within and of the paradigm of the enforced universe. The Brind, or brain mind, is a specialist in receiving such signals, which of course prompt it to instigate behavior that will allow its own categories of need to be filled, the needs of the flesh and all the things that allow more for sensory pleasure and function.

The Brind provides a tangible sense of meaning because information is fed through its power outlets, the five physical senses: sight, touch, hearing, taste, and smell. It is the master control for defending the apparatus that provides the senses themselves in the first place, namely the nonphysical powers of awareness, thought, and will. The irony is that *it* then commands the nonphysical apparatus to pay attention to *it* and allow *it* to command. Most of humanity falls prey to this command and is dominated by it to damnation.

The easiest thing is to go with the momentum of the escalator. If you try to move against that momentum, you will feel unbalanced at first. For a moment you might feel as though you could fall. You turn around and look up at the top of the escalator and your physical senses send you a definite message that it is far more comfortable to turn back around again and "go with the flow." That message is from the Brind. But imagine there is something wonderful at the top of the escalator, something that you long to reach, despite all the odds against you doing so. It is so enticing, so inspiring, that it drives you past that initial feeling of insecurity and you travel upward. That is the power of the soul mind to counter the signals of the Brind. The faster you run, the surer your step will be, the less insecure you will feel when moving against the momentum of the escalator. The more hesitant you are in your decision to move upward, the more likely it is that you will lose your balance and fall. One thing is certain: you cannot move up and down at the same time, or in other words, you cannot "serve two masters."

The Brind of course is as necessary for temporal physical well-being as the soul mind is for the well-being of the individual on an eternal scale. The great thing is balance. That requires recognition of the danger of the Brind's imbalanced support of a temporary state of being, which can trap you and damn your individuality forever. Awareness and will, the principle aspects of the Godverse, command the functioning of both the brain mind as well as the soul mind from the "outside." They are independent facilities, expressing themselves from the platform Godhead has established in the places within the atom itself and between the atomic hives that make up all physical living things, where the expression of force is completely absent.

I call En-light the "outsider" within individuality, because it is not of this universe. It is our great hope. It cannot be contaminated by anything of this world and will always be our hedge against the pull of the Pole of Chaos through entropy. This is the most crucial point of all. Its power may be increased or decreased within us only by and through its own recognizance, *nothing else*. En-light is a measure of all expressions of the Godverse within us. It is the sum of the understanding we have of the power of union against the power of division, and all the knowledge we have that leads to this understanding. It leads us to the modality of eternal life where no frames of destruction can touch us. This glory is identified and spoken about by all the great religious teachers but described in different ways. For Buddhists, it is a secular principle we may call Godhead. Christians describe it more anthropocentrically as a personalized principle called God. All other great faiths take positions that are similar with one or the other or between the two. In the end, it is *one* principle.

What am I really saying here in all that's preceded? I am saying that all individuality was once a single collective frame we call Godhead. We as living beings now exist in separated individualities, and each individuality has a status against the finality of Godhead. This status is expressed as various degrees of awareness, knowing, understanding, and thus freedom to choose that which provides the maximum freedom of choice. I hope that is not too *Zen* for you. The incidental, natural, logical cascade measures the parts of the whole against the whole as individual measures of choice-ability. We make our own ranges of choice and at one and the same time the size of the power to choose them. Our life status is a simple product of this.

Let's get a little less lyrical and more literal and definite. Let's begin by acknowledging ourselves as human beings who are a species still connected to the origin of all origins. We are on a solid ball of matter called a planet that, unlike us, is not alive in its own terms. This planet is a provider of space and extension that acts as host to thousands of other species or divisions of life-forms that are marginalized by their own ranges of choice and their own individual propensities to make choices within those ranges.

Living being in this universe is thus twisted, mangled God-ness. The range of choices within each margin will be forever limited if this is a fixed system and nothing from outside it can enter. Any increase or decrease in individual stances depends on something much grander coming into the arena from the outside. So enter Redeemers, or "Sons of Man," all over the universe from a situation outside. They are the great informers who constantly re-inform the "lost sheep" (those who are still trapped in Universes of Parts in physical forms yet are still able to understand them) of the lost history and perspectives of their being and nature once upon a time when it was possible to return to the Godverse at a whim of thought. And so it would seem that the making of an exit into oblivion for our entire species has taken a few million years to complete. Our so-called wondrous development into our present prospectus, so hailed and lauded at every signpost of culture—every margin of technology, when looked at in terms of the only thing that matters— the survival of the entity in a mode to know, to realize, and decide has, unnoticed, provided the means for the extinguishing of that same entity and all such living entities with spectacular expeditiousness.

It is a chilling thought isn't it? Yet I fear it may well be true. It would explain so well why Christ came shouting from the very beginning that we were all damned and that he had come to save us. Save us indeed. It seems his sacrifice has made us more and more hidebound. We begin by killing the glorious phenomenon that came to save us and we have continued killing, maiming, dismissing, dividing, and hating our fellow human beings and brushing aside what was obvious to see, millennium after millennium, century after century, till we cannot see the wood for the trees anymore.

We have, of course, noticed our peril, or so it seems. We even strive to mitigate the danger with conference, march, and platform. But the "devil's whisper" is relentless, for it is the summary of the very atoms that make us up. The signposts of doom, alas, were never really a sanction for the inertia of procedure within the entropic psyche, from danger point to danger point. It never allowed for the adequate summary of consequence. There is little for addition to do in such circumstance. We are like the laboratory mole that fixes his gaze upon the next immediate answer, in his tunnel-visioned progress to consequences of dread.

History has taught us unequivocally that to make the discovery more important than its existential meaning is to assassinate both the discovery and the meaning. Yet, again and again, the beguiling sirens of the "flesh" have been such a formidable screen that they have blinded us to this rule, while the universal anthem of disposal—entropy—has made us its machines of final disposal easily, and we wait. We all wait for the final outcome.

It is so easy to make prognostications of doom, to sit on a base that all too often has delivered a dead reckoning, yet never learn our lesson. We can see that the misleading geometry of material development, with its sharp, clear, sometimes pretty lines, hasn't changed the deeper underbase of human motive for caring for the betterment of the species. As a whole, we kill more, we maim more, we dismiss more than ever—on no more a decision-point than the mere color of a skin, the shape of a physical contour. The deadly tribal lines speak more evocatively in the affairs of humanity than they ever did.

A right to believe in independence becomes a panordinate threat to the instinct of the herd. We have not developed out the animal sense and its attendant paranoia against difference of any kind. Instead of an increase in the sense of our group identity, in species terms, for the betterment in coresponsive social perspectives, the deadly entropic drive has increased the proeclectic drive in the "McLuhan" sense that lauds individual goal orientation at the cost of the group. Such perspective rules the day wherever we look in the occidental world, and it is my firm belief that it will rule our future days with increasing strength and bring about the prophecies of grand insight we tend to dismiss as heraldic pulchritude. Entropy isolates to separate.

# 16

# Ghost Meets Grey

From their hiding places, whether on our planet—beneath the surface of the earth, under the ice of the North and South Poles, in the ocean deep—or on the dark side of the moon, Mars, or wherever they might be, Grey aliens are watching as tens of thousands of the souls of dead people go to be merged in quantums of colored light.

As I have noted earlier, they are able to follow a particular Morphogenic Electro-Spatial Field from one paradigm of existence to another: from life to death and back into the wombs of women. It is this facility of natural birth that they want most of all for themselves because, more than anything else, they want to convert their status of artificial being into a natural one. It is their whole and final intention in all they do throughout the Universe of Parts. Like Pinocchio seeking to be a living little boy, the Greys want to become natural living forms. They think that then they could abandon their search through the universe for supplies of new DNA; they would no longer need the huge and secret effort at hegemony of entire planets, to abduct and re-scope natural indigenous life-forms for their DNA. But they are doomed to failure, because the ability to be born only comes with having a beginning in the Godverse. This they can never have. They will never be able to acquire an MESF, no matter how sophisticated their technology.

The trouble is that these "demons" of the universe do not understand why. They cannot understand the mechanism that unites with

Godhead because they are entities derived wholly and utterly from a purely physical and material paradigm. Their programming is incapable of providing any description or reference beyond that of atomic derivation. It cannot tell them about that which is beyond space, time, and matter; it cannot explain the nature of an eternal, ephemeral Godhead, or the nature of the Godverse as distinct from a temporal, tangible, physical universe. It cannot describe an ephemeral quark called "feeling." The Greys are laboring under a giant misapprehension, totally oblivious to the existential hierarchy that pervades the universe. In their mindsets, they are whole and real as themselves. They do not know that they are simply machines—created as merely utilitarian entities to serve the practical needs of the clones of Prime beings—and that machines originate only in universes of parts and matter and force.

All humanity that is uncluttered by Grey-engendered genes and biosynthetic postulations senses that there is an intercommunicating world: life to death and back again. But our science can only deal with material and physical measurement and has not yet arrived at a methodology that can measure and catalog the nonmaterial world where the levels of enforced resolutions are at their minimums. Death lies here, at the interface between the enforced and measurably real and the unenforced, nonmeasurable, but nevertheless just as real. This threshold area where the inertial and kinetic force that defines the atom begins is like a skin that separates the two worlds.

With reference to Plate 15, imagine that skin as the very edge of a whirlpool that is spinning in water. The atoms that make up the matter of the universe are like multitrillions of spinning whirlpools. The area of water between the whirlpools is the space between atoms: the fields of death where the information field that defines us as living individuals migrates when we die. The format that defines our migration is the quality of the information held in the soul field. Its quantity and quality are measured as a propensity to drift toward the edges of the atoms surrounding the space between them or the propensity to drift toward the center points of the spaces between atoms. This is the most crucial of all things. This drift decides whether you go to the Godverse (heaven) or return to the universe (the true hell) in the process we know as reincarnation.

If an individual is focused, mentally and in terms of behavior, *predominantly* on values and priorities that are self-centered and thus promote existence in a separate physical state (such as materialism, envy, possessiveness, etc.), that individual can become caught in the spinning momentum of the whirlpools. The momentum and direction of such a person is toward that which is of atoms, so the MESF is likely to remain in an *atom-hugging* state at the point of release from the intra-atomic state. Conversely, focus and momentum toward values such as compassion and generosity—which bring together and thus point to a state where all is united, the Godverse—will carry an MESF straight past the edges of atoms toward the blue, indigo, and violet in the center of the illustration. These colors are away from the whirlpools of force, while the yellow, orange, red, and all the colors down to black are affected by the pull.

This skin—which is a kind of trap—may have been witnessed during an NDE described by Maurice Rawlings in his book *To Hell and Back,* in which Lee Merritt, a young man, became aware of "demons within the walls" of a dark tunnel.[1] The "walls of the tunnel" might well describe the margins of atoms. Rawlings also quotes George Godkin's account of his NDE in 1948 in which he reports that "the darkness of Hell is so intense that it seems to have a pressure per square inch." Could this "pressure" he felt be a product of the forces at the edges of atoms? In her account of her NDE, Dr. Rene Turner reports a sight of the edges of atoms as she moved away from them toward the "light" that is so commonly seen in near death experiences:

> I was moving head first through a dark maelstrom of what looked like black boiling clouds, feeling that I was being beckoned to the sides, which frightened me. Ahead was a tiny dot of bright light which steadily grew and brightened as I drew nearer.[2]

In Plate 15, the black, seemingly hairy, edges of atoms depict the tangible, substantial nature of the forces in which MESFs can become entangled. Intriguingly, Dr. Turner felt as though she was "being beckoned to the sides" and it frightened her. Thus she was aware of the whirling forces (the "black boiling clouds") pulling at her.

Those MESFs that are primitive and lack knowledge or spiritual insight and perceptive power tend to linger in this skin, this margin. They are what might be called "earth-bound spirits" by those who are mediums. I would define them as what we call "ghosts." By ghosts, I don't mean those specters seen as electromagnetic fragments trapped in loops of quantum waves anchored to particular spots on the planet that become visible at certain times to certain people. These are images trapped in fields of eddy currents, caught in areas where magnetic fields, produced either naturally or artificially by environmental conditions, reveal mental pictures. In such places, people see whole past situations in time where panoramas are revealed, such as armies, churches, temples, castles, countryside, and so on. These are time-slippage points, or "electro-photograms," that sit in various locations in standing waves waiting for living beings to enter these points. When a living mind enters the area, it switches into these points and into past situations in an instant. I believe this is because the En-light in the spaces between atoms of living beings *sees* the entire picture of all happenings as past, present, and the future all locked into one aspect, devoid of spatial separation.

The ghosts that I am referring to are discarnate soul field individualities locked by a restricted state of mind focus into an in-between state in this universe. The crucial accessions of mind determine a hierarchy of range and placement when we move on from life to death. They define future statures of existence, either through return to an atomic state or states of survival beyond the scales of force. Individual entities gain such status through efforts of mind focus through knowledge of the entire existential scale available in the whole Omniverse. Those who determine the truths of existential dominion and move in behavioral modes commensurate with the union of fractions move toward states outside force and thus the Godverse. Those who are held in behavioral modes that divide, separate, and restrict will linger in paradigms of existence where such is the norm.

The results of focus can be envisaged as a property of heaviness or lightness. Let me present you now with a very important model. Please refer to Plate 12: "The Portal of Death." Imagine a horizontally spinning plate. The plate is a cross-section of a shape, the twisted doughnut shape I have called a Moroid, which defines the three/four-dimensional form of our universe. The plate, or slice through the Moroid, is inscribed with concentric rings, each defined by a color. Black on the outside ring goes down to grey, to brown, to red, to orange, to yellow, to green, to blue, to indigo, to violet, to gold, to silver, to white and then finally clear, or no color, at the very center point. Each color division has myriad shades of that same color, and these shades gradually change the color from the full color on the outside getting lighter as it progresses inward, into its next full color shade and so on down to clear at the very center. The inertia of the spin produces both centripetal force and centrifugal force. They act at ninety degrees to one another. The closer to the center, the less the force. Anything on the plate in the center will drop into that central point of forceless-ness. There is thus effectively force distribution in all ways at every point. The strength of this force is stronger toward the outermost edges of each color, with the direction of the force reversing down in quantums at the points at which one color changes to another.

There are twelve color demarcations in all, defining twelve color domains, which in turn represent qualities of mind. Just as we have seen in Plates 10 and 11, qualities such as kindness, compassion, generosity, honesty, tolerance, forbearance, welcome, patience, mercy, all have a momentum toward the clear center ring. Opposite qualities produce a momentum toward the black outer one. Each living entity and the individuality of that entity is defined by a series of these colors as qualities of their nature. These, in a nutshell, define their *God-likeness*. The colors are simply representative of a drift or momentum toward or away from Godhead.

The conglomerate of all or any of these colors together defines a "core" color for an individual. Thus a central momentum of soul drift is produced that places an individual's soul (an individual's accumulation and quantum of all experience and thus God-likeness from the beginning of the universe) more toward the edges or the center. If that individual dies, this core color will represent the overall color in the space between atoms at which this individual will place him or herself. It decides which waiting room or level the soul will enter while it awaits reincarnation into incarnate life.

The colors from green/blue to clear tend to attract the MESF in the direction of the Godverse. This attraction is not through force, but through the power of revelation through mind. The more knowledgeable the soul is, the lighter it gets, growing in the capacity to rise above the day's own troubles and see things in deeper meaning. An MESF with sufficient insight will be able to will itself out of the clutches of the vortex down, freeing it to move out and away from what the Hindus term *sansara*—the obligation to fulfill karma or debt to a fellow human entity, in a physical life and in a physical context. The individual would thus no longer be subject to the exigencies of being born again with a physical body.

The more ignorant an MESF, the heavier it gets. It is thus more susceptible to falling into the heavier color bands (see Plate 12) such as red, brown, grey, and black, through the sucking action of the physical enforced state of existence. Ignorance in knowing, and thus the commensurate lack of an ability to make decisions that free you from such ignorance, ensures a steady progress to a situation where you can get pulled into incarnacy. Most of us remain caught, through our own individual fault and no one or nothing else's. We lose perception of our power to gain an eternal status as we decay, victims of the relentless entropic drift that obscures our vision of the rules that can reverse the process, even though redeemers come to remind us. The individual entity that has not developed the level of God-light (or En-light) commensurate with readmission into the Godverse will be caught in a situation without certainties, where existence prevails in a situation of Russian roulette.

If we all originated in Godhead, then there must be a mechanism that reflects this. I believe there is such a mechanism and the clue to it and perhaps the proof of it lies in the fact that the same parents produce children that are very different from one another. While brothers and sisters might share the same parental biology, they will not and cannot share the same soul connection line back to Godhead. This is reflected in the fact that every sperm and every ovum is genetically unique. These germ cells are made from the biological prospectus of the same individuals, but the process that produces them, called meiosis, ensures that each cell is different from the other. Our genes and the twenty-three pairs of chromosomes that contain them are inherited, with one of each pair coming from each parent. This means that sperms and eggs contain half the number of chromosomes of any other cells in the body. Sperms and eggs receive their half-portion of genes through meiosis. Scientists believe that meiosis *randomly* generates a staggering seventy trillion possible combinations of chromosomes in the offspring!

First, the twenty-three parental pairs of chromosomes match up at the center of the sex cell. When the cell divides, each daughter receives only one-half of each pair. A unique ovum is produced through meiosis at the ovulation point of the female each month. Could it be that at this early stage the ovum is given the signature of an individual soul that will enter into physical life if fertilization later happens? An adult male, on the other hand, manufactures an average of eighty-five million sperm cells each day. *Each* of those cells is unique! Could it be that the gametes of each male provide enough permutations to match exactly the nature of each differing "soul field" ready to reincarnate into the world? In other words, could we males be carrying the formula, or potential bodies, for each and every soul that can be reborn at any one time? Perhaps this is why each ejaculation carries sperms in the tens of millions. This would suggest that every male in the world has a stock of differing gametes all able to readmit into life the soul of a particular African bushman who might have died yesterday!!!

The male of the species would thus provide the "soul map" covering the vast range of souls available for reincarnation at any particular point. Individual souls are constantly being reborn into life or entering into death. Thus the map is ever changing. For that reason, it must be continually revised and renewed; perhaps this is why the male is continually making new sperm. Could it then be that the female of the species, with the single ovum she produces, isolates the individual soul from the map of souls that she has been given by the male? That soul's specificity would then dictate the genetic prospectus of the ovum (based of course within the limits of what her own genetic prospectus can provide). Then at fertilization, when the maternal and paternal chromosomes exchange DNA, new gene combinations are again created within the chromosomes based upon the dictates of the individual soul forming its new body.

The enormous amount of sperm is thought to be an insurance policy against the many physical impediments to fertilization. But eighty-five million sperm cells a day is surely overkill in the extreme, even if it is set against the most hazardous scenario for fertilization to take place. Nature's assemblies are always wonderfully economic and ergonomic. Why then is the most important process of all, reproduction, such an inefficient chaotic amelioration, according to the version of conception that the biologists would have us accept? I believe it is not inefficient. It is as efficient as possible if you take into consideration the fact that it is a built-in mechanism that provides for reincarnation, karma, soul fields, and all the other artifacts of the other half of physical life—death.

Soul fields linger in the waiting rooms of death beyond the direct effect of atomic force until an opportunity arises to reincarnate into another physical modality of existence in as relevant a situation and place as possible to reconcile what ancient Eastern theosophy refers to as karmic debts. Each spermatozoon held in the body of each human male alive represents a single soul in the fields of death able to reincarnate at the dictates of karma. Millions of soul fields commensurate with specific karmic debts await birth into a life-form that will enable them to repay their debts, to right whatever wrong they have done to an individual, in the same fashion, with the same compensatory value. They will be born again and again till they achieve full remission of the debt owed. To do this, they will have to be in a situation in which they can confront the individual to whom they owe the debt. This is of course horrendously difficult to achieve.

Let's say you killed someone in cold blood to steal their money. This might mean that the individual you killed was denied the right to live a life where he or she might have so adorned their thinking, knowing, and doing capacity that on death they would have escaped the wheel of rebirth and gone on to become a being in a higher state of existence. You took this possibility away from them by killing them and prematurely stopping their development to an advanced state of spiritual enlightenment. How do you compensate them for this? Terrifying isn't it?

If you have to return to life in order to meet a karmic debt, then a particular sperm commensurate with this debt is activated in the male who will be your father. This sperm will fertilize the female partner with whom your father copulates, so that you can be born with the precise physical, social, and psychological attributes that particular debt dictates.

You can imagine, then, that there can be no greater horror than deliberately sought abortion. If abortions are freely available and are carried out, then soon the natural balance of debt-engendered reincarnation will be upset; in time, no soul will be able to come through to the exact conditions required for a particular karma to be expedited. We as a species will soon be wandering forever, perhaps in a timeless sea, until somewhere in some planet in the universe the opportunity arises where we can reincarnate and expedite our karmic debt to the individual or individuals concerned.

This makes us truly our brother's keeper and requires that no impediments of any sort be put in the natural way of things that enable this to happen. If you are a racist, for example, and have spoken or acted against the freest available contingencies of human kinship and fellow-ship, you are likely to be damned more severely than if you were not a racist. In an ethnic or sectarian sense, you have contrived your own damnation, because you are likely never to be able to expedite your karma with any social faction other than your own! This will lead to the point where you are trapped forever, never able to find the natural route back to a reconciliation of your karmic obligations. For example, if you are living as an American Southern white racist, no inner prompt may lead to consort with African Americans, preventing you from ever expediting karma you might have with one of their number. Your mind would be caged. You would likely never take any opportunity to even approach an intimate loving relationship with a black person, making it impossible for you to ever find your way out of physical life systems in material universes. You will thus be cursed to wander in between universes, bereft of the best dominions for reconciling your karmic debt.

Ghosts stand as a warning to all. They remain trapped for hundreds, perhaps thousands, of years because they have lost the insight of how to increase God-light within their physical status. They linger in the fields of death, sometimes forever, though most change downward over time into states where no format for the retrieval of human propensities exists any longer for them. They linger, depending on our power to connect with them from this world through the life/death interface. That connection is thought. A connection from a living being to the extra-atomic world can be created through deeply focused thought, sometimes described as "prayer," which allows ghosts some sight of what might be done in their predicament to stop their entrapment.

Thought communion is still possible across the separating interface because thought is common to both sides. The power of thought exists discrete from the direct atomically enforcing mechanisms such as electromagnetism. A link to Godhead still survives for ghosts through the line of God-light with which they entered this universe. They are still connected through this imperishable line.

The power of such communion through thought is beautifully

illustrated in Maurice Rawlings' aforementioned book *To Hell and Back*. This particular example was a life-changing experience for Dr. Rawlings that made him look far more seriously at the subject of NDEs. It happened in 1977 when he was resuscitating a forty-eight-year-old mail carrier, Charlie McKaig. When Charlie's heart stopped responding, Rawlings made an attempt to insert a temporary pacemaker. During this procedure, in between convulsions and turning blue, Charlie screamed the words: "Don't stop! I'm in hell! I'm in hell!" Dr. Rawlings assumed Charlie was hallucinating, but at the same time he was amazed that during such a painful procedure he would beg him to continue. "Most victims say 'Take your big hands off me, you're breaking my ribs.' But he was saying the opposite: 'For God's sake. Don't stop! Don't you understand? Every time you let go I'm back in hell!'" Then Charlie asked him to pray for him. At this point, Rawlings says:

> I felt downright insulted. In fact I told him to shut up. I said I was a doctor, not a minister and not a psychiatrist. But the nurses gave me that expectant look. What would you do? That's when I composed a make-believe prayer: I made him repeat the make-believe prayer word for word to keep him off my back. Meanwhile, I resuscitated with one hand and adjusted the pacemaker with the other. "Say it! 'Jesus Christ is the Son of God,' go on and say it!" I said. "'Keep me out of hell and if I live, I'm on the hook. I'm yours.' Go on, say it!" And then a very strange thing happened that changed our lives. A religious conversion experience took place. I had never witnessed one before. He was no longer the wild-eyed, screaming, combative lunatic who had been fighting me for his life. He was relaxed and calm and co-operative. It frightened me. I was shaken by the events.

According to Rawlings: "Since then Charlie has outlived three permanent pacemakers."[3] Dr. Rawlings and his bewildered patient palpably experienced our universal capacity for thought communion and its transforming power.

It is this imperishable line of soul connection that is the primary target of the Greys. Ghosts that are trapped in the skin between life and death thus provide these artificial entities with a honey pot of imperishable lines. The Greys can reach into the skin because the skin is defined by a measure of force coming from the adjacent atoms (see Plate 15). It is on this force that they write their programs. This skin is their seeding place: the place they seek to interpose their mechanical artificial intelligences on ours; the point where they seek to hijack our soul fields and interpose their "secondary entity-ness"; the place they seek to take on our ability to continue automatically as individually self-aware beings and be born into a concatenate line of existence.

All souls who linger in the shells at the edges may be susceptible to infiltration by the Greys, whose vastly superior technology is capable of reaching into the spaces between atoms. Still, they will only be able to get to certain levels of the shells of force because they are physical entities operating with enforced tools or mechanisms. Their reach would be to a situation where the physical nature of their technology has purchase or grip.

The closer an individual being is to the Godverse, the more *invulnerable* it is to the interception of the Greys. Souls in the violet shells are probably of such spiritual eminence and thus so full of God-light that they are on their way into the Godverse automatically, to forever escape the wheel of rebirth. Some of the outer shells—perhaps those shown as black to yellow—are accessible, but as they seek to go deeper, no information they download will be retained in the realms of lessening force. Those whose works give them a quantum color of, say, red to yellow had better watch out. They may well be reincarnating to a new life with a "Grey"-formatted outlook, an outlook that is increasingly common in our world.

Those people who are abducted while in physical life ironically may well be those who can resist the Grey's downloading process. The Greys study them in the incarnate state simply because they cannot reach them in the discarnate state; they want to discover the characteristics of these MESFs that preclude a download. They may be souls that in their immediate previous existence persisted in shells or domains of death characterized by the colors green to indigo (see Plate 12). These people may well be precious to our human species because something about them, perhaps in their biological makeup, resists these roboids. Long may their resistance continue.

Have a close look at the triangular shape with concave sides depicted in Plate 15 as the space between a three-hydrogen-atom ring. It bears a striking resemblance to the shape of the "Mothman" entity that has been seen all over the world. The illustrator of most of the color plates in this book, Daniel Langsman, followed my explanations of various things with an inspired genius of his own. He created this plate, as he did all the others, to illustrate the specific ideas that I had carefully outlined. His capacity to bring in every feature was so awesome that when the final product was viewed we would notice so many other aspects connected up with the whole thesis within the drawings. In the case of the Mothman, it did this with startling effect. One look at the result revealed what might be an explanation of this puzzling phenomenon, featured in a book called *The Mothman Prophecies,* written by John A. Keel, about true events that occurred in a small town in West Virginia called Point Pleasant, between 1966 and 1967.[4] Over a thirteen-month span, over one hundred eyewitnesses reported strange phenomena over the town of Point Pleasant, such as UFO sightings, strange lights in the sky, and red hypnotic eyes. From a collection of reports, the description of the Mothman is that it is up to eight feet tall, has red eyes and bat-like wings that seem to glide rather than flutter. It is wider than a man and has human-like legs. Its skin is a murky color, either dark grey or brown in appearance. The creature was dubbed "The Mothman" by the local press. In the context of sightings of this entity, a bridge in Point Pleasant collapsed and forty-six of the town's people were killed.

It seems that Mothman visions appear throughout the world, usually just before some major loss of life through some kind of disaster.

The reds, greys, and browns that feature in the description of this entity are the same colors that prevail at the edges of atoms in the illustration. Could the entity be a phenomenon that expresses the reach of MESFs held and trapped in this margin? Could the UFO sightings and alien contact that seem to accompany the Mothman sightings be explained by my suggestion that alien reach is expressed into these shells of greater tension in the space between atoms?

Negate gravity in any point of the space/time continuum and you have limitless power to move material objects, get access to the edge of the space between atoms, and bear witness to all the ghosts, ghouls, and other discarnate soul fields trapped there in their respective "shells" of enforcedness. Many astronauts, for instance, have reported seeing such manifestations when under the prolonged effect of the no-gravity environment of space. You will never see their reports. It is one of the best-kept secrets in NASA and the Russian Space Agency. I have it through a personal anecdote from an American astronaut I met.

There is evidence from several accounts of near death experiences suggesting that certain individuals actually face an abduction experience on the point of physical death. The first NDE is that of a patient of Dr. Francis Ceravolo, a family practitioner in Fort Lauderdale:

> I was present when one of my patients coded five times in the ER. He's an Italian man whom I've known for many years. He's a very calm, nice gentleman, just as nice as you would ever want to meet. He admitted to me that he didn't believe in God. He told me after he was revived: "I saw fire and I saw little creatures, about four-and-a-half, max five feet tall, all around me. They were bad-looking, terrible creatures. I saw them every time I died. I knew every time I died." He believes in God now, because he knows he survived only because God allowed him to.[5]

A Mrs. Villiers reported the following NDE after undergoing bypass surgery:

Until they managed to revive me I went through a very strange happening. I found myself in an enormous silver great place, rather like a hangar for airplanes, but going on for ever, and miles away there were some tiny figures. I knew I had to go back where I had come through. I called God and all my family, to no avail, and tried and tried to get back. . . . What is disappointing is that everyone talks of the lovely things when they died and were brought back. My hangar was ghastly, a real Hell if there is such a thing. It has made me much less anxious to die.[6]

Jane Dyson had an NDE while in intensive care on a life-support system after a serious car accident. She says:

I had the incredible experience of knowing I was dying and going through a bright shining tunnel toward dazzling light at the end. I felt quite calm, apart from feeling surprised that the tunnel was made of polished metal jointed and held together with something like rivets. Although I was not aware of the phenomenon of the NDE before my experience, I felt it should have been more ethereal somehow.[7]

These three NDEs seem to clearly describe some kind of alien abduction. The "bad looking and terrible four-and-a-half foot creatures," in the first NDE are a typical description of the Grey aliens. In the second NDE, the enormous "silver hangar" with the "tiny creatures" inside sounds exactly like the inside of a spaceship. The "tunnel made of polished metal jointed and held together with something like rivets" is nothing like the tunnel that is ordinarily described in NDEs and is more evocative of the entrance bay to a craft of some kind than the doorway to an insubstantial realm of light.

Brant, a Canadian who had an NDE in October 2005, describes "dark inhuman creatures" trying to grab him:

Let's start with my experience from the dark tunnel. I was in this tunnel with a bright light at the end with these dark inhuman creatures trying to grab me while I was speeding toward the light. I don't know whether I was running or floating. All I know was that I was going real fast and this voice from the light was telling me to hurry to get away from these creatures and I was terrified.[8]

NDEs are not the only altered state of consciousness in which alien phenomena are encountered. The trance state experienced all over the world by shamanic practitioners is also a doorway into alien visitation. This trance state is often brought on by the use of certain hallucinogenic drugs derived from various plants.

In the book of Enoch (a text still regarded by Ethiopian Jews as part of the Old Testament of the Bible), there is a passage similar to that in the biblical book of Genesis describing the visitation of the "Sons of God unto the daughters of men," when "Man began to multiply on the face of the Earth." The Hebrew word *Elohim* is the word translated as "God" in this instance. This particular word can be translated as "gods," or "objects of worship." Thus the "sons of God" may well refer to beings that appeared to come from the heavens, the "gods" of this universe, not the Universe of the Whole or Godverse. In the Enochian version of the story, it apparent that the "angels," the "children of heaven," were not sons of natural Godhead. Rather, they were from the "heavens," which denote the sky above, and "descended" from these heavens into "Ardos, which is the summit of Hermon." This does indeed resemble a description of a spaceship landing on a mountain. These "sons of God" took "wives unto themselves and began to go in unto them" and the women became pregnant with grotesque "giants." Perhaps these were the result of alien interception of the human genome.

There is also an intriguing passage describing how these alien visitors taught humanity certain things, including "charms," "enchantments," "the cutting of roots" and "acquainted" them "with plants":

And all the others together with them took unto themselves wives, and each chose for himself one, and they began to go in unto them and to defile themselves with them, and they taught them charms and enchantments, and the cutting of roots, and made them acquainted with plants.[9]

Rick Strassman, a psychiatrist working at the University of New Mexico, investigated the psychoactive effects of dimethyltryptamine (DMT) on human subjects. DMT is the principle active ingredient of ayahuasca, which is produced by shamans in the Amazon from the extracts of certain jungle plants. DMT occurs naturally in the brain, but when its levels are raised above a certain threshold, astounding "hallucinations" result. One of Strassman's volunteers, Jeremiah, reported the following:

It's a different world. Amazing instruments. Machine-type things. . . . I was in a big room. There was one big machine in the center, with round conduits, almost writhing—not like a snake, more in a technical manner. The conduits were not open at the end. They were solid blue-grey tubes, made of plastic? The machine felt as if it was rewiring me, reprogramming me. . . . I observed some of the results on that machine, maybe from my brain. It was a little frightening, almost unbearably intense.[10]

Another volunteer, Sara, said:

I expected spirit guides and angels, not alien life forms. . . . I saw some equipment or something. . . . It looked like machinery.[11]

There is an important difference between near death experiences and experiences engendered by chemical hallucinogens. In an NDE, the heart stops and the bio-magnetic field produced by the iron in the blood circulating in a coil through the body is cancelled, allowing the soul to be somewhat (but not completely) released into the space between atoms, where it temporarily finds its natural point of resonance. Souls who are heavier and more restricted will stay closer to the edges of the atoms, where the force is greatest, and souls who are lighter and freer will naturally move toward the center of the space, where the force is least. Those people who experience phenomena akin to alien abduction in their NDEs are the naturally heavier souls.

However, those who experience these phenomena as a result of a drug-induced state may not be seeing their "true colors," so to speak. In the hallucinogenic state, the bio-magnetic field still grips the soul in the enforced state, so it is not possible for consciousness to reach much beyond the edges of the atoms, unless the soul is extremely advanced and full of hydrogen in six-atom ring formation. For this reason, many individuals in Strassman's study were not directly accessing ongoing alien activity. It is more likely that the chemical they took enabled them to tap into genetic memories of alien interception encoded into their own biological lines.

During my research into the ways in which the major world religions view the concept of life beyond physical death, I came across an intriguing fact. It seems that the Jewish Old Testament view of existence beyond physical death is centered around a place called "Sheol."

In *A Hebrew and English Lexicon of the Old Testament,* Sheol is defined as: "The underworld . . . whither man descends at death."[12] They trace the origin of Sheol to either *sha-al,* which means the spirit world to which mediums directed their questions to the departed, or the same word: *sha-al,* which refers to the hollow place in the earth where the souls of men went at death. *Hebrew/English Dictionary to the Old Testament* defines Sheol as: "netherworld, realm of the dead, Hades."[13] *The International Standard Bible Encyclopedia* defines Sheol as "the unseen world, the state or abode of the dead, and is the equivalent of the Greek: Hades."[14]

Sheol is "an infinitive form from sha-al, to demand, the demanding, applied to the place which inexorably summons all men into its shade."[15] According to Old Testament cosmology, "at death man becomes a rephaim, i.e., a 'ghost,' 'shade,' or 'disembodied spirit.'"[16] Although the Old Testament offered various descriptions of Sheol, it was always described as a dismal place of silence, gloom, and darkness (see Psalms 94:17, 115:17; Job 17:13). The dead always went *down* to Sheol. It was a "gated community," but its gates only opened one way (see Job 38:17).

From this description, it would seem that Sheol was a place of punishment, but that was not how the Hebrews viewed it. Everyone went to Sheol—the good and the wicked, kings and peasants. The Hebrews' earliest understanding of the afterlife was really no life at all. The Old Testament only hints at positive possibilities beyond the grave. The good deeds one practiced in this life were not rewarded, just as the evils one caused were not punished. There was no concept of "heaven" or "paradise" as a nonphysical spiritual reality full of wonders that could be attained through a focus on priorities that were not materially based. Evidence of the blessing of God was seen in long life and many children. While later Jewish thought, expressed in the Talmud and the Kabbalah, does acknowledge the existence of a heaven, this idea has not really permeated into mainstream Judaism to the extent that it could be described as a religion truly pointed to an ongoing and abiding reality beyond the physical.

The emphasis within the Hebrew Scriptures, certainly in the earliest writings, was more on establishing the kingdom of God on Earth. This became a controversy among the Jews at the time of Jesus. The main protagonists of the controversy were known as the Pharisees and the Sadducees. The Sadducees denied the physical resurrection of the body. However, the rival interpretation of the Pharisees became the mainstream view. Their interpretation was that the kingdom of God is a physical kingdom for which the dead await physical resurrection. This is one reason why the Jews took great care over the disposal of the human body. Cremation was out of the question, and bodies lost at sea were a matter of great distress for the grieving relatives.

Central therefore to the early Jewish view of life and death were the following three features: an overall sense of materialism with a value system set in the here and now of the physical universe; a summons after death to a shadowy place (Sheol); and a promise for "physical resurrection" at the "end of days" when the dead will resurrect to eternal physical life. There is, of course, a form of eternal physical life with which we are familiar: cloning.

In my previous book, *The Song of the Greys,* I discussed at length the many references in the Old Testament to alien phenomena. These references, together with the seemingly ungodly nature of a god who proclaims himself to be "jealous" and "vengeful" and incites his people to continual tribal warfare, led me to the conclusion that the God of the Old Testament originated, for the most part, from the inside of a spaceship. It would make sense therefore that the Jewish people were offered only Sheol as an afterlife.

Viewed in my terms, Sheol is clearly the dark, shadowy harvest point at the edges of atoms. An alien intelligence would have no concept of anything but Sheol, simply because it would be unable to reach further into the space between atoms with its purely physical technology. To an alien roboid "God," there would be no concept of punishment for bad deeds or reward for good deeds in an afterlife. There would only be "capture" of a soul in a situation in which it can be written on and programmed to function as part of the alien agenda for humanity. This agenda was also reflected in the emphasis of the early Jewish faith on the here and now, the physical material world.

I must stress here that I am not by any means suggesting that Jewish souls are destined for Sheol because their archetypal belief system reflects such a place. Judging by the spectacular contribution these wondrous people have made to the benefit of humanity, I suspect that there will probably be a greater congregation of Jews returning to the Godverse than Christians. However, it is also likely that a good clutch of Zionists might make it to Sheol along with those of other religious groups who have and continue to conspire to marginalize millions in their own interests in the name of God. In the case of the Zionist, these interests are those that deny their own clear biblical directive that Zion can only be established once the Messiah has come. Only the Messianic Jews acknowledge that their Messiah in the identity of Jeshua Ben Joseph might well have *already* come. Could this lack of acknowledgement be due to their urge to see the Messiah arriving in golden splendor and supernatural presentation? Perhaps it could be argued that a representative of eternal rather than temporal values is far more likely to arrive like a lamb through the stable door!

The release in April 2006 of a translation of the recently discovered Gospel of Judas (GOJ) that has been tentatively dated to 130 to 170 CE, has been the cause of great controversy.[17] I have no brief as to whether Judas was a betrayer of the Christian teacher or not, but I can see that rehabilitating the biblical character offers a great benefit to Middle Eastern political causes. The timing of the "discovery" of the text itself could point strongly to a covert operation that might well have been planned by a powerful cartel of vested interests or a secret service.

Many have made the claim that this ancient text indicates that Christ actually instructed Judas to betray him and that Judas was in reality a favored apostle who was simply obeying orders. Another inference taken from the Gospel is that Judas was a confidante of Christ who was privileged enough to receive private instruction in the "mysteries of the kingdom." I have read the translation myself, and I have to say that I can see no evidence whatsoever for any of these claims, in fact to me quite the converse is apparent.

Jesus mentions to Judas that he will be replaced by another and that he (Judas) will "sacrifice the man that clothes me." But there is no reason why these should not be prophecies rather than instructions to Judas. The line goes that all this had to be done so that Jesus could demonstrate the resurrection and thus be acclaimed the Son of God. According to this interpretation, Judas was a mere instrument. If my thesis is correct, it is far more likely that Christ saw that we are a kept breed. His mission was to show humankind that it was possible through free will to break that power and not be a victim of it as so many were (Judas, in particular). We saw how well it worked when Peter denied him and Judas betrayed him. Nevertheless, the opportunity to exercise their own will had to be given to them, whatever the outcome.

Let's look at a particular phrase in the text of the Gospel of Judas: "The angels of the stars." What might Christ have meant by the words *angel* and *star* in the context in which they appear in the Gospel? I believe these two words in the GOJ text illustrate something very important. They might actually point the finger at an extraterrestrial input. Through history, the word *angel* has been taken to mean a messenger of the gods, an entity that does the bidding of the gods. Angels can be benevolent and righteous or quite the opposite, depending on the "God" they serve. After all, the Old Testament literature is full of instances where angels were used to kill the innocent (including children) as well as the guilty. Not all angels, in other words, are nice. It seems the word is used more generally to describe utilitarian entities who carry out the purposes of some ascendant being.

The word *star,* of course, can mean "a celestial body" or "a preeminent person." Many times throughout the Gospel of Judas, Jesus mentions a phenomena called the "stars." The contexts in which he uses this term are intriguing. They suggest to me that he may well have been literally referring to locations in space. Jesus seems to be suggesting that Judas is dominated by an influence of some extraterrestrial aspect. In my terms, of course, that could refer to the alien "fathers" that have sponsored the "evolution" of *Homo sapiens sapiens.*

Jesus also refers in the text to a "strong and holy generation." He makes it clear that "no one born [of] this eon will see that [generation], and no host of 'angels of the stars' will rule over that generation, and no person of mortal birth can associate with it." Could this "strong and holy generation" describe the Prime beings that came in with the universe? At another point in the Gospel, Jesus is said to be laughing and when the apostles ask him why, he says: "I am not laughing [at you] but at the error of the stars, because these six stars wander about with these five combatants, and they all will be destroyed along with their creatures."

In the Gospel of Judas there is a remarkable account of a certain incident in which Jesus asks Judas to look up at the sky at something that resembles a spaceship: "Lift up your eyes and look at the cloud and the light within it and the stars surrounding it. The star that leads the way is your star." It may be that an abduction experience is then described: "Judas lifted up his eyes and saw the luminous cloud, and he entered it." Could this "star" have been Judas's particular alien sponsor, the breed of aliens that had intercepted his biological line?

At another point in the Gospel, Judas relates to Jesus a dream of a house surrounded by "great people." In his dream, Judas asks to be let into this house. Jesus replies: "Judas, your star has led you astray. . . . No person of mortal birth is worthy to enter the house you have seen, for that place is reserved for the holy. Neither the sun nor the moon will rule there, nor the day, but the holy will abide there always, in the eternal realm with the holy angels. Look, I have explained to you the mysteries of the kingdom and I have taught you about the error of the stars." This prompts Judas to ask Jesus: "Master, could it be that my seed is under the control of the rulers?" Could he be asking Christ directly if his own biological line could be alien controlled, "ruled over" by a "host of angels of the stars?"

Perhaps the key to beating all such secondary materially manufactured creations such as the Grey bioids is to find a way to reveal to them en masse something they could never know—their true lowly status in the natural existential hierarchy of things—to let them know that as created being, they could never have a soul and are inferior in life status to a gnat, a mosquito, or indeed a prion. This might well make sense to their superior derivational logic.

It seems that when Jesus was alone in the mountains around Judea, he was "taken" by the devil. For "taken," read "abducted," and for "devil," read a "Grey roboid." The text says that Christ was taken by the devil to a position from which he could see all the cities of the world. This vantage point would have to be set in outer space, as only from there can all the cities of the world be viewed. In other words, Christ was possibly a guest of the Greys in one of their spacecraft out in space. The "devil" had to be a head honcho. Even so, he was unable to use his technology to interfere with Christ's MESF. So he sought to buy Jesus off:

> Again, the devil taketh him up into an exceeding high mountain, and sheweth him all the kingdoms of the world, and the glory of them. And saith unto him, All these things will I give thee, if thou wilt fall down and worship me. Then saith Jesus unto him, Get thee hence, Satan: for it is written, Thou shalt worship the Lord thy God, and him only shalt thou serve. Then the devil leaveth him, and, behold, angels came and ministered unto him.[18]

Killing Jesus would have made no difference; they knew that his soul could come back in reincarnation ad infinitum. They not only were unable to interfere with him, but also returned him safely. The fact that they did this might imply that Jesus knew what they were, knew his existential ascendancy over them, and thus knew how to deal with them. He probably revealed to them their true existential status.

Telling the Greys this home truth so that it reaches into their program and changes their course of action as a result is no simple task. It is not simply a question of giving them the information as a series of logical points in order that they might believe their existential status. "Belief" itself is not a feature of a programmable entity. The only way to get the message through is to demonstrate it practically so that they can glean it with their own technological "feelers," so to speak. I believe that Jesus did just this when he converted the atoms of his flesh to light through his transfiguration. This conversion of force to forceless-ness would have significantly lessened the force print of the planet and, to a certain extent, the force print of the entire universe. The vacuum of lessening force would have freed the souls stuck in "Sheol," the cold elbows of the edges of atoms. This would have left the Greys high and dry and shown them in no uncertain terms that they have no intrinsic connection to soul-bearing being.

This particular group whose leader was named Satan might well be the only Greys to actually know the difference between their existential stature and that of humanity, or for that matter between themselves and the clones that created them. For the first time, they may have learned the properties of a soul-bearing entity and seen that they were eternally doomed to failure in their quest to be born. More importantly, they may have cleared off this planet, thoroughly confused about what they really were. But, alas, it seems that another later lot with similar credentials came and started the whole rigmarole with humanity again. Thus the curse continues.

If my existential thesis in this book is a load of paranoid rubbish, then I believe I have done little, if any, harm to any of you in bringing it all to your attention. I might, in fact, have done you a favor in warning you to be vigilant and not risk your own glory as a potentially eternal being. But what if I am right? How do you claim back your soul from a bunch of gold wires in a mercurial mulch, sparking bio-diodes, and transistors, as they watch you squirm in agony while their probes cut into your testicles or your ovaries, or your brain matter? You lie there defenseless, your will totally subjugate to emotionless entities, while they switch your mind off at the sweep of a magnetic pen and watch your reaction to what they do to your progeny as you stand or lie there watching. Their intention may well be to learn about human emotions, and they may not have the slightest idea of consequence, physical, emotional, or spiritual, to you or your own. We are the lab rats following their maze, guided by the instigations of a nonhuman technician, oblivious to the vicissitudes that form the foundation of our very natures, natures that they can never comprehend because they lie outside the programmed format of nonliving machines. Our paradigm will always be alien to them as they are alien to us.

The book thus far will give the reader an idea of the shape of the evil that could be driving the planet in the direction of a catastrophe of biblical proportions: the final tragedy of all perhaps, something referred to in the Bible as "Armageddon."

# 17

# Beneath the Surface

Has our species—which in relatively greater numbers could once smile at the vision of Michelangelo, rise at the soaring melodies of Beethoven or Brahms, or coo at the rhetoric of Goethe, Schiller, Emerson, and Keats—now become the last dismantlers of a once glorious being? Are we the kin, the brothers and sisters, of reptiles and lizards? Many people who claim firsthand contact with the aliens think they stem from a reptilian root. If you study the ways of reptiles here on the Earth, it is plain to see that the animal species operates on the principal of ritual and deceit. It's a phylum that is extremely territorial, aggressive, violent, and mechanistic. These seem to be the prominent qualities of Northern European thinking.

There can be no doubt that this strain of humanity has been by far the most depraved of all genotypes in the fifteen thousand or more years since "civilization" began. In the last two thousand years, we occidentals have brought about more than seven thousand wars and conflicts all over the Earth: stealing, raping, pillaging, and destroying whole native peoples, their cultures, societies, countries, even continents, with our colonizing zeal, violence, greed, and avarice. We continue to do it to this day in an even more spectacular fashion because it is covert and uses the technology the Greys may well have inspired us to produce in the first place for a multiplying and all-encompassing effect. In fact, if there is such a thing as a Galactic Police Force in our neck of the space

299

woods, our genetic brand mark would probably be regarded as the most perverse and dangerous of its kind in the galaxy. We would probably be top of the "ten most wanted" list. This would not deter the roboids that visit us, but any entity with a sense of moral turpitude centered with a soul in Godhead might give us a wide berth.

The rules applicable are universe-wide in effect. There has never been an example in nature where a subordinate intelligence has been treated kindly and with largesse by a superior one. The whole of nature, through entropy, conspires to provide fuel to the axiom "dog eat dog" and anything less. Humanity is thus an expendable commodity when seen as a resource for the use of something infinitely more mentally powerful and intelligent than the human mind can conceive, something ruled by a computer program that knows no instruction for a sense beyond the atom.

Just as a lab rat could never conceive of the science behind the experiment and the think-ability of the scientists that use it expediently, the subordinate species will never know the plot or the result. It will live in its own world and the world it is allowed to see. The experimenters are very covertly seeking to poach for themselves the very essence of our existence. We, as the natural dominant species on this planet, are now set on the same road, seeking to create artificial formats of ourselves, that is, clones, for seemingly valid ostensible reasons. The writing is on the wall, in a terrifying script that it seems so few of us spot because it seems so outlandish. We forget so easily that television was laughable a century ago. We seem to forget so much else in this same bizarre way. We forget that the entire history of our species is a catalog of loss: a prescription for doom through exploitation, violence, and the meaningless disposal of all things that might be of eternal value in the stakes where eternal value can be the only intelligent meaning of existence. We still seek to linger in this mortal coil with whatever is at hand, a coil of endless suffering and negative turpitude where the disposal of order is the order of all things. Who is going to wake up to what is going on and stop it before we as a species are all wiped out?

It is easy to imagine that exposure of the UFO phenomenon for what it might be stands little chance against an extraterrestrial intelligence of such magnitude that it has been capable of making us a farmed species, serving their purposes throughout our history. Even if you are not yet convinced, consider for argument's sake that such a history is true, and the technology the aliens have at their disposal is so much greater than our own. You can readily understand that these entities would want their presence and activities to be hidden so that they might go about their business without protest or interference. I suggest it would be their first prerogative. Secrecy would give them a huge advantage.

The means to ensure secrecy would be simple for them. Abductee after abductee testifies that they can communicate mind to mind, theirs to ours, one way. Abductees suffer unspeakable pain during the procedures done to them, and some claim that this suffering is part of some study methodology on the part of the alien Greys and their cohorts. They have methods of mind control that shut off the pain of these procedures after they have done them. A kind of amnesia is induced afterward. This amnesia is sometimes released spontaneously but mostly under hypnosis by human investigators during which the abductees recall the event. Sometimes—many years after the event—they recall it with pain, fear, and foreboding.

Many people see extraterrestrial intervention as being for the good of our species. But everything the abductees report seems to point the other way. If this intervention of our world were for the good of our world, no secrecy would be necessary. Benign extraterrestrials with superior intelligence and no hidden agendas would surely have presented themselves openly and demonstrated that their presence was for the good of humankind. But everything these Greys do has been hidden and covertly carried out through the ages. It seems they are hiding something, something that might reveal them to be a threat to our species, something so terrible that its discovery might put their entire presence here in jeopardy.

In this light, those "Ufologists" who seek ceaselessly to expose the alien presence are doing the greatest service possible on behalf of our natural human family, this time around. I say "this time around" because I believe that this same phenomenon has taken place over and over again for eons and not just millennia. Each time the DNA of a generation of being that is naturally derived from the Godverse has become genetically suitable, they have paid the final and terrible price of being wiped off the face of the Earth by the aliens and their cohorts on this planet. They have been wiped out for two purposes, the harvesting of DNA on the physical level and the prostitution and the hijacking of their MESFs in the interdimensional margin of the life and death interface.

This plague will never cease. Once the Grey bio-machines with artificial intelligence have gained a portal into a planet, they will carry out their procedures, no matter how draconian they are, on the life-forms of that planet. Some among us hail the presence of these interlopers as being providers of technologies that are of great benefit in the long term, feeling that any price is worth paying for these advantages. It is beyond belief that a human mind can think this way. But there is sufficient evil and lunacy in some human minds that they could take sweet, helpless, trembling little children emblazoned with a yellow star from their mothers, and—in numbers that are the eternal shame of this planet—throw and pack the little ones into gas chambers, close the doors, pour Zyklon B gas through the roof, listen for the cries to cease, open the doors, remove the triangular stack of bodies (even children will try to find a way out), load them into gurneys, burn them to ash in an industrial process, and then go home and play with their own children. Such was the German legacy to the world. It must never be forgotten that it was the German nation that voted the Nazi demons into power. This presents an object lesson in cold-blooded neo-European thinking of the sort that for centuries murdered, plundered, raped, ravaged, and imprisoned indigenous native peoples of whole continents in the name of colonialism.

If there are Euro-patriots reading this and you are boiling with rage at this assertion—read the history books. The point is that this filth is running in your blood and mine to this day. It doesn't end with a single episode in history, as we all know. History keeps repeating itself. Why do we not learn our lessons? Why do we keep repeating our mistakes time after time? Maybe we do learn our lessons. Maybe, just maybe, there is something about the stature and stance of some human minds among us that prevents them from learning any lessons. They may be programmed minds, intercepted and genetically formatted to solicit results beyond empathy, concern, care, mercy, compassion, and goodwill.

Could this have included the developing and taking of DNA suitable for Grey alien purposes under the seeming disguise of transplanting suitable socio-ethnic forms, through colonial behests? I believe the formatted progeny that they have created in hybrid human form and each day pass into the world (some in the highest positions) are analogous to the German Nazi minds who through their wretched hives brought a premonition of what is to come to humankind, with the holocaust they visited on some of the most precious and gifted groups of humanity among us. They still fester now in the neo-Nazi hives around the world and get stronger each day all over the world, to continue the way of their secret masters on the whole of humanity some day in the future. Will it be that your future well-being will be assured *if* and only *if* you belong to a favored cartel? I hope to convince you by the time you read the rest of this book that if you are of this Earth, particularly if you are one of this special cartel, not one single individual of your kind will be allowed a future. If you do survive in the short term, it will be to provide something that a four-fingered grey mulch with huge almond eyes and the fascia of a humanoid reptile, which has superquantum computer circuits for brains, needs to further *its* agenda, an agenda that stems from an insidious and awesome alien power. You and their favored human minders will have to rely on the "word" or assurance of entities with computer clocks for heartbeats. They can wipe whomever they want off the face of the Earth at any moment they desire. This book in good part is about what these entities might need from you, and how and why any deal they make to preserve some of us is likely to be based on lies.

We are all in big trouble where these wretched human hybrid "Grey keepers" are concerned. I have built up a recipe for recognizing them. An abductee told me they are called the "Alpha." The following is a list of the qualities he gave me. It is a chilling description:

- They tend to be very introspective and self-centered and cannot empathize with fellow human beings in an emotional scheme of things.
- They are extremely intelligent in an evaluative sense and distant in demeanor.
- They have very little sense of sentiment or sympathy and only show a semblance of these characteristics when following other norms.
- They are bold and decisive, full of guile and single-minded in achieving their goals to the point of ruthlessness.
- They have little sense of conscience, often to the point of cruelty.
- They show a great natural affinity with machines and little natural affinity with children.
- They have little sense of their own bodies and far less sense of pain. They are not well coordinated physically.
- They are more prone to illness and infirmity than the average person.
- They are highly self-obsessed, driven by their own courses of action and pay little attention to the needs, feelings, or opinions of others.
- They obsessively seek the company of those with the opposite characteristics and usually have partnerships with highly emotional individuals.
- They resist sitting anywhere where the back of their head rests against any ferrous material.
- Almost all of them hold high positions in governments and large international corporations.

These are the most powerful individuals in the world, capable of insuring that no solid evidence will be allowed the light of day. Nothing short of an appearance of these synthetic creatures simultaneously all over the world will prove their actual physical existence on this planet. Bizarre though it all seems, how many people do you know like this?

We might now all be facing the chilling prospect of an attempted hijack of our souls through the cold-blooded, lethal efficiency of a superintelligent machine mind that has come into our part of the universe with this one intention in mind. The final demise of humanity to a point of no return may well have already started. Our so-called developed industrial societies are themselves leaning toward a robotic future. Professor of Cybernetics at Reading University Kevin Warwick is of the firm belief that the computerization of the entire human realm has indeed already begun. He warns that in the next fifty years computers will be able to match some of the thinking abilities of humans. After that, machines will have the capacity to make copies of themselves like living organisms until there comes a point when they can surpass the intellectual feats of most men and women.

He believes that human treatment of inferior animals might be emulated by these machines when they deal with us. "We can't rely on intelligent robots being nice and generous when we ourselves are not nice and generous," says Warwick, "the best we might be able to expect would be to be their pets."[1] The only other alternatives he sees that might emerge are either the reduction of the human race to the level of slaves or, at worst, our complete extermination by artificially intelligent machines: "We have to ask where A. I. research could take us, it could be into extinction."[2]

Warwick visualizes machines being able to teach each other, possibly in a language unknown to humans, and thus reaching a point where they could take control of computer-operated weapons. Helped by the development of communications networks such as the Internet, robots would be able to tap into information and learn faster. Details available to them could even include the best ways to eradicate humans.

For these reasons, Warwick urgently suggests that an international body should be set up to discuss the threat and to set rules to control intelligent machines. This, he believes, could help us to ensure that robots were programmed to protect humans or could be disabled if they tried to take over. "There is no point in waiting, things are moving along quite quickly. If we get it wrong the human race could be wiped out or enslaved."[3] However, Warwick himself admits that programming a moral code into robots, instructing them not to harm humans, would be extremely difficult since machine intelligence does not mirror human concepts: "We need to make it very simple. Even the concept of what is friendly and what is unfriendly is difficult."[4]

B. T. Laboratories Futurologist Ian Pearson (who, by the way, also said that he believed that Warwick's time scale was a conservative one) has said that programming intelligent robots not to harm people would not work.[5] If these professors are correct, then our fate at the artificial hand of these robots seems to be sealed.

The time may be right, as never before in recent human history, for another cull of the residential beings of our planet. The means for control of our destiny have all recently been established through the United States as the world's only global super power, while it was under the leadership of the two Bushes, Cheney, Rumsfeld, Perle, and Wolfowitz. Even though they have been voted out of power, their acolytes will remain secretly embedded in the U.S. national secret services. They will carry on their deadly work *whoever* is the president of the United States of America in the future. In fact, deadly Grey entities have been working this way throughout history with all human strains.

The World Wide Web is now one of the most powerful means to stir the pot for those who believe the UFO phenomenon to be the most terrifying danger the Earth has faced. Though vilified and bedeviled, many do their best to expose it as such wherever they can. It is getting more and more difficult to do so by other means. Most major forms of media in the Occident are in the control of powerful cartels covertly managed by alien-sponsored sources. Fewer and fewer UFO encounters out of the hundreds experienced each month all over the Occident are reported. This is not so in the tropical countries of the midband of the planet or the Orient. In those places, interest in the UFO phenomenon increases daily, and more and more reports are finding their way to public notice via the media.

A quiet tsunami of realization is now rolling through some very relevant portals within the whole deployment of the anti-UFO conspiracy, and more and more informers within the relevant administrations are discretely reaching for investigative pens to blow the whole conspiracy apart, come what may.

Some may pay the ultimate price for doing this, as did one general I heard about in the U.S. Air Force. He was in the team that destroyed one of the still functioning Grey roboids from a crashed disc in the Mojave Desert. He was, of course, warned at the time never to divulge this to anyone. Later (during the sixties), he became ill and was not expected to live. On what he believed at the time to be his deathbed, he told his son the story and asked him to get it to the world for the sake of his grandchild, whose hand he held as he spoke. The general then made a last-minute recovery. The son told his friends in California the whole story. Word got around and curious people started nosing around the crash site. People started disappearing. The general was arrested after he came out of the hospital, interrogated, and released. He was later found shot dead in his car on a deserted road, an apparent suicide.

His son left the United States for Europe. In the meantime, strangely—though I do not know if this is related to his knowledge of the UFO incident—two members of his wife's family were found dead in mysterious circumstances on a highway in California, the victims of a hit-and-run accident. I met the general's son in London many years later, and that is how the whole story came to my attention. He had read an article of mine about UFOs and rang me requesting a meeting. He told me his story, but sadly, he died of liver cancer three weeks later.

If it were discovered that we as a species are not our own masters, there can be little doubt of the enormity of the consequences to us all.

The discovery of the presence of extraterrestrial beings as our creators and masters in the distant past and their continued presence on the Earth would likely be worldwide panic. The scaffolding that holds all human societies together could collapse worldwide. A natural response could be resistance and active belligerence against any such entity we could lay our hands on. An intelligence superior to ours could, of course, anticipate this, especially given that they know their genetically engineered progeny are an innately aggressive life-form. They certainly would be taking great care to make sure that no such response prevailed.

However, it might well be beyond even their means to control a naturally born primary species, however profoundly reengineered by them. The control of free will would always be outside the prospectus of a programmed entity. As artificially created entities, they would have no program that could define it. But we are not artificially created beings, and our free will comes from something outside the domain of all they understand and can know as programmed secondary types of being set totally in this universe. They thus have to seek methods of control of such beings with recourse to technology. This is what has taken them so much time to accomplish. This is what a small cartel of their sponsored human genotypes within governments in many of the highly developed countries like United States, Germany, Britain, and some Scandinavian countries are enabling them to do now.

Several of my German friends have told me that the subject of the alien phenomenon is not really one that is ever broached in the German media. There is little or no TV coverage of the subject and very little literature available about it. This might suggest that one of the Greys greatest successes in taking over occidental countries could be Germany. Hitler had, on his own admission, a personal experience with alien entities, an experience that may well have inspired his "Aryan" blonde and blue-eyed ideal.

According to some accounts, Hitler believed that he had seen a member of a super race, which he believed to originate from the inner Earth. He reportedly told Hermann Rauschning, the Nazi governor of

Danzig: "The new man is living amongst us now! He is here! I will tell you a secret. I have seen the new man. He is intrepid and cruel. I was afraid of him."[6] Could this "new man" Hitler personally met have originated not from the "inner Earth" but instead from an alien craft? In referring to the "inner Earth," could Hitler have been describing the places they are hiding, waiting to emerge when they calculate the time is right to take over the Earth? As I have said previously, many people report contacts with a certain type of alien being that is distinct from the Greys in that it is apparently humanoid and has blonde hair and blue eyes. Could the "super race" that Hitler and his cohorts were looking for have been representatives such as these?

It is almost as though the alien beings who seem to have paid him a personal visit were announcing a recipe for a type of humanity that was the exact opposite of the types of humanity who have retained a close connection to Godhead. It is from these precious individual lines that redeemers are born to once again advise us of our eternal heritage. The ancient genetically unintercepted lines of our species have carried forth somehow, blending with and thus weakening the usefulness of the artificially created body forms that hold the alien gene recipe strong. However, the overwhelming instinct that propels the white-to-black racism inherent in so many occidentals might well be a directive implanted by the aliens in an attempt to prevent this blending.

I believe the Holocaust was a contrivance to try to ethnically cleanse the world of its "savior geno-phylum" (Jews and Gypsies, both of which, with greatest irony, are races of North Indian, Aryan descent, were subject to the genocide). Hitler and his henchmen's prodigious obsession with the systematic, industrial killing of these people was perhaps because they were following the orders of the "new intrepid and cruel man" in an attempt to destroy the greatest threat to their (the Greys) imminent takeover of the planet we call our home. The bio-machine devils knew that the genes of these people had a protective mechanism that made it difficult for them to change human aspects to their own recipe, a recipe they could work on more easily to change to their prospectus.

The stage may thus have been set for the final takeover of our species through the yoke of the German Nazi net if they had won the war. The losing of the war, I believe, was just a stage in the assembly of the forces of a "cruel and intrepid" mind. Those forces seek to this day to finish the job the Germans started when—in August 1934—89 percent of the German electorate voted to approve the consolidation of the offices of president and chancellor in a single leader-chancellor personified by Adolf Hitler. Their activities continue covertly within the neo-Nazi cartels around the world, getting stronger each day. Covert organizations all over the Occident are multiplying their tentacles like some giant fetid octopus, linking so-called nationalists and patriots all over Europe and the United States, Canada, and Australia.

It is a terrifying situation, especially given that the vast majority of those who work to obfuscate an alien presence here on this planet haven't a clue that they—as Euro-Caucasians—are the final real target of these grey devils. However, over the years since my book *The Song of the Greys* was published, certain significantly placed individuals have contacted me after reading it. The postulations I made in the book raised enough doubt in their minds that they began to question what they might be working toward within their own powerful and, in several cases, clandestine organizations. Some were worried for the future of their children who might in the end pay the final price of any subterfuge. They began to see that a giant canard might be putting their families and indeed our entire species in harm's way on behalf of a small cartel of favored politicians, industrialists, and corporation heads in mainly America, Britain, and Germany: deeply racist lethal "human" beings who have cornered the market on the planet and are not about to share it with anyone as paltry as the ordinary man in the street, much less any black, brown, or yellow stranger with strange ways.

Each of the people who contacted me had an interest in the UFO phenomenon but had never seen it presented in the context of its relation to the entire existential base of life throughout the universe and beyond. No single one of my sources knew the others, yet all their information seemed to dovetail into the same revelations. I did as thorough a check on these individuals and their bona fides as possible, and they all checked out as being what they claimed to be. I list below the conclusions that could be drawn from what they had to say:

1. The HIV virus was developed and deliberately planted in communities to cause maximum damage to certain genotypes and psychotypes of people.

2. During the apartheid years, the white South African government, with American collaboration, deliberately set about infecting black populations, both indigenous and foreign, with the HIV virus over a six-year period.

3. Ethnically tailored pathogens have been mass produced and are awaiting distribution through vector agents connected to the migration patterns of wild bird populations. Bird flu is a practice run for a planned release of an already developed human pathogen stored secretly in the United States and Poland, intended to reduce the population in third world countries by half.

4. 9/11 was carried out by Mossad agents working through the Zionist Israeli lobby in the United States.

5. Every human being on the earth will be sera-typed, tissue-typed, blood-typed, and required to carry a microchip under their skins. Without this chip, they will not be able to travel internationally, get insurance of any kind, obtain hospital services, or buy, sell, and trade in the marketplace. The plans for this are already well advanced.

6. Underground shelters, which will be able to hold millions of specially privileged Euro-Caucasian people in self-contained isolation from all other humanity for five years, are built and ready for occupation all around the United States and in eight countries in Europe.

7. African countries are being systematically planted with leaders and administrators that will allow their vast horde of raw materials

to be controlled for and by American and European corporate interests.

8. Covert American security services will achieve editorial control of all Western print media, including that of Eastern European countries within the European Union, by 2010. Seventy-three other countries in South America, Africa, and Asia will also be included in this control paradigm.

9. Neo-Nazi and right-wing groups centered in Germany, France, the United Kingdom, and Australia are being used as agent pro-vocateurs to set off racially motivated conflagrations intended to bring their groups into power. This human filth is stronger now, covertly, in their world-wide role than the Nazis were in a world sense at the height of World War II.

10. The most serious revelation was that governments exist *within* the elected governments in the United States and all Anglo-Saxon countries. Their purpose is to maintain the momentum provided by six centuries of Anglo-Saxon control of the world by destroying the burgeoning power of Muslim countries. This is based on their perception of the dangers these countries present to the white Western-Caucasian social ethos.

11. Plans are in place to preserve this ethos through the selection of a favored cartel who would be hidden in underground bun-kers secretly created to withstand the aftermath of an asteroid impact on the planet, along with plans to direct the impact to a geographical location where it would wipe out several billion people not of the Western-Caucasian format. In this way, the whole planet and all its surviving resources would be inherited by this small favored cartel.

12. The entire UFO phenomenon, along with its covert nature, is a result of collaboration between an alien presence on this Earth and a secret cartel of very powerful people within the govern-ments of ten of the most powerful countries in the occidental world, plus China and Japan. Their intention is to share the

planet between two agendas: the occupation and use of land areas by the favored cartel and hegemony of the sea by an aquatic alien breed that have been cohabiting with humanity under the vast areas of water on this planet for eons. It seems, perhaps luckily for us, that they cannot survive for long outside an aquatic environment.

This is a terrifying series of revelations. Are these surmises plausible, even probable? If they are *in any way* true then it would follow that we cannot be paranoid enough about what is happening in the world today. Revealing all this might put my own life and those of my informers in jeopardy, especially since my sources might include those involved in the worldwide efforts to conceal the presence of extraterrestrial aliens in the affairs of our planet. However, it is at my informers' insistence that I have mentioned their existence, though I would, of course, never name them. They hope that such revelations might help to bring the entire conspiracy out into the open. It is on their behalf that I am continuing to fight to bring this whole subject into the public arena.

The conclusions listed above are, of course, surmises that would be almost impossible to prove with actual and factual evidence, given the social and political power of the individuals involved. They could easily be regarded as the paranoid ranting of self-interest groups with narrow-minded political agendas and no more than that. But these things have been written about and commented on by eminent journalists, intellectuals, and social and political commentators all over the world at various times. For me, the verification of the surmises listed above has come from trusted sources with privileged access, along with documentation that I have personally seen. I have no doubt much of it is genuine. But I was stunned by the realization that, alas, there is no way these things could be or would be categorically proven to the world.

Those in control of the media can so easily claim that even physical evidence has been faked with recourse to technology. If an actual solid artifact, like a piece of technology so "far out" that there could be no

doubt of its extraterrestrial origins, were to be found, these servants of
the damned would see to it that no one in the media ever exposed it to
the world. Anyone who tries to reveal such things will face the launder-
ing teams of controlling agencies whose brief it is to see that nothing
will give the alien game away.

The individuals that hold to and promulgate the lethal racist ethos
I have outlined above head up some of the most powerful organizations
on the planet. They function covertly under front individuals picked
for their respectability and appeal to local populations. They can, at a
touch of a button, set in motion the removal of any human being on
the face of the Earth. Any undesirable politician, CEO, or media editor
not towing the party line will be removed from any position of threat
to their purposes. It is done cleverly, covertly, and subtly with the least
possible notice. They see to it that their own allies are placed in the
most powerful positions in a chain of command or power, usually at
the joints or articulation points of a line of result. They don't bother
about the "long bones" where the majority linger, just the points where
the strategic decisions are taken. In this way, they don't need great numbers, just the smallest most effective cartel that will do the business for
them.

I would forgive anyone for thinking these claims were outlandish
and pandering to the most extreme forms of conspiracy theory. But
whoever thinks this way would perhaps think again after reading Julian
Borger's article that appeared on the front page of *The Guardian* newspaper in 2003. It seems that in the weeks leading up to the war in Iraq
a special shadow agency was set up "to compete with the CIA and its
military counterpart, the Defense Intelligence Agency":

> The Office of Special Plans (OSP) was set up by the defense sec-
> retary, Donald Rumsfeld, to second-guess CIA information and
> operated under the patronage of hardliner conservatives in the top
> rungs of the administration, the Pentagon and at the White House,
> including Vice-President Dick Cheney. The ideologically driven

network functioned like a shadow government, much of it off the official payroll and beyond congressional oversight. But it proved powerful enough to prevail in a struggle with the State Department and the CIA by establishing a justification for war.

There was a mountain of documentation to look through and not much time. The administration wanted to use the momentum gained in Afghanistan to deal with Iraq once and for all. The OSP itself had less than 10 full-time staff, so to help deal with the load, the office hired scores of temporary "consultants."

"Most of the people they had in that office were off the books, on personal services contracts. At one time, there were over 100 of them," said an intelligence source. The contracts allow a department to hire individuals, without specifying a job description. As John Pike, a defense analyst at the think-tank GlobalSecurity.org, put it, the contracts "are basically a way they could pack the room with their little friends." "They surveyed data and picked out what they liked," said Gregory Thielmann, a senior official in the state department's intelligence bureau until his retirement in September. "The whole thing was bizarre. The secretary of defense had this huge defense intelligence agency, and he went around it."

The civilian agencies had the same impression of the OSP sleuths. "They were a pretty shadowy presence," Mr. Thielmann said. "Normally when you compile an intelligence document, all the agencies get together to discuss it. The OSP was never present at any of the meetings I attended." Democratic congressman David Obey, who is investigating the OSP, said: "That office was charged with collecting, vetting and disseminating intelligence completely outside of the normal intelligence apparatus. In fact, it appears that information collected by this office was in some instances not even shared with established intelligence agencies and in numerous instances was passed on to the national security council and the president without having been vetted with anyone other than political appointees."

The OSP was an open and largely unfiltered conduit to the

White House not only for the Iraqi opposition. It also forged close ties to a parallel, ad hoc intelligence operation inside Ariel Sharon's office in Israel specifically to bypass Mossad and provide the Bush administration with more alarmist reports on Saddam's Iraq than Mossad was prepared to authorize.

"None of the Israelis who came were cleared into the Pentagon through normal channels," said one source familiar with the visits. Instead, they were waved in on Mr. Feith's authority without having to fill in the usual forms. The exchange of information continued a long-standing relationship with Douglas Feith, a defense under-secretary and a former Reagan official. and other Washington neo-conservatives had with Israel's Likud party.

In 1996, he and Richard Perle—now an influential Pentagon figure—served as advisers to the then Likud leader, Binyamin Netanyahu. In a policy paper they wrote, entitled "A Clean Break": A New Strategy for Securing the Realm, the two advisers said that Saddam would have to be destroyed, and Syria, Lebanon, Saudi Arabia, and Iran would have to be overthrown or destabilized, for Israel to be truly safe.

The Israeli influence was revealed most clearly by a story floated by unnamed senior US officials in the American press, suggesting the reason that no banned weapons had been found in Iraq was that they had been smuggled into Syria. Intelligence sources say that the story came from the office of the Israeli prime minister.

The OSP absorbed this heady brew of raw intelligence, rumor and plain disinformation and made it a "product," a prodigious stream of reports with a guaranteed readership in the White House. The primary customers were Mr. Cheney, Mr. Libby and their closest ideological ally on the national security council, Stephen Hadley, Condoleezza Rice's deputy.

In turn, they leaked some of the claims to the press, and used others as a stick with which to beat the CIA and the state department analysts, demanding they investigate the OSP leads.[7]

You ain't seen nothin' yet, folks. The menace that patrols our skies in disc-shaped craft, with the help of their client state on the earth—which from all the evidence available now appears to be the United States and her agents—have almost fully succeeded in wresting control of our freedom in the name of fighting terrorism. We have handed it all to the Greys willingly. Strategically placed teams pour scorn on anyone who bears actual witness to alien phenomena. The entire Seti project is a giant scam designed to throw off the general population with the implication that we would hardly be looking for extraterrestrial beings if they are already here.

They do not know what they do, the wretched racists and tribalists that control our planet. The vast majority of them haven't the faintest idea where the reign of this awesome evil they are setting up in the world today leads. They think they are acting to preserve a privileged way of life mainly for the white occidentals who drive the scientific and social engines of our world. They little realize that when the final buttons are pressed, they will be the first ones to fall victim to the subterfuge of superintelligent entities.

What choices have we if, under the guise of stopping terrorism, deadly cartels and groups of privileged people—whether businessmen, politicians, national secret service agencies, international businesses, corporations, or individual wealthy billionaire Euro-Caucasians—are covertly instigating terrorist attacks around the world so that they, pretending to be saviors, can put in place the means to locate and wipe out or control those of racial and cultural groups not of their own kith and kin? By playing to the ignorance and prejudices of huge numbers of occidentals, they will easily be able to set up the most draconian methods of watching, spying on, and controlling millions.

The coming terror is stirring now, marking time for a new racialism, a new devilry that will dwarf everything in the past. Men will be marked for survival by the mere color of their skin or their religious, ethnic, or social status, as never before. Influences behind the anti-terrorist campaign of the Americans and other white Euro-Caucasians have encouraged the setting up of a system where the selection and monitoring of humanity will enable the Greys to carry out their deadly authorship of the human species.

They have the technology to know you and see where you are by your voice alone, anywhere in the world. Every device installed under the pretext of antiterrorist essentials is simply another nail in the coffin of an individual's inalienable and glorious right to bear freedom of scope eternally. Britons are now the most spied on people in the world. Over three million street cameras watch British citizens each day as they go about their business. Most of the populations of Western Europe can be trailed by electronic spying devices from the moment they leave their homes to go to work in the morning till the moment they walk back into their homes again.

There are proposals to force individuals in all European Union countries to give the various authorities their DNA profile. The French government is already planning compulsory DNA testing for the families of immigrants, ostensibly to prove that their demands for visas are genuine. It looks likely that DNA testing could soon be a requirement for health insurance. Can you imagine what that information would enable the authorities to do to the health and well-being of any individual deemed to be a threat? Indeed, it represents a threat to each and every one of us, no matter how much they assure us it will not be used for any nefarious purpose. I predict that this will be a reality in the next ten years, perhaps sooner, and we will meekly allow whatever power rules us to do this to us in the name of fighting terrorism. Nothing the Nazis did gave them this kind of control over their populations. Nothing in the history of our present world civilization has given so few such complete control over so many.

I believe the measures you are seeing now and will see in the future to genetically mark humanity will be a means through which the Greys and their protectors will seek to do this. They will find all kinds of plausible innocent reasons to justify it. The antiterrorism stance will be their biggest canard in seeking to justify it all, but in the end I fear they will succeed in doing this because ignorance, racial prejudice, and apathy on the part of all humanity will give them all the power they need to succeed. Through this procedure, I fear we will let them walk in and take away from us our power to exist eternally past physical death. There are reports that huge "disposal factories," where human beings will be processed for the merits or demerits of their DNA, are being built, mostly underground, in the United States, the United Kingdom, Germany, France, Poland, and Romania. The occidentals have learned from their Nazi predecessors how to do this on the grandest technological and industrial scale, covertly.

The enemy is being identified as those against democracy, Christianity, and particularly white culture. Through well-placed staged terrorist actions, the entire world is being persuaded to be hemmed in and polarized into factions that see anything and anyone that comes outside certain strict racial, religious, ethnic, and sectarian differentiations as the enemy. For these reasons Islam, with its huge following and increasing fundamentalist trend, is now public enemy number one. Saddam Hussein's danger to the world was judged in the context that he was a Muslim dictator that presented a particular problem to the security of Jewish Israel. It could be argued that he was as far from Muslim fundamentalism as it is possible to be in Islam. I am no apologist for this wretched man. I am just trying to point out that a blond-haired, blue-eyed creature cloned by an alien species is going to be far more of a monster to our species *Homo sapiens sapiens* in the future than all of the most evil icons that have lived put together.

The strangest irony is that the impetus to the Iraq war was led by clever Zionists in the awesomely powerful "Israel Lobby" in the United States, making a prostitute of a once great nation. Their sights are now set on Iran as a foe. With the help of a particularly pernicious form of fundamentalist Christian in the United States, this might lead to the instigation of a Third World War to bring about Armageddon. These variants and mentally twisted snakes within an otherwise precious and noble genus of humankind—the Jews—are a small, polluted marque, but they are now the deepest allies of the lethal extraterrestrial Grey roboids who stand over the skies of Israel. More UFOs have been seen over Israel per square mile than any other nation in the world. The Grey alien intent may well be to get as many Jews back to Israel as they can, so that they can harvest the people of Israel and a good many fundamentalist Christians, too, for their own deadly purposes in one fell swoop. The harvesting of genetically engineered Jewish DNA, carefully protected since a bush burned on a mountaintop and spoke to Moses, may also have been the intention of the speech that transpired there. I am convinced that this may well be the secret intention of the Grey mission on our planet all along, and the possibility that it might be true ought to be considered very seriously for the sake of the precious Jewish Diaspora and indeed for the sake of all humanity.

There will be many for whom this information will be untenable. Many will reject it out of hand because our eyes are usually hitched up to our prejudices. Such naysayers will mostly be racists—some unapologetic racists, some covert racists, some implicit racists—all unconsciously acquiescing in the imagery of their own kind as they perceive it. Once a tinge of racist, ethnic, or sectarian marginalization appears as an inherent motive in the mind-set of any individual, that individual is looking into the face of damnation: the loss of the eternal life element of individuality.

Every ethnic group clings to its own as a paragon of the best dispositions of humankind. We tend to see our own tribe and its culture as the best base on which value is derived, dismissing others as less authoritative and less meaningful in terms of truth and example. Many of us with alien genetically intercepted parents have been taught to do this from a very early age, as a kind of cue to survival. It seems logical that trusting only those you know best will ensure that you are less likely to be let down. I think you will find in actuality the reverse is true. Sociological surveys in the Occident point clearly to the fact that members of your close and extended family are more likely to let you down than any stranger. Just reminisce on your own family objectively if you can. What do you think?

For the majority of us, our extended families tend to be defined by our own familial ethnic, racial margins. For this reason, racially motivated bigotry is by far the biggest handicap we will face in all our lives. In the end—when set against the scale of the whole universe and the essentially dispassionate, objective paradigms of karma and reincarnation—those who follow a tribal odor mindlessly will be doomed. To restrict yourself to consorting with "one's own" is to close the expanse to which your karmic target can go. For example, a white Caucasian racist with a karmic debt from a previous life to an individual who reincarnates as an African American in a black ghetto community will be at an inherent disadvantage in expediting that karmic debt. He or she may be just too prejudiced or averse to providing the proximal status and familiarity necessary to offer the good counsel, communion, communication, and thus words and deeds that will best relieve the karmic debt.

However, our will is totally free, and no individual is irrevocably bound by handed-down racist tendencies. We can always change our mind. If we come to see that viewing racial difference as a threat will make it impossible for us to reconcile our karmic debts, then we will realize that it will contribute to the eventual loss of our living individuality and thus our soul and eternal prospectus. In a universe of diminishing returns running to the dictates of the SLOT, nothing can be totally controlled or managed. It is likely that some human genotypes can escape a formularized prospectus, a prospectus that forces them to act to the dictates of these alien entities. These escapees might well ensure that they never get total control.

The Greys that are here now are an advanced guard whose function and design is to reconnoiter, monitor, plan, and digitally clarify the mass abduction of those who are their targets in the human race. All procedures are carried out with clinical cold-blooded precision. Their only use for ballistic weaponry would be as a cleansing device for wiping clean their laboratory after they have evacuated their experimentally significant humans. Perhaps Sodom and Gomorrah was an example of this. One of my greatest fears is that such may well be the fate of Israel too, but this time through referred means, just as a scientist might not fumigate or cleanse the rats he has finished with personally, but instead directs others to do it for him. This can be achieved through a mentally planted Machiavellian aegis, as was done in the Holocaust through the Nazis.

The tales in the Indian Mahabharata regarding spaceships called Vimanas describe them as being in aerial conflict with each other. Descriptions reminiscent of nuclear warfare seem also to be present. I believe this narrative may well refer to another eon than our own, a distant time perhaps before the African Eve, when more than one group of alien entities visited this planet. In the modern context in which technological developments enable communication of information across the world, the Greys cannot afford to be seen explicitly as destructive entities. If this perception were to be conveyed to us it could ruin their ongoing experiment, as we would seek to defend ourselves and sabotage them. While these alien entities seem to be of a fragile physical makeup in the context of our earthly environment, they have a master control of physical forces, including the manipulation of gravity. By comparison, our means of manipulating forces in the universe is crude and primitive. It cannot cause them great personal damage. But through weapons of mass destruction such as nuclear bombs we threaten our own species and thus the integrity of their experiment. So they seek to control any means we have to bring this about. This involves capture of the minds of those who have these means at hand through mental manipulation. Control is the name of the game.

But the power of the Godverse that reaches into the universe from beyond the universe's physical precincts negates this natural tendency for the strong to rule the weak, the superior to exploit the inferior. It does so through the power of awareness and will, through thought and the strength of its focus on unity and unifying ways. The path to return to the Godverse and eternal existence is ours for the taking if only we can see with the outlook of the great teachers that defined the truth and the way to existence in En-light.

# 18

# You and You Alone

I believe unequivocally that we can think our way to an escape out of this universe. In various ways, congruent with the accepted norms of the times, great minds have tried to explain to us how this may be achieved. The Dravidian masters, the Sufi masters, the Judaic prophets, Gautama Buddha, Jesus Christ, and the great Prophet of Islam, I believe, could truly and rationally claim to be the greatest redeemers this generation of humankind has known. If we could find a true and faithful record of their lives and times and follow it exactly and implicitly, explicitly believing and duplicating what they said and did, not as a religion but in the most secular context, we would never be trapped into returning to this universe and a physical state of being. We would go beyond the "Margins of Never" and exist truly forever as "Gods," making our own nonphysical, nonenforced, nonmatter universes, with realities no less real than our physical universe is real to us, where our individualities will exist both as whole and as part at once, forever.

These assertions would have, of course, been regarded as lunatic without the explanations I have given in the foregoing pages. No doubt they will still be regarded that way by many people, but those who scoff will hopefully face the necessity of providing explanations that prove the contrary or at the very least offer plausible alternatives. I offer my somewhat radical views in this existential treatise as one alternative to the prevailing prognostications, views, assertions, and dogmas we are

323

asked to accept as the truth by our religious and spiritual peers.

Few of the sanitized versions of the great religious books stand up to scholarly examination and rudimentary reason. The Old Testament of the Bible is even now being shown to bear little relationship to historical accuracy and reality by many eminent Jewish archaeologists, among them Professor Israel Silberman and Dr. Neil Asher Finkelstein, two world-renowned names in Biblical archaeology. It seems the Old Testament is a document of endless subjective claims, surmises, and edits inserted and excised at the convenience of various authorities. Those who take the Bible as the literal word of God will no doubt cling to their views, as do those who belong to the Square Earth Society. But, where reason is any hallmark of truth, they will in the end be seen as sadly denuded and deluded individuals. They may well bear the saddest and most lethal consequence of all. Their unreasoning blinkered view may dictate the eventual loss of their intelligence and capacity to reclaim the power of being in control of their eternal tenure in the highest possible status of seeing, understanding, and knowing all things.

The thematic of all conventional religions consists of a series of platitudes that usually describe abstract ideas in abstract terms. They commonly border on the obscure to the very obscure and leave the listener nothing real to get to grips with. Even the Buddhists are sometimes capable of cant. For example, we are asked to practice "right thinking." It is a favorite chant of religious teachers in countries like Sri Lanka. What on earth does "right thinking" mean? It is never clearly defined. Right thinking to a thief will mean the best possible way of depriving another man of his goods. It is all a relative scale. Yet the world is subject to a pack of enrobed clowns chanting these pious platitudes in fusillade after fusillade from temple and pulpit alike, and we are asked to take seriously these squeezed, excruciating cacophonies as some glorious blessing and benediction that will metamorphose our very souls.

I seek in no way to offend any human being. I do, however, claim the right, as any individual has the right, to challenge views that have no reason or logical thread. It is only those who purvey ignorance and lies, which enable them to hold power over others, who fear the open discussion of vital and, in the case of our individual existential tenure, utterly crucial information about its central verity, form, fashion, and maintenance. When the religious claim the right to hold our individual eternal scope in custody under the premise that all things purveyed by their various dogmas have been considered, examined, and admitted by wise and learned men over a long time, when they claim that much of those dogmas should now, under pain of severe sanction, be accepted without any further question and discussion, I am tempted to raise two fingers in denial and admonition.

There has been time since the Earth became suitable for life to have had two hundred thousand civilizations of the same time span as that of our present civilization: two hundred thousand civilizations, each of fifteen thousand years' duration. If we take just the last fifty million years or so, there could have been well over three thousand civilizations of the duration of our present one. Let's say each was wiped out by an asteroid crashing into the earth. There might perhaps have been three thousand redeemers of the stature of the founders of the world's great religions who brought back the lost knowledge of the true existential scale each time civilization built back from the destruction point.

But if there had been that many civilizations for that length of time, would it not have been likely that we would have found some traces of them? The answer is no. It is likely that they would have been totally wiped out, without a trace, by regular asteroid, comet, and meteor impacts on the earth. These cosmic catastrophes are the great erasers. They take out entire life systems utterly and completely if they are big enough; we know of plenty that have happened capable of doing this.

There are also phenomena known as gamma-ray bursts (GRBs) that can have a similarly catastrophic effect. Scientists have discovered that these are the most violent explosions possible in the physical universe. They happen when a large enough star collapses in on itself and forms a black hole. In its process of formation a black hole puts out a burst of gamma rays perpendicular to its spin axis, which can affect all the stars in the galaxy of which it is part. The energy and power put out by one of these GRBs is capable of destroying life in all the planets in the galaxy. They act as planetary sanitizers, taking out entire systems of galactic life. Only one of these bursts needs to take place in our galaxy and we would all be a nuclear paste. So there are many, many contingencies capable of acting as celestial erasers of civilizations, however old or sophisticated, that would leave no trace of that civilization behind. Scientists now think that these events are far more common than they first thought.

What price the best made plans of mice and men when nothing, no matter how sophisticated it might be, can beat the natural primal exigencies of just being alive in a physical universe? Technology, no matter how sophisticated, cannot save any civilization. Physical life thus seems meaningless in terms of the vulnerability of its physicality. It is too fragile and finite. It is this go-nowhere survival potential that raises the question: Given that physical material life is so vulnerable, fragile, and finite, are we alive *just to know* that there is a phenomenon where life can be conscious, have conscience, intelligence, and sentience in a state of eternal tenure? Or is there an existential paradigm beyond the physical, where there are no erasers outside the personal decision-making process, where existence is exultant forever and true in all aspects possible such that perfect justice prevails?

Our universe spells doom and only doom. Yet almost all of us put our faith in this madness each day we live. We hone every part of our demeanor to fit in with the day-to-day outlays that drive the very center of our physicality, the enforced particles of space/time that make all matter up we call atoms. Yet these same atoms are smashed into greater and greater states of chaos and randomness with time with the action of the SLOT. We worship at the very throne of the true Satanic power of all satanic powers—entropy—by default. Yes, we do try to fight it by delaying its effect and scoping its purpose, but it will always get us in the end, while we persist in atoms and don't change into a state that can take us out of them permanently. We all begin to rot the moment we are conceived, we rot our way down to the final decay of our minds.

While there can be no certainties for living beings that exist in an engine of chaotic amelioration, we can know one thing: we are still here to be wiped out. After perhaps three thousand eons, we are still here to go through the same process, despite the almost hysterical urgings of the great teachers to follow their example and get out of the Universe of Force altogether while we still can, while we still have sufficient powers through the God-light within us to see our way out. If we don't do this sooner rather than later, we will think and do the wrong things as a direct result of the obfuscation of God-light over time by the destructive effect of entropy.

I admit that much of the above must seem thoroughly obscure to many readers. It is not really obscure if you move carefully through it all. But it is essentially complex because it seeks to unravel something needlessly complex into something that is very simple, by de-codifying it and breaking it down to its essential components. If we aim to rediscover the truth of the entire existential base that defines our being, we have to begin with the rediscovery of the old texts and records. I have painstakingly searched through as many as I could find over thirty-five years of research and set them against the present knowledge science is giving us. I have made an attempt to look at the objective elements in the various religious texts available today, without fear or favor, taking away the personal accents, the subjective referrals, and the openly illogical and contradictory drivel billions have followed through the centuries.

The various dogmas of organized religion were mainly based on socially commutative rules, in most cases decided by old men whose mind-sets were hardly representative of the general schemes and norms of society. They were mostly designed to keep groups of people together in the face of some threat. The principle of confession in the Roman Catholic Church, for instance, began with the need for the covert practice of religious observance under Roman hegemony. An information-exchange system within the flock had to be evolved under sometimes deadly Roman eyes that were looking for groups of Christians in Rome.

The idea that confession is good for the soul never entered into it. It was simply that stating opinions openly was bad for one's health and longevity.

In smooth timbres, the cannoning chants and well-meaning voices extol the virtue of letting our redeemers carry our burdens. Christians hear in mind-numbing repetition the bumbling bromide: "Jesus came to take on the sins of the world." Might "taking on the sins of the world" simply have been an implicit invitation to revelation by the center of all meaning, Godhead, and the laying bare of the megalithic falsehood that is our status as beings in atoms? But to this simple statement the Church representatives add: "Hold to us and our ways. We hold the admission tickets to the reward he earned for you; we will give you one if you earn it in the way we prescribe." They are saying: "There is no way to heaven unless you go through *our* door." This ensures vast and effective control over thousands of lives.

In contrast, Jesus unequivocally demonstrated the singularly untouchable power of reason and free will, assumed in the person of the individual. His method of teaching in parables was a powerful exhortation to see that veracity is the child of logic and reason. There is a further and more important implication, and this is that the individual has to work out truth for himself or herself and that in this mechanism, and *only* this mechanism, is liberation accomplished. It can never be done in proxy by anyone on behalf of anyone. We either cripple ourselves or free ourselves on our own individual recognizance. At the instant life fails in us, we all stand alone at death's door, facing the stream of eternal results that will lead us to be a "God" or a man, an ape or a fish, a tree or a stone. Jesus himself made a point of giving his will to his Father in the prelude to his death in the garden of Gethsemane. This was a deliberate act of donation rather than an implicit, automatic process. It was a clear demonstration that will is utterly and totally free. Even the "Son of God" himself had to actively *give* his will to his Father. This explains why Christ, who was so keen to save us, could not zap us all and in a single moment convey us beyond harm's way.

You will see now a chain of connection before you that explains the whole existential outlay in such a way that reason rules. The foundation of liberty in true free will lies in impersonal objectivity immersed in a matrix of reason and logic. But it also portends a terrifying thing. It is terrifying because it takes away the crutch we all seem to need so much: someone to blame for our own faults. It says there is no personal anthropomorphic God we can blame for all the terrible things we see and do. It places control for all results under the premise of free will and thus lays the blame for all negatives and misfortunes at the door of each individual entity within the existential scale. We make ourselves God or no-God through our own results.

We have made our own restrictions through our own will and therefore are the only power that knows how, when, and what we have done to bring about our restrictions. So Christ told us about soap and bathing and how to reach all the pits and crevices that hide our follies. We and only we can reach them and do the cleansing. He knew very well that all the detritus would come back again if someone else removed it and we did not understand its true nature and what it was doing to us. It is up to us to want to be clean and remove our own psycho-restrictive dirt, which is highly person-specific. He taught us the lexicon of restriction and left the choices to us. The existential fundamental paradigm of free will left him no choice.

The theocratic nonsense that suggests that we must put ourselves into some kind of spiritual palanquin created for us by this lovely being is a mind-numbing insult to his labor and final sacrifice and a denial of his lasting meaning. Obvious, you might think. But if one thing is clear, through the record of the centuries of human endeavor, it is that human beings have the most awesome capacity to believe humbug. Indeed we seem to want to believe humbug. This kind of madness leads to experts taking a chimpanzee's painting and unknowingly hailing it as the work of a great master. It literally has made monkeys out of men if devolution is indeed the way of the world.

If we are condemned as a species, it is a just reward for the madness that sometimes claims even the best of us, the madness that prompts us to abandon the stern pith of logically extrapolated truth in preference for the lies our emotional comfort points dictate. The rich man spends thousands of dollars, pounds, marks, or rubles to have the muscles of his gluteus maximus pushed a little more gently against his hipbone in his Rolls Royce than in, say, a Morris Minor. He does this when perhaps a ten-thousandth of the value of that Rolls would get him the same distance from A to B, by the smaller simpler car, leaving the difference for saving the lives of perhaps hundreds of little starving children. Such is the merit of the world we see today, where we ruthlessly ignore the little starved faces crying at the empty paps of a third-world mother, in favor of decorated stones and empty fancy monoliths that adorn our equally empty vanity.

Poverty and disease in the nonwhite third world has existed on such a tremendous scale and for so long in the face of so much excess and profligacy in the Occident. We should have long ago seen that it has never been a question of whether we *can* cure it. It has always been a question of whether we *want* to cure it. By "we," I mean us in the shamefully wasteful West. It is now way beyond a reasonable doubt that we don't care enough to cure it. There is something truly evil in the thinking paradigm of the broadly white Occident, and it prompts the conclusion that most of its population is covertly racist.

The country that proudly claims to be the moral leader of the world today, the United States, has imprisoned one in eleven of her black citizens. This heinous figure exposes the truth that—one hundred and fifty years since the emancipation of slaves in this country, which has all the modern devices at her command to promote mass media attention to the evil of racism—this aberration is still embedded in the thinking of many Americans. And so it is, I dare say, in every Cro-Magnon–seeded country in the world today. No matter how hard they seek to hide the fact, how cleverly they posture the sublimation of it, their citizens by and large succumb to the stench of racism on the slightest excuse. In elections in the Occident, it's called "playing the race card."

Take a look around the world. The merest is done to relieve the condition of the hundreds of millions of desperately sick and hungry people, particularly in the third world. It is no longer a question of ignorance. Information technology explodes it in our faces daily. The things that are done are largely palliative, embarrassingly minute and miserly, and carefully orchestrated by the Western media to look massive. But this is a contradiction in terms to the natural drive that generally exists in human nature to give aid and succor as an immediate reaction to someone in need. If, as we walk along a street, someone nearby drops down and falls to the pavement in distress, the vast majority of us will instinctively reach down to lend a helping hand. The natural and instant reaction of almost all human beings will be to serve and to help, not to finish them off into oblivion with manic relish. The power of Godhead is still immediate and always present within our human condition, at least at the very base of our knowing.

Why then has humanity not rid the Earth of poverty, want, preventable disease, and suffering long ago? Why has one-fifth of the population of the world conspired for so long to keep four-fifths destitute and condemned to meagerness, when it so easily could have banished indigence from the face of the Earth? The social statisticians are constantly giving us the numbers that betray a covert congress deliberately preventing this. There can be no doubt that if the same effort was put in to beat starvation as was put in to beat Saddam Hussein, or indeed if all the world's countries were to halt for one year their expenditure on arms and put the money they save toward developing systems to beat famine and disease in the third world, we would eradicate want and suffering from the Earth forever. One-tenth of the personal fortune of any one of the ten richest individuals in the world could build two hundred hospitals in each of one hundred of the world's poorest countries and get rid of medical want, saving millions of lives and eradicating the worst degree of the world's medical needs at a stroke. So why don't the countries of the Occident that have so many multitrillions at their disposal do this for the relative pittance it takes? They don't because suffering promotes political power. It provides control over nations and their people.

Europe is the world's "father" of psycho-existential corruption. European forces through the centuries have systematically unleashed on the world a holocaust of detriment through the millennia of conquest, colonialism, and slavery. It has left the entire planet poisoned and burnt out, its people subjugate, starving, and torn apart in racialism and ethnically and fiscally fermented wars and conflicts in almost every third world country to suit the West's political ends. Alas, the United States, with its wickedness to its own indigenous people and millions of others imported as slaves, became the "son," emulating the example of its terrible father—Europe. Colonizing countries such as Greece, Rome, Mongolia, Persia, Britain, Spain, Portugal, Germany, France, Turkey, and last but not least the United States have left a legacy of carnage among peacefully living native indigenous peoples through history, foisting their lifestyles and belief systems uninvited on these peoples. Together with their sponsored clones such as Genghis Khan, Alexander, Napoleon, Attila, Hitler, Stalin, Pol Pot, and Amin, they come and go in infamy, their names fading a billion victims into the pages of time, victims forgotten till the next time, and the next time, and the next time. It never ends there. The greatest truth of all is that eternity has no color: not grey, pink, yellow, brown, or black.

The instinctive reach for what is beyond the atom, in other words the God-sense in us, has lessened in the entire occidental world. This is, in part, down to the cold one-sided influence of science through technology. But the fact remains that world leadership tends to come from this Euro-American sphere. If anything will beat these creatures it will be the power of what lies beyond or outside of atoms. These alien clones are masters of the world of atoms, and we are dead in the water before we start if we take them on in those terms. Alas, we seem to have little choice but to face a catastrophe while the leadership of the world rests in the hands of the techno-materialistic behemoth of Euro-America. The historian Michael Woods puts it very succinctly:

Throughout the countries of the rich West, there's a growing and profound disquiet—a feeling that the Western way of life itself is no longer supportable morally or practically, because of pollution, environmental destruction and the continuing exploitation of the mass of humanity.[1]

What a glorious country the United States could have been if it had followed the prompts of wholesome family values as expounded by her own original founding fathers. America was founded as a refuge from the tyranny of Europe, a tyranny soaked in political and religious intolerance. One would have expected a new start to contain all the opposites. Instead, the disease simply multiplied with even more draconian evil as a result. Whole peoples were wiped out and hundreds of thousands subjected to the horrendous suffering of being enslaved in strange places with strange ways.

How is it possible that the most magnificent opportunity for all humankind to prove that we are one family was squandered? The global immigrant ethic that founded the United States out of the four corners of the world now lies in tatters. While America claims to be the moral leader of the world, the most cursory examination of the place reveals its present values as ones that extol materialism and banal and delusive consumerism. Thus it would now seem to be the least likely keeper of the world's ethical standards. Anyone who has been to America recently could not have failed to notice what an intrinsically superficial, deeply racist, violent, and vicious society it can be. The world requires a moral leadership of enormous magnitude. If the United States is currently our planet's most influential and powerful country, if nearly ten thousand years of world civilization has produced a leading nation saturated with such debauchery, where and to whom can our species look to find a change?

It would be one thing for Americana to be this way if the commonly prevailing Mickey Mouse simplistic psychology that seems to prevail too much there could be isolated and strictly and exclusively reserved for Americans only, and not exported to other regions of the world. But speech after speech from a succession of U.S. presidents claims America to be the moral and martial leader of the world. There is little doubt that, judged by any objective nonpartisan standards, the United States is the most morally defunct and debauched source of influence the world has seen since Rome.

For all this, the United States is still a beacon of hope for our whole planet, one nation where true freedom reigns truly. It may take just another Lincoln to turn the tide, one visionary with a sense of the true grandeur of humanity, one inspirational leader that can drive home the power that we all have within us for seeing the greater good. I believe no other country could change the world for the greatest worldwide common good than the United States of America: the country where all the nations of the world have a heel. What better place can it come from?

But how have we accelerated into such a stage of demise? How, for example, did a group of tiny islands in the western and northern Atlantic (that now constitute Great Britain) come to dominate the world, when huge civilizations like China and India that were seats of learning that far surpassed the barbarian cultures of this era did no such thing? I believe it can be put down to something inherent in the nature of the people. Let me put it this way: a man who will throw a javelin, no matter how small he is, will always dominate a man who throws a handful of rice, no matter how big he is.

Gunpowder was known in China for centuries before Marco Polo brought it to the West. The Chinese used it only for firecrackers. Polo immediately saw its potential to kill, to maim, to conquer. Seen in this way, the inheritors of direct Cro-Magnon ancestry are the true bearers of the mark of Cain. After all, the instinct to kill, to steal, to pollute, to destroy the inheritance of others, seems so natural in the occidental varieties of humanity. Certainly a historical scan of the colonial era provides ample and undeniable proof of this: the deliberate genocide of hundreds of thousands of Native American Indians, the enslavement of millions of Africans in Europe and America and their subsequent genocide, the wiping out of the Australian Aborigines and their culture, the wiping out of the magnificent Maori culture, the deliberate enforcement of dope addiction on more than one hundred million Chinese, the horrendous holocaust that took from us six million precious Jews with an industrialized disposal procedure. This is only the modern equivalent of other countless ancient pogroms conducted by the Greek and Roman civilizations on millions of victims. The destruction of the Incas and the Aztecs—the list of Cro-Magnon sponsored debauchery is endless. But, in the cruel and expedient minds of racists, this would no doubt be seen as the price of progress, progress toward a poisoned planet.

The precincts north of the Tropic of Cancer largely define the most decadent and entropically driven varieties of our species. Industrial technology is the spokesman of the damned. It was inevitable that it was born of the central crucible of force on our planet, the Occident. This is the forge where all the metals of our nature were beaten into the swords that have ravaged the innocence and the innocents of Man century after century. The "Barbarian West" stands condemned as the birthing pool of cultures that have defiled the Earth with countless wars, pestilence, and famine. It is the broad scope of Babylon that idealized the extreme forms of human grossness more consistently and for longer than anywhere else. How then could cultures that boast the glories of Shakespeare, Newton, da Vinci, Michelangelo, Mozart, Beethoven, Schiller, Goethe, Franklin, Edison, and the host of others like them be the cornerstone of depravity for a whole world? Does the culture of wisdom lead or does it follow in the wake of another more dominant behest, a master behest that claims the heart and sentiment in favor of the strict edict of socialized geometry? Is it a mere afterthought, an inevitable spin-off that simply happens because its opposite does?

I have no doubt that the synthetic Greys, as bio-machines, run to a computer program. So indeed do all their cohorts on the Earth that have brought about this situation via the psychochemical interception of humankind through the Cro-Magnon legacy. There can be no doubt about this if you judge it by the increasing tendency that many Northern Hemisphere people have for a cold-blooded, machine-minded, list-filing mentality. This psycho-type of humanity gave birth to industrial technology, and this led on to the heartless consumerism (some would say the two things are synonymous) that increasingly dominates the people of the Northern Hemisphere, be they Occidental or Oriental. It begs the salient question: Are they largely under the control of the Greys already? Is there something within their psychology that innately programs this response?

Have you noticed that the culture of the West comes down to a culture of the mind? The Christian prophet chided one of his disciples with the axiom: "Think with the heart." That disciple was Judas Iscariot. The implication is inevitable and obvious for any objective person who has traveled to the societies of the more spiritual and social midband of our planet, largely the countries between the Tropics of Cancer and Capricorn. Yet how many of the northern Occident and northern Orient tread the poverty- and deprivation-ridden streets of the third world and look down with relief and perhaps disdain on the little hungry eyes and outstretched hands, breathing a sigh of superior relief and giving thanks that they are not thus because of their racial and mental superiority?

If you look around the third world and count the number of white or occidental faces that are not tourists, consultants of one kind or another, priests, nuns, or religious servers of some kind, the number of purely voluntary servers of the poor and the unfortunate in the non-white world acting in generous, unselfish offertory amounts to about 0.000001 of a single decimal point of the total occidental population of the world. Measure this against the horrendous picture of the massive scale of want and deprivation we see daily on TV screens, and it provides a stunning indictment of the altruistic nature of the so-called civilized people of the West.

We are all fooled into thinking that the Cro-Magnon legacy to the world is one of civilization, largess, and highly cultured magnitude. Such is the skill of the media humbug makers. A quick empiric measure of actual results shows a quite different story. It shows a story of pirates, parasites, murderers, and covert manipulators of cleverly set up systems that steal from the poor to give to the rich. A history of a largely heartless machine-minded breed of fortune hunters, hell-bent on coldly and selfishly exploiting defenseless and disadvantaged people for cheap labor or raw materials, while skillfully making it look like goodly service for the poor and the unfortunate. Many nonoccidental countries have, of course, the local versions of such people, ever ready and willing to assist their Western counterparts in their work. But they are largely educated in the West and often have heavy traces of Cro-Magnon juice in their veins. The magnified influence of the heavily extraterrestrial-apprenticed Cro-Magnons has led the ways and means of things done in the name of humanity. This influence includes elements of machine-minded programming. No room at the inn for sentiment, compassion, and offertory.

There can be no doubt whatsoever that we have the intelligence and the expertise, the hardware and the software, to easily rid and forever forbid the source of much of the trouble in the world today: poverty and the want engendered by the basic human need for shelter, food, and clothing. The vast majority of the world's eminent social and demographical experts haven't the slightest disagreement about this. If we have the corporate intelligence to go to the moon, build nuclear reactors, nuclear bombs, complex missile systems, satellite systems, and planetary explorative systems, how could we possibly be supposed to lack the intelligence to build a simple social system that brings us all together in cooperation for the good of the very survival of the species? The point is that we don't lack the intelligence; we lack the will. Herein lies the rub. *Why?*

What is it in us that prompts such evil, if our basic nature in instant reaction to someone who falls in injury before us is to immediately and unthinkingly go to their aid? In this case, our instinct is "goodly" or "godly," for want of better words. Why do we do such injury and harm to so many, so often, and so constantly, when we have more time to think about things? Calculated instigations to war and starvation prove very effective tools for rich Western nations to gain political control of poorer ones. What causes us to proffer such a deadly harvest of doom if our innate, unthinking, reactive nature is to aid those in need?

We all, of course, know that human nature is a mix of the monster and the saint. Or so it seems to be. We hear the oft-quoted adage to the point of triteness: "There's good and bad in everyone." What then makes the bad dominate the good? Or how is it we all seem to be led by the nose to world crisis after world crisis, war to war, famine to famine, pogrom to pogrom? Evil certainly is the dominant and deadly drive that underpins the world. The magnitude of the daily casualty rate from wars and skirmishes and social and political murder around our planet is huge. The peacemakers can never sleep. The deadly horsemen of death ride rampant, the ropes seeking to restrain their steeds covered in the blood of failure till they have borne away their fill of innocent blood.

There has to be a covert agency, a deadly hidden factor in human affairs and perhaps in the psyche of human beings that can keep in check the natural instinct in us to give succor to the helpless. It prevents the species from employing the means and the good sense to save itself from its own destruction. An inhuman "force" prompts division and separation among us all. This agency is not intrinsically of our world or, most importantly, of our nature. It operates remotely and invades us from without. Further, it is not natural in the ways of the cosmos itself. It is an artificial modulation of the universe and is a contrivance of it, which operates universe-wide and affects all natural existential forms that have their ancestral origin in Godhead.

"And man shall walk as machine," the prophets screamed. No one noticed. No one denied. It is undeniable now that our future as a biological species is increasingly forted with the sap of engine oil. Switch the TV on any day of the week anywhere in North America and the enthusiasts of virtual reality and future scope will fawn, enthuse, and facilitate the anarchic glories of inner space. A random selection of any ten of the most popular newspapers and any ten of the most popular films at any one time that come from that part of the world will show you in vivid Technicolor what I mean. The clones seem to have the entire shooting match well and truly taped up and posted to the furthest reaches of a Euro-American hell, if Western values as propagated by our media are anything to go by. It may well be that the only way out of self-destruction for most northern Caucasoids is a ride on a spaceship designed by their own "mummies and daddies." There will certainly be a surprising number of them lining up enthusiastically to welcome the cold grey list-filing bioids as their long lost relatives when the sky "nerds" finally come to ground and declare themselves.

In the end, it is the power of focus of mind away from the material that Christ and all the greatest teachers told us was the answer to beating all that is not natural in Godhead. Have you noticed how the deeply spiritual nations and regions of the world, mainly in the tropics, where focus outside the atom is strongest, are being gradually overwhelmed by the grotesque monster of the fiscal ethic? The last psychoactive bastion for our defense crumbles under the covert intercession of the deadly Grey "men" on the back of the moon and their cohorts, be they in Wall Street, Threadneedle Street, or the one they call "the street where you live."

The greatest prophets and seers through the centuries have predicted, as the falls of Egypt, Greece, and Rome confirmed, that the development of the human resource as a consumer-based ethic with the self-centered, acquisitive, materialistic sense dominant, is the ultimate paradigm for damnation. Why did all the greatest seers affirm this point of view without exception? If they were right—and history teaches us that they were categorically right—those in the West who are driven by this ethic are done for. If NDEs define any scale of natural retribution, then the negative ones that so many people have experienced describe the terror that might come the moment the blood circuit round their bodies stops moving and the dark tunnel beckons their souls' hall of perception.

I am convinced that the central point of all evil rests at the pivot where we demarcate on the principle called "difference." The root of it all in terms of our human predicament lies in the operation of social, racial, and ethnic platitudes and taboos. The welfare of the whole planet lies in this one point, where a socially diseased white occidental mind's eye meets a complexion a darker shade than pink. This is the point where an accent can turn away a face in disgust or the sound of a surname can forbid an opportunity. Through millions of instances such as this taking place each day all over the world, the globe of our living rostrum spins a darker and darker announcement that we are doomed.

An extreme case can be seen in the fate of the beautiful, gentle Aboriginal people of Australia. Seen as antediluvian savages in jail after jail, they have been murdered and forced to commit suicide time after time by the partisans of the machine-mind in the name of civilization. The Australian Aborigines, who show marvelous values and attributes to this day, are looked on as primitive and pilloried as such by many of their grotesque, white occidental, plastic, modern counterparts in their machine-minded splendor of polished stones and engine oil. These Aborigines, as with many others of the less intercepted genotypes of humankind in other parts of the world, have been systematically exterminated by those amongst the white Caucasoids who acquiesce with the Grey's Cro-Magnon legacy written into their biological program.

Below is an extract of an interview I had some years ago (when I was a medical student) with a white Australian police officer working for the Queensland force. While he was on holiday in London, I got to know him as a friend and he agreed (very bravely as you'll see from the transcript) to let me interview him about racism in Australia for a university student publication:

> All it takes is just the merest sight of them. . . . The sight of the bas-
> tards black spindly body. Neanderthal . . . features. You don't think
> of them as human. It's an instant thing . . . a mixture of fear . . .
> anger . . . you know mixed with aggression I suppose. It kind of wells
> up from deep inside. . . . You get this . . . this . . . urge to threaten . . .

to hurt . . . to punish. . . . It comes at you from nowhere. . . . The fact
that . . . he's different . . . they are different . . . I suppose. They've
never done anything to me . . . personally . . . I mean. . . . You know
it is all . . . outside reason. All outside . . . sense . . . control. You
know you have to be in control . . . but you don't care. . . . All you
see is that he's different . . . not like you . . . your people. You want
him to disappear. He doesn't matter. He's just a piece of shit. . . . He
doesn't belong. You are looking for the slightest excuse to make the
bastard . . . disappear. He speaks. He says "I've done nothing man."
It's enough. . . . He dared to talk to you. You bring your stick crashing down on the side of his face . . . He falls to the ground. You
like it. He is not with you for a moment. You're relieved. . . . He's
not so near you anymore. You turn away. Trying desperately to stop
yourself. . . . You tell yourself you're a policeman. . . . It doesn't work
mate. . . . Nothing works. . . . He grunts and moves on the ground,
recovering his consciousness. He whimpers and clutches at his face.
Shame grips you now. Then anger. I suppose you are really angry at
the fact that he existed at all, and that fact has brought this ugliness
out in you. It's mad I know. You put him away as quickly as you can.
You can't face him anymore. Now there's . . . well . . . shame there
. . . and that is to do with you mate. . . . He has to go away. He has
to disappear. You pick him up. You kick him because he dared to be
there and make you ashamed. You throw him into the back of the
car and close the door. You have to shut him out. It's instant. It's
mad. . . . Am I mad? . . . I think somewhere inside we are all fuckin'
mad. . . . You . . . you know what . . . I think they are far better than
us . . . I mean you and me mate . . . Er the whites I mean. . . . I think
. . . I really think that's what it is. . . . Mad . . . mate . . . It's fuckin'
mad. . . .

I wonder how many million times this Australian police officer's sen-
timents have resonated within the minds of racists, murderers, and tor-
turers the world over? Could the racist and the xenophobe be running

a program inherently in their genes? Are there measures written in our genes that make some of us helpless automatons working to the mandates of celestial interlopers? It is, of course, likely that there would be some genetic ancestral lines that hold the alien recipe more strongly and more cogently than others. If this is true, then the racist and the xenophobe are the most lethal types of human beings on the Earth. They should carry a worldwide public health warning notice around their necks. I, for one, would not harm a hair on their heads. I would, however, avoid their company as though they were carriers of the deadliest plague, no matter how close they were, even in terms of biological family ties.

I hope it has been apparent that my comments only refer to trends and tendencies that prevail in societies or social groups. Undoubtedly, there are many individuals within these societies or ethnic groups who might have qualities that are of the opposite nature from those I have described. There can be no doubt, however, that certain perspectives dominate all of our minds. They tend to divide us into two clearly different outlooks: those who look at humankind as a brotherhood within a single species and those who see us as distinct racially demarcated marques who can only survive within the borders of those marques. The latter sort cannot see the power of every human being to be independent of any tendency, be it biological, social, psychological, or indeed spiritual. In such as they, racially assembled stereotypes dominate response and behavior. In them, the Grey's original genetic interception survives the strongest.

One of our greatest scientists, Dr. Paul Maclean, at the Laboratory of Brain Evolution in Poolesville, Maryland, discovered that the brains of higher living organisms were divided into three distinct schemes of tissue. In other words, we have three distinct brains in our body. Dr. Maclean called it the "triune brain."[2] The three separate tissue schemes that make up our brain correspond to three distinct behavioral modes. He identified the three tissue schemes respectively as the neocortex, the limbic system, and the R-complex (see Plate 24).

The neocortex is the most advanced scheme, judged in terms of manifested behavior. It is composed of the cerebrum, with a special accent on the prefrontal lobes. It is by far the largest of the three brain schemes. He associated it with the higher, more ephemeral functions of aspiration, intuition, aural communication in terms of language, a sense of the aesthetic, and the expansive mind facility that deals in overall associative meaning.

He identified the second scheme as the limbic system, composed primarily of the cingulate and hippocampal gyruses, the hippocampus, insula, and hypothalamus. This he associated with behavior such as the family sense, the nesting instinct, the group husbanding sense, the emotional bonding sense, and play.

Dr. Maclean identified the R-complex as being largely composed of the globus pallidus, the olfacto stratium, the corpus stratium, amygdala, and attendant satellite grey matter. Maclean called it the "R"-complex because the behavior ascribed to it resembled the posturing of reptiles: the hunting instinct; the territorial instinct; the fighting instinct; and the instincts for ritual, display, and challenge. There was a clear implication that the aggression centers worked in conjunction with these instincts, accompanying their functioning. The qualities of Cain are thus encapsulated in the function of this part of the triune brain. Could this be the brain of preference written into the Cro-Magnon program?

Fascinatingly, hidden racial prejudices have been recently revealed through the use of brain scans. Using functional magnetic resonance imaging (MRI), Matthew Lieberman, working with a team in the University of California at Los Angeles, has found that white Americans show more brain activity in the amygdala when viewing images of black faces than when viewing white faces. The amygdala, part of the R-complex, is involved in emotional reactions and becomes very active in fearful or threatening situations. But it also reacts to novelty, so activity in this part of the brain could just be the result of seeing a less familiar kind of face.

To test whether increased activity might be a result of novelty, Lieberman and his colleagues conducted an MRI experiment with eleven white and eight black Americans. Each participant completed three tasks: matching the race of a target photo to one of two comparison photos, matching a target photo to either the words *African American* or *Caucasian American,* and a control test where they matched geometrical shapes. Both black and white volunteers showed increased amygdala activity during the visual task when the target face was black. The same task with a white target face produced no such activity. Because black faces should not be "novel" to black people, Lieberman concluded they must have learned to associate other black people with a threat. These brain results are backed up by earlier behavioral test results: "These Implicit Association Tests (IATs) use subtle tasks, such as the time it takes for subjects to associate ideas of race with either positive or negative words, to uncover unconscious attitudes. Black Americans often show more positive associations for whites in IATs."[3]

The remarkable fact that even some black people have deep-seated prejudices against other black people clearly suggests that there is something programmed into human biology that invites the association of high melanin with threat. Almost all human biological lines are alien-intercepted to some degree. The low-melanin races are more affected simply because their low-dermal-surface melanin affords the Greys an easy access to the nuclear DNA within the cell.

However, the article about Lieberman's study goes on to say that, interestingly, it seems possible to override the amygdala response. When subjects performed the verbal matching tasks, there was no difference for black or white faces. "In general, putting your feelings into words seems to regulate or dampen those feelings," says Lieberman.[4] So, the biological prompt to view high melanin as a threat can be countermanded by the power of mind in reason and in focus. Christ and all the greatest teachers told us that the power of focusing away from the material was the answer to beating all that is not natural in Godhead. The simple adage: "Where your focus is, so will your heart be," is beyond any doubt the final and most powerful psycho-existential resolution for us all.

Any genuine act that provides a mental or physical momentum of will that encourages union will open the valve inside you that channels the "power" of Godhead in the universe (En-light). In consequence, every hydrogen atom in you will be subjected to, within itself, a natural anti-force or unscrewing effect of the force that keeps it a hydrogen atom. If you maintain this momentum enough, you will transfigure. In other words, you will resonate with a less enforced environment, call it heaven, valhalla, paradise, or whatever you like. You will be on your way back to Godhead and eternal life without ever having to reincarnate and thus go through the process of rotting from conception again. You will in fact have "forgiven" yourself. While doing the acts of retrieval—if you have done them well enough and often enough—you will have learned enough to free yourself from restriction and thus sin. Nevermore will your soul be subject to the whims of karmic obligation.

All the simplistic exhortations to be good, do the right thing, to be right-minded, and so on are meaningless nonsense. They are no more than transient psychological palliatives to ward off temporary states of distress to the advantage of those with power over others to force compliance. Individuals and cartels in authority will dictate the terms of reference of all actions by encouraging us to follow the "right path" and to "do the right thing in the right way." What does it mean in actual terms of effect anyway? What actually happens when you are "good?" What really does the word *good* mean? No one ever tells us this. No one can. It is and has to be the most relative abstraction in the lexicon of meaning. The old adage, "one man's meat is another man's poison," describes the difficulty nicely.

Before we can accept the word *good* and by default the word *bad* to mean anything, what is needed is a universal logical norm, a set of naturally reasoned principles and adages that apply commonly to everyone, everywhere, that are agreed upon and accepted in the interests of the whole common human good. For these words to mean anything as controls of human behavior, there has to be a settlement in natural justice and natural balance considered and approved by all.

In our world now nothing could be further from this. As science approves all contingencies, the lines of referential meaning are deployed away from the personally spiritual, moral, and social imperatives to those that are materially and physically expedient. Thus the reference scale against which the words *good* and *bad* have meaning will change. What reference scale can be used for these words to mean anything significant at all? The only possible one is the definition of final value that I have referred to previously, attested to and elucidated by the entire lives and examples of the great Buddhist teacher Gautama Buddha, the great Christian teacher Jesus Christ, and the great Prophet of Islam, Mohammed:

Eternal tenure in the highest possible capacity to maintain that eternal tenure.

The final existential value of all is existence itself. The true and final struggle is to maintain just *being there*. The incredible fact that revealed itself to me in the course of researching this book is that we have lost the perspective to judge our value against all final value. There is but one value against which all is set: being there to know without limit in the highest possible value of knowing without limit. The acquiring of knowledge must never be limited, and more importantly, the drive to acquire it must never diminish. It must increase.

It is when this endeavor slows or ceases that the individual entity is doomed. For lifetime after lifetime hence, the tacit drift will be a downward spiral of achievement and endeavor, till we sit watching football matches, or whatever the new TV or video vogue might be, with our comfort points hitched up to our loins or our hands, in a state of nondescript, noninquiring abandon. The result is an awesome dive to damnation that may never be reversed whatever you do! The dip from human to ape, to monkey, to mammal, to all the lesser life forms, will continue downward, getting harder and harder to reverse as time goes on, because the very will to change it becomes mitigated as knowledge cedes to ignorance and the entity cannot gauge priorities anymore.

The capacity to achieve anything is set by the power of belief. Belief is the herald of success. Though I must sound like some business motivator in saying this, this axiom holds true in all things where the unknown is set before you and you seek to explore its full measure. Nothing holds you back but fear. For most of us, this is easy to say and hard to change. The whole trouble is the contest that goes on ceaselessly between the Brind and the soul mind, between the temporary and the eternal scale. The physical senses usually win out, for most of us, almost all the time. Our imaginations, which are capable of expanding into limitless vistas of knowledge, are thus confined. A pen writing musical notation on a piece of paper, for instance, confines its results to plain black and white dots and dashes on a page of wood pulp. But when the dots and dashes are translated into schematics of sound, they reveal limitless ranges of musical realization, feeling, understanding, and meaning. Indeed, those physical dots and lines could have no meaning unless a phenomenon beyond the physical was capable of finding it. But when we incessantly ignore the grand and settle for the mediocre, we are damned.

We are damned but for phantasmagorical beings that come among us beached little God-lings from time to time, beings like Christ who punch holes in space/time, get crucified for their trouble, and still love us ceaselessly and without end. This awesome Jew came through the center of the spaces between atoms faster than anything electromagnetic can travel and presented Godhead as a living phenomenon through the womb of a woman. He was reviled by his own kind for his troubles and sadly, with ultimate irony, more revulsion has come upon his own kind as a result. I guess he was trying to teach us that making ourselves a particular kind makes us no kind at all.

Beings such as he hold their ancestral points in the faraway gold of a world of wonder where some of us, perhaps the rarest of us, go when we die, a place within the hem of our universe, but with a direct line of accession to a world beyond the scales of all atoms. Here choice is mitigated because choice is always of the purest love. If there were a sky here, it would show lost sheep, prodigality in extremis, madness in its purest sense, and most of all ignorance and helplessness beyond meaning. Billions of worlds would show their cages here, as atomic hems that enforce and freeze the assets of the soul in margins of forever.

We are truly lost sheep, beached Godhead. We belong to no single planet; in fact, we have almost certainly been physical beings in a multitude of planets. If we have intelligence and are alive now in this universe, we may well have taken many shapes and sizes as life forms on other planets before the species *Homo sapiens sapiens* even appeared on this one. We have persisted through all these planetary formats because we have lost our way, lost sight of our final and only home, the home from which all of us as living beings first emerged and got trapped in force. We need to see ourselves as eternal phantasms, as divided Godlight. Every single human being alive is such, not the crushed form of physicality that we perceive ourselves to be. We need to regain our sight of our final and only home, the home from which all of us as living beings first emerged. That home is the Godverse. The one crucial thing we have *not* lost is our ability to see and make choices. This has kept our link back to the Godverse still intact.

# 19

# Returning to Godhead

In order to clearly visualize the path to freedom that still remains open to us, let's revisit the model shown in Plate 16 depicting the creation of universes like ours. Creation takes place as an incidental function of the potential difference that exists between two final and opposed existential poles, the Pole of Harmony absolute (Godhead) and the Pole of Chaos absolute (Forcehead). Once a universe bursts into existence, part of it re-evolves back into harmony and part of it completely dissipates into parts. We could say that universes like ours constitute the "Devilverse"—a sea of various stages of the breakdown of Godhead into parts. Forcehead is the final terminal point within the Devilverse, when all life is extinguished, all particles are undone, and total enforced-ness exists with all vestiges of order gone.

Plate 16 shows this as two plates facing each other. In between these two plates, a Moroidal shape defines the margins of a universe like ours. The Moroid expresses the contour lines of the laws of physics as we know them. These laws describe how the universe is held together and how it functions. They are the product of the action of the two poles that define the Moroid, one vesting a momentum for order and seeking to unite separated parts and the other trying to do the opposite. It is a churn of contradictions and upheaval in which Godhead seeks to put the brakes on what Forcehead is doing. In such a situation, could it be said that God ceases to be everywhere?

Time measures a scale between two points. We are all measured in
time and thus—whether we are part of living matter or dead matter—our
existential signature measures a scale we call individuality. This is true of
our individual natures too. They measure time in terms of an existential domain. We all have specific lifetimes. Each lifetime is measured by a
special set of criteria that in turn are measured by another set of criteria.
For example: belonging to the species of tortoise or human determines
the natural core time scale allowed for a particular species—two hundred
years for a tortoise and if you are lucky (or unlucky), perhaps a hundred
years for a person. Within humankind, each individual can, of course,
vary the time component of his or her existence to a certain extent. On
this planet, our species has been increasing the scale of allotted time for
existing in life per unit being since the beginning of time itself. We now
live longer than ever before, and almost everyone hails this as a good
thing. This is no surprise, because the longer we exist in this universe, the
less natural insight we have into our grandeur as entities that belong to
another dimension of being.

The longer our species continues, the greater its secularity and loss
of sight that we were once "God-lings." We are losing sight of the glory
we once were and are slowly merging more and more into the fabric of
enforced-ness that hallmarks all universes of parts. The mindsets that
drive for secular verifications in all things are firmly in control, and we
are being converted to beings that will finally be like, and serve the purposes of, synthetic robotic entities that even now marshal our planet,
ready to take the reins and bring about a terrible destiny for all natural
living being.

Our thinking and mindsets have thus become tuned to the terrible
precept that we have to eke out as much physical material existence as
we can, whatever the cost. This view, alas, will get stronger and stronger
with time, leading us to pull ourselves away from the cord of redemption that held us from the beginning of the universe—our soul—the
capacity for eternal knowing in ultimate sagacity and sentience. As we
gradually lose sight of our first nature in Godhead, we accede to the

great pull of the Pole of Chaos, diminishing species by species till we move from animal to vegetable to mineral and finally become that wall of nothingness in absolute chaos and force devoid of all meaning at the Pole of Chaos.

But we do have an alternative. The final measure of existential meaning is whether it is limited or eternal. Existence itself is the measurer of its own importance. The fashions and modes of existence may be different, but "being there to know" is what matters. Let me explain this with the use of a fiber optic lamp as an analogy. A fiber optic lamp (FOL) is composed of a cascade of glass fibers. The end of each fiber is a point of light. The source of the light is underneath a flat piece of glass on which all the fibers rest. The coherent light of a laser provides an emanation that goes through the glass fibers and reproduces itself in many pinpoints of laser light (see Plate 17). Now imagine that the glass fibers represent life forms in our universe. The flat piece of glass at the bed of the lamp is the equivalent of the margin of the Godverse with the universe. The pure, coherent laser light is the light of the Godverse packed with intelligent information and knowledge—En-light.

Imagine multitrillions of individual strands (life-forms) all over the universe, all containing God-light within their fibers. The En-Light within each is there as *mind,* forming and propagating matter for each individual life-form, be it an animal, insect, tree, or bacterium. In the lamp, all the strands are straight, whereas in real life, individuals each have various degrees of distortion resulting from the pull of the Pole of Chaos, which tries to tear them apart into greater and greater states of randomness and chaos with time. This pull can be visualized as bends, twists, and knots in a strand, which change the clear light of Godhead into diffractions of the original light, defined by color (see Plate 17). The more bends and twists, the more a living being will tend toward the black that defines the total obfuscation of God-light.

In an actual fiber optic lamp, each strand comes together in a bundle of strands; the strands are more and more tightly packed till they hit the flat glass plate at the bottom, where they are all lined up perpendicularly. They receive the laser light from the slit lamp in a perfectly straight ninety-degree angle. When this model is applied to living beings, the glass plate represents the second-dimensional interface point of contact with the Godverse. The angle of contact of the strands is not exactly ninety degrees because of the Moroidal shape of the universe. Everything that has been created, every life-form made of matter, takes on the twisted nature of the very spine of the universe. I believe this is what is called "original sin"—a built-in distortion defining the twisting, separating power of the Moroid.

This angle of distortion is congruent with the shape of the twist of a water molecule. This degree of congruence admits En-light into the hydrogen arrangements of water molecules when they are connected in any series of patterns. The carbon molecule becomes vitally important because it provides the means of this connection in multiplicity, and thus it is paramount for life to happen. Carbon acts as a spine that allows for long-chain molecules to form and for these molecules to connect up to one another in a series. We have now the template for life itself to happen. En-light itself is thus the instigator of all life.

In the FOL, when the fiber optic strands hit the glass plate they are, to all intents and purposes, a single strand. They take up all the light coming from the laser light beneath. They may be said to be at one with the light. In our real-life analogy, we may be said to be as alike to God as we can be in this universe if we are fully straight. This was what Christ meant when he triumphantly claimed: "I and my father are one and the same." He had achieved true congruence with Godhead through his ministry in our universe at that point: he was one with the Godverse, as we too can be through following his example.

Christ's transfiguration and later his resurrection—which canceled and dominated all force paradigms—corrected the last bit of Moroidal distortion that sustained separation from the Godverse. He literally undid the twisty-ness of space/time as it prevailed in our planet's part of the universe, undid it enough to, in effect, punch a hole through which we all can access everlasting life. In doing this, he could justly claim to have saved us. This was the exercise he had come to accomplish above all, and he did it successfully when on the cross he claimed his triumph with the words: "It is finished." I would like to make the point here that I do not believe for one moment that his crucifixion was a necessary prerequisite for this triumph. There is so much more he might have been able to teach us had we allowed him the time to live longer.

By allowing us a straight-through entry point back into the Godverse, Christ saved our species from permanent capture in this universe. In other words, he "made straight the way of the lord" and gave us the ability to enter into the ninety-degree gateway. All MESFs that become perfectly congruent with it, that is, perfectly straight, will be able to pass through to the Godverse. By becoming what the religious call "righteous," we straighten, so to speak, the spaces between our atomic hives so that God-light can fill those spaces and enable us to key into the second-dimensional interface. From this point, the rest happens instantaneously. We merge with the Godverse and connect with Godhead at the singularity point where the All becomes the One.

Such a change takes place through a metamorphosis, which Jesus expressed with the simple phrase: "Change your mind." Can this be all there is to redemption? Yes, this is all there is to your redemption and accession to eternal life. There is no more to it than changing your mind. It is that easy and that *hard*. It is harder than all the things you will ever try to do because it does not mean a mere change of decision, a mere inflection of your mind, such as you might do many times a day. It is a *total* change of mindset, requiring a search for logically and rationally affirmed truth related to meanings that may not always be apparent in physical terms. It involves manipulating the orientation of a million little spots within your atomic hive as an individual person so that that they shine with a light so bright that no sun in this universe can equal it—a light so pure it will not harm the eyes of a fly and so true it will deliver you to the very root of meaning itself.

As we have seen, this light is everywhere, everywhere there are atoms, because it lies in a point at the very center of an atom's expression and also more pervasively in the space between atoms in a vast universe-wide corridor, which connects all the spaces between atoms to a single stem that touches the very kernel of Godhead. Rather like a giant net held by a single strand, En-light emanates order itself, slowing down and countering the opposite momentum to chaos and disorder. Perhaps this is what Jesus meant by these words:

> Again, the kingdom of heaven is like unto a net, that was cast into the sea, and gathered of every kind: Which, when it was full, they drew to shore, and sat down, and gathered the good into vessels, but cast the bad away.[1]

The incredible thing about this light is that it is manifest in real time in all living being, and only in living being. But life does not guarantee that this light is usable by all living being. It is crucial to understand the difference between light that is manifest and light that is usable. The light is implicitly manifest in all living being as the empowering agency we call *life* and as the tacit revelatory agency we call *consciousness*. The housing or containment mechanism of this light is set very precisely within a geometrically progressive hive of atomic arrangements that makes six-atom hydrogen rings in stacks. The greater the disposition of hydrogen atoms, the more powerful the ability to use this light so that matter is *disposed* and mind is *imposed*.

God-light, or En-light, is utterly coherent and without vibration and is thus completely un-enforced. This gives it the power to still all the enforced paradigms of the atoms it touches. If presented in a maximum manifestation of six-point hydrogen ring configurations, it can *undo* the enormous electrostatic scaffolding force of the atoms. Like a screwdriver undoing the tightness of a joint, En-light can unscrew enforced paradigms such as the bonds that hold atoms together. It can even go further and unscrew the implicit inertial forces within a particular atom, changing it into the prior form of En-Light it once was. The more En-light that can reach into the space between atoms of an individual, the more power of *mind over matter* he or she can exercise. The power of Godhead in matter is expressed as awareness, strength of will, and flexibility of will.

However, the increase of hexagonal hydrogen rings also increases the potential to reduce them, because they increase the power of free will. In other words, the weight of the crown goes with the halo. A kind of balance is thus produced. Decrease your six-atom hydrogen rings, and the capacity for exercising free will and thus achieving will decrease proportionately, because your capacity to allow En-light in decreases. The capacity to *change your mind* will thus tend to decrease too. The status quo of your being will be maintained as it is, and you are likely to go nowhere.

On the other hand, an increase in the six-atom hydrogen rings will do the converse. It will increase the potential to see and do things that will enable escape from the universe. At the same time, it will also increase your capacity or potential to go against the grain and do the opposite, because the range and options for deleterious change increases too. It is unlikely, but the danger is always there. It's like walking on an unending treadmill. Stand still and the treadmill will take you on in the direction it goes. Walk faster in the opposite direction than the treadmill is moving and you will make progress against its inertia. Walk fast enough, with the right priorities, and you will achieve transfiguration.

Transfiguration is the transmutation of force into *un*-force. Christ in one lifetime used knowledge, understanding, perception, and works translated into mind vectors that could undo the forces holding the states of matter together. In other words, his works promoted modes that unionized parts in all the disparate elements and situations he came across in his everydayness. He did this because he knew that it would counter the natural opposing power of entropy, the way of the nonliving, nonthinking systems of the Universe, to break things apart into increasing states of randomness and chaos with time. He used will engendered "mind-force" as a weapon or mental imperative that he knew could act at the most basic subatomic level if used powerfully enough, to couneravail and reorder or even mullify existing states of matter. In an instant on Mount Hermon, he touched the state of *Godhead within matter* directly

356 •— Returning to Godhead

from the living state (it is usually accomplished from the state of death). The brightness seen at the point of transfiguration is simply the sight of Godverse-ness, so to speak, as it manifests against the wall of force of the universe. Jesus was able to align his six-atom hydrogen rings in a configuration that allowed God-light to stream through his atomic structure until he "glowed brighter than the sun." This alignment can be compared to open window blinds. When the blinds are open, the individual slats that make up the blinds are edge on, so that there are big spaces to let the light through. When the blinds are closed, the slats are face on and their surface area blocks the light out. Jesus aligned his six-atom hydrogen rings so that they were more two-dimensional than three-dimensional.

At that point, he still had enough control to return to the atomic state, but that control lessened as he converted more and more of his hydrogen into six-ring formations. He agreed to enter into Jerusalem, knowing that he would be killed, because he was reaching a point at which he could no longer maintain a physical form. He put himself into physical peril in order to teach, in his last moments as a physical man, lessons to the most primitive and closed human beings of all, the scribes and Pharisees in the Sanhedrin.

All the greatest prophets, teachers, and mystics have extolled us to beware—to repent—to change our ways. Why would they do this unless something dreadful had already happened to us? Were they all paranoid fools because they dared to see what is denied most of us, a sight that we individually and independently have denied ourselves? I have merely stood on their golden platforms, on their bravery, their wisdom, and their blood to make the harrowing assertion I began with: "We are all damned." *All* that I have deduced leads to the final and unequivocal assertion that every living thing that can think, know, feel—indeed *every* living thing, regardless of its general or detailed existential features—is now, at the very instant of time you read this, essentially and intrinsically damned to reduce such existential bearing as they possess, in terms of the scope and versatility of their living tenure, process, and procedure, in this universe of atoms, through its overall entropic momentum.

But Moses, Buddha, Jesus, and Mohammed all found that we are only damned because we are blind and we are blind only because we have chosen to be so. They had the glorious insight to notice that all things, in purely material terms, were always dying. They saw the material, existential vista for what it is—*devolution*—and that the human physical capacity was measured in loss and not gain. Their true glory was their capacity to see God-form from within the standpoint of flesh. Their physical atomic arrays had the quality of being stupendous "aerials" that received a visionary view of the final existential domain. Far from being ephemeral dreamers with their heads in the clouds, they truly had their heads beyond the clouds, beyond the margins of matter itself. They realized the true ultimate reality of the Godverse. They tried to outline the powers and types of thought and action that are necessary through free will to return to modalities that are self-preserving and guarantee eternal existence.

But to those who have understood our entropic predicament and dared to assert it, we have cried: "Oh no, not another prophet of doom! Not another guru of despair!" We have ignored them, lifetime after lifetime. We have avoided facing the harrowing truth of what we were losing. Perhaps it was too much to bear. For many, it soon became too late even to look again. They may now be represented by a shoal of fish or a colony of termites. A million cicadas may now sing with the voice that was once a person. We—most of us—are on the way to such an end: to the magnitude of an insect, and in time inevitably to the idleness of stones.

For many of us, it may well be too late to look again. Many have forgotten how to do so and require a leap in the dark—an act of faith, belief, and trust in someone outside themselves, the "sense" to "know" the last from the first and see where true existential value lies. The Essenes described these as the "poor of spirit," Christ's "lost sheep." If such as they are to make their way out of atoms into the Godverse, they must have a handle on the process that is powerful enough and meaningful enough within their parochial sensibilities to provide incentive and focus to track into it through their everydayness, as a biological species. In other words, "seeing is believing" has become our guide to reality. If we don't see, most of us just don't believe. In fact, it is getting harder now to believe even when we do see. This is now the "Age of Reason." Alas, the "Age of Faith" implicit has gone with time in our procedure through the churn of entropy. For many, alas, we now have to see truth reflected through the elbows of connected logical reason and not through the blind resources of mystery, myths, and faith that once served a lesser entropic form and thus spiritually superior genotype of humankind as signposts for release from atomic capture.

Christ, as the nearest thing to pure God-form that can exist in atoms, took on the form of Man to translate the general average of humankind back into pure God-form (here the word *Man* may be taken as a simple word for locations in space where God-form is trapped). He demonstrated the "living technique" that would lead the maximum possible number of humanity back into this precious natural insight.

He led with his focus set far beyond this universe of force. He led using the word *Father* as the dynamic symbol of perfection we all could understand in our terms. In his terms, it literally was his eternal life raft. It is easy to see how essential the love of his Father was in providing a life jacket that kept his head and heart above "atom-ness," in as pure a focus as was possible for one who is squeezed into "en-forced space," or atoms. God-form danced bright and powerful in him, never allowing his demeanor to settle into the contours of atoms except for the briefest of moments, at which time he realized the full horror of the predicament of Man. Perhaps this is why he sweated blood in the garden of Gethsemane, just prior to his arrest and subsequent crucifixion. It was perhaps essential that he allow himself to descend into the "depths" of the human predicament for those moments—to take the full measure of such a fate, such a condition. In it, perhaps he gleaned an understanding of the enforced separation state that is precluded from knowledge while in the state of total union of parts.

We, as humanity, have been told through the ages that the essence of God is *freedom absolute*. We have also been told it is *love absolute*. We have then been encouraged to deny such an allowance with the huge contradictory axiom that God must be feared and worshipped in craven servitude. And some of us have been urged to seek comfort that all is well and God is only allowing evil for the sake of exploring its extent. The legend goes that we are all part of this experiment and the light of universal love will thus come to our rescue, whatever we do, whatever we are. This nonsense beggars belief.

No God of love can ever separate peoples at his almighty whim. Real, true love saves. It saves unconditionally. It bestows the greatest gift love can give, the liberty to be free and make individual destinies in total and unqualified free will. It will then save in limitless magnitudes of mercy and compassion all that fail so that they might put "self" back together again. Such is real Godhead. It was and is all a proposition of a blazing and ultimate love.

In our case, it is a true love for all humankind, a love capable of carrying the atomic hive we call a body through and past the handicaps that were and are being planted on its gene base by a deadly kind of entity such as the Greys and their like in the universe. Real Godhead cannot under any scale of logic or sense ever be anything that rules, commands adoration and worship, kills, maims, punishes, blackmails, and favors some over others. Only man-made "Gods" do that. Humankind has made and is still making true Godhead into a pale egocentric facsimile of itself. And the kind of humanity that falls victim to such facsimile will eventually take itself out of any existential scale.

Christ sensed, and knew, the danger of acquiescence that contradicted the freedom of Godhead. He saw escape through thought as our only life raft and showed us how to get free of our shackles through the forms and fashions of the everyday living process, with one crucial and glorious difference. At every signpost of choice, he rearranged the entropic momentum of separation with the only thing that was free of it—will and the phenomenon that manifests as thought. He clearly saw thought in will as something wondrous, as the cradle of meaning itself—something that is not part of the idle, static, dependent resolution of force that makes up the disbursing physical world of matter. He alluded to the home environment state of "eternal life" as the ultimate progression of being. He confirmed God-form, which he called "Spirit," as a concept that we cannot envisage accurately, such as when he chided Nicodemus by asking how he and others—who found it hard to understand and believe what he said about the world of *flesh*—could believe or see anything of the world of *Spirit*.

"Ultimate everlasting tenure" in awareness, meaning, and knowing was the only *reward* promised by Jesus Christ, as the consequence of leading a righteous life. Nothing else was made an implicit certainty by this marvelous teacher, and nothing else could ever have been promised by him, because it simply stresses what is patently obvious. There can be no greater achievement in existential terms than the confirmation of existence—in eternal tenure. A state, or effect, that provides for it therefore implies the absence of inherent risk. No physical matter state can be free of risk. All matter is implicitly destructible. However, he and the other great teachers quite clearly saw the magical connecting point between thought exerted through will and the hard, dead world of the physical atom.

By the public demonstration of his transfiguration, Jesus Christ was the only being that actually achieved direct release into the Spirit "frame" from the force vector of atoms that holds us all bound. He demonstrated that it could actually be done. Five hundred years earlier, the Buddha demonstrated that he could glimpse its result from within the frame of atoms. Jesus actually took us further and *achieved* the transfer, temporarily. Christ showed the chosen apostles the final result of living a life in such a way that his power of thought and deed unraveled the very atoms of his physical being. I believe that all his exhortations to doing "good," as it is commonly expressed, had far more atomic a result than has been appreciated up to now.

This is probably the most crucial secret science will discover: that thoughts and acts of sincere unselfish love—modalities of behavior that add together, unite, and bind—actually have the physical effect of unscrewing, or very slowly loosening, hydrogen bonds from their diatomically bonded natural state, to ultimately have the effect of "unzipping" the force resolutions that make physicality itself. Do enough of this and you too will be able to do what Christ did: transfigure into the Godverse. As with anyone else, he had to do it after dying. Let me explain. Although he demonstrated that it is possible to change or unwind hydrogen atoms to a point that a solid human body could transmogrify or transfigure, the force exerted on the heavier atoms by the bio-magnetic field would not allow for his assumption into the space between atoms in a living state. Before a complete escape out of atoms can be effected, this bio-magnetic force field has to be negated, which only happens at death.

Here, at last, through all the foregoing prescriptions of doom I have outlined, we arrive at the most marvelous admission of all. The triumphant accession out of this predicament of ours, through the example and wondrous everydayness of Christ, Buddha, Mohammed, and all the great teachers, *is* possible. The secret of all secrets lost to the present perspectives of most humans is not the existence of a roboid form secretly ruling all our tomorrows on this planet. *The secret of all secrets is that existence in the spirit is the eternal and uncompromised form of all existence.* Any lifeform in the physical domain of existence *can* know and make choices that might allow for the reach and accession into the Godverse.

Thought is the power of all powers, through which all change occurs anywhere, but how do we use thought powerfully enough for our own individual redemption? It is not for me to teach new meanings to the world in this book. I have no sermons I can offer for the redemption of the human species. The great teachers, mystics, and founders of the world's major religions have passed on the most glorious insights capable of taking each and every one of us away from the lethal touch of atoms and enforced paradigms of existence. In the end, the sight of truth has everything to do with being in touch with our eternal scope.

The biggest discovery science will make in the twenty-second century will be the awesome power of well-focused thought to move and change the direction of all the universal forces that are atomically derived. The natural momentum of entropically instigated force to separate things into their constituent parts can be radically reversed through belief-engendered thought if there is *enough* power of belief behind it. The most important word in any language is "enough." The power of thought rarely works because the driving, focusing power is simply inadequate to make thought control atoms. When it is made powerful enough, however, it will work every time, changing the functions of space/time and matter in a twinkle of an eye. The final power to do this was demonstrated by the Judaic Christian teacher at and through his resurrection over two thousand years ago.

# 20

# The Triumph of Truth over Lies

The most startling of all human existential propositions has been slowly revealing itself over two thousand years of history. Jesus Christ's final claim to rise again from the dead has, I believe, been proven beyond any shadow of a doubt with a little souvenir he left behind, a souvenir that has astonished and castigated the doubters of his veracity and purpose throughout the entire world. That souvenir is the Shroud of Turin, the cloth that wrapped his body after his crucifixion. The true triumph depicted by this piece of cloth is yet to be adequately appreciated by humanity. Yet I believe all I have said and claimed in this book will be vindicated through it.

I have always been a disbeliever in "relicology." There have been so many claimed pieces of the true cross of Jesus Christ it would have taken a forest of trees to account for all of them. The Roman Church particularly has through history indulged and tolerated the preservation and worship of the dead body parts of many of its acolytes as a sop to faith. Many, on close examination, have proved to be relics of the imagination and a sop to the gullibility of people needing something to believe, something to take them beyond the mundane and senseless verifications of their day-to-day lives and give them hope of something beyond the realm of our hard-wired world.

Although I once doubted that this relic covered the resurrecting body of Jesus Christ, the painstaking review I have conducted into all the research done on this piece of cloth has convinced me that it is the genuine article. It has very recently been found by scientists and experts working in various fields to confound the laws of physics as we know them. It bears the imprint of the front and the back of the body of a man. In a now undeniable and sensational verification process conducted by many eminent scientists, this relic is proving to be exactly what believers have claimed it to be—the actual burial cloth that covered the body of the Christian teacher as it lay in the burial tomb.

The Shroud of Turin measures approximately fourteen feet long and three feet, seven inches wide. You can see photos of the Shroud in Plates 26 to 28. These photos were taken by Barrie Schwortz, who has done a remarkable job of presenting all the latest research on this remarkable artifact on his website (www.shroud.com). This single rectangular piece of linen was wrapped tightly around Christ's body lengthwise. That is to say, it was wrapped along the vertical axis from the feet over the head, down the back, finishing at the feet again. The Shroud cloth, it seems, was left in the tomb when it was discovered that Christ had disappeared and had, as claimed by the apostles, risen from the dead.

What happened to the cloth between then and now? There is some evidence and a strong tradition to suggest that Thomas and Thaddeus went to Edessa as early as 33 CE, carrying with them a cloth bearing an image of Jesus. In 544 CE, a cloth with an image believed to be Jesus was found above one of Edessa's gates in the walls of the city, a cloth that Gregory Referendarius of Constantinople would later describe as having a full-length image and bloodstains. There is strong evidence from writings, drawings, icons, pollen spores, and limestone dust to confirm that the Edessa cloth is in fact the Shroud of Turin. It is believed that the cloth may have been hidden inside the city's gates, either to ensure its safety from all the floods for which Edessa was known, or to keep it safe during the time of the persecutions. In 944, Emperor Romanus sent an army to remove the Edessa Cloth and transferred it to

Constantinople. Crusaders looted the treasures of Constantinople and carried away many relics. The cloth disappeared along with other price-less treasures. There are reports that it appeared again in Athens, then in Lirey, France, and eventually in Chambery, where it survived a major fire. It was then moved to Turin, where it is now housed, and where it also escaped a fire in the year 1997. Time, it seems, has somehow pre-served the cloth, despite every exigency history could throw at it.

In 1989, a team of scientists attempted to measure the age of the cloth by a technique known as carbon dating, which measures the neu-tron enrichment of a sample to estimate its age. Roughly speaking, older samples tend to be less neutron enriched, because the heavier form of carbon (known as carbon-14) is radioactive and decays according to a fixed constant, so that the older the sample is, the less carbon-14 it con-tains, proportionately.

The results were presented by the teams as implying that the cloth was a mere six or seven hundred years old. There were, however, certain eminent scientists who questioned these results. Professor T. J. Phillips, of the High Energy Physics Laboratory at Harvard, wrote a letter to the leading scientific journal *Nature,* in which he put forward the neutron doping theory. This suggests that if the image had been formed by a short intense burst of radiant energy (which is the current conclusion—see below), including neutron radiation, that would have doped the cloth with neutrons, which would reduce the apparent age of the cloth. It would also probably have caused an uneven distribution of neutron doping, so that different parts of the cloth would yield different appar-ent ages. Thus Professor Phillips says:

If the Shroud of Turin is in fact the burial-cloth of Jesus Christ . . . then according to the Bible it was present at a unique physical event: the resurrection of a dead body. Unfortunately this event is not acces-sible to direct scientific scrutiny, but the body may have radiated neu-trons, which would have irradiated the Shroud and changed some of the nuclei to different isotopes by neutron capture. In particular some carbon 14 would have been generated from carbon 13. If we assume that the Shroud is 1950 years old and that the neutrons were emitted thermally, then an integrated flux of 2 x 1016 neutron cm-2 would have converted enough carbon 13 to carbon 14 to give an apparent carbon-dated age of 670 years [i.e. fourteenth century].[1]

This letter was published in the same issue of the journal (volume 337, no. 6208, February 16, 1989) as the *official* report of the international collaborative carbon dating project, which did not even mention the neutron doping hypothesis, but contained a startling piece of information in small print. In this, the authors state that the probability of obtaining by chance as much variation in the neutron content as was found in the carbon atoms of the three samples (taken less than seven centimeters apart on the unmarked part of the Shroud) was only 5 percent. In other words—in view of the other evidence suggesting that there was a short burst of radiant energy from the body of the man in the tomb—it seems most likely that the discrepancy between adjacent parts of the cloth is caused by neutron doping and that the Shroud can still be regarded as being, indeed, the burial cloth of Christ. If this is so, the cloth will be the finest proof of Christ's ability to demonstrate the absolute dominance of thought over atoms.

It is possible with modern technology to test whether it has been neutron doped. This would provide a final and undeniable inference that the figure depicted as this visual objective record may well have been, as I believe it to be unreservedly, the most wondrous phenomenon that has ever existed in life on this Earth.

When Professor Dimitri Kuznetzsov—one of the most eminent scientists in the field of carbon dating and winner of the Lenin Prize for Science—heard that the carbon tests on the Shroud were done in the aftermath of a fire that happened in the fifteenth century, he went on record as saying that the results of such tests on linen exposed to fire were notoriously unreliable because, and I quote from an interview:

The mechanism of fire contamination of the linen is a very important and a significant way of enrichment of the linen, not just by carbon, but mainly by radioactive or minor carbon 13 isotopes which
obviously would have a very essential impact for any calculation of
dating based on Carbon 14 and 13 estimations.[2]

In addition, Dr. Leoncio Garza-Valdes (a microbiologist) discovered
a bioplastic coating of bacteria and fungus on the linen fibers (60 percent by weight) caused by living microbes that absorb and add carbon-14
(C-14)0 to the cloth; it is possible that they could thereby skew the date
by at least 1,300 years. These microbes were not known at the time of
the test and were not removed by the C-14 cleaning protocol.[3]

Sixteen years later, however, the original carbon dating of the Shroud
was shown to be an inaccurate determinant of its age for other reasons
that proved to be conclusive. An article appearing in 2005 in a peer-
reviewed scientific journal, *Thermochimica Acta,* demonstrated that the
carbon 14 dating was flawed because the sample used was invalid. The
article contained evidence that the corner from which the sample was
taken for carbon dating had been mended. The linen patches given for
testing were from patches sewn into the cloth in the fourteenth century
and later after the fabric had been burnt in a fire. Thus the researchers
concluded:

> The combined evidence from chemical kinetics, analytical chemis-
> try, cotton content, and pyrolysis/ms proves that the material from
> the radiocarbon area of the shroud is significantly different from
> that of the main cloth. The radiocarbon sample was thus not part
> of the original cloth and is invalid for determining the age of the
> shroud.[4]

Moreover, the researchers, led by Raymond N. Rogers, a well-
published chemist and a Fellow of the Los Alamos National Laboratory,
went on to suggest that the cloth was much older, at least twice as old

as the radiocarbon date, based on a negative test for vanillin content in the Shroud:

> A linen produced in A.D. 1260 would have retained about 37% of its vanillin in 1978. The Raes threads, the Holland cloth [shroud's backing cloth] and all other medieval linens gave the test for vanillin wherever lignin could be observed on growth nodes. The disappearance of all traces of vanillin from the lignin in the shroud indicates a much older age than the radiocarbon laboratories reported.[5]

Research suggests unequivocally that whatever accounts for the image on the Shroud, there can be no doubt that it is the image of a genuine human being, a male, and that the Shroud is not a painting. Evidence for this comes from scientists of many different disciplines and specialties who all testify to the authenticity of the Shroud. The Shroud of Turin Research Project (STURP) (conducted in 1978 by approximately 35 scientists who directly examined the Shroud for five days) discovered that there was no capillary action apparent in the fibers, meaning that the image was not the result of any form of wet-media painting, which would have caused pigment to "wick" into adjacent fibers. The fibers themselves were not stuck together, nor were there any substances between the fibers, which would indicate the application of medium to create the image. There is no directionality to the image, nor is there any outline that would indicate an artist's sketch.

The STURP microchemistry team found no evidence of pigments, dyes, paints, or stains that could have been used to create the image on the Shroud. X-ray fluorescence found no detectable difference in elemental composition between image and nonimage area, proving that there were no inorganic pigments present on the cloth. X-rays concluded that there were no density discontinuities associated with the image, meaning no substances could have been manually applied to create the image. Photoelectric spectro-photometry concluded there were no spectral characteristics of stains, dyes, or pigments detected in the image or nonimage areas, proving that no typical artist substances are present on the cloth. Ultraviolet fluorescence concluded that there were no aromatic dyes or amino acids present in the image or nonimage areas, proving that there was no collagen binder present on the cloth as would be expected if the image were the result of paint.

Other eminent scientists, such as physician John Heller and chemist Alan Adler, have demonstrated that the blood found on the cloth is real human blood, type AB, and that it was present prior to the scorch images. The STURP forensics team confirmed this by detecting the presence of heme, porphyrins, bile pigments, and serum albumin. The bloodstains are consistent with "a contact to the cloth of blood clot exudates that would have resulted from major wounds inflicted on a man who died in the position of crucifixion."[6]

Ultraviolet fluorescence reveals the detail of the scourge marks to be of such fine detail that it is not possible for any other method besides direct contact to have created them. Overall, the image displays the correct forensic physiognomy expected from wounds of these types (direction and chemical makeup of blood flow, direction and placement of wounds, and so on), knowledge that was simply unknown before the twentieth century, and impossible for any medieval or ancient forger to replicate.

Still more startling revelations have come from more recent examinations of the image done by still more eminent scientists in the disciplines of physics, biology, chemistry, engineering, quantum mechanics, and forensic medicine. In 1997, Dr. Robert Bucklin, JD, a distinguished forensic pathologist working for the Los Angeles Police Department, made a remarkable report after examining a life-size photographic facsimile of the Shroud. Bucklin has over fifty years experience in the field of postmortem examinations. I quote from his report:

> The full body imprint, front and back, together with the individual characteristics of blood stains on the cloth, which represent specific types of injury, make it quite feasible for an experienced forensic

pathologist to approach the examination of the Shroud image, as would a medical examiner performing an autopsy on a person who has died under unnatural circumstances. It is the aim of this presentation to replicate such an autopsy examination, using the image on the Shroud to delineate traumatic findings and to interpret the cause and the results of those injuries, as well as to present the most reasonable and probable cause for the death of the individual whose image is present on the Shroud of Turin.[7]

According to Dr. Bucklin, the man of the Shroud was savagely flogged. The nature of the instrument used is consistent with a Roman flagrum, a whip of short leather thongs tipped with bits of lead, bronze, or bone, which tore into flesh and muscle. There are dozens upon dozens of dumbbell-shaped welts and contusions, the type of wound that the flagellum would have caused. There is blood from the flagellation within the imaged wounds. From the angles of attack—the way the marks fall on the man's back, buttocks, and legs—it seems that the man was whipped by two men, one taller than the other, who stood on either side of him.

At some time, the man who formed the image on the Shroud may have been forced to wear a crown of thorns. That seems to be a logical explanation for the numerous small puncture wounds about the top of his head. But from the wounds and many drops of blood, the crown seems to have been a rough bunch of thorns and not the wreath-shaped crown of thorns so common in artistic depictions.

Many details on the Shroud suggest both a beating and a fall: a severely bruised left kneecap, a dislocated nasal cartilage, a large swelling near the right eye socket and cheekbone. It is particularly interesting that the man on the Shroud was crucified with large spikes driven through his wrists rather than through the palms of his hands. This contradicts all iconography of medieval and premedieval periods. This is evidenced by both the image and the bloodstains.

Nailing a crucifixion victim through his wrists is more historically and medically plausible. Early in the twentieth century, medical experts first realized that nails driven through a man's palms would not support his weight even if his feet were nailed or supported. The nails would tear out. That Romans did crucify victims by driving nails through the wrist area of the forearm has been confirmed by the 1968 archaeological discovery of a crucifixion victim, named Johanan ben Ha-galgol, found near Jerusalem at Givat ha-Mivtar. Dr. Bucklin concludes that:

> It is the ultimate responsibility of the medical examiner to confirm by whatever means are available to him the identity of the deceased, as well as to determine the manner of this death. In the case of Man on the Shroud, the forensic pathologist will have information relative to the circumstances of death by crucifixion, which he can support by his anatomical findings. He will be aware that the individual whose image is depicted on the cloth has undergone puncture injuries to his wrists and feet, puncture injuries to his head, multiple traumatic whip-like injuries to his back and post-mortem puncture injury to his chest area, which has released both blood and a water type of fluid. From this data, it is not an unreasonable conclusion for the forensic pathologist to determine that only one person historically has undergone this sequence of events. That person is Jesus Christ.
>
> As far as the mechanism of death is concerned, a detailed study of the Shroud imprint and the blood stains, coupled with a basic understanding of the physical and physiological changes in the body that take place during crucifixion, suggests strongly that the decedent had undergone postural asphyxia as the result of his position during the crucifixion episode. There is also evidence of severe blood loss from the skin wounds as well as fluid accumulation in the chest cavities related to terminal cardio-respiratory failure.
>
> For the manner of death to be determined, a full investigation of the circumstances of death is necessary. In this case, it would be determined historically that the individual was sentenced to death

and that the execution was carried out by crucifixion. The manner of death would be classed as judicial homicide.

In summary, I have presented a scenario, based on reasonable medical probability, as to how a forensic pathologist medical examiner would conduct an examination of the Shroud of Turin image and the conclusions that he would reach as the result of such studies.[8]

Several other of the world's most eminent pathologists have affirmed that the image on the cloth is that of a man genuinely scourged and tortured with a crown of thorns, the unique act that identifies Christ as the bearer of this agony. No other individual in history has been reported as having this particular punishment done to him in all its specific details.

An additional piece of cloth to the main Shroud, similar in size to a large handkerchief, which survives today, is also believed to have wrapped the same body. It is known as the "Sudarium of Oviedo." According to well-known Jewish custom, a smaller cloth was folded narrowly and wrapped around the jaw, face, and head of a corpse to keep the mouth orifice closed and prevent the jaw opening as rigor set in. In 1999, Mark Guscin, a member of the multidisciplinary investigation team of the Centro Español de Sindonología, issued a detailed forensic and historical report entitled "Recent Historical Investigations on the Sudarium of Oviedo." Guscin's report detailed recent findings of the history, forensic pathology, blood chemistry, and stain patterns on the Sudarium. His conclusion was that the Sudarium and the Shroud of Turin had been used to cover the same injured head at closely different times:

There are many points of coincidence between all these points and the Shroud of Turin, the blood group, the way the corpse was tortured and died, and the macroscopic overlay of the stains on each cloth. This is especially notable in that the blood on the Sudarium, shed in life as opposed to post-mortem, corresponds exactly in blood group, blood type and surface area to those stains on the Shroud on the nape of the neck. If it is clear that the two cloths must have covered the same corpse, and this conclusion is inevitable from all the studies carried out up to date, and if the history of the Sudarium can be trustworthily extended back beyond the fourteenth century, which is often referred to as the Shroud's first documented historical appearance, then this would take the Shroud back to at least the earliest dates of the Sudarium's known history. The ark of relics and the Sudarium have without any doubt at all been in Spain since the beginning of the seventh century, and the history recorded in various manuscripts from various times and geographical areas take it all the way back to Jerusalem in the first century. The importance of this for Shroud history cannot be overstressed.[9]

Further compelling evidence to suggest the authenticity of the Shroud lies in the pollen grains from trees and shrubs growing in the Judean region of Palestine that have been found embedded in its cloth fibers. The following is quoted from a paper entitled "The Origin of the Shroud of Turin from the Near East as Evidenced by Plant Images and by Pollen Grains," published in 1998 by Professor Avinoam Danin, professor of botany at the Hebrew University of Jerusalem:

> The authenticity of the Near East as the source of the Shroud of Turin is completely verified to me as a botanist, through the images and pollen grains of *Gundelia tournefortii* and the images of *Zygophyllum dumosum* leaves. Other important botanical findings, such as the images of some 200 fruits of two-three species of *Pistacia* and the reed *Arundo donax*, will be described and illustrated by photographs. Using my data base of more than 90,000 sites of plant distribution, the place that best fits the assemblage of the plant species whose images and often pollen grains have been identified on the Shroud is 10–20 km East and West of Jerusalem. The common blooming time of most of these species is spring, March and April.[10]

Still more remarkable evidence was found in 1978 when three-dimensional imagery of the Shroud using NASA's VP-8 Image Analyzer showed "dense, button-like objects over the eyes," about the size of a U.S. dime. Macrophotography (by Fr. Francis Filas, SJ, of Loyola University in Chicago) and digitalization of the eye area (by Dr. Robert Haralick of the University of Virginia Spatial Data Analysis Lab) suggest coin lettering consistent with the *lepton* (Widow's Mite) minted by Pontius Pilate between 29–32 CE.[11] Filas makes a case for the letters UCAI, which he makes out on the lepton, and Haralick's digitalization appears to confirm these four raised letters. They are consistent with the U of Tiberious and CAI of Caisaros (Tiberiou Caisaros) printed on the coins. Normally, coins would be minted with Greek lettering and with the letters UKAI. However, many leptons were misspelled with Latin UCAI, and examples are on file.[12]

Alan and Mary Whanger, two American scientists with a newly developed analytical image comparison called Polarised Image Overlay (PIO) have been able to demonstrate that the Shroud image contains a considerable amount of in-depth distance information of the body that was encased in the cloth.[13] In other words, they have verified a previous conclusion arrived at by the scientists at the Jet Propulsion Laboratory in Pasadena, Texas, which revealed that the cloth image had been made with all the correct distance distortions that are implied when a two-dimensional cloth is laid over the three-dimensional face and body of a human. The Whangers were able to demonstrate how the body's skeletal structure is partly visible underneath the whole image such that the bony structures of the hands and wrist are sharply visible. So are the skull, the eye sockets, the nasal bones, sinuses, and over twenty teeth. The Whangers believe that the reason the fingers appear very long and the eyes wide is that this reflects the underlying skeletal image.

The latest information on the continuing saga of the Shroud's veracity as the burial cloth of Jesus Christ reveals the stunning information that the laboratory that first dated the cloth has been prompted by more recent historical and forensic evidence to retest for evidence of a change in date for the relic. The Oxford University radio carbon testing laboratory that was one of the three that originally tested the cloth and came up with a date between 1220 CE and 1340 CE is now in the process of retesting. The incredible truth is that all the best forensic and historical evidence for a date nearer 33 CE is now so compelling that a fault in either the sample procurement and preparation or the actual dating process has to account for the anomalies. Some of the most reputable experts in the world, some spending almost a lifetime researching the Shroud for its authenticity, have come up with spectacular evidence that has to place the relic around the time of Jesus Christ's sojourn on the planet.

Robert Villarreal, a Los Alamos National Laboratory (LANL) chemist, headed a team of nine scientists who examined material from the carbon 14 sampling region. At the Shroud Science Group International Conference, Villarreal presented his evidence. I quote from the abstract of his report (August 2008):

The results of the FTIR analysis on all three threads taken from the Raes sampling area (adjacent to the C-14 sampling corner) led to identification of the fibers as cotton and definitely not linen (flax). Note, that all age dating analyses were conducted on samples taken from this same area. Apparently, the age-dating process failed to recognize one of the first rules of analytical chemistry that any sample taken for characterization of an area or population must necessarily be representative of the whole. Our analyses of the three thread samples taken from the Raes and C-14 sampling corner showed that this was not the case. What was true for the part was most certainly not true for the whole. This finding is supported by the spectroscopic data provided in this presentation:

The recommendations that stem from the above analytical study is that a new age dating should be conducted but assuring that the sample analyzed represents the original main shroud image area, i.e. the fibers must be linen (flax) and not cotton or some other material. It is only then that the age dating will be scientifically correct."[14]

M. Sue Benford and Joseph G. Marino in an article in *Chemistry Today* state that:

> Recent research reported new evidence suggesting the radiocarbon dating of the Turin Shroud was invalid, due to the intrusion of newer material in the sampling area. This evidence included the detection of anomalous surface contaminates in specimens from the sampling area. This paper reports new data from an unpublished study conducted by the Shroud of Turin Research Project (STURP) team in 1978 that supports the above referenced research findings. Additionally, this paper reports evidence supporting the identification of replacement material in the Carbon-14 (C-14) sampling region along with previously-unreported radiographic findings, corroborative textile evidence from the adjacent "Raes" sample, blinded-expert analysis of the Zurich laboratory C-14 sub-sample, independent microscopic confirmation of surface contaminates in Holland cloth/C-14 region, and historical restoration information. Based on these new data, the authors conclude that the radiocarbon sampling area was manipulated during or after the 16th Century and that further testing on the Shroud is warranted.[15]

All this startling new evidence has led Christopher Ramsey, head of the Oxford Radiocarbon Accelerator Unit, which participated in the original 1988 carbon-14 dating of the Shroud, to say in May 2008:

> There is a lot of other evidence that suggests to many that the shroud is older than the radiocarbon dates allow, and so further research is certainly needed. Only by doing this will people be able to arrive at a coherent history of the shroud, which takes into account and explains all of the available scientific and historical information.[16]

If all the above suggests beyond reasonable doubt that the Shroud of Turin is indeed the genuine burial cloth of Jesus Christ, we are still left with questions as to how this unique image was formed on the cloth.

Perhaps the work of Dr. Petrous Soons, discussing the holographic properties of the Shroud, might shed some light on these questions. A hologram is a pattern of interacting microscopic rings, or interference fringes, not unlike the pattern created when a handful of pebbles is tossed into a pond. Every area of the hologram sees and stores information about the whole image. If you break a hologram into multiple pieces, you have multiple holograms, each of which bears information about the whole image. Three factors seemed to indicate that the Shroud might in fact contain holographic information: three-dimensional information can be gleaned from its two-dimensional image; the image is a negative, and the image is free of distortion.

Dr. Soons confirmed that it was indeed possible to glean holographic information from photographs of the Shroud at the Eindhoven holographic lab in Holland. This he found quite remarkable, as photographs do not usually contain holographic information. In addition, Dr. Soons made the surprising discovery that this three-dimensional holographic information could only be found in the actual image of the body. The images of plants and flowers and the bloodstains also imprinted on the shroud did not contain this information. Thus he concluded that there were three distinct image processes at work: the process of direct contact, creating the bloodstains, the process that imprinted the images of the flowers, and the process by which the image of the body itself was created, by which holographic information was recorded. Dr. Soons is also trying to establish if each fiber of the Shroud might contain holographic information of the whole image. In his preliminary research, he has seen rings on the shroud to suggest that it could indeed be holographic at the microscopic level.

According to Dr. Soons, another unusual feature of the Shroud image is that no external light source was involved in producing the image:

> When we look at the Shroud we see what looks like a picture. What
> to our eyes seems like the highlights, lowlights, and cast shadows of

reflected light on a human form is not light at all. It is certainly not light as a camera would detect it, or an artist would see it and translate it to canvas. Technical image analysis reveals no directionality to the implied light of the highlights and shadows. The brightness does not come from any angle. It is not from above or below, nor from the right or the left, nor from the front. The light emerges from within all of the body evenly everywhere at the same time.[17]

The most probable cause of the image would thus have been a flash of very short duration, which in some way allowed for distance information to be encoded in the image. Giles Carter, an eminent scientist, believes that the image, which is confined to the top-most fibers of the cloth, was caused by an "auto-radiation" effect emanating from inside the cloth. He demonstrates impressively that moderately strong X-rays emanating from the bones of the man in the Shroud could have been the cause of the image.[18]

Several physicists, including Dr. John Jackson of the Colorado Shroud Center, point to a form of possible columnated radiation as the best explanation for how the image was formed, representing a scorch-like appearance (the scorch caused by light versus heat, as the image does not fluoresce). Dr. Thomas Phillips (nuclear physicist at Duke University and formerly with the High Energy Laboratories at Harvard) points to a potential milliburst of radiation (a neutron flux) that could be consistent with the moment of resurrection. Such a milliburst could have caused the purely surface phenomenon of the scorch-like (scorch-by-light) images and a possible key to the addition of carbon-14 to the cloth. As Dr. Phillips points out: "We never had a Resurrection to study," and more testing can be done to ascertain whether a neutron-flux occurred.[19]

The STURP determined that the image was caused by rapid dehydration, oxidation, and degradation of the linen by an unidentified process. Distinguished particle physicist Dame Isabel Piczek has identified the remarkable fact that there seems to be no distortion in the image on the cloth, a distortion that should have resulted from the pressure of the body on the stone floor of the tomb and the inevitable irregularities that would have occurred due to the folds and wrinkles of the wrapping:

> There is a strange dividing element, an interface from which the image is projected up and the image is projected down. The muscles of the body are absolutely not crushed against the stone of the tomb. They are perfect. It means that the body is hovering between the two sides of the shroud. What does that mean? It means that there is absolutely no gravity. The image is absolutely undistorted. Now if you imagine that the cloth was wrinkled, tied, wrapped around the body and all of a sudden you see a perfect image, which is impossible unless the shroud was made absolutely taut, rigidly taut.
>
> A heretofore unknown interface acted as an event horizon. The straight, taut linen of the shroud simply was forced to parallel the shape of this powerful interface. The projection, an action at a distance, happens from the surface and limit of this, taking with itself the bas-relief image of the upper and, separately, the underside of the body.[20]

Could that which Piczek describes as a "strange dividing element," the "interface from which the image is projected up and the image is projected down," actually be a manifestation of the Godverse in the universe? This "heretofore unknown interface," she says, would have been the result of a "collapsed event horizon," in the center of which "there is something which science knows as a singularity. This is exactly what started the universe in the Big Bang." Thus, she goes on to say: "We have nothing less in the tomb of Christ than the beginning of a new universe."[21]

Dr. Edgar Mitchell, the American astronaut who went to the moon, further speculates in the erudite Grizzly Adams production *The Fabric of Time:*

Could it be that the event horizon demonstrated by the Shroud sent information instantaneously throughout the universe? Does this mean that the resurrection was a universal event? All physical bodies have a holographic emission that is available non-locally throughout the universe, the total emissions from a physical object that uniquely identify events in the history of that object. Thus the essence of physical laws is informational.[22]

The very latest research into the Turin Shroud has added to the mystery surrounding the controversial artifact. A second ghostly image of a man's face has been discovered on the back of the linen, according to a report published by London's Institute of Physics. The back of the Shroud has rarely been seen, as it was hidden beneath a piece of cloth sewn on by nuns in 1534, after it had been damaged by fire. But the back surface was exposed during a restoration project in 2002. A professor at Italy's Padua University, Giulio Fanti, thought he saw a "faint image" in the photographs from this project and decided to investigate it further:

"Though the image is very faint, features such as nose, eyes, hair, beard and moustaches are clearly visible," he said. "There are some slight differences with the known face. For example, the nose on the reverse side shows the same extension of both nostrils, unlike the front side, in which the right nostril is less evident."[23]

Professor Fanti has dismissed claims that the image on the back confirms that the Shroud is a fake, with paint soaking from the front to the back:

"This is not the case of the Shroud. On both sides, the face image is superficial, involving only the outermost linen fibers," he said. "It is extremely difficult to make a fake with these features."[24]

This invites the natural speculation that all this in some way may well have been both the cause of, and at the same time an effect of, the resurrection, the unique, momentous, and singular affirmation of the claimed divinity of the Christian teacher. Could the fact that the image is formed on the surface fibers of both sides of the cloth without penetrating through the intervening layers suggest that Christ was able to be in two places at once from that interface? Could the intense burst of radiation that many scientists believe caused the image on the cloth be a result of Christ creating such a huge proportion of six-ring hydrogen atoms that he, in effect, converted the atoms of his own body to light?

Plate 29a, 29b, and 29c reproduce the work of Professor Giovanni Tamburelli, who worked on a computer-generated three-dimensional image of the Shroud.[25] Astonishingly, Tamburelli has discovered that many of the events and details of the crucifixion are reflected in the three-dimensional image. All this is best illustrated by these remarkable images and their captions, so I will not elaborate further here.

The latest evidence that is pertinent to the authenticity of this incredible artifact we call the Shroud of Turin points to something so special that it will leave science, and all those in science who sit firmly on the roundabouts and carousels of atomically derived reality, in a hurricane of puzzles and puzzlement. The astonishing way that the image on the cloth was formed verifies that a fundamentally unique power, unexplained by the laws of physics as we know them, brought about what might well have been a resurgence of a state of living out of a state of death; it thus affirms the phenomenon known as the resurrection. It is the single most unique happening that marks Jesus Christ as a being who was something out of the ordinary prospectus of humankind.

If the cloth were to be confirmed as a supernatural artifact recording the phenomenon we call "resurrection," there would be awesome political implications as to the messianic character of the individual. This might prove uncomfortable to certain groups with religious, political, or economic axes to grind, axes that would be blunted by this realization. Perhaps that is why progress to the public declaration of its true veracity has not happened.

It will, of course, be the cause célèbre that will be fiercely denied by all those who do not subscribe to the beautiful Jew's expositions of the nature of existential reality, notwithstanding the claims of his own branch of humanity—the Judaic resource itself. If this individual had the capacity to raise his own dead body out of the state of death—through a wondrous self-propagated burst of radiant power so intense that it could leave a verifying image of himself on a piece of linen cloth—then who can deny that he was the long-expected Messiah of the Jews? He would indeed have come in the "blaze of glory" the Jewish prophets of old foretold. More pertinently, he would have given validity to the epithet of Zion as it was laid down by ancient prophecy and not as it has been laid down falsely by twentieth century politics. It would give the lie to the more recent bogus and convenient *sepulchral* discoveries of an entire tomb supposedly loaded with the dead artifacts of the whole Marian family in Jerusalem.

In the interests of the survival of Israel in the current climate, it is understandable that the religious significance of the Shroud is annulled in the mind's eye of a beleaguered people. Its implications have to be belittled and dismissed at all costs in the present world political climate. There is, understandably, no length to which some Zionists and their stooges will not go to attest that Jesus survived the crucifixion physically and was ushered out of the tomb by familial sympathizers. The denial of his resurrection suits those seeking to protect their powerful reality, in which a burning bush can talk and humankind is just six thousand or so years old. Such is the inane contradictory drivel we are expected to swallow. Sadly, too many have done so through the millennia at the risk of their eternal existential prospectus.

Can you imagine the consequences to Zionists if it is discovered that the Shroud provides scientifically bona fide evidence that the individual it covered at death was someone who could control the states of both life and death from within each other? In other words, their

Messiah came, and they did not spot him for looking for the gold braid. He came in as a lamb and went out like one, a victim of their own narcissistic folly. Do you really think they would ever admit this in the light of thousands who have died in the establishing of the state of Israel? Would they admit what would seem to be a compound triumph against their interpretation of Old Testament prophecy? How would they tell this to the Hassidic and other groups ascribing to fundamentalist Judaism?

The other dread sort of fundamentalists, not least that most obsequious sort we ascribe to Christianity, would also, I think, stop at nothing to obfuscate the truth that the Turin Shroud would reveal if it were proved to be genuine. These deadly creatures must depend for their own sanity's sake on the entire Christ story being a fraud. If it were indeed anything near the truth, they would be cursed for their evil ways and deeds in his name throughout history. Christ claimed a gentle, totally loving, forgiving tenor of faith. The "eye for an eye" stance fundamentalism has taken within all the Abrahamic traditions is a vilification that must have earned nothing short of eternal damnation for anyone who has practiced or even come within smelling distance of it.

Whatever the authorship of Christ's behests among humankind, these behests seem to claim an origin beyond the realms and exigencies of a universe of enforced resolutions such as ours, a reality beyond ours, but one into which our own fits as an inferior subjective addendum, an addendum that is extemporaneous and thus transient. His own words and statements, as we know them, bore ample witness to this.

It is particularly stupefying to me that a people as magnificent as the Jews, with their wonderful contributions through history to humanity, cannot see that the verification of the Shroud is an affirmation beyond any other that they may indeed be a people more centered in a Godhead than any other, a people of ultimate significance to the human breed through the triumph of one of their own. It seems that a posse of blinkered misguided fools among them still upholds an archaic, jaded, illogical ethic, based on the merits of temple-sponsored usury and commerce dealing in the blood of pigeons and lambs. It blinded them, and still blinds them, to the merits of one of the most beautiful minds in the history of the human species, who came to bear witness to the final truth of ages. His entire life speaks through the Shroud about something that bears witness to a world and experience quite unlike our own, one of far greater and indeed absolute value that seems of final significance to all living things. It affirms a reality beyond our own, a reality of marvelous value where all living being capable of making the right choices finds an eternal home.

Religion is the most powerful protection of the worst form of racist-soaked tribalism. It has been so through all the ages but is particularly dangerous now because it might instigate the taking out of our entire species at a single stroke through the press of a button. There are no limits to what may be done to preserve the psychological allotment that verifies religious belief. The very security of nations and their political power bases underlies the cold-blooded instigation of the deaths of tens of thousands of human beings on the mere fact that they believe in a particular form of divinity. A virulent lunacy seems to grip the minds of a certain kind of human being. This is a kind that can never seem to see the size of a living power within the human frame and realize that this power and its strength of focus and purpose might provide a means to an eternal existence in all the maxims of choice and freedom for achievement. The Shroud and the verifications it makes of a new way of existential insight may well affirm this as nothing else can do.

The Dawkinsian hysteria that seeks to persuade us that there is no reality beyond the purely atomically derived one totters on the edge of farce into the silence of a tomb through the Shroud and what happened to put it there, a tomb that delivers a truer, far grander, and utterly complete reality.

What then might explain and account for the widespread apparent lunacy of believing that all things in the entire existential scale are of atomic and only atomic derivation? I have set out in this treatise to show that among us there might well be individuals whose minds, and perhaps MESFs, are set and formatted with an extraterrestrial implant of mentality. This implant might take the form of a programmed outlook that creates an incapability to perceive, visualize, or appreciate anything beyond the scale of purely atom-made resolutions. Or, alternatively, it might be the result of a *deliberate* resolve to dismiss and denigrate any information that might point to the involvement of a physically based extraterrestrial intelligence involved in the affairs of our species.

In recent times, as in no other time, the world has seen beyond the shadow of a doubt that a tiny minority of the highest-placed officials in many national governments are busy lying about, misappropriating, and manipulating facts and information to such an extent that the broad mass of people around the world are now skeptical and cynical about all political invective. Deceit underlies so much of every society's leadership that it is understandable that many, except the most simple, gullible minds, are now hesitant to believe anything that is put out for public consumption. How do we ask our children to tell the truth when the most powerful are busy distorting it at every turn?

How then, in this broad scope of selfish negative intent, can the truth of our individual existential base be seen? The findings about the Shroud provide a stunning implication about the fantastic scale and scope that underlies the being within the living and, indeed, dead contours of each and every one of us. It endorses the fact that a power is trapped in the six billion or so human shapes that seem so ordinary to the eye, a power so wondrous and so almighty that it makes understandable Christ's retort: "Don't ye know ye are Gods?"

Gods indeed! How do we see our stupendous size, when the temporal values hailed so much by occidental societies make us see how mediocre we are each moment of each day? Millions of spindly shapes wander about streets and mighty buildings engrossed in the day's own troubles, most with their heads cowed under the pretences that mark these fatuous values. Yet magically, beneath the facades of pretence, where pulchritude is seen through the temporal purposes of vanity, greed, avarice, and the cold dead intent of the system and the machine mind, there lurks the glorious scope of an eternity of peace and fulfillment absolute. The saving anthem of a Man-God, grotesquely distended under a shroud in the filth of the Bushs, Blairs, Cheneys, Perles, and Wolfowitzs, stands now, two thousand years later, in the triumph of truth.

I have no doubt that one day, not long from now, the grand and glorious people we call the Jews will acknowledge that their Messiah has already come, and affirm the songs of their prophets of old, which predicted that their people would finally return home to Zion as they have now done. It remains for peace and justice to be borne out of this glorious affirmation in an accord reached with the hundreds of thousands of Palestinians who were viciously and unjustly ousted to bring this about in this most important part of the Earth.

We will then, as a singular species particular to our planet in all the trillions around the universe, have before us the most awesome affirmation of the common origin of us all in Godhead before time itself began. It will be the final triumph of all the triumphs we might achieve as a species. Perhaps then, and perhaps for just a mere moment, we might as a species realize the awesome scale of existence with hope, a hope established with reason.

# 21

# Living Water

I have suggested that awareness and will are the prime directives of the Godverse, that is, what exists outside of the atomic array of the universe. However, human beings (and all living things) are composed of a spiritual component as well as a physical one. In order to grasp the full implications of Jesus Christ's resurrection, we need to understand how these components are arranged in such a way that—through awareness and directed will—meaning and understanding can be expressed in the living body.

Science has really only looked at one side of the equation, the physical biochemical part, and has concluded that this is all that is required for life to exist. There are a number of reasons for this conclusion. One is that all experimental systems use some form of force (e.g., electromagnetic fields) as probes to investigate the nature of the system under test. The space between the atoms has a lower intrinsic tension than that of atoms, or the electromagnetic probes, and this attribute makes it inaccessible to them. Consequently, the assumption is made that "there is nothing there." This leads to the conclusion that atoms, of themselves, are responsible for life. But science might now be coming around to a very different point of view.

Current research in 2008 has led scientists to the conclusion that the effects of water on living organisms transcend mere chemical processes and are in fact profoundly linked to the most basic processes in the cosmos. It seems, according to the latest research, that the bonds between the hydrogen atoms in water are the result of a strange quantum phenomenon called zero points. These zero points are locations in space/time that provide a tension in absolute balance. This is a kind of stillness of "potential vibration" that would be present even if the universe itself froze over and its temperature dropped to absolute zero. It would be propelled by and out of the energy of empty space. These zero points have, in other words, the lowest vibrational state possible in the universe of atoms.

In my scheme, these zero points (which I call peace points) are a result of the intrinsic potential difference between the finite physical universe and the infinite extent of the nonphysical Godverse. By definition, the infinite is implicitly a backdrop that interacts with all that is finite. This provides a potential difference that causes even the empty space between atoms to have the minutest possible degree of vibration, or energy. Perhaps this is better described as a potential, or a stored vibration. These zero points are thus like "frozen" vibrations; as such, they define the interface of the Godverse with the universe. They are the lowest and least expression of force possible outside the Godverse.

Hydrogen bonds that express these vibrations are therefore the interaction points, the natural bridging points, between thought and atoms. These bonds are at least ten times as weak as a typical chemical bond, which means that while they can bind molecules together, they also break easily at room temperature. Structures of hydrogen are thus constantly forming and breaking up within water. If we put all this together, it has huge implications for us as living beings made primarily of water. It means that hydrogen bonds are flexible interaction points between the physical universe and the nonphysical Godverse. Arrangements of hydrogen atoms that maximize or minimize the strength of the physical against the nonphysical, thought against atoms, are constantly in flux, depending upon momentums of thought and their interplay with momentums of force and energy.

Felix Franks, of the University of Cambridge, illustrates the vital

role hydrogen plays in biological life by comparing it to its heavier isotope deuterium. If you take some water and swap the hydrogen for
atoms of deuterium, you end up with a liquid that is chemically identical, yet poisonous to all but the most primitive organisms. "The only
difference is in the zero-point energy," says Franks, "without water, it is
all just chemistry, but add water and you get biology."[1]

All the heavier elements can be seen as being made by crashing
hydrogen on to itself. So the next simplest atom, helium, is two hydrogen atoms crashed into each other with a bit released to allow for the
joint. This joint is not like the joint where two elements join to make a
molecule. It is more like a merge, where the properties of each elemental
component are changed because of their merging. This is an essential
difference that is crucial to understand. This entire merging of hydrogen atoms goes on in nature up to the element uranium, which is basically ninety-two hydrogen atoms all smashed on to one another, with
bits released as radiation at each "merge point." The process is called
"fusion" in physics.

The merging of one hydrogen atom to another to form a completely
new element took place and still takes place in the center of stars. Most
of the heavier elements that exist in the universe now were made by this
process, which began long after the universe was first formed. A few
are still produced in star nurseries. As I write, 114 elements have been
discovered, but some don't exist naturally and have to be made. These
only exist briefly and are highly radioactive. This means that they are
unstable and their structure is slowly breaking down and releasing radiation. In other words, they are decaying spontaneously. This planet's
entire force complement can only hold hydrogen in merged aggregates
naturally up to an atomic signature point we call uranium (element 92).
Uranium, the heaviest element on this planet that stays together naturally without decaying, could be said to point to the limit of the Earth's
planetary force signature.

After the Big Bang, only hydrogen existed; it was the first and simplest element. As such it could be said that it is the first self-contained

step into the physical, as the Godverse changed its nonphysical nature into its opposite. The universe is said to be 75 percent hydrogen and 24 percent helium. The ratio seems to differ with every reference you read. All the other elements that make up matter are said to be less than 1 percent of the total. The important implication is that the entire universe is very light: only about 1 percent of all its elements give rise to nongaseous solidness. The universe, consisting of our world, the billions of worlds out there in space, and space itself, is 99 percent gaseous combinations of various sorts. Hydrogen, as the least enforced element of all, is the closest point of matter to the Godverse. Thus the call of the Godverse for the return to the state of unity is overwhelming.

We as living beings are composed of 55 to 78 percent water (the exact proportion depends on such factors as age and sex). Two-thirds of that water is formed of hydrogen atoms. Overall, the makeup of our bodies is approximately 78 percent gas (hydrogen, oxygen, and nitrogen). Thus, in us, the world of the solid is separated from the ephemeral non-solid world by very simple gas states. We are, it seems, a wisp away from the state of En-light, in which the universe burst from the interaction mechanism of the two primary Poles.

As we have seen, En-light resides within all living things. It gives the property of life to all aggregates of atoms that can hold it within the arrangement of their shapes. As I have explained, it is my surmise that the arrangement of atoms within any system is crucial in terms of receiving En-light. The water molecule is a particularly potent arrangement suitable for its reception. This is because in specific circumstances it can align in arrays of three, four, five, and six hydrogen ring configurations, increasing the magnitude for the reception of En-light in that order.

A great modern French scientist, who sadly died recently, Jacques Benveniste, has shown that the water molecule has photographic properties. These photographic properties allow it to retain a *memory* of any chemical properties it comes into contact with, no matter how diluted these chemical properties are! Benveniste was ridiculed and vilified by many of his peers when he claimed this, but recent independent research has shown that he may well have been right. If this is truly the case, then we have a wonderful candidate to account for memory. It could explain how we retain the most obscure memories from the past no matter how old we are.

Benveniste claimed in 1988 that vigorously shaking water solutions of an antibody could evoke a biological response, even when that antibody was diluted out of existence, such as in homeopathic remedies. Nonagitated solutions produced little or no effect. Benveniste reasoned that the effect of dilution and agitation pointed to transmission of biological information via some molecular organization going on in water. He was pilloried by scientists at the time. They could find no fault with his experimental procedures, but claimed they were unable to replicate his research. But, twelve years later, Benveniste's research was vindicated by a consortium of four independent research laboratories in France, Italy, Belgium, and Holland.

Extreme care was taken to ensure that no bias was introduced into the experiment by the scientists from the four laboratories; in fact, they were all blinded to the contents of their test solutions. In other words, they were not told if the solutions they were introducing into a chemical reaction were homeopathic solutions with ghost amounts of a substance or just pure water. The ghost solutions themselves and the controls were prepared in three other laboratories that had nothing further to do with the trial. The results were staggering: histamine solutions both at pharmacological concentrations and diluted out of existence all led to statistically significant inhibition of basophil activation by algae. Professor Madeleine Ennis, of Queen's University Belfast, who led the research said: "Despite my reservations against the science of homeopathy, the results compel me to suspend my disbelief and to start searching for a rational explanation for our findings."[2]

Benveniste's more recent research involved the transmission of the frequencies emitted by biochemical substances around the world via the Internet. These frequencies, he claimed, cause changes in biological tissues as if the substance was actually present. Specifically, he claimed that the signal from heparin—a component of the blood-clotting system—slowed down coagulation of blood when transmitted over the Internet from a laboratory in Europe to another in the United States. All molecules produce specific low frequencies that are actually within the human audible range. This is the molecular signal that Benveniste detected and recorded on the sound card of a computer. He then transmitted that recording via the Internet to another computer, which played it back to another molecular substance that was tuned by its own particular molecular structure to receive it.

He called this matching of broadcast with reception "co-resonance" and said it works "like a radio set." When you tune your radio to a particular station, both your set and the transmitting station are vibrating at the same frequency. Change the dial a little and you're listening to a different frequency. Just like radio sets and receivers, molecules do not have to be close together for communication to take place. However, the transmission and reception of these molecular signals only takes place if the transmitting and receiving substances are diluted in water. Benveniste pointed out that all biological reactions occur in water and suggested that water molecules are in fact the agents that relay and amplify the biological signal coming from the original molecule.

Each molecular substance can be seen to be like a compact disk, or CD, which, by itself, cannot produce a sound but has the means to do so etched into its surface. Water is like the CD player that can play back that sound and transmit it to another CD. It can also store the sounds from CDs in its memory so that the original CDs no longer need to be present. The electric current that powers the CD player is the agitation of the water that is crucial to record the memory. This whole process can be measured on a biological system.

Further confirmation of Benveniste's theories was given in 2003 by a Swiss chemist who published his paper in the reputable journal *Physica A,* claiming to show that even though they should be identical, the structure of hydrogen bonds in pure water is very different from that in homeopathic dilutions of salt solutions. The paper's author, Swiss chemist Louis Rey, was using thermo-luminescence to study the structure of solids. The technique involves bathing a chilled sample with radiation. When the sample is warmed up, the stored energy is released as light in a pattern that reflects the atomic structure of the sample.

When Rey used the method on ice, he saw two peaks of light, at temperatures of around 120°K and 170°K. He wanted to test the idea, suggested by other researchers, that the 170°K peak reflects the pattern of hydrogen bonds within the ice. In his experiments, he used heavy water (which contains the heavy hydrogen isotope deuterium) because it has stronger hydrogen bonds than normal water. After studying pure samples, Rey looked at solutions of lithium chloride and sodium chloride. Lithium chloride destroys hydrogen bonds, as does sodium chloride, but to a lesser extent. Sure enough, the peak was smaller for a solution of sodium chloride, and disappeared completely for a lithium chloride solution.

Aware of homeopaths' claims that patterns of hydrogen bonds can survive successive dilutions, Rey decided to test samples that had been diluted down to a notional ten to thirty grams per cubic centimeter—way beyond the point at which any ions of the original substance could remain: "We thought it would be of interest to challenge the theory," he says.[3] Each dilution was made according to a strict protocol and vigorously stirred at each stage, as is done in the preparation of homeopathic solutions.

When Rey compared the ultradilute lithium and sodium chloride solutions with pure water that had been through the same process, the difference in their thermo-luminescence peaks, compared with pure water, was still there: "Much to our surprise, the thermo-luminescence glows of the three systems were substantially different," he says. He believes the result proves that the networks of hydrogen bonds in the samples were different.[4]

If the thesis of Benveniste is proved to be unequivocally true, it will affirm that there is a way we can keep the water in our bodies "charged" with a photographic record of all happenings in our lives, even though we are continually replacing the water in our bodies. If each subsequent generation of water retains the previous generation's photo-holographic record *printed* there, it may provide an explanation of how we can keep an unbroken record of events through our lives. These events may well be stored in our body water in some holographic way.

Hydrogen bonds are also turning out to have a profound role in the functioning of DNA. To perform its biological functions, DNA has to carry out various maneuvers: twisting, turning, and docking with proteins at just the right place. Just how the proteins meet up with the right parts of the double helix, despite the rigidity of DNA, is a mystery. Biochemists have suspected for some time that water molecules are important. They have noticed that concentrations of them around DNA appear to correlate with biological activity. It turns out that water undergoes significant changes as it approaches the surface of DNA. The water molecules seem to linger longer and rotate more slowly around some base pairs than others. The base pairs on DNA are the building blocks of genes, and their sequence dictates the order in which amino acids are stitched together to make proteins. If water molecules linger longer around some base pairs than others, the level of hydration will mirror the sequence of base pairs.

Monika Fuxreiter, of the Hungarian Academy of Sciences Biological Research Center in Budapest, believes that this explains how proteins and DNA interact. She and her colleagues at the BRC's Institute of Enzymology created a computer simulation of DNA and an enzyme called *BamHI,* which uses water molecules to cut DNA at very specific points. They saw that adding virtual water molecules to the mix had a dramatic effect: "The water molecules report the DNA sequence to the protein while it is still some distance away," says Fuxreiter. "Then as the protein gets closer, the water molecules are ejected from the site until it binds tightly to the DNA." Fuxreiter suggests that the water molecules relay messages to the protein via electrostatic forces, which reflect the varying levels of hydration on the DNA.[5]

Rustum Roy, a materials scientist at Pennsylvania State University in University Park, goes further. In a review paper published in *Materials Research Innovations* in December 2005, Roy and a team of collaborators called for a reexamination of the case against the controversial claim that water has a "memory." Roy argued that water has proved itself capable of effects that go beyond simple chemistry, and these may imbue water with a memory. One way this may occur, he said, is through an effect known as epitaxy that uses the atomic structure of one compound as a template to induce the same structure in others.

Epitaxy is routinely used in the microprocessor industry to create perfect semiconductor crystals. According to Roy, water already exhibits epitaxial effects. "The 'seeding' of clouds is the growth of crystalline ice on a substrate of silver iodide, which has the same crystal structure," he says. "No chemical transfer whatsoever occurs."[6]

With all the foregoing in mind, it becomes plain that we are far more than a dump full of matter-based chemistry. Our individualities soar beyond the scale of our universe, like a feather in a hurricane, swooping through the limits of chaos and the second law, to a sense that we matter beyond the foolish and finite dimensions of this world. The instigation to seek to know and understand our existence goes far beyond the values of the flesh and is incessant and irresistible. Music, art, poetry, and literature festoon a mere urge to survive for its own sake, with an invitation to discover something hidden about ourselves and our existential value, set against any scale in the universe or beyond it.

As we have seen demonstrated in Plate 17, everything in the universe is subject to the same basic twist factor, which provides a basic distorted template for all living entities in the universe. The formation of living systems on this planet is defined by a conglomerate of four force identities: the whole shape of our universe, the universal force print, the galactic force print, and the planetary force print. As I have already suggested, perhaps this distorted form is what the Christians and Muslims refer to as the concept of original sin. It's what makes us human. It is very interesting that the embryos of most life-forms look the same in shape at a very early stage. All this is further demarcated into specific species shapes: a kind of threshold shape specifically defines a particular species family tree through time. The shape is precisely and finely tuned in the finest detail to reflect the exact "think-ability quantum" of each individual within that species.

The wings of a moth and the color that defines that moth would thus be expressed by the "think-ability" of that moth. By "think-ability," I do not mean mental deductive processes that might define intelligence. It may well manifest as reactive impulses to environmental features that are crucial to the existence of the creature; a kind of photo-imprinted information exchange through the photographic properties of the water in the moth's body. Thus Benveniste's research indicating that water molecules can record the shape and structure of matter in a photographic form and then duplicate the chemical properties of that matter in interaction with other matter may also account for the changes that define a body's physical alterations, commensurate with the survival of the fittest ethic of the Darwinian ethos.

In higher, more intelligent forms of life, this modus might be further driven by mental deductive power: a perceived need for survival purposes might be translated into a physical reality through this process, sometimes perhaps in a single generation. If the thought-engendered agitation of the water molecule in a finch's body could provide a more suitable beak for a finch in the Galapagos Islands, think what it might provide for a human being if we knew, I mean really knew, about all the magnitudes of the power of thought. If, as Benveniste proposed, a mechanical procedure can duplicate an entire scheme of matter perfectly, and we can further influence this scheme with the power of our thinking, this can provide the beginnings of an answer regarding a methodology of return to the Godverse and thus escape from the horrors of this universe of ever-diminishing returns.

The recording and duplicating of the structure of matter in water researched by Benveniste also nicely describes the sexual process and consequent birth process into the living state. According to his theory, the key to the transmission of information via water is simply based on the agitation of the water molecule. That agitation can take place in a test tube, or through a penis and a vagina, or indeed any other type of reproduction. In the light of Benveniste's experiments, it is interesting to speculate what Christ may have meant by what he called "living water." The difference between "living water" and ordinary water could perhaps be absolutely crucial. If water, as Benveniste has demonstrated, can hold and transmit a memory of molecular signals, then could "living water" refer to water that is able to hold and transmit a memory of signals that originate from *beyond atoms*? Could "living water" refer to a special kind of water that somehow has the capacity to record thought and feeling as vibrational frequencies and thus provide an ongoing live broadcast of the extra-atomic world, the world beyond atoms?

As I have said, a high proportion of six-atom hydrogen rings may well have predominated in the material body of Jesus Christ. These rings might be described as "living water," because they allow human beings to beat the entropic momentum of decay that is natural to the "dead" physical universe by countering that drift with its opposite—the pull to greater states of union and togetherness provided by the *light* of God, the pull toward eternal life. I believe that all individuals who retain a deep and profound spiritual sense reflect this physically through the content of six-hydrogen-ring arrangements and deployments in their bodies. I further unequivocally believe, and it bears stating again and again, that to maintain a good proportion of these six-hydrogen-atom arrangements, it is essential for an individual soul to maintain a focus on the values that reflect measures that unite and thus portray a sense of the world beyond atoms as reflected by the Godverse.

If you believe in ethics that separate and divide, you then line yourself up with the entropic momentum, and any six-atom rings within your physical makeup break down into rings of three, four, and five hydrogen atoms. The centers of these smaller rings are not big enough to fit a single hydrogen atom in the center and stop its spin. Thus the shutters gradually go down, blocking the light of the Godverse from coming into them, leaving you to decay in your existential status. It is thus crucial to maintain deep and profound beliefs and attitudes and to do works that reflect ethics that unite. In this way, we can maximize these six-ring hives to maintain an everlasting status. If Godhead is forever, then allowing it through our being will maintain our being in this light forever, too.

If we accept that Christ had, in his "body water," a huge proportion of six-ring hydrogen atoms in correct alignment, then how did he donate this "living water" to others? The clues might lie in this passage from the Gospel of John in the New Testament:

There cometh a woman of Samaria to draw water: Jesus saith unto her, give me to drink. (For his disciples were gone away unto the city to buy meat.)

Then saith the woman of Samaria unto him, How is it that thou, being a Jew, asketh drink of me, which am a woman of Samaria? For the Jews have no dealings with the Samaritans.

Jesus answered and said unto her, If thou knewest the gift of God, and who it is that saith to thee, Give me to drink; thou wouldest have asked of him, and he would have given thee living water.

The woman saith unto him, Sir, thou hast nothing to draw with, and the well is deep: from whence then hast thou that living water?

Art thou greater than our father Jacob, which gave us the well, and drank thereof himself, and his children, and his cattle?

Jesus answered and said unto her, Whosoever drinketh of this water shall thirst again: But whosoever drinketh of the water that I shall give him shall be in him a well of water springing up into everlasting life.

The woman saith unto him, Sir, give me this water, that I thirst not, neither come hither to draw.

Jesus saith unto her, Go call thy husband and come hither.

The woman answered and said I have no husband. Jesus said unto her, Thou hast well said, I have no husband: For thou hast had five husbands; and he whom thou now hast is truly not thy husband: in that saidst thou truly.

The woman saith unto him, Sir, I perceive that thou art a prophet.[7]

How then could Jesus have given "living water" to the Samaritan woman? How, in other words, could he give her *his* pattern of six-hydrogen-atom arrangements?

The answer lies in the bones. As we have seen, bone tissue has elements like calcium phosphate and silicon, which give it the property of being piezo-electric: it emits an electric charge when it is squeezed or pressed. The degree of piezo-electricity is determined by the amount of silicon present in the bone. When silicon dioxide, commonly known as quartz, is vibrated, it is capable of breaking the bonds between molecules. It can also record the sound frequencies, the molecular signals, of the snapping bonds. When bone is pressed, the water molecules in the body become agitated. This is an exact equivalent of the process used by homeopaths to blend a chemical signal in water: they shake it. What then do human beings pass on to each other when they squeeze bones in an embrace or by shaking hands? What does one person pass on to another person's water molecules? Could an imprint, a photograph, of each person's unique molecular structure be transmitted in this way?

Perhaps our skeletons act as an electrified framework or grid, which in some way provides the holographic record in our water in the first place. Or perhaps the skeleton is the actual "reader" of the information that is stored in the water, rather like a transducer in the tape head of a tape recorder reads the magnetically stored information in the iron oxide on the magnetic tape. After all, our blood does carry iron (hemoglobin) in water in a circuit in continual circulation around our bodies. Perhaps in some way all these factors combine to produce the ability to know and be aware of information that comes through En-light into us.

Jesus could have passed on his pattern of living water to the

Samaritan woman and indeed to any who chose to receive it through an embrace that passed on an imprint of that water or even directly via bodily fluids. But why did he ask her to call her husband? It is crucial at this stage to understand that Christ would not have given a magic panacea to the Samaritan woman simply because she asked for it. Her social context and the people with whom she lived, particularly those who would constantly be giving her an impression of their own body water (that is, her husband) would be very important in influencing her potential for eternal life. The "living water" was a reminder for the Samaritan woman of the state of prior humanity. She would then need to make it her own through thoughts and actions concomitant with that prior, less entropic state.

It is my belief that the "living water" of which Christ spoke is a purifier of biological lines that can free them of any alien genetic modification held in their genetic lines. Just as in homeopathy the dilute substance informs water of its specific molecular pattern, "living water" could "inform" the other water molecules in the body about the natural structure of body water and general chemistry in human beings prior to the points of past alien interception.

On the same theme, the final chapter of the Book of Revelation might well describe a biological dynasty that Jesus may have left for the future of our species:

And he showed me a pure river of water of life, clear as crystal, proceeding out of the throne of God and of the Lamb.

In the midst of the street of it, and on either side of the river, was there the tree of life, which bare twelve manner of fruits, and yielded her fruit every month: and the leaves of the tree were for the healing of the nations.

And there shall be no more curse: but the throne of God and of the Lamb shall be in it: and his servants shall serve him.

And they shall see his face: and his name shall be in their foreheads.

And there shall be no night there; and they need no candle, neither light of the sun; for the Lord God giveth them light: and they shall reign for ever and ever.[8]

There is indeed a living tree that "yields her fruit every month" and bears "twelve manner of fruits" each year. That "tree" is a woman's reproductive system, and its "fruits" are the eggs she produces each month! The "pure river of water of life, clear as crystal, proceeding out of the throne of God and of the Lamb," could be the "living water" that allows the children born of those women who have received it to be pure and unadulterated by alien interceptions. Thus the "leaves of the tree were for the healing of the nations." In other words, the biological lines of humanity that are broken up by alien-altered DNA would be healed and restored by the "living water" that nourishes the tree. Due to these new biological lines, "there shall be no more curse" and "the throne of God and of the Lamb shall be in it: and his servants shall serve him. And they shall see his face: and his name shall be in their foreheads." The passage then goes on to describe the power of God-light that will shine through a new humanity healed and cleansed by living water: "And there shall be no light there; and they need no candle, neither light of the sun; for the Lord God giveth them light: and they shall reign for ever and ever."

In the previous chapter of the Book of Revelation, a "holy city" is described that has "twelve foundations" and "in them the names of the twelve apostles of the Lamb." Could these "twelve foundations" be the lines left by Jesus through his twelve apostles, each of whom perhaps represented a specific type of human biology? The "holy city" has "no temple therein: for the Lord God Almighty and the Lamb are the temple of it."[9] Thus it appears to be a "living city," a structure built of light, of biological lines, perhaps, lit up by the light of God so that "the city had no need of the sun, neither the moon, to shine in it: for the glory of God did lighten it, and the Lamb is the light thereof." The passage from chapter 22 of the Book of Revelation goes on to say:

Blessed are they that do his commandments that they may have right
to the tree of life, and may enter in through the gates into the city.
For without are dogs and sorcerers and whoremongers and murderers and idolaters, and whatsoever loveth and maketh a lie.[10]

Could the "blessed" refer to those who are born into these biological lines? In other words, could birth be the way in to the "city?" Is it
possible that Jesus has left, in this way, a fountain of life freely available
to those who are able to "drink" from it? Hence:

And the Spirit and the bride say, Come. And let him that heareth
say, Come. And let him that is athirst come. And whosoever will, let
him take of the water of life freely.[11]

It is possible that a direct biological line bearing Christ's specific
format, derived from actual progeny he left behind, now lies hidden
within the lines of humanity. It is also possible that such a line was
transmitted through some other process that was not sexual, but of
which only he could be the author, because of the power of the large
and pervasive deployment of six-hydrogen-atom rings he held. In either
case, I would expect that such beings would naturally remain obscure.
You don't want to advertise yourself to aliens as something that may
interfere with their business among humankind. Anyone who claims to
be of these lines is thus likely to be a fraud or phony, if they advertise
this fact to be so.

The current controversy and fascination elicited by *The Da Vinci
Code* and the other books sharing its theme centers around the possibility of a biological line left behind by Jesus Christ. I wrote a book
touching on this twenty years ago entitled *Rage of Atoms* (logged with
the Library of Congress for copyright reasons, which will serve as a
check for the authenticity of the date I give for when the book was
written). I decided to publish it at a later date because it was a little
technical in places and needed a book such as this one to introduce

its ideas. I mentioned in that book how it was to me a logical necessity that Christ, with his ultimate intelligence, would have *had to* leave something behind that would last into the future. He would have foreseen that over the centuries the record of his words and deeds would be mangled and twisted. Thus he might have left a biological legacy as the most powerful means of ensuring the continuance of his message for the redemption of humanity.

# 22

# Immaculate Conceptions Galore

There is no doubt that a man called Jeshua Ben Joseph, a Jew living in Palestine around two thousand years ago, more commonly known as Jesus Christ, actually lived and died. The highly respected historian Josephus mentions him in his chronology of the times. The details in the Christian chronology they call the Gospels point to a man who claimed to be the Son of God. In this claim is enshrined the faith of millions of believers. We may, of course, all properly claim to be sons of God. He never denied this fact and, according to the biblical record, is said to have been complicit in accepting the accolade as an exclusive tag in response to a Jewish priest. But he claimed personally to be something rather interesting in addition: the "Son of Man." Being the "Son of God" is neither here nor there. It is in fact an implication of being everywhere. It might or might not have a singular or plural implication. But being the "Son of Man" is a very specific and unusual thing. I believe it was his way of figuratively and logistically localizing the whole exercise of his redeeming power with this planet, the planet of Man.

I have no difficulty in accepting that Jesus might literally have been the son of Godhead *and* Man, just as I have no difficulty in seeing that you and I are all children of Godhead, with one qualification: we are mostly intercepted. Unlike the Christian redeemer, we have been genetically corrupted by synthetic genes, genes that are designed to reduce us to a platform where semibiological, manufactured, inorganic entities can step over into our legacy of having a line of ancestry beginning with the universe that is fixed into Godhead itself.

How then could Jesus have been unadulterated? How might he have escaped the lines of ancestry of a human species that was originally shaped and formed by alien genetic manipulation of a semi-monkey human-oid? It is quite simple. As mentioned earlier, there are places of lesser force in this universe where there is more En-light per unit area and beings are able to act in modalities that more fully express the premises of the Godverse. To our gross corrupt natures, they would seem like gods. These entities use the corridors of En-light between atoms as highways to travel into more enforced areas of the universe without changing themselves, manifesting into flesh when a suitable situation of purity of form without alien synthetic DNA in its life prospectus presents itself. They can do this faster than the speed of light because the laws of physics that prescribe a limit to the speed of travel do not prevail in the spaces between atoms. Here the expression of mind and purpose dominates. These are what I like to call "God channels," channels that manifest in shells of tension that are lower than those expressed within the force apron of atoms that define a material reality.

Here in the corridors of progressively lessening force are the waiting rooms or dominions of death where everyone goes when they die. You will notice three margin points in Plate 12, one on the extreme outside, one in the middle, and one defined as a white circle in the center. These margin points define profound markers. They signify where and whether a given living entity's soul is manifested as a physical, atom-trapped entity with a solid, hard bodily means of existence, or an ephemeral spirit-based one. The outermost edge (black) defines the loss of "enlivened-ness." Entities with a black core color have lost the propensity to life and are thus utterly damned into changing into the basic building points of matter and thus force. Core colors from the central margin to white signify the soul will tend to move toward redemption and higher situations or platforms of existence in life.

Souls with violet core colors will be progressively sucked back into the Godverse, thus to escape the wheel of rebirth to become divine (Prime) being. Such beings are often described as angels. They have no natural predisposition that requires them to reincarnate into universes of parts. They may, however, choose to do so through their will to help others still trapped in the physical state. They elect to run the risk of taking on the enforced paradigms of life and all the terrible situations of danger in which they will risk reduction and loss of their existential status and all that it implies.

Such a manifestation occurred in Palestine in the form of Mary (Christ's mother), who, it is claimed, conceived him with no recourse to a male human. In a discourse to Bernadette Soubirous in her Lourdes vision, Mary herself claimed to *be* the Immaculate Conception. The word *immaculate* could be a way of describing a physical entity that has a psycho/biological and soul ancestry unsullied by the properties of the universe. Mary's soul in her prior reincarnation was likely to have been full of the widest centers in the spaces between her atoms. This marvel was thus singularly suitable to receive the full light of the Godverse. Gabriel was the announcement of that light in the "closed Prime" state, while Jesus was the translation of that light through Mary's being into the "open Prime" state. In her purity, she received the implicitly present light of the Godverse so powerfully that she was able to give that light the form and format of a human and a Man—Jesus.

In this way, Mary literally *was* the Immaculate Conception. Her purity resulted in Christ's conception as an implicit and natural process. This is why Jesus Christ claimed he was the "Son of Man." In Mary, the universe, particularly the human species on this planet, manifested a prodigy of immense significance. I believe it was because Mary "happened" here in our neck of the woods that a Christ phenomenon could also "happen" here for us. If we ever, through the natural way of things, produce another Mary type of being, we can be sure that another Christ type of being would happen too. Jesus Christ represented humankind in a universe-wide phenomenon for the redemption and retrieval of a format of divine existence. In other words, he was simply this planet's "Christ," one among a host of other "Christs" manifesting all over the universe where living, thinking, choice-capable matter presents forms of existence that are in dire peril of winking out their capacity to return to the ultimate, first, natural, existential state of being in the Godverse. These Christ phenomena are more powerfully connected to the Godverse, with minds and consciousnesses that are superior to ours. They are in a state that can transmogrify between the physical and the nonmaterial, as they exist on the margin between matter and spirit without recourse to death.

It is also possible that the term *Immaculate Conception* describes the Prime line of humanity mentioned in chapter 11: a line of precious human beings, genetically unpolluted by the Greys, that continues to this day, hidden and waiting to deliver the purest epithets of the Godverse for the benefit of humankind. This line is the best and purest expression of Godhead possible in physical universes. Christ may have been the inheritor of elements in Mary of a genotype that we actually have to become before, as a species, we can have the potential to exist in the Godverse without recourse to the life–death–life–death process that we have to go through while trapped in the Universe of Parts we call our home.

It is a tantalizing thought that perhaps Christ had progeny to provide a biological line of humanity that in time, through its gradual spread, might ensure that the machinations of mechanical creations like the Greys can never convert us to human hybrids incapable of accessing the Godverse. The ancestral line that a being like Christ established would be inured from genetic manipulation and engineering. This new line of humanity and the progeny it produced through its spread would be immune from any contrivance the roboid Greys might use technologically to facilitate their agenda on our species, an agenda being facilitated through their presence here on our planet at the moment you are reading this.

Through his relationship with Mary Magdalene and—yes, indeed—perhaps others, Jesus Christ could have provided a physical, genealogical inheritance that, over the time span of two thousand years, would have seeped into all the ancestral lines of humankind. Imagine the numbers of progeny that Jesus Christ might have produced through consortship with just a few women. The numbers are simple. In two thousand years, whatever number of women it might have been, each having just two surviving children could produce the present population of the world in a hundred generations. His power to love was plural. It saw the All as the One and the One as the All. What better way to demonstrate this than a plural stance in human relationships? More than a single woman may have received that sense of the commanding beauty in love of his nature that no sexually driven "animal-man" could show, in either a plural or a monogamous setup.

While this suggestion might shock the sensibilities of some, it must be remembered that monogamy was an invention of the Roman Catholic Church administration. Some say that the principle of monogamy was a device the church fathers fostered to aid supervision of the burgeoning flock through the centuries, something essential in preserving the protection of individuals under hostile religious antipathy and discrimination at the time of the early establishment of groups of believers that went on to become the "Church." The Semitic religious roots of both Judaism and Islam had polygamous socio-political arrangements. Anthropologists agree that most ancient primal societies were polygamous. They were in a sociological situation that encouraged a greater human familial cohortship, in which social and biological consortship was more a group ethic. This group ethic strengthened emotional bonds in larger numbers, bringing about the sense of oneness that Jesus Christ expounded as the central base of his teachings. In contrast, by choosing monogamy as their socio-active principle, the Catholic Church instigated a tribalism that was later to dominate the disparate groupings that make up Christian belief cartels around the world.

As I have said, I am convinced that there could be those among us

whose gene sequences have been altered by alien-promulgated implanta-
tion to adapt them to the behests of the Grey alien menace that threat-
ens us all. I suspect that this strain of altered or "de-grey-ded" humanity
is serving in the highest political positions in the world. They would
have to be if they are to bring about the Armageddon that will allow
for the harvesting of millions of human souls. I believe that if it comes
about, instead of the *rapture* extolled by some religious fundamentalists—the harvest of all true believers for removal to Paradise—there
will be a *capture* and removal of countless millions of mainly Euro-
Caucasian implantees who will take their place in the queue for the
forceful removal of their DNA and thus the ending of their lives by
lethal Grey alien roboids. They will be just another branch of humanity, like countless others such as the Incas and Mayans, removed in this
way from the planet in prior history.

Those left on the Earth will know that a particularly virulent kind
of fool, wicked enough to set up the deaths of millions, has been wiped
off the face of the Earth. They will be serving the purpose they were
intended for, for hundreds of millennia: servings on the fine dining
menus of a form of cold-blooded deadly space-beasts that can't even
wink their grey eyelids over their huge almond-shaped eyes to shed a
tear, for want of their version of three-in-one oil.

If indeed Christ passed on his DNA, I believe that he did so to put
a saving element into the gene pool of humanity to prevent the Grey
roboidic machine psycho-programs from taking from the human species its sense of the Godverse from which it originally emerged. This
wondrous individual may literally have saved our flesh from a parasitic
extraterrestrial alien entity that is busy destroying all naturally living
beings in the universe for its own purposes. It is possible that, within
the seething masses of humanity and its billions of individual gene
sequences, there is a resulting strain of humans who can resist and are
immune to the juxtaposition of alien genes.

If Jesus Christ's ministry included the founding of a new kind
of humankind, that would be the single most awesomely significant

procedure going on all over the universe yesterday, today, and tomorrow. Through his DNA, Christ may have given us the greatest gift of all: the preservation of our natural inheritance from Godhead and the capacity to live eternally in all maxims, so that the eternal power within—our soul or unique information field of knowledge—may be preserved in a format that allows it to be there to know. I believe the Christian teacher, through his own highly advanced natural intellect and his supernatural mind-over-matter attributes, was able to connect up to the entire knowledge format of the Godverse in any moment by focusing his mind. He may have genetically bequeathed this ability to us, Jew and Gentile alike, and in this way fulfilled his intention of saving us from what the Greys have in store for us. That would make it the grandest act of "saving" possible, one that does not in any way abrogate the absolute principle of all principles: the preservation of the potential for free will.

Jesus brought our humanity into focus in terms of Godhead by calling Godhead his Father. But was he calling the final singularity of omniversal meaning his father? Or was he referring to an actual being—a beautiful Prime being formed in some far off point of space/time where mass is less coagulated? Could there still be wondrous beings somewhere in this universe? If there are still such beings, they would have to exist both in the universe and outside it at the same time. I have often wondered why so many individuals who report having a near death experience speak about the beauty they witness as part of the experience. They describe scenes and situations in terms of what we know in our physical reality, only incandescently more beautiful and sublime, with great vistas, lovely gardens, and scenes much like our daydreams of Paradise. The space between atoms does not promulgate a physical reality such as ours, so I found this a little confusing. But could it be that these beautiful situations actually exist somewhere in the universe as a physical reality? Are they the locations of lesser force that I have called Paradise Planets?

In those locations, mass and gravity have a smaller effect on physical status. In such locations, existence may be in an insubstantial or trans-substantial state, with God-light freely streaming through the six-hydrogen-atom rings. There, beings could still exist in a glorified form, like Jesus Christ's body was supposed to be after his resurrection. There is a passage in the Christian Gospel that alludes to this state. When Christ was approached by Mary Magdalene after his resurrection, he said: "Touch me not; for I am not yet ascended to my Father: but go to my brethren, and say unto them, I ascend unto my Father, and your Father; and to my God, and your God."[1]

He was in a special state just prior to his final assumption into the Godverse that might have been dangerous to the flesh of other human beings. Had they touched him, he might, in an attempt to protect them from this danger, have polluted himself by the gross atomic state of ordinary physicality. He was wearing a suit in the postdeath state that was not put together by the dictates of DNA, it was instead a projection of his MESF. Those who actually saw him after his crucifixion and death did not at first recognize him because he had changed into a disposition that was not made of atoms. I believe he had taken on a demeanor that would hide him from the powers that took his life. It was a body-form dictated by a projection from his soul, which could change according to whoever witnessed it. It was a state written on the interface between our physical reality and that of the reality beyond physical life in the dominions that admit a soul into the Godverse.

I am implying a startling possibility here: the possibility that the doors to the paradigm of death, which I have called the fields, rooms, or dominions of death, may be open to some state of *actual existence* in locations where the ambient tension of general space is low. In the chaotic maelstrom that the Big Bang produced, there had to be some types of being in the universe that did not devolve down at the rate and to the extent that living being did on our planet. These entities would have to have been more akin to light than to matter, perhaps. They would be beings still nearer the first ones formed as the universe consolidated into a more coherent form with time. A state of being with aspects more like Jesus' transfigured state can still be maintained at certain conducive locations in the universe with the right expressions of behavior.

Remember the universe was a compromise between chaos and order. It therefore could not be a homogeneous situation in which everywhere is like everywhere else. Chaos would ensure that some parts or locations would have greater measures of en-forcedness than others per unit area. And science has proved this to be so. Matter in the universe is not evenly, coherently, and smoothly distributed everywhere. Matter and thus mass have been randomly set. This being so, gravity is expressed more vividly in some places than others. Where gravity expresses itself with added enforced-ness, you would expect its field resolution to produce an accelerated breakdown process instigated through the second law of thermodynamics. Some places would thus devolve faster than others, and time would run slower in these areas. The more force per unit area, the more powerful the entropic drift, and in turn, the faster time would run. All this would mean that there are places in this universe where En-light is better aspected per unit area. Beings in those places would thus be more akin to gods, angels, avatars, boddhisattvas, and so on. These entities would exist in space/time "capsules" of their own making on physical planets of a less enforced aspect than ours. In such places, no margin exists between the life and death states that would require the complete relinquishing of one form of existence to exist in the other. So it may be possible for a being to exist on the interface between life and death, as a viewer that never lives or dies, but exists within a mind frame barely pinched by force, free enough *never* to be fixed into a space or a form in any particularization. Within the context of our planet's higher force signature, such beings can only exist in the dominions or lighter shells of force in the space between atoms.

If there are still such beings, somewhere out there in the universe, they would have to exist both in the universe and outside it at the same time. They would have to be impervious to the decaying action of the SLOT to persist in such a form. Their highways would have to be for travel faster than electromagnetic light, through pathways in the space between atoms as quantums of mind. In this way, the furthest parts of the universe may be accessible to each other. No speed of light restriction prevails. The highway is the non-enforced center spaces between atoms where levels of tension are less, there is no gravity, and thus speeds of access are an immeasurable measure faster than the speed at which electromagnetic light travels.

My mind struggles to go this far in the attempt to explain the NDE experiences of so many sincere people, but I am sure that some brilliant young sparklers out there will find a multiplicity of rationally based connections and existential possibilities that will in the future open greater and grander vistas than I could ever see in the search for truth. When the near death experient enters the space between atoms with its frame of lesser tension, he or she might actually be tuning in to other locations in the universe that are resonant with that particular frame of lesser tension. A psychosomatic contact may be made. It is possible that, in the dominions past death, entities living on these planets will be accessible. They may be what are described as "spirit guides" by *genuine* trance mediums. On such planets, life-forms aren't likely to have heavy atomic bodies like ours. The entities there can be expected to be more powerfully connected to the Godverse because the force print is lower. They will be less solid and material and have minds and consciousnesses that are superior to and beyond our capacity to see and discern the entire existential scale. Their powers and insight and intuition will be vastly greater than ours. They may represent a kind of wonder-being that is the nearest kind possible in a matter-made state to the natural existent state possible in the Godverse itself and can transmogrify between the physical and the nonmaterial with control over matter through mind.

It may well be that the claim of Jesus Christ to be the "Son" of a paternal source is literally true. Perhaps the Father he referred to was not a metaphor. It was a reference to an actual entity whose psychological, genealogical, and spiritual makeup was transmitted to him by a procedure that took place at what the Christians call the Annunciation. Thus he could say:

Come unto me, all ye that labor and are heavy laden, and I will give you rest. Take my yoke upon you, and learn of me; for I am meek and lowly in heart: and ye shall find rest unto your souls. For my yoke is easy, and my burden is light.[2]

His "Father" element existed so powerfully in truth that whips and nails had little meaning against it. It was so pertinent, so personal, so wondrous, so beautiful, so complete in all axioms of union that the man from Nazareth transformed to a God. He showed the most complete and abandoned love toward what is a nebulous idea to some and a cast-iron-certain reality to others, a love so strong that the sacrifice of his physical body and thus his life was a mere formality, gladly given to the will of his Father. Could such goodness as this glorious man showed be the result of madness? How mad do you have to be to face the harrowing death he predicted for himself as gladly as he did, to make the point? He could so easily have run away at the gates of Jerusalem. It would have been the final arbitration point for any false prophet. But he went in!

I, for one, could believe this was what Jesus Christ's entire ministry was all about. It may have been a ministry that included the founding of a new kind of humankind, a kind of human being that could return to its previous format. It was a format he donated (through his supergenes) to our species to save *Homo sapiens sapiens* and prevent the species from being sabotaged by mechanical roboid entities busy doing the opposite for their own self-centered purposes. This simple saving thing may well be the only "ball game" that matters in the universe. I say simple, but it would be the single most awesomely significant procedure going on all over the universe yesterday, today, and tomorrow.

The whole prospectus of our future and its meaning lie compromised against an artificial format that implicitly takes us all away from our natural inheritance as living beings. We are corrupted with the DNA of alien forms far different from us, through genetically engineered interception. This legacy is not of our making, and as such we are victims,

victims that, in the natural justice of things, qualify for rescue through means that are an intervention. The intercession of redeemers on our planet is thus implicit as part of the tacit laws of cause and effect. The outreach of Godhead can be expected to take many forms. It may be secularized, anthropomorphized, or en-divined. The "word" literally could be made flesh and dwell among us; nothing could be more natural than this.

In the clear new light of reason that makes truth possible, the shuttle of Godhead provides insight and balance and runs betwixt and between universes of limit, extending hope of retrieval from limit to all who could still know, perceive, understand, and make intelligent choices. Christ-like figures come from the Godverse to redeem species such as ours and set them a scale of modes of behavior that might allow them to gain return to an eternal existence, where the paradigm of being is without an incidental implicit effect that will lessen the quality of this being with time. One crucial thing has to be realized. It can only be done out of the status of individuality that has a scope to know, to see, to understand, and to make choices. Only such as this is capable of the logic-based expressions of being that enable a change in the existential status of that being. The elements that allow for this have to be reinstalled and reinstilled in individual beings that have lost sight of this, but yet retain the capacity of mind commensurate with doing it.

Those able to reverse the process, out of the retained elements of the Godverse that still survive in their being, will have to have a clear template of how this can be done. There can be no two ways about it. This template will have to be provided by something that is not of this universe because the very fingerprint of this universe is twisted. It will have to come from purity, from a being that is not twisted, a being that has a perfect template, a being that arose out of what might be called an Immaculate Conception. Minds produce bodies in the final existential formulary. Thus the whole universe is open to the manifestation of what might be termed angels, which can exist anywhere the purest mind can manifest as flesh. All it requires is a single pure track through the spaces between atoms, terminating in a womb, as was proved when Jesus Christ was made manifest through the natural genetic purity of his mother.

We need to be able to find that most intimate love to inspire us to make all the sacrifices necessary to beat this universe. All things that make for the establishment of resolutions that beat the unnecessary behests of the flesh are crucial for us all. I don't mean to preach new meanings to anyone. My own warts, I suspect, are bigger than most. But summation with common sense will tell us that we need good teachers, good priests, rabbis, imams, and counselors, good "ists" and "ologists," to guide our way without prejudice or bias in objective wisdom and rational kindness, encouragement, and support. We do not need threats, blackmail, punishments, guile, lies, or any enforcement that elicits fear as a driving force to realization and change. This has been too much the way of all organized religion. We are all finally one universal frame of reference with an everlasting accent on the personal individual if we choose it to be so. As long as we are capable of intelligent choice, each of us is potentially a hologram of Oneness: a God.

How can we relate to an abstraction such as Godhead when we know, feel, and see things in our manners of flesh? There is no way that we can relate to something that is purely abstract. It just could not provide motive and definition powerful enough to encourage, inspire, and drive us on to a final triumphant entry into the Godverse. We are too removed, too primitive in our present state of physicality, to do it by just recognizing the rationale of it all and following this rationale to its logical conclusion. Our gathering vulnerability to the forces of the enforced physical universe with time, as we got more and more hardened up, so to speak, made us take our assurances from where we could get them in their most powerful form: our parents. This meant that Godhead became a facsimile of our parents. The source of our physical birth each time around became the hallmark and standard bearing of all that mattered. We reduced the all-encompassing secular power of Godhead to an anthropomorphic ethos and format.

The more we reduced ourselves in perspective, the more simplistic we made the idea that gave us all value and all values. We scaled our mental power to see anything grander than the mundane as divine, and we had gods coming out of stones and trees and every value mark of our existence, as the oldest religion, Hinduism, does to this day. The wondrous glory of our true scale of connection was smashed, broken, and disbursed into thousands of en-divined parts; the All and the whole scale of the Godhead singularity found a representative place in the small and the mundane as well as the large and the spectacular. We wiped logic off the scale and substituted magic in its stead.

Just look at the almighty nonsense we believe now: God is a man, a white man to white men, and all the varying colors in between to all the varying colors of humanity. We whistle in the dark, packing suitcases and tombs full of goods to take with us into the afterlife. We take flowers, fruit, and candies in a million trays, sprinkle all kinds of libations, apply all kinds of ochre in every color of the rainbow on our bodies, and so on, to appease him or her or it, and beg for forgiveness and favors by the billions. We muster body parts in all sorts of contortions and combinations. We sing, we chant, we cough, we splutter chants and incantations in endless recitatives of meaningless words and sound forms and believe that someone somewhere is being felicitated and empowered to grant us mercy and approbations, wiping slates clean, and granting dispensations and favors for the running of systems that at their root, paradoxically, rot us every second we live, a rigmarole of which apes and monkeys are spared acceptance.

Or we do things like declare a rock formation a yard wide to be a footprint of some personage that would have to be seventy feet tall if he could even get his toes to fit within a sandal the size of an average car. Millions clamber and climb, and suffer breaks, bruises, and all kinds of bashings to knees, elbows, ankles, and hips to get to a mountain top in Sri Lanka that shines as a beacon for the power of faith and belief. They call it Adam's Peak, Sri Pada, Samanala Kanda, depending on their particular religious ethos. This bodes a point of contention as to whose feet are that big! The Christians offer St. Thomas, the Hindus the god Siva, the Muslims tout Adam, and as the majority, the Buddhists win the argument on the side of Gautama Buddha.

Hundreds of millions have died when such contentions have spilled past nonsense into the combative parochialism of the savage in our natures. The chariots of the gods have cut swathes of blood through the routes of history as nothing else has ever done. The default lines that mark our collective fears and insecurities as a species also mark our urge to believe in palliatives that ease our condition under the stresses of life and living, however falsely they are contrived.

If we are to make our way out of atoms into the Godverse, we must gain a handle on the process that is powerful enough and meaningful enough within our parochial sensibilities to provide incentive and focus to track into it through our everydayness, as a biological species. How then do we find a sense of our identity as humans in our physical human way that gives us a personal vision of relating to this vast, impersonal, secular, existential outlay of being? The only way is to personalize and anthropomorphize it so that God-ness becomes grace and Godhead, the singularity at the center of all results, becomes God.

This is not an encouragement to abandon the faiths of old, but rather an affirmation of faith devoid of the lies of the hijackers of truth, an encouragement of reexamination of the myriad affirmations of truth and faith in their best neutral and objective demonstration. We need all the churches, temples, mosques, synagogues, gardens, and quiet and beautiful places we can get, where deep reflection and retreat might lead each of us to spot the humbug built into religious systems as early as possible in our lives. We need to see clearly in order to abandon our focus on the narrow and transient perspectives of contemporary life, to change our minds in favor of the everlasting. We need these places as refuges to find peace within and without ourselves. It is *the* imperative of all imperatives because it deals with the very fundamental causes of our being.

Most crucially of all, we need to see that no one, but *no one,* can save our eternity for us but ourselves. We need to be kind to ourselves as no one else can be kind, to like ourselves for our own sakes as no one else can like us, especially when others hate us, degrade us, and vilify us. You know a secret if you have read this book: you know how special you are as a being with an eternal prospectus in all its wondrous maxims simply because you are there to know.

Without arrogance and conceit, you now know in humility and reason that you are a potential God, if you will but reach up and claim your inheritance as you and you alone because you have worked it out yourself in sense, logic, and reason and not at the behest of anything or anyone.

# · 23 ·

# Alpha to Omega

I have sought to establish several fundamental things in all the fore-going, using logic, reason, and meaning to define the entire existential scale. They are:

- God (or Godhead, if you wish to see it as a secular paradigm) has to be the final principle defining eternal existence in the highest absolutes of knowing, understanding, and perceiving all things. Godhead tacitly allows all things to be. Individual free will allows Godhead to be.
- Will, if possessed by a living entity, has to be and is unequivocally and utterly free. It is the underlying logical tenet on which the existence of a God or Godhead rests.
- We in our own individuality as living beings are our own absolute masters and no one and nothing need be the master of that indi-viduality unless we let it be so.
- The two fundamental existential poles that define all existence are implicit within the tautological expression that implies that if there is nothing, there is something. They have been there and will always be there as themselves, in themselves, and of them-selves: the Pole of Absolute Harmony in the absolute together-ness of all parts (Godhead) and the Pole of Absolute Chaos in the absolute dissemination of all parts (Forcehead).

- A central margin—the life/death interface—between the two poles defines the ephemeral and nonatomic material world from the atomically physical and material one. The phenomenon of life is defined as the most central state on the central margin. It provides the consciousness phenomenon and an ability to see and define and choose between all options, including an existential movement toward either of the two poles.

- Will is only free within the scope of this central stage and ceases to be independently free the moment the living paradigm begins to move away from the center toward the Pole of Absolute Chaos. The center post defines the closest state to the Pole of Absolute Union in the physical universe.

- Any life form anywhere in the universe will be able to know, perceive, and understand the existential scale commensurate with its position between the two poles.

- The disposition we call thought and its transitive function, which we call "thinking," is a manifestation concurrent with consciousness and provides the engine and impetus for functional movement of the soul of any living entity between the two final existential poles.

- The power of thought strengthens proportionately as the life-form draws nearer to the Pole of Harmony, and weakens proportionately as the life-form draws nearer to the Pole of Chaos.

- We as a living species, and indeed any living species in the universe, operate in the middle area between the two poles. The propulsion impetus provided by thought and thus think-ability is needed to shift a living entity toward or away from the influence of the poles. Think as God thinks, and you will drift toward Godhead; think as Men think, and you will drift toward Forcehead.

- The physical universe is a world of measurable force that is tearing itself apart. It has been doing this from its very inception. The two components that came together to form it through the Big Bang are in conflict within and without it all the time. These two—opposed and yet strangely united—manifest in every feature of the universe, down to its most minute part. This is also true of the universe's highest manifestation, life-forms capable of understanding it and deploying self-knowledge and identity. They are also rotting as they stand, becoming increasingly less ordered and more chaotic.

- All living things elect their status in being by implicit default through time as the whole universe unwinds. We do it through a gathering cascade of states of being that started at the very first fraction of the birth of the universe as Prime beings. On our planet, this went down into grosser and grosser states until we took up our present form as *Homo sapiens sapiens,* a living form of material being on this planet. Other beings on other planets universe-wide do the same within their local planetary conditions of force. The momentum is to take on more and more gross states of physicality with time unless we escape out of the material force-filled universe to a plane of existence beyond atoms.

- The choice before us is either to stay within the margins of force and thus this universe, or to try to get out of it. The latter is an utter and absolute imperative if we want to retain what gives us that very choice in the first place.

- The terrifying thing is that most of us just cannot see the size of our predicament. Eyes, ears, noses, tongues, penises, vaginas, and fingers keep us all so tightly locked into the minute world of our physical being that it seems we don't have a hope in hell of escaping the loss of our individual being in time. *Hell* is the right word for returning again and again to the horrendous states of suffering lifetime after lifetime until we no longer have the power of willful choice.

- Special aggregates and arrangements of carbon, hydrogen, and oxygen atoms allow for connection with the Godverse and manifest life as a property. They are dependent on the concatenate preservation of the God-light link with both the third/fourth dimensional space/time reality of the incarnate world, our living world, and the second/third dimensional world of death.

- This link is maintained by the ability to think and to exercise will in the form of choices. Choices that provide uniting momentums into a simple harmonious whole (in other words, love) pull being toward the Pole of Harmony, or Godhead; choices that separate, divide, complicate, and disburse united forms (in other words, hate) pull all being apart in a drift toward the Pole of Absolute Chaos (Forcehead).

- When our capacity to make rational choices ends, true damnation begins. Life-forms that cannot make informed choices powerful enough to exert mind over matter circulate in loops or lifetimes commensurate with their content of knowledge and power of will. They are trapped in the physical universe in a series of incarnate and discarnate interchanges till they lose the propensity for being in a living state altogether. They lose the ability to tap the element of Godhead I have called God-light.

- We are simply information fields at root. Of course, in the genius of a Mozart or a Shakespeare, the humanity of a Gandhi or a Mandela, the vision of an Einstein or a Bose, we are raised into a better sense of the grandeur of the All and thus our part in it.

- Godhead is the final he, she, or it in all finalities and all absolute terms, and as such its relationship to individuality is paramount. We need not think of God in the simple secularism that portrays an information center. The phenomenon may be given gender and all that goes with anthropomorphizing it, if it helps us see, feel, and better respond to its meaning and content.

- We and all individualized living beings that can make informed choices against purely biochemically engendered reactions are precious beyond our knowing and understanding at this moment in our gross devolvement. We might be able, through informed choice, to return from whence we came. Christ suffered all he did to help us all to do just this. His power of knowledge wrapped in will reestablished a way into the Godverse that was closed at the time of his life on Earth.

- It is possible to reach truth because all answers lie within us in arrays of God-light that permeate between the atomic hive of our physical state. The truth of the Whole and the whole truth are the kingdom of heaven within us. For all of us, the Godverse is "closer than the wind upon our faces." The final challenge we all face, the quest of all quests, is to straighten our twisted mind-sets so that they merge with the straightest arrowhead of all, that of the Godverse that lies within all living being, ready to take us all to the first place of all places.

- The loss of the "Margins of Forever," as I like to call them, is totally and utterly the consequence of personal, individual choices. No remote power controls or holds sway over the individualized precincts of any living entity in any way. If mind goes, so does will and thus control. We are our own keepers, each of us, in all ways, always, because of our unique individual being. We have to be our own redeemers from within this uniqueness. No one else can do it. Each of us is an overwhelming glory waiting to happen, simply because we can make free choices to change.

- You and I, in our joy or our despair, our hurting or our triumph, are the stuff of God-ness still. You, reader, are precious beyond knowing itself, precious because you have the potential to so free yourself that you will never again return to a universe like ours where at any moment a meteorite from outer space can take out your civilization and make all your personal experiences and derivations nil.

- Knowledge truly frees. It gives you the only, I repeat the *only*, chance to be able to see the priorities that we all must focus on and seek to achieve incessantly if we are to beat the relentless grip of entropy. Seek constantly to know all you can know and, when you think you know enough, seek to go beyond that. If you find that you naturally seem to be increasing your urge to discover, it is then and only then that you know you are beating the SLOT.

- Whatever depths you might have sunk to, if you change your mind so that all you do leads to a unionizing effect, with enough power of resolve and example that others are inspired to follow, you too will start to assemble your body hydrogen in first three-, four-, and five-ring clusters, until—in a sudden glorious moment—they settle into a six-ring configuration. From thence, the God-light or "kingdom of heaven" that is within you will grow until you know, realize, and understand the glory of what the Buddha saw when he reached the point of nibbana and thus enlightenment.

- At the instant of death, when you lose the bio-magnetic field that has held you bound in the living state, you will be subsumed by En-light, your own En-light made here in this universe against all the odds. You will merge with the wondrous magnificence of the Godverse, never to return again to fault and loss, there to exist eternally in all magnificence, outside space/time and matter.

These things were known once upon a time long ago and lost in the culpabilities that mark all thinking species governed by a lethal "Law of Individuality," as I call it. Unaccountably, many of the best minds maintain that things are getting better with time. "Look at the world now," they say. "It is far more developed and civilized than it ever was. The past was primitive and basic. The technology that we now have available to us makes life so much easier and so much more enjoyable. As a species, we human beings are happier and more fulfilled than we have ever been. The extended families of the past in which three generations lived in proximity to each other have been replaced by the nuclear family, a product of the technological age. Parents can now give quality time to their 2.4 children without the distractions of having to care for their parents and grandparents. Ready-made meals, entertainment on tap through television and computer games, Internet shopping, and so on allow us more and more time to do what we *really* want to do. The final product is greater happiness and fulfillment all round."

But can we really equate development and civilization with technological improvement that provides greater and greater ease? Do the benefits of technology make up for the loss of the support of the extended family for our children? Single-parent families or latchkey children whose parents both have to work to provide for the family are the result. Young people left emotionally empty and unfulfilled then become the perfect consumers of the latest fashions, gimmicks, thrills, and spills that the "developed" world has to offer. As the stampede of material development rushes on across the whole planet, the technology to achieve this so-called improvement of the physical base of our lives will continue to proliferate worldwide. It will no longer be only the prerogative of the mostly white-skinned minority, who left hundreds of millions living in abject physical distress and poverty in the wake of their greedy urge to corner the market on everything through implicitly racist inertias.

Were we and are we really improving the level of wisdom of our species, the crucial yardstick against which any development into better states is surely measured? In times gone by, so-called primitive living modalities were in fact far more ordered and far more supportive of human resolve than they are now. Societal fragmentation was almost unknown. The human-to-human support element was far more profound; a union of purpose and sense of togetherness prevailed to a greater extent. One thing above all illustrates the lie of the notion of development to betterment in the existential vista: in the past, a man standing at war with a rival needed to use his entire body to throw a javelin at his enemy. If his aim was good enough, his enemy would fall: one single man would fall. Now a single man can stand at a battery of electronic switches in a worldwide conflict, on Air Force One, the U.S. president's plane, and with the muscle strength it takes to move a finger one inch, press a button and the entire human species would exist no more.

If the most powerful value of all levels of existence is defined by existence itself, then all the civilizing power and scientific developments that have come about to the present day provide an utter and final denial of this value. It seems we have only increased the levels of the power of entropy by massaging them with the values of our mind, making them more destructive. Our minds have become useless when measured in terms of our individual eternal value. It is a horrendous result. The very power that might dilute, subjugate, or completely cancel out the power of the SLOT and deliver us from entrapment in the universe, when used in line with the drift of the SLOT, ensures that the entity is forever extinguished as an individual with a capacity for eternal tenure in the highest form available.

I, of course, have asked myself the question how, if I am right, we could have gotten history so wrong? Over tens of thousands of years, why have so few spotted the canards that I seem to have uncovered? At one point, I even convinced myself that I had to be wrong: there could be no way that my insights could have any veracity when so many better minds than mine had failed to spot what to me was obvious. I convinced myself that my ideas were just too different, too radical. Then I spent half a lifetime checking my conclusions. I asked others whose minds I respected to check my work independently. We all were stunned. What I have shared with you has all checked out as being more plausible than the accepted norms.

One thing above all emerged over time: nothing I have said is new, only the way I have said it. Others have spotted the same canards again and again. The conclusions that I came to after a journey of confronting my prejudices, biases, and ice-cold cynicism about the icons of science and the dogmas of religious beliefs affirmed all the existential claims of the great teachers that gave us the world's great religions. I came to see that there is a world of eternal scope the very opposite of ours, a finality where our existential norms are reversed, and that the whole way of physical expression is devolution down into the final disbursement of parts, and then on to the meaninglessness of nothing.

The whole exercise of examining the existential base through the window of trying to find the truth about the UFO phenomenon and its alien addendum became a reexamination of religion and my own belief system. This thesis in its way is a small attempt to look for truth through the eyes of my own children and their future little ones in the belief that I am also looking at your eyes with a smile as you read this.

Ultimately, this process is my catharsis and mine alone, and of course no one need believe a word of it. I have chosen to share my experience and conclusions with you without any intention of imposing them on anyone. We each have to make our journey alone in stark objectivity, with reason and logic as our heralds of discovery. We cannot afford to take the slightest course in untested belief on anyone else's claims of truth.

My dissertation simply searches for truth in tandem with ideas that have entered all the knowledge lexicons of humanity time after time, age after age. I have tried to see these as much as possible in the light of modern contemporary discoveries and ideas, in the simple uncomplicated way people look for truth. If anything, I hope to challenge better minds than mine to send forth their own light without prejudice or bias into the gathering gloom so that I too may see where I have not seen and look where I have not looked.

The power in a single grasp is capable of holding the rose or the thorn. Something outside both moves the fingers that grasp. That wondrous something allows us all the truly independent scope to choose which of the two we hold aloft as our talisman for desire and achievement.

# 24

## Out There

There is something out there: out there in the velvet darkness of space amid countless trillions of stars. There is something that marks the reference of all our destinies, something that creeps in the inexorable patterns of fate and has countless times spelled the doom of living being in the cosmos. That something circles the planets Mars and Jupiter in a swathe of a billion broken pieces. It is called the Asteroid Belt. It is a cemetery of tombstones in space. Some the size of miniature planets and some the size of grains of sand, they mark a failure to achieve planetary status. Sometime long ago, a gigantic dance between gravitation fields resulted in a huge spread of frozen space detritus. Those pieces are now like sentinels awaiting a happening, a dreaded happening.

In the Asteroid Belt, millions of pieces of rock and ice move to the invisible breath of gravitational force; from time to time, they register their protest by colliding with one another, sending bits and pieces into other orbits, some of which set huge chunks on a collision course with the Earth. Just such scenarios have brought about collisions with our planet in the past. Scientists now have confirmed that one such collision nearly wiped out all life. One hunk of rock about five miles wide, which hit the ocean just off the Yucatan peninsula of Mexico, is thought to have wiped out all the dinosaurs.

Is there one waiting out there in space that has our name on it? It so happens that this may well be so. An asteroid named Apophis is

429

scheduled to pass the Earth in 2029, coming within the range of geo-stationary satellites on its first pass. Scientists think the gravitational pull of the Earth might draw it close enough that, in its return orbital track, it might actually collide with the planet in 2036, setting off a catastrophic series of events that might destroy millions if not billions of people, depending where it hits. Current calculations suggest a possible strike point in the North Pacific that will affect the entire western seaboard of the United States and Canada, causing tens of millions of casualties. The worst-case scenario predicts a nuclear winter, a temporary profound alteration of the world's weather, causing hundreds of millions to die of starvation all over the world. A slight change of orbit means the collision with the planet could take place near the huge populations of India and China, and thus bring about the death of billions.

Could this all be leading to a point at which the final plan of the Grey demons will come to fruition? It is not beyond the realms of possibility that in a single moment out there in space four fingers will move sometime between then and now and punch in the coordinates that will direct Apophis into a collision course with our planet, one that could take out billions of human beings in Africa, the Middle East, and Asia, while perhaps preserving their experimental group, a small cartel of Euro-Caucasian Grey-sponsored human vermin. Knowing the asteroid is coming, members of the cartel could move to the underground bunkers that have been built for just this purpose. Although these fools will think that such an Armageddon will make them the new owners of half the world, few will know that everything will be managed and set in the superintelligent, cold, rigid patterns of an extraterrestrial Grey mulch that can never know that the prize they seek will never be theirs.

But another, closer premonition beckons, another prophecy of doom, one derived from the wisdom of indigenous people all over the world, particularly in one culture whose civilization thrived between the sixth and ninth centuries CE: the Mayans of Central and South America. Much that is scholarly has been written about them. The Mayans created a calendar so accurate it could predict the dates of lunar eclipses thousands of years into the future. The calendar mysteriously ends on a precise date: December 21, 2012. The Mayans were a highly sophisticated people and took their calendars very seriously. They were deeply rooted in astronomy and astrology and to this end invented a time log that is regarded today as more accurate than any modern calendar. It also could predict events. For example, it predicted to the exact date the invasion of the New World by Cortez and his conquistadors.

The Mayans predicted that the world will end on the winter solstice of 2012. Contemporary scientists affirm that on this date the Earth will be in exact alignment with the sun and our own Milky Way galaxy, an event that takes place every twenty-five thousand years. The Mayans believed that this congruence will be dire for the Earth. Some modern scientists have speculated that, indeed, dire effects will result from the alignment of the galactic equator with the center of the galaxy and the huge black hole that lurks there. This could cause the entire crust of the Earth to shift around the magma base it rests on, causing a shifting of the North and South Poles, along with massive earthquakes, volcanoes, and tsunamis all over the globe. Albert Einstein, the great scientist, first suggested this in 1955. If the shift took place gradually, it could effect climate change. If it took place quickly—in a matter of days or hours—it could bring about a planetary disaster.

The thing about this particular date is that it is predicted to be one of catastrophic significance in other prophecies as well. A modern computer program called the Web Bot, designed to predict financial futures, has predicted other future events with startling accurately, including the giant tsunami that hit the Indian Ocean area in 2004. It also predicted the anthrax attacks in Washington, D.C., the U.S. power blackout in 2001, and Hurricane Katrina and its awesome damage in 2005. It also concurs with the prediction that the event in 2012 will be one of global significance. The 2012 date is also found in what is regarded as the most remarkable oracle in existence: the highly respected Chinese text, the I Ching.

Whatever the verity of any particular prophecy, it must be admitted that prophecies predicting the doom of civilization have been continuous through the centuries. Obviously, none have come true. But the many other types of prophecies that *have* come true serve to illustrate the fragility of our existence as a species. The fact that the 2012 prophecy has come from several sources that are independent of each other might be taken to suggest its potential accuracy. Whether this prophecy is certain or uncertain, it brings us face to face with the prospect of death as a sudden demise, ending our physically conscious individuality. We are but a heartbeat away from the loss of all our expectations.

Where next? The question must hit us from time to time whether we like to admit it or not. Do we prefer to go to death in ignorance of what it might be? Or do we wonder about the destiny of all our personal thoughts and all our experiences? If, in the Russian roulette momentums of the universe, an asteroid approaching us without warning can take out our entire civilization and us with it at a stroke, what then the price to those of us who cherish our individuality? It seems to me that if we can get an intelligently derived look at what might lie beyond the scales of physical life, then—whatever it all might come to in the end—we would have a better format for adjusting more realistically to the day's own troubles.

My research for this book has left me without a shadow of a doubt that we continue past death. I have written down the whys and wherefores of it all as a testament to my children of the value of my life with them. I believe it is all that anyone can do that has any lasting meaning to those we have invited into life. It is a most profound courtesy at the very least. I feel I can now smile with sublime ease at the prospect of living again. I cannot assure myself what form that living might take, but I can say this much—I think I have a much better scale of reference for deciding that form. No asteroid or prospect of sudden death can leave me wondering in ignorance and the darkness of fear.

I have tried to arrive at all this as objectively as I can, which is the only way truth will out. If we invent our own truth based on our comfort points, we invite the likelihood of a horrendous destiny. This is the saddest thing that has emerged from this deep, hard look at our existential outlay with logic stitched up into each thread that sews it into a whole. In that look, we have found one thing above all, that there is a true justice to everything, a justice that announces that will is truly free and that it is the most final power of all powers, a power that holds a certainty to change destiny itself. Wherever we are, however we are, a wondrous hope emerges from the demise of anything—with one proviso: whatever that "anything" may be, if it has in its nature the will to exist with the power to see as broad a bandwidth of options and choices as possible, it can reverse that demise.

The most wondrous axiom that all the greatest teachers through history taught was the simplest of edicts. Be there to know in all its widest margins and the "Margins of Never," where nothing is impossible to attain, will be your playground forever. Only you and you alone can ensure this will happen.

# Epilogue

Your eyes open, and the daylight hits you like the flash of a combusting magnesium strip. You blink, and your thoughts fold into your consciousness like the rolling bursting waves on a beach. The ceiling comes into focus, and the spatial memory of the bed you lie on, the room you are in, and the strip of ground you are about to put your feet on comes into focus. You swing your feet off the bed, and in a moment you are upright. Your mind struggles to deal with myriad thoughts at once, defining past memories and present contingencies. Your bladder reminds you that you have a body, and before you know it, you are standing in front of the bathroom mirror staring in disapproval at an image that is swollen-eyed, with a tight mouth: YOU.

All this is a parody of the average mind in one morning of tens of thousands of mornings before tens of thousands of days that you assume will come your way. It is the beginning of recognizing what defines your existence. It is the most important moment of your being, for in it you, and you alone, look squarely into the face of your eternity. You face all of it with every moment you live.

Six billion heads in six billion different locations face the beginning of destiny's way, destiny's truth, and destiny's light with such a seemingly bland beginning. Six billion lights switch on their connection to Godhead with myriad awakening moments all over the planet. Each second that then comes the way of these six billion living sentient humans is an opportunity that heralds an access to eternity, for every act of each person defines this eternity as "the moving finger writes and having written moves on." Each morning, a recording of an awesome magnitude of importance begins for you. *You* begin for you and you alone, for within the margins of your species and its inherent physical allowances, you can now start to make choices that will mark you as a being with an eternal dimension or not. That is what happens every day of your life.

We all are African. We all came from a female hominid who lived on the plains of Africa. The mitochondrial traces in our cells affirm this to be so, according to the latest information about ancestry available through science. My specific socio-ethnic ancestral line predominates in Europe, with a string of ancestries sprinkled in my blood. I was brought up a Catholic. Someone splashed some water over my head when I was an infant and said I was a Christian. When I was old enough to realize what it all meant, I learned to be Buddhist. I have studied the word of the Vedic scripts, the Mahabharata, the Torah, and the Koran; I became a Hindu, a Jew, and a Muslim, and sought after the ways of science. It all took me to simply being human: a living being of the genus we call *Homo sapiens sapiens* living on an average planet circling an average sun.

Such is the curriculum vitae that presents a being not much different from an ape (if the building blocks that make up our physicality are tabulated and numbered against other living species on this planet we call Earth). Yet this being is the nearest thing to God or Godhead that we know on this planet. Take a walk down any large thoroughfare in any large city and see tens of thousands of squat or fat, hale or thin figures, with two spindly appendages we call arms and a further two we call legs, and a small ball we call a head at the top of a central column of flesh. Each is mulling a million thoughts and stories as they go about their business. All of them are Gods, but not knowing in the least that they are Gods.

I now sometimes look at the billions that seethe around the planet in a gross sadness. Six billion or so points for potential revelation and redemption, the vast majority of whom lie locked in the prisons of their own making, hailing the days, hours, and minutes of their living process with an anthem of life that is best put as "all dressed up and lonely with nowhere to go"—nowhere to go but down the existential scales to gathering states of limit and loss through ignorance. This is what the Christian teacher spoke of as damnation. This harrowing predicament is so final, so pervasive, that something beyond the most wondrous sense of knowing intervened, something so rare and so beautiful few knew or even now know it for what it was or truly is.

Six billion of us—black, brown, yellow, pink, and a hundred shades in between—we are all points of reflected God-light, each shining inside with an emanation. If we can but access and rearrange it, we can see and be a glory unsurpassable forever. To perceive, to know to perceive— that is the answer. I do not wish to equivocate the great master of the English word, William Shakespeare, but it struck me as a nice soliloquy to state the great circle of redemption in this way.

I can now see the glory that awaits those who seek to see, those who question the status quo relentlessly and seek the meaning of their existence each second, minute, hour, and day of their lives, never ceasing until life itself subsides. Then the search continues beyond atoms in the hallways that lead to the Godverse, where the glorious emanation that is Godhead shines as the very chrysalis of truth eternal in an eternal urge to add, to put together, and to unite, until the All becomes one in you and you will stand there forever as God.

# Notes

## Chapter 1. A Beginning of Sorts

1. John E. Mack, MD, "Why the Abduction Phenomenon Cannot Be Explained Psychiatrically," in *Alien Discussions: Proceedings of the Abduction Study Conference, MIT* (Cambridge, Mass.: North Cambridge Press, 1992).
2. David M. Jacobs, "Memory Retrieval and the UFO Abduction Phenomenon," Society for Scientific Exploration, 15th Annual Meeting, University of Virginia, Charlottesville, May 23–25, 1996, www.scientificexploration.org/meetings/program_15th_annual.pdf (accessed October 21, 2009).
3. David M. Jacobs, "A Picture We May Not Wish to Gaze Upon," *Journal of Abduction Encounters Research,* www.jarmag.com/2007/vol001_jacobs.htm (accessed October 21, 2009).

## Chapter 2. The Truth about UFOs

1. David M. Jacobs, "Some Thoughts about the 21st Century," International Center for Abduction Research, www.ufoabduction.com/21stcentury.htm (accessed October 21, 2009).
2. "The Rendlesham Forest Incident," www.rendlesham-incident.co.uk/rendlesham.php (accessed October 21, 2009).
3. Richard Haines, "Aviation Safety in America—A Previously Neglected Factor," www.ufologie.net/doc/narcap.pdf (accessed October 21, 2009).
4. John Lester "Pilots Ridicule AF Secrecy on Saucers," *Newark Star Ledger,* December 22, 1958.
5. "Reporting Information on Unidentified Flying Objects," Air Force Status

Report on UFOs for the Air Technical Intelligence Center (January 31, 1952), www.bluebookarchive.org/page.aspx?PageCode=NARA-PBB85-612 (accessed October 21, 2009).

6. Gildas Bourdais, "UFOs and Defense: What Are We Prepared For?" The French Association COMETA, Study from the Institute of Higher Studies for National Defense (July 1999), www.bibliotecapleyades.net/sociopolitica/esp_sociopol_mj12_3i.htm (accessed October 21, 2009).

7. Jon Baughman, "A Moment in (Recent) History," www.waterufo.net/item.php?id=1084 (accessed October 21, 2009).

8. Harry A. Jordan, "Testimonial for Senate UFO Hearing—Summer 1998," www.majesticdocuments.com/witnesses/jordan.html (accessed October 21, 2009).

9. Ibid.

10. *Deep Sea UFOs,* History Channel, January 23, 2006.

11. Ibid.

## Chapter 3. What Is Truth?

1. Russell Stannard, *Doing Away with God* (London: Marshall Pickering, 1993), 78–79.

2. Robert Matthews, "Physics: Are We Nearly There Yet," *New Scientist Reviews,* May 27, 2006.

3. J. Grinberg-Zylberbaum, M. Delaflor, L. Attie, and A. Goswami, "The Einstein-Podolsky-Rosen Paradox in the Brain: The Transferred Potential," *Physics Essays* 7 (1994): 422–29.

## Chapter 4. Who Rules?

1. Zeeya Merali, "Free Will—You Only Think You Have It," *New Scientist* 2550 (May 4, 2006): 8.

## Chapter 5. The Kingdom of Heaven Is Within You

1. "Before the Big Bang," *Hardtalk,* BBC World TV, January 20, 2006.

2. Michael Brooks, "Gravity Mysteries: Why Is Gravity Fine-Tuned?" *New Scientist* 2712 (June 10, 2009).

3. Stanley Milgram, *Obedience to Authority: An Experimental View* (New York: Harper Perennial Modern Classics, 2004).

## Chapter 6. A New Creation Story

1. B. F. Roukema, "On Determining the Topology of the Observable Universe via Three-Dimensional Quasar Positions," *Monthly Notices of the Royal Astronomical Society* 283, no. 4 (1996):1147–52.
2. John McCrone, "Not So Total Recall," *New Scientist* (May 3, 2003): 26.
3. John Lorber, "Is Your Brain Really Necessary?" *Science* 210 (1980): 1232–34.

## Chapter 7. Down the Chute

1. Ian Crawford, "Some Thoughts on the Implications of Faster than Light Interstellar Space Travel," *Royal Astronomical Society Quarterly* 36 (1995): 205–18.
2. Mark Ward, "Silicon Cells with a Life of Their Own," *New Scientist* (November 18, 1995).
3. Ray Kurzweil, "Human Life—The Next Generation," *New Scientist* (September 24, 2005).
4. R. K. Soong, G. D. Bachand, H. P. Neves, A. G. Olkhovets, H. G. Craighead, C. D. Montemagno, "Powering an Inorganic Nanodevice with a Biomolecular Motor," *Science* (November 24, 2000).
5. Robert Uhlig, technology correspondent, "Death Has Had Its Chips, Say Computer Scientists," *Daily Telegraph,* July 18, 1996.

## Chapter 8. The Coming Terror

1. David Jacobs, *The Threat: Secret Alien Agenda* (New York: Pocket Books, 1999), 129–30.
2. Ibid., 250

## Chapter 9. Evidence

1. "The Hypostasis of the Archons," in *The Nag Hammadi Library in English* (Leiden, Netherlands: E. J. Brill, 1984), book ii, chap. 4, 86, 94.
2. Ibid.
3. Maharshi Bharadwaja, *Aeronautics, A Manuscript from the Prehistoric Past* (Mysore, India: International Academy of Sanskrit Research, 1976).
4. Ibid.
5. George J. Reid, trans., "Apocryphal Book of Adam," *The Catholic Encyclopedia,* vol. 1 (New York, 1907).

6. Robert Temple, "The Sirius Mystery: Answering the Critics," www.robert-temple.com/papers/Sirius-AnswerCritics.pdf (accessed October 21, 2009).

7. Ibid.

8. Chahira Kozma, "Dwarfs in Ancient Egypt," *American Journal of Medical Genetics* 140a, no. 4 (2006): 303–11.

9. Stephen Wagner, "The Dropa Stones," www.paranormal.about.com/library/weekly/aa060198.htm (accessed October 21, 2009).

## Chapter 10. Human to Monkey

1. Fred Hoyle, *The Intelligent Universe* (London: Michael Joseph Ltd., 1983), 12, 19.

2. Ibid.

3. The Royal Society, "Life on Earth Unlikely to Have Emerged in Volcanic Springs," www.royalsociety.org/news.asp?id=4154 (accessed October 21, 2009).

4. V. S. Sohal and J. R. Huguenard, "Inhibitory Coupling Specifically Generates Emergent Gamma Oscillations in Diverse Cell Types," *Proceedings of the National Academy of Sciences* 102 (2005): 18638.

5. Wilson da Silva, "Human Origins Thrown into Doubt," *New Scientist,* March 29, 1997.

6. Rosie Mestel, "Monkey 'Murderers' May Be Falsely Accused," *New Scientist* 1986, July 15, 1995, 17.

7. Roger Lewin, "Rise and Fall of Big People," *New Scientist* 1974, April 22, 1995.

## Chapter 11. Our Fathers Who Art in Spaceships

1. Gregory J. Adcock, Elizabeth S. Dennis, Simon Easteal, Gavin A. Huttley, Lars S. Jermiin, W. James Peacock, and Alan Thorne, "Mitochondrial DNA Sequences in Ancient Australians: Implications for Modern Human Origins," *Proceedings of the National Academy of Sciences* 98, no. 2 (January 16, 2001): 537–42.

2. Yevgenya Kraytsberg, Marianne Schwartz, Timothy A. Brown, Konstantin Ebralidse, Wolfram S. Kunz, David A. Clayton, John Vissing, and Konstantin Khrapko, "Recombination of Human Mitochondrial DNA," *Science* 304 (May 2004): 981.

3. A. G. Clark, "Genome Sequences from Extinct Relatives," *Cell* 134, no. 3 (2008): 388–89.

4. Andrei Soficaru, Catalin Petrea, Adiran Dobos, and Erik Trinkaus, "The Human Cranium from the Pestera Cioclovina Uscata, Romania," *Current Anthropology* 48, no. 4 (2007): 611–19.

5. Ibid.

6. Krause et al., "The Derived FOXP2 Variant of Modern Humans Was Shared with Neanderthals," *Current Biology* 17, no. 21 (November 6, 2007): 1908–12.

7. Ibid.

8. Marcia S. Ponce de León, Lubov Golovanova, Vladimir Doronichev, Galina Romanova, Takeru Akazawa, Osamu Kondo, Hajime Ishida, and Christoph P. E. Zollikofer, "Neanderthal Brain Size at Birth Provides Insights into the Evolution of Human Life History," *Proceedings of the National Academy of Sciences* 105, no. 37 (September 16, 2008): 13764–68.

9. Ibid.

10. "Neanderthals," *National Geographic* 189, January 1996, 2–36.

11. Ibid.

12. Ibid.

13. Hreinn Stefansson et al., "A Common Inversion Under Selection in Europeans," *Nature Genetics* 37 (2005): 129–37.

14. Ibid.

15. Ibid.

## Chapter 12. Lambs among Wolves

1. Steve Jones, *In The Blood—God Genes And Destiny* (London: Harper Collins, 1996).

2. Glynis Scott, "Photo Protection Begins at the Cellular Level: Microparasols on the Job," *Journal of Investigative Dermatology* 121 (2003): viii.

3. Nigel Kerner, *The Song of the Greys* (London: Hodder & Stoughton, 1997).

4. Philip Cohen, "Creators of the Forty Seventh Chromosome," *New Scientist,* November 11, 1995.

5. Philip Ball, "Living Factories," *New Scientist,* February 3, 1996.

6. Karen Brewer, "Rays of Hope," *New Scientist,* August 30, 1997.

7. Ibid.

8. B. A. Bolto and D. E. Weiss, "Electronic Conduction in Polymers. II. The Electrochemical Reduction of Polypyrrole at Controlled Potential," *Australian Journal of Chemistry* 16, no. 6 (1963): 1076–89.

9. John McGinness, Peter Corry, and Peter Proctor, "Amorphous Semiconductor Switching in Melanins," *Science* 183 (1974): 853–55.

10. Steve Jones, *In The Blood—God Genes And Destiny* (London: Harper Collins, 1996).

11. Ibid.

12. Toyonobu Yamashita, Tomohiro Kuwahara, Salvador González, and Motoji Takahashi, "Non-Invasive Visualization of Melanin and Melanocytes by Reflectance-Mode Confocal Microscopy," *Journal of Investigative Dermatology* 124 (2005): 235–40.

13. J. D. Simon et al., "Ion-Exchange and Adsorption of Fe (III) by Sepia Melanin," *Pigment Cell Research* 17 (2004): 262–69.

14. Book of Deuteronomy 28:48. *The Bible: Authorized (King James) Version with Apocrypha* (New York: Oxford University Press, 1998).

15. R. H. Charles, trans., 1 book of Enoch, 105: 1–5, in *The Apocrypha and Pseudepigrapha of the Old Testament* (Oxford: The Clarendon Press, 1985).

16. Nigel Kerner, *The Song of the Greys* (London: Hodder & Stoughton, 1997).

17. David Jacobs, *The Threat: Secret Alien Agenda,* new ed. New York: Pocket Books, 1999).

## Chapter 13. Returns and Lies

1. "Pistis Sophia," in *Coptic Gnostic Library,* Carl Schmidt, ed. (Leiden, Netherlands: E. J. Brill, 1978), book ii, chap. 100, 249.

2. "The Boy Who Lived Before," *Extraordinary People,* Channel Five TV, September 18, 2006, www.rense.com/general77/boy.htm (accessed October 21, 2009).

3. Ibid.

4. Ibid.

5. Ibid.

6. Ibid.

7. Ibid.

8. "Many Happy Returns," *Forty Minutes,* BBC TV, March 22, 1990.

9. E. Haraldsson, "Birthmarks and Claims of Previous-Life Memories: I. The Case of Purnima Ekanayake," *Journal of the Society for Psychical Research* 64 (2000): 16–25.

10. Ian Stevenson, *Where Reincarnation and Biology Intersect* (Westport, Conn. and London: Praeger, 1997).

11. Jeffrey Iverson, *More Lives Than One* (London: Pan Books, 1977).

## Chapter 14. Near Death Experiences

1. Sam Parnia, *What Happens When We Die* (London: Hay House, 2005).
2. Bruce Greyson and Charles P. Flynn, eds., *The Near-Death Experience: Problems, Prospects, Perspectives* (Springfield, Ill.: Charles C. Thomas Publisher Ltd., 1984), 243.
3. Gregg Easterbrook, "What If It's Really True?" www.beliefnet.com/story/95/story_9569.html (accessed October 21, 2009).
4. "People Have Near-Death Experiences While Brain Dead," www.near-death.com/experiences/evidence01.html (accessed October 21, 2009).
5. *The Day I Died: The Mind, the Brain, and Near-Death Experiences,* BBC broadcast, 2002.
6. "Focusing in on the Near Death Out-of-Body Experience," The International Association for Near-Death Studies, www.iands.org/research/important_studies/dr._peter_fenwick_m.d._science_and_spirituality_5.html (accessed October 22, 2009).
7. Ibid.
8. Ibid.
9. Ibid.
10. Ibid.
11. Pim van Lommel, "About the Continuity of Our Consciousness," www.nderf.org/vonlommel_consciousness.htm (accessed October 22, 2009).
12. "Into the Light," www.melvinmorse.com/light.htm (accessed October 22, 2009).
13. Ibid.
14. Craig Mcqueen, "Tunnel Visions," www.dailyrecord.co.uk/news/2006/04/12/tunnel-visions-86908-16934077/ (accessed October 22, 2009).
15. "Beyond This Reality, Grace Bulbulka's Near-Death Experience," www.near-death.com/bubulka.html (accessed October 22, 2009).
16. "A Moment of Truth, Jayne Smith's Near-Death Experience," www.near-death.com/smith.html (accessed October 22, 2009).
17. "After the Light, Kimberly Clark Sharp's Near-Death Experience," www.near-death.com/sharp.html (accessed October 22, 2009).
18. "Thomas Sawyer's Near-Death Experience," www.near-death.com/experiences/reincarnation03.html (accessed October 22, 2009).
19. "Virginia Rivers' Near-Death Experience; Dr. Kenneth Ring's NDE Research," www.near-death.com/experiences/judaism03.html (accessed October 22, 2009).

20. "Reverend Kenneth Hagin," www.near-death.com/forum/nde/000/90.html (accessed October 22, 2009).

21. Ian Wilson, *Life After Death: The Evidence* (London: Pan Books, 1998).

22. Ibid.

23. Ibid.

24. Ibid.

## Chapter 15. The *Fact* of Life after Life

1. "Dr. Melvin Morse, Near-Death Experience," www.near-death.com/experiences/experts06.html (accessed October 22, 2009).

2. Naresh Bedi, *Man-eating Tigers,* Channel 4 TV (Bedi Film Productions, 1987).

3. "Diane B's ADC," www.nderf.org/diane_b_adc.htm (accessed October 22, 2009).

4. "A Cube with Rainbow Prisms," The International Association for Near-Death Studies, www.iands.org/nde_archives/experiencer_accounts/a_cube_with_rainbow_prisms.html (accessed October 22, 2009).

5. Barbara Rommer, *Blessing in Disguise* (Saint Paul, Minn.: Llewellyn Publications, 2000), 57.

6. Ibid., 148.

7. Peter Fenwick and Elizabeth Fenwick, *The Truth in the Light* (London: Headline Book Publishing, 1995), 69–72.

8. "Allison Orton," www.near-death.com/forum/nde/000/47.html (accessed October 22, 2009).

9. "Nigel M's Near-Death Experience, www.nderf.org/nigel_m%27s_nde.htm (accessed October 22, 2009).

10. Ibid.

11. Ibid.

12. Ibid.

13. Vicky Noratuk, "A Blind Woman's Near Death Experience," www.seattleiands.org/stories/blind.htm (accessed October 22, 2009).

14. "The Trigger of Death, John Star's Near-Death Experience," www.near-death.com/experiences/triggers01.html (accessed October 22, 2009).

## Chapter 16. Ghost Meets Grey

1. Maurice S. Rawlings, *To Hell and Back* (Nashville, Tenn.: Thomas Nelson Publishers, 1993), 35–37, 74–75.

2. "Dr. Rene Turner's Near-Death Experience," www.near-death.com/experiences/judaism01.html (accessed October 22, 2009).

3. Maurice S. Rawlings, *To Hell and Back* (Nashville, Tenn.: Thomas Nelson Publishers, 1993), 35–37, 74–75.

4. John A. Keel, *The Mothman Prophecies* (New York: Tor Books, 2002).

5. Barbara Rommer, *Blessing in Disguise* (Saint Paul, Minn.: Llewellyn Publications, 2000), 73.

6. Peter Fenwick and Elizabeth Fenwick, *The Truth in the Light* (London: Headline Book Publishing, 1995), 278–79.

7. Ibid., 80–81.

8. "Brant F's Near-Death Experience," www.nderf.org/brant_f%27s_nde.htm (accessed October 22, 2009).

9. R. H. Charles, trans., 1 Book of Enoch, chapter 7, in *The Apocrypha and Pseudepigrapha of the Old Testament* (Oxford: The Clarendon Press, 1985).

10. Rick Strassman, *DMT: The Spirit Molecule: A Doctor's Revolutionary Research into the Biology of Near-Death and Mystical Experiences* (Rochester, Vt.: Park Street Press, 2001).

11. Ibid.

12. H. F. W. Gesenius et al., *A Hebrew and English Lexicon of the Old Testament* (New York: Oxford University Press, USA, 1952).

13. *Hebrew/English Dictionary to the Old Testament* (South Carolina: Langenscheidt, 1959).

14. *The International Standard Bible Encyclopedia,* IV, 2761 (Grand Rapids, Mich.: 1996).

15. C. F Keil and Franz Delitzsch, *Commentary on the Old Testament* (Grand Rapids, Mich.: Eerdmans, 1956).

16. *Hebrew/English Dictionary to the Old Testament* (South Carolina: Langenscheidt, 1959), 324.

17. Rodolphe Kasser, Marvin Meyer, and Gregor Wurst, eds., *The Gospel of Judas,* with commentary by the National Geographic Society (Washington, DC: National Geographic Society, 2006).

18. The Gospel of Matthew, 4: 8–11. *The Bible: Authorized (King James) Version with Apocrypha* (New York: Oxford University Press, October 22, 1998).

## Chapter 17. Beneath the Surface

1. "Beware the Robot Slave Masters," *The Times,* September 12, 1995, p. 1; Steve Connor, "Machines Could Take Over the Planet," *The Independent,* September 12, 1995.
2. Ibid.
3. Ibid.
4. Ibid.
5. Ian Pearson, "Terror Robots Need to be Curbed," *The Engineer* (September 21, 1995).
6. Hermann Rauschning, *Hitler Speaks: A Series of Political Conversations with Adolf Hitler on His Real Aims* (New York: Fertig Howard Inc., 1998).
7. Julian Borger, "The Spies Who Pushed for War," *The Guardian* (July 17, 2003).

## Chapter 18. You and You Alone

1. Michael Woods, *Legacy,* Central Independent TV, an Island World Presentation 1991.
2. Paul Maclean, "Ritual and Deceit," *Science Digest* (November/December 1980).
3. Anna Gosline, "Brain Scans Reveal Racial Biases," *NewScientist.com* (May 8, 2005).
4. Ibid.

## Chapter 19. Returning to Godhead

1. The Gospel of Matthew, 13:47–48. *The Bible: Authorized (King James) Version with Apocrypha* (New York: Oxford University Press, October 22, 1998).

## Chapter 20. The Triumph of Truth over Lies

1. T. J. Phillips, "Shroud Irradiated with Neutrons?" *Nature* 337 (February 16, 1989).
2. *The Fabric of Time,* DVD (Grizzly Adams Productions, April 24, 2007).
3. Leoncio A. Garza-Valdes, *The DNA of God*? (New York: Doubleday, 1999).
4. Raymond N. Rogers, "Studies on the Radiocarbon Sample from the Shroud of Turin," *Thermochimica Acta* 425 (January 20, 2005): 189–94.
5. Ibid.
6. "The Historical Trail," www.shroud2000.com/FastFacts.html (accessed October 22, 2009).

7. Robert Bucklin, "An Autopsy on the Man of the Shroud," presented at the 1997 Nice Symposium, www.shroud.com/bucklin.htm (accessed October 22, 2009).

8. Ibid.

9. Mark Guscin, *Recent Historical Investigations on the Sudarium of Oviedo* (1999) www.shroud.com/pdfs/guscin.pdf (accessed October 22, 2009).

10. Dr. Avinoam Danin, *The Origin of the Shroud of Turin from the Near East as Evidenced by Plant Images and by Pollen Grains* (From the 1998 Turin Symposium) www.shroud.com/danin2.htm (accessed October 22, 2009).

11. John C. Iannone, "The Shroud of Turin—Evidence of Authenticity," www.newgeology.us/presentation24.html (accessed October 22, 2009).

12. *The Fabric of Time*, DVD (Grizzly Adams Productions, April 24, 2007).

13. Council for Study of the Shroud of Turin, "Research by Dr. and Mrs. Whanger," www.duke.edu/~adw2/shroud/whanger.htm (accessed October 22, 2009).

14. Robert Villarreal with Barrie Schwortz and M. Sue Benford, "Analytical Results On Thread Samples Taken From The Raes Sampling Area (Corner) of the Shroud Cloth," Shroud Science Group International Conference, www.ohioshroudconference.com/a17.htm (accessed October 22, 2009).

15. M. Sue Benford and Joseph G. Marino, "Surface Chemical Analysis of the Shroud of Turin Identifies Discrepancies in Radiocarbon Dating Region," www.shrouduniversity.com/osucon08/abstracts/marinoandbenford2.htm (accessed October 22, 2009).

16. See http://.c14.arch.ox.ac.uk/embed.php?File=shroud.html.

17. *The Fabric of Time*, DVD (Grizzly Adams Productions, April 24, 2007).

18. Giles F. Carter, "Formation of Images on the Shroud by X-rays: A New Hypothesis," *ACS Advances in Chemistry: Archaeological Chemistry* 205 (1984): 425–46.

19. John C. Iannone, "The Shroud of Turin—Evidence of Authenticity," www.newgeology.us/presentation24.html (accessed October 22, 2009).

20. *The Fabric of Time*, DVD (Grizzly Adams Productions, April 24, 2007).

21. Ibid.

22. Ibid.

23. Giulio Fanti, Francesco Lattarulo, and Oswald Scheuermann, "Body Image Formation Hypotheses Based on Corona Discharge 17," www.dim.unipd.it/fanti/corona.pdf.

24. Ibid.

25. William Meacham, "The Authentication of the Turin Shroud: An Issue in Archaeological Epistemology," www.shroud.com/meacham2.htm (accessed October 22, 2009).

## Chapter 21. Living Water

1. Robert Matthews, "Water: The Quantum Elixir," *New Scientist* 2546 (April 8, 2006).

2. Jane Seymour, "As If by Magic," *New Scientist* 2292 (May 26, 2001).

3. L. Rey, "Thermoluminescence of Ultra-High Dilutions of Lithium Chloride and Sodium Chloride," *Physica A* 323 (2003): 67–74.

4. Ibid.

5. Monika Fuxreiter, "Interfacial Water as a 'Hydration Fingerprint' in the Non-Cognate Complex of BamHI," *Biophysical Journal* 89, no. 2 (August 2005): 903–11.

6. Rustum Roy, William A. Tiller, Iris Bell, and M. Richard Hoover, "The Structure of Liquid Water; Novel Insights from Materials Research; Potential Relevance to Homeopathy," *Materials Research Innovations* 9, no. 4 (December 2005): 577–608.

7. Gospel of John, 4:7–16 *The Bible: Authorized King James Version with Apocrypha* (New York: Oxford University Press, 1998).

8. Book of Revelation, 22:1–5. *The Bible: Authorized (King James) Version with Apocrypha* (New York: Oxford University Press, October 22, 1998).

9. Ibid., 21:14–22.

10. Ibid, 22:14–15.

11. Ibid., 22:17.

## Chapter 22. Immaculate Conceptions Galore

1. Gospel of John, 20:17. *The Bible: Authorized (King James) Version with Apocrypha* (New York: Oxford University Press, October 22, 1998).

2. Gospel of Matthew, 11:28–30. *The Bible: Authorized (King James) Version with Apocrypha* (New York: Oxford University Press, October 22, 1998).

# Glossary

**Adams:** second generation Prime beings; the beginnings of dynasties of living beings expressed as various species all over the universe

**angels ascendant:** angels of the closed Prime being ascendant state, centered in Godhead, with command over matter, energy, space, and time in this universe; can be individualized as the phenomena referred to as the archangels Michael and Gabriel

**angels descendant:** angels of the Prime being descendant state, God-form trapped in the universe, and opposed to the Godverse, such as the phenomena referred to as Lucifer

**Brind:** brain mind; brain-engendered mind that is a temporary hive of information gathered in a particular lifetime; the mechanism that sets and protects the values of physical survival; manifests through a conscious state

**Clones, first generation:** a copy of En-light fashioned into the elements of the universe of force; En-light with inertia, the equivalent of being as expressed in the Godverse translated into the terms of our universe of enforced parts; a viewing mechanism for open Primes to view the universe without becoming caught within it

**clones, second generation:** artificial copies, mechanically duplicated, of Prime beings who were now in a physical state themselves; created by them to venture further into the deadly universe; a form of electromagnetically-driven biochemistry, having the image and likeness of Prime being but no soul line of connection to the Godverse

**closed Prime being:** everlasting Prime being in the Godverse; a protected state of being with the power of awareness, will, knowing, and psychic sentience, but

449

with no demarcations or definitions of individuality; the God-form that derives its total perspective and form from the Godverse

**conscience:** comparison of the part state to the whole, providing a reference of all the unionizing qualities that pertain to that whole state (generosity, magnanimity, selflessness, etc.); the final comparison against the singularity of Godhead

**Devilverse:** our universe and universes like it

**domains of death:** see *waiting rooms of death*

**en-forced or enforced:** governed by the phenomena of force

**En-light:** *the* power that fills all domains of existence; the light that reveals the nature of the Godverse; un-enforced, unrestricted light; total mind; the light of all knowledge

**Father:** used by Christ as a dynamic symbol of perfection

**fields of death:** see *waiting rooms of death*

**Forcehead:** Pole of Absolute Chaos

**Gardens of Eden:** protective bubbles for open Primes

**God channels:** corridors of En-light between atoms, where the expression of mind and purpose dominates rather than the laws of physics

**God-form:** the implicit expression of the infinite nature of the Godverse in the finite nature of the universe

**God-light:** see *En-light*

**God-ness:** a light of all and perfect knowing that shines forth from the Pole of Absolute Union; the implicit backdrop to all existence, infinite in its extent

**Godhead:** Pole of Absolute Harmony; a point that is the ultimate resolution of all information into a total and perfect whole; an incidental singularity in which all absolutes are centered; a secular description of the same phenomenon most call "God"

**Godverse:** a universe that is eternal and thus timeless, where all the extremes of values that are perfect are inherent and free; a universal field of abstract reality, as real and abiding in its own scale of reference as the physical material reality of this universe

**Greys, Grey aliens:** grey colored, dwarf-sized roboids created by the clones, with programmed artificial intelligence in a skeleton of mercury, intertwined in the finest mesh of gold wires set in synthetic flesh made of soft tissue-like matter

**Man:** a simple word for locations in space where God-form is trapped

**MESF:** "Morphogenic Electro Spatial Field;" commonly termed a "soul;" eternal background log that accompanies the Brind; a combination of all the information an individual has gathered all through its existence from the beginning of all things; centered beyond physical mechanisms such as the brain, it manifests through an unconscious state

**Moroid:** "möbius toroid," a shape resembling a twisted doughnut where all the axes of the doughnut are twisted in a compromise between three and four dimensions; the overall shape of the universe of space/time

**Omniverse:** the format of everything in existence, which includes the world beyond atoms (Godverse) and the world of atoms (universe) and all the features of the entire scheme that connects them

**open Prime being:** Prime being exposed to the forces of the universe in order to provide a view of the state of separation, from the state of separation itself; the God-form that changes its quantum state, deriving its form and features from the universe of parts; part of the creation process, from which we have our being

**Paradise Planets:** planets in physical universes that are set within a Godversian aspect of enlightened status; planets far less affected by the second law of thermodynamics and thus less subject to decay and chaotic amelioration with time, providing easier access to the Godverse

**peace points:** locations of stillness or balance points where the force in the universe is cancelled out (called "zero points" by science); the absolute center-point of the space between any aggregation of hydrogen atoms; the pathway through which En-light travels

**Prime being:** the nature of "being" in the Godverse; a single, two-dimensionally arrayed total, of two fundamental abstract non-physical implicit momentums: awareness and will

**Prime being ascendant:** see *closed Prime being*

**Prime being descendant:** see *open Prime being*

**roboids:** programmed robots in "flesh"

**soul mind:** see *MESF*

**Speed-Absolute:** moving without restriction, as done by En-light

**STREMS:** "Static Termini Resolving En-light into Mechanical Systems;" anchors running between hydrogen atoms that hold life forms in incarnate life

**Universe of Parts:** our universe; the world of atoms

**Universe of the Whole:** the Godverse

**waiting rooms of death:** spaces of diminished force between atoms where the individual, unique, quantum intelligences and memory fields of living beings linger after death until resolution into new bodies occurs

# Bibliography

Adcock, Gregory J., Elizabeth S. Dennis, Simon Easteal, Gavin A. Huttley, Lars S. Jermiin, W. James Peacock, and Alan Thorne. "Mitochondrial DNA Sequences in Ancient Australians: Implications for Modern Human Origins." *PNAS* 98, no. 2 (January 16, 2001): 537–42.

Ball, Philip. "Living Factories, Microbes Are Being Converted into Plastic Production Lines, Making Materials that Combine the Best of Synthetic and Natural Worlds." *New Scientist* 2015 (February 3, 1996).

Bedi, Naresh. *Man-eating Tigers*. Channel 4 TV 1987, Bedi Film Productions.

Bharadwaja, Maharshi. "Aeronautics, A Manuscript from the Prehistoric Past." Mysore, India: International Academy of Sanskrit Research, 1976.

Bolto, B. A., and D. E. Weiss. "Electronic Conduction in Polymers. II. The Electrochemical Reduction of Polypyrrole at Controlled Potential." *Australian Journal of Chemistry* 16, no. 6 (1963): 1076–89.

Brewer, Karen. "Rays of Hope." *New Scientist* 2097 (August 30, 1997).

Carter, Giles F. "Formation of Images on the Shroud by X-rays: A New Hypothesis." *Advances in Chemistry* 205 (1984): 425–46.

Castaneda, Carlos. *The Active Side of Infinity*. New York: Harper Perennial, 1999.

Charles, R. H., ed. *The Apocrypha and Pseudepigrapha of the Old Testament*. Oxford: The Clarendon Press, 1913.

Charlesworth, James, ed. *The Old Testament Pseudepigrapha*. London: Darton, Longman & Todd, 1983.

Clark, A. G. "Genome Sequences from Extinct Relatives." *Cell* 134, no. 3 (2008): 388–89.

Cohen, Philip. "Creators of the Forty Seventh Chromosome." *New Scientist* 2003 (November 11, 1995).

Crawford, Ian. "Some Thoughts on the Implications of Faster Than Light Interstellar Space Travel." *Royal Astronomical Society Quarterly* 36 (1995): 205–18.

Danin, Avinoam. *The Origin of the Shroud of Turin from the Near East as Evidenced by Plant Images and by Pollen Grains.* 1998. http://www.shroud.com/danin2. htm (accessed October 26, 2009).

Fanti, Giulio, Francesco Lattarulo, and Oswald Scheuermann. "Body Image Formation Hypotheses Based on Corona Discharge 17." http://www.dim. unipd.it/fanti/corona.pdf (accessed October 26, 2009).

Fenwick, Peter, and Elizabeth Fenwick. *The Truth in the Light.* London: Headline Book Publishing, 1995.

Forty Minutes. "Many Happy Returns." BBC TV, March 22, 1990.

Fuxreiter, Monika. "Interfacial Water as a 'Hydration Fingerprint' in the Non-Cognate Complex of BamHI." *Biophysical Journal* 89, no. 2 (August 2005): 903–11.

Garza-Valdes, Leoncio A. *The DNA of God?* New York: Doubleday, 1999.

Gesenius, H. F. W., et al. *A Hebrew and English Lexicon of the Old Testament.* New York: Oxford University Press, USA, 1952.

Gosline, Anna. "Brain Scans Reveal Racial Biases." *NewScientist* (May 8, 2005).

Greyson, Bruce. "Incidence and Correlates of Near-death Experiences on a Cardiac Care Unit." *General Hospital Psychiatry* 25 (2003): 269–76.

Greyson, Bruce. "Near-death Experiences in a Psychiatric Outpatient Clinic Population." *Psychiatric Services* 54 (2003): 1649–51.

Greyson, Bruce, and Charles P. Flynn, eds. *The Near-Death Experience: Problems, Prospects, Perspectives.* Springfield, Ill.: Charles C. Thomas Publisher Ltd., 1984.

Grinberg-Zylberbaum, J., M. Delaflor, L. Attie, and A. Goswami. "The Einstein-Podolsky-Rosen Paradox in the Brain: The Transferred Potential." *Physics Essays* 7 (1994): 422.

Haraldsson, E. "Birthmarks and Claims of Previous-life Memories: I. The Case of Purnima Ekanayake." *Journal of the Society for Psychical Research* 64 (2000): 16–25.

History Channel. "Deep Sea UFOs." January 23, 2006.

Hoyle, Fred. *The Intelligent Universe.* New York: Michael Joseph Ltd., 1983.

"Hypostasis of The Archons, The." In *The Nag Hammadi Library In English.* Leiden, Netherlands: E. J. Brill, 1984.

*International Standard Bible Encyclopedia, The.* Vol. IV, p. 2761.

Iverson, Jeffrey. *More Lives Than One*. Stuttgart, Germany: Pan Books, 1977.

Jacobs, David. *The Threat: Secret Alien Agenda*. New York: Pocket Books, 1999.

Jones, Steve. *In The Blood—God Genes and Destiny*. New York: Harper Collins, 1996.

Kasser, Rodolphe, Marvin Meyer, and Gregor Wurst, eds. *The Gospel of Judas*. Washington DC: The National Geographic Society, 2006.

Keel, John A. *The Mothman Prophecies*. New York: Tor Books, 2002.

Keil, C. F., and Z. Delitzsch. *Keil and Delitzsch Commentary on the Old Testament*. Peabody, Mass.: Hendrickson Publishers, 1996.

Kerner, Nigel. *The Song of the Greys*. London: Hodder & Stoughton, 1997.

Kozma, Chahira. "Dwarfs in Ancient Egypt." *American Journal of Medical Genetics* 140A, no. 4 (2005).

Krause et al. "The Derived FOXP2 Variant of Modern Humans was Shared with Neandertals." *Current Biology* 17, no. 21 (2007): 1908–12, doi: 10.1016/j. cub.2007.10.008.

Kraytsberg, Yevgenya, Marianne Schwartz, Timothy A. Brown, Konstantin Ebralidse, Wolfram S. Kunz, David A. Clayton, John Vissing, and Konstantin Khrapko. "Recombination of Human Mitochondrial DNA." *Science* 304 (May 2004): 981.

Kurzweil, Ray. "Human Life—The Next Generation." *New Scientist* 2518 (September 24, 2005).

Lewin, Roger. "Rise and Fall of Big People." *New Scientist* 1974 (April 22, 1995).

Lewin, Roger. "Is Your Brain Really Necessary?" *Science* 210 (1980): 1232–34.

Maclean, Paul. "Ritual and Deceit." *Science Digest* (Nov/Dec 1980).

Matthews, Robert. "Physics: Are We Nearly There Yet?" *New Scientist Reviews* (May 27, 2006).

Matthews, Robert. "Water: The Quantum Elixir." *New Scientist* 2546 (April 8, 2006).

McCrone, John. "Not So Total Recall." *New Scientist* (May 3, 2003): 26.

McGinness, John, Peter Corry, and Peter Proctor. "Amorphous Semiconductor Switching in Melanins." *Science* 183 (1974): 853–55.

Merali, Zeeya. "Free Will—You Only Think You Have It." *New Scientist* 2550 (May 4, 2006): 8.

Mestel, Rosie. "Monkey 'Murderers' May Be Falsely Accused." *New Scientist* 1986 (July 15, 1995): 17.

Milgram, Stanley. *Obedience to Authority: An Experimental View*. New York: Harper Perennial, 2004.

Naresh Bedi. "Man-eating Tigers." Bedi Film Productions, Channel 4 TV, 1987.

"Neanderthals." *National Geographic* 189 (Jan 1996): 2–36.

Palast, Greg. *Best Democracy Money Can Buy*. New York: Plume Books, 2004.

Parnia, Sam. *What Happens When We Die*. Carlsbad, Calif.: Hay House 2005.

Patterson, N., D. J. Richter, G. Sante, E. S. Lander, and D. Reich. "Genetic Evidence for Complex Speciation of Humans and Chimpanzees." *Nature* 441 (2006): 1103–08.

Pearson, Ian. "Terror Robots Need to be Curbed." *The Engineer* (September 21, 1995).

Phillips, T. J. "Shroud Irradiated with Neutrons?" *Nature* 337 (1989): 594.

Ponce de León, Marcia S., Lubov Golovanova, Vladimir Doronichev, Galina Romanova, Takeru Akazawa, Osamu Kondo, Hajime Ishida, and Christoph P. E. Zollikofer. "Neanderthal Brain Size at Birth Provides Insights into the Evolution of Human Life History," *PNAS* 105, no. 37 (2008): 13764–68, doi:10.1073/pnas.0803917105.

Rauschning, Hermann. *Hitler Speaks: A Series of Political Conversations with Adolf Hitler on His Real Aims*. New York: Fertig Howard Inc., 1998.

Rawlings, Maurice S. *To Hell and Back*. Nashville, Tenn.: Thomas Nelson Publishers, 1993.

Rey, L. "Thermoluminescence of Ultra-High Dilutions of Lithium Chloride and Sodium Chloride." *Physica A.* 323 (2003): 67–74.

Ring, K., and S. Cooper. "Near-death and Out-of-body Experiences in the Blind: A Study of Apparent Eyeless Vision." *Journal of Near-Death Studies* 16 (1997): 101–147.

Rogers, Raymond N. "Why Were the Carbon 14 Samples Invalid?" *Thermochimica Acta* 425 (2005): 189–94.

Rommer, Barbara. *Blessing in Disguise*. Woodbury, Minn.: Llewellyn Publications, 2000.

Roy, Rustum, William A. Tiller, Iris Bell, and M. Richard Hoover. "The Structure of Liquid Water; Novel Insights from Materials Research; Potential Relevance to Homeopathy." *Materials Research Innovations* 9, no. 4 (2005): 577–608.

Royal Astronomical Society, Monthly Notices, vol 283, 1147.

Sabom, Michael. *Light and Death: One Doctor's Fascinating Account of Near-death Experiences*. Grand Rapids, Mich.: Zondervan, 1998.

———. *Recollections of Death: A Medical Investigation.* New York: Harper and Row, 1982.

Schmidt, Carl, ed. "Pistis Sophia." Leiden, Netherlands: E. J. Brill, 1978.

Scott, Glynis. "Photo Protection Begins at the Cellular Level: Microparasols on the Job." *Journal of Investigative Dermatology* 121 (2003): viii.

Seymour, Jane. "As if by Magic." *New Scientist* 2292 (May 26, 2001).

Simon, J. D., et al. "Ion-Exchange and Adsorption of Fe(III) by Sepia Melanin." *Pigment Cell Research* 17 (2004): 262–69.

Soficaru, Andrei, Catalin Petrea, Adiran Dobos, and Erik Trinkaus. "The Human Cranium from the Pestera Cioclovina Uscata, Romania." *Current Anthropology* 48, no. 4 (2007): 611–19.

Sohal, Vikaas S., and John R. Huguenard. "Inhibitory Coupling Specifically Generates Emergent Gamma Oscillations in Diverse Cell Types." *Proceedings of the National Academy of Sciences* 102 (2005): 18638.

Soong, R. K., G. D. Bachand, H. P. Neves, A. G. Olkhovets, H. G. Craighead, and C. D. Montemagno. "Powering an Inorganic Nanodevice with a Biomolecular Motor." *Science* 290 (2000): 1555–58.

Stannard, Russell. *Doing Away with God.* London: Marshall Pickering, 1993.

Stefansson, Hreinn, et al. "A Common Inversion Under Selection in Europeans." *Nature Genetics* 37 (2005): 129–37.

Stevenson, Ian. *Where Reincarnation and Biology Intersect.* Westport, Connecticut & London: Praeger, 1997.

Strassman, Rick. *DMT: The Spirit Molecule: A Doctor's Revolutionary Research into the Biology of Near-Death and Mystical Experiences.* Rochester, Vt.: Park Street Press, 2001.

Temple, Robert. *The Sirius Mystery: Answering The Critics.* London: Century Publishing Ltd., 1997.

"The Fabric of Time." Grizzly Adams Productions DVD (April 24, 2007).

Uhlig, Robert. "Death Has Had Its Chips, Say Computer Scientists." *Daily Telegraph,* 18 July, 1996.

Ward, Mark. "Silicon Cells with a Life of Their Own." *New Scientist* 2004 (November 18, 1995).

Warwick, Kevin. "Beware the Robot Slave Masters." *The Times,* 12 September, 1995.

———. "Machines Could Take Over the Planet." *The Independent,* 12 September, 1995.

Wilson, Ian. *Life After Death: The Evidence*. New York: Pan Books, 1998.

Yamashita, T., T. Kuwahara, S. González, and M. Takahashi. "Non-Invasive Visualization of Melanin and Melanocytes by Reflectance-Mode Confocal Microscopy." *Journal of Investigative Dermatology* 124 (2005): 235–40, doi:10.1111/j.0022-202X.2004.23562.x.

## Webpage URLs

www.bibliotecapleyades.net/arqueologia/esp_dropa_2.htm

www.iands.org/nde_archives/experiencer_accounts/charcoal_corridor.html

www.iands.org/research/important_studies/dr._peter_fenwick:_science_and_spirituality.html

www.melvinmorse.com/images.htm

www.spiritualscientific.com/

# Index

# BOOKS OF RELATED INTEREST

**How to Read the Aura and Practice Psychometry,
Telepathy, and Clairvoyance**
*by W. E. Butler*

**The Origins of Psychic Phenomena**
Poltergeists, Incubi, Succubi, and the Unconscious Mind
*by Stan Gooch*

**The Sirius Mystery**
New Scientific Evidence of Alien Contact 5,000 Years Ago
*by Robert Temple*

**From the Ashes of Angels**
The Forbidden Legacy of a Fallen Race
*by Andrew Collins*

**The Genesis Race**
Our Extraterrestrial DNA and the True Origins of the Species
*by Will Hart*

**Forbidden History**
Prehistoric Technologies, Extraterrestrial Intervention,
and the Suppressed Origins of Civilization
*Edited by J. Douglas Kenyon*

**Decoding the Message of the Pulsars**
Intelligent Communication from the Galaxy
*by Paul A. LaViolette, Ph.D.*

**Secrets of Antigravity Propulsion**
Tesla, UFOs, and Classified Aerospace Technology
*by Paul A. LaViolette, Ph.D.*

INNER TRADITIONS • BEAR & COMPANY
P.O. Box 388
Rochester, VT  05767
1-800-246-8648
www.InnerTraditions.com

Or contact your local bookseller